David Herbert (D. H.) Lawrence,

whose fiction has had a profound influence on twentieth-century literature, was born on September 11, 1885, in a mining village in Nottinghamshire, England. His father was an illiterate coal miner, his mother a genteel schoolteacher determined to lift her children out of the working class. His parents' unhappy marriage and his mother's strong emotional claims on her son later became the basis for Lawrence's *Sons and Lovers* (1913), one of the most important autobiographical novels of this century. Lawrence completed his studies at University College, Nottingham, in 1908 and taught for a few years at a boys' school. In 1912, he left teaching to devote himself to writing—and to run away with a married woman, Frieda von Richthofen, sister of the famous German World War I flying ace and wife of Lawrence's French professor at Nottingham. The elopement marked the beginning of Lawrence's lifelong clash with accepted morality, as well as the start of a ceaseless wanderlust prompted by the tuberculosis that would eventually kill him.

In 1915, his masterpiece *The Rainbow,* which like its companion novel *Women in Love* (1920) dealt frankly with sex, was suppressed as indecent a month after its publication. *Aaron's Rod* (1922), *Kangaroo* (1923), set in Australia, and *The Plumed Serpent* (1926), set in Mexico, were all written during Lawrence's travels in search of political and emotional refuge and a healthful climate. In 1928, already desperately ill, Lawrence wrote *Lady Chatterley's Lover.* Banned as pornographic, the unexpurgated edition was not allowed legal circulation in Britain until 1960. D. H. Lawrence called his life, marked by struggle, frustration, and despair, "a savage enough pilgrimage." He died on March 2, 1930, at the age of forty-four, in Vence, France.

THE LOST GIRL

by
D. H. Lawrence

*With an Introduction
by
Jeffrey Meyers*

BANTAM BOOKS
NEW YORK   TORONTO   LONDON   SYDNEY   AUCKLAND

A   BANTAM   CLASSIC

THE LOST GIRL

A Bantam Classic Book / August 1996

PUBLISHING HISTORY
The Lost Girl was first published
in England in 1920.
Cover art: *Dreams* by Vittorio Matteo Corcos. Galleria Nazionale
d'Arte Moderna, Rome.

ISBN 0-553-21448-9

Published simultaneously in the United States and Canada

Bantam Books are published by Bantam Books, a division of Bantam
Doubleday Dell Publishing Group, Inc. Its trademark, consisting of
the words "Bantam Books" and the portrayal of
a rooster, is Registered in U.S. Patent and Trademark Office
and in other countries. Marca Registrada. Bantam Books,
1540 Broadway, New York, New York 10036.

PRINTED IN THE UNITED STATES OF AMERICA

OPM   0 9 8 7 6 5 4 3 2 1

CONTENTS

Introduction

by Jeffrey Meyers

*T*he Lost Girl, with its picaresque plot and multiple characters, is a crucial transitional work that appeared exactly halfway through Lawrence's literary career. The book is both a postscript that recalls past themes and a prelude that anticipates future ones: the attraction of a lady to a passionate working-class man in *The White Peacock;* the conflict of generations and sexual rebellion in *The Rainbow;* the destruction of love by war in *Women in Love;* the escape to Italy (which recalls Lawrence's elopement with his wife, Frieda) in *Women in Love, Aaron's Rod,* and *Lady Chatterley's Lover;* the homosexual motif in four major novels; the submission of a woman to a dominant male in *The Virgin and the Gipsy* and *The Plumed Serpent;* and the resurrection theme in *Lady Chatterley's Lover* and *The Man Who Died.*

The composition of *The Lost Girl*—like that of *Ulysses, A Passage to India,* and *The Magic Mountain*—was interrupted by the Great War. In 1913 Lawrence began the novel as "The Insurrection of Miss Houghton" (other titles were "Mixed Marriage," and "The Bitter Cherry") in Gargnano, in northern Italy, where he wrote about 200 holograph pages. He revived it after his return to Italy in November 1919, and concluded it while living in Taormina, Sicily. In

December 1921 the novel won the only honor Lawrence ever received in his life: the James Tait Black Prize of £100. We do not know how much of the final version had been completed earlier. The original manuscript has not survived; the extant novel, entirely rewritten and completed between March and May 1920, is probably a very different kind of book from the 1913 version.

The Lost Girl raises two questions that are central to Lawrence's work: "What is one's own real self?" and "How does one realize one's own true nature?" Lawrence insists that "extraordinary people [have] extraordinary fates" and that Alvina "*was* her own fate." At the very end of the novel, as she urges Cicio to come back from the war, she exclaims: "We have our fate in our hands." Throughout the novel the principal characters struggle to fulfill their difficult destiny.

Alvina's impressive ability to determine her own fate resolves the novel's secularized paradox, expressed in Matthew 10:39: "He that loseth his life for my sake shall find it." At various times in the novel Alvina is mentally, morally, physically, and geographically lost. She loses her parents, her friends, her fiancés, her social position, her career, her inheritance, her self-respect, her virginity, her reputation, her security, her language, and her country. She is "lost to Woodhouse, to Lancaster, to England . . . cut off from everything she belonged to." Cicio feels he cannot bear to lose her; she fears she will lose him—in the war, or afterward. Despite these formidable difficulties, her attitude remains: "All for love, and the world well lost." She finds, in characteristic Laurentian manner, salvation not of the soul but of the flesh.

Each phase and major experience of Alvina's life prefigures Cicio and prepares her for Italy. She comes from an ugly, provincial, class-constricted mining town, from a family declining in both health and fortune. Her mother is a professional invalid, her father a frantic failure, Miss Frost and Miss Pinnegar rather cold and bitter examples of spinsterhood. The lives of the women in the household provide a grim warning about Alvina's future, just as their deaths release her from a repressive life. She has nothing to gain by remaining "buried alive" in Woodhouse, and almost any other mode of existence appears more promising.

The five disastrous business ventures of James Houghton (which resemble the dismal careers of Joyce's Simon Dedalus) parallel the five suitors of Alvina, foreshadow her fate, and force her toward Cicio. Houghton is a flamboyant but unrealistic draper who organized sensational exhibitions in his shopwindow on Friday nights when the miners got their pay, and "hovered in the back-ground like an author on his first night in the theatre." He then fails as a Klondyke brick manufacturer, a Throttle Ha'Penny colliery manager, a would-be proprietor of a private hotel, and finally—encouraged by the persuasive impresario Mr. May—the owner of a shabby, ill-situated cinema and music hall.

Each of Alvina's five beaux—Australian, English, South African emigrant, American, and Scotsman—anticipate an aspect of the Italian Cicio. The passionate receptivity of Alexander Graham, who has strong teeth and dark blood, "dark in colouring, with very dark eyes, and a body which seemed to move inside his clothing," overwhelms Alvina, as Cicio does. Though she cannot bring herself to marry him, Graham's love gives her the confidence to break away from Woodhouse, to seek her own career and travel to an exotic country.

Alvina, who (like Connie Chatterley) has been visibly fading away, blooms as a maternity nurse (a symbol of her commitment to life) and flirts with all the physicians. Dr. Young, her second suitor, with his "deep, half-perverse knowledge of the other sex," touches, kisses, and rouses her. But her inflexible virginity prevents her from yielding to him.

Alvina is genuinely attracted to the married plumber Arthur Witham. His "vulnerable, hairy, and somehow childish leg" reveals the kernel of the real man beneath the workman's trousers as he passes her hand over his broken shin after an accident in the chapel. But she is courted by his brother Albert, whose Oxford education makes him brittle and flat. Albert prefigures Cicio's shallow "little modern education" that oppressed his natural instinct and "made money and independence an *idée fixe*."

The fourth beau, the plump and perky Mr. May, is not as brilliantly drawn as the real Magnus in Lawrence's introduction to his *Memoir*, but he is still the liveliest character in the book. He is sensitive, dainty, manicured, fastidious; sports immaculate clothes and silk underwear (he later dresses as a girl to act with the Indian troupe); stays at the best hotel, though down-at-heels; has a quick but pedestrian mind; is evasive and unscrupulous. He has been a journalist and a manager "for Miss Maud Callum [Isadora Duncan], the *danseuse*." Mr. May introduces Alvina to the music-hall world and the Indian troupe. She must free herself from his influence, after they quarrel about money while playing cards and drinking, before she can commit herself to Cicio. Mr. May, in an ironic twist of the plot (for his model, Magnus, had been pursued by detectives throughout Italy), pretends to concern himself with Alvina's virtue, curries favor in Woodhouse, and takes revenge by sending detectives to determine if she is involved in white slave traffic.

The last suitor, Dr. Mitchell, is a domineering male who hates to be thwarted. In a brilliant tragicomic scene, he brutally flings Alvina against the wall when she refuses to kiss him—just as Cicio does ("he seemed to throw her down and suffocate her") when he first has sex with her. And Mitchell's ludicrous self-abasement, when he falls to his knees and begs forgiveness and love, recalls Alvina's slavish degradation with Cicio.

Alvina's character predetermines her impulsive acts and unconventional behavior. This very proper and well-bred young lady's eyes are sardonic and mocking, her tone mad and jeering, her expression deliberately derisive, her "ancient sapience . . . deeper than Woodhouse could fathom." She scorns protection, is reckless, fascinated by the outlawed look of navvies, and seems as knowing as a prostitute. Her employment as a maternity nurse and music-hall piano player makes her déclassé even before she meets Cicio.

The descent into her father's mine is an exploration of her own subconscious desire for sexual as well as social experience. For the subterranean creatures, swooning in the drafts of darkness, suggest "something for ever unknowable and inadmissable." The miners "brought with them above ground the curious dark intimacy of the mine, the naked sort of contact . . . [and] preferred to take life instinctively and intuitively." They make Alvina realize that she wants "a Dark Master from the underworld."

The peripatetic pattern of Alvina's life also prepares her for Cicio and the flight to Italy. She escapes from Woodhouse to become a nurse in London and to join the Indian troupe in Sheffield. She runs away from the troupe to meditate in Scarborough and becomes a nurse in Lancaster. She finally escapes from her enforced engagement to Dr. Mitchell, meets Cicio in Scarborough, and lives with him in London before leaving for Italy.

Alvina's passion for Cicio is the crux of the novel. He is physically attractive, with catlike tawny-yellow eyes and gleaming teeth, muscular, graceful, sensual, passionate, exciting, an expert horseman. But his negative qualities are dominant. He is, Lawrence emphasizes, stupid, inarticulate, childish, common, loutish, crude, violent, servile, and surly. In sex (his strongest card) he is emotionally unresponsive, insensitive, heartless, domineering, and even brutal—though Alvina seems to like his bestial behavior. He is also mercenary and exploitive and uses Alvina to gain wealth and social status. Cicio's love for Geoffrey, the French actor in the troupe, seems stronger than his love for Alvina, though his passion for her is much greater.

Despite these formidable faults, Alvina is instinctively attracted to Cicio and establishes "an implicit correspondence between their two psyches." She must learn to respond to his sensual nature without losing her self-respect and becoming degraded. Soon after they first meet, Alvina, who had noticed his Mediterranean hand, "prehensile and tender and dusky," reaches for him in the dark outside her house and meets his groping fingers. After Cicio fights with the actor Max and stabs him with a stage knife, Alvina kisses the violent hand and convinces him to rejoin the troupe.

Immediately after she is released by her father's death, Alvina declares her love for Cicio, "and smiling, he kissed her, delicately, with a certain finesse of knowledge." The conjunction of death and love is not ironic, as in the funeral-wedding sequences of *Antigone* and *Hamlet* (Lawrence refers to "The funeral tea, with its baked meats"). Instead, it suggests the kind of acceptance of death and affirmation of life, both part of the same process, that Lawrence so admired in Etruscan culture. As he wrote in his last work, *Apocalypse:* "The dead may look after the afterwards. But the magnificent here and now of life in the flesh is ours, and ours alone, and ours only for a time." Her mother's illness encouraged Alvina to break her engagement to Alexander Graham, just as her father's opposition prevented her marriage to Cicio. Only after she quarrels with Miss Pinnegar and Mr. May, and breaks the last bonds with the people who influenced her maiden life, is she physically and emotionally free to give herself to Cicio.

Their first sexual encounter occurs after Alvina has escaped the well-meaning but unwelcome advice of family friends in Woodhouse and joined the absurd troupe of Indian impersonators (an imaginary group based on Lawrence's knowledge of the Natchez and Tawasa tribes and his early reading of the novels of Fenimore Cooper). She is on probation with the troupe (just as she had been on her first nursing job) and unwittingly adopts the obscene name of Allaye, which is derived through association with the Italian and French euphemisms *viale, voie, petit chemin, allée* and suggests vagina. Though Madame Rochard has promised to protect Alvina (who had previously said she did not mind being unprotected), she acts as procuress and gives Cicio the key to Alvina's lodging-house room. "So he took her in both arms, powerful, mysterious, horrible in the pitch dark . . . and made her his slave. But the spell was on her. . . . How she suffered no one can tell." After he treated her brutally and enslaved her, she cried hysterically and "turned her face to the wall, feeling beaten. . . . She lay inert, as if envenomed." After sleeping with Cicio she is torn between desire and humiliation, and forced to bribe her all-too-inquisitive landlady. Cicio simply ignores her and wears an ugly, jeering expression.

Alvina's second sexual encounter is even more brutal than the first. It takes place in her parents' bed, as if to exorcise the spirits of her family, Miss Frost, and Miss Pinnegar, when she returns to Woodhouse with Cicio to consult her lawyer and settle her father's affairs. Once again he takes her savagely, against her conscious will, and tears away her defense and dignity: "She struggled frenziedly. But almost instantly she recognized how much stronger he was, and she was still, mute and motionless with anger. . . . Recklessly, he had his will with her—but deliberately, and thoroughly, not rushing to the issue, but taking everything he wanted of her, progressively, and fully, leaving her stark, with nothing, nothing of herself—nothing." She responds to this treatment by fighting her slavish desire to fall at his feet (she is later dumbfounded and disgusted when Dr. Mitchell does the same thing after she rejects his proposal), and becomes ridiculously happy. She clearly takes masochistic pleasure in being reduced to nothingness by Cicio as punishment for her sexual guilt. When friends see her in the street immediately afterward, they cheerfully remark how well she looks: "A change does you good."

When Alvina is told she is to receive virtually nothing from her father's estate, she realizes she must endure both the insolent contempt of Madame Rochard and the officious yet ineffectual patronage of the Woodhouse magnates. So she leaves the troupe, gets a second job as a maternity nurse, suffers the rather repulsive courtship of Dr. Mitchell, and nurses the pregnant Mrs. Tukes. In a rather contrived moment of the plot Cicio turns up in Lancaster as suddenly as he had in Woodhouse, when he played his "wildly-yearning Neapolitan songs" under her window after taking her virginity. Now he plays the mandolin under the window of Mrs. Tukes with a despairing, "clamorous, animal sort of yearning." As Alvina goes downstairs to meet him, he becomes the active suitor for the first time, declares his love, and begs her to come with him to Italy.

Cicio's agonizing wails somehow induce Mrs. Tukes's labor, and an implicit connection is made between sexual desire and (its consequence) the pain of parturition. Mrs. Tukes is drawn to Cicio because, she says, they are both tormented by the flesh: "I'm howling with one sort of pain, and he's howling with another." In a birth-love scene that parallels the death-love scene when James Houghton dies, Mrs. Tukes invites Cicio into her bedroom, presumably to distract her from her agony. Wildly clutching at the sheets, she begs her husband to go away. The would-be composer Tommy Tukes is virtually annihilated by the instinctive music of Cicio, whose life force and animal brutality seem more powerful, during emotional extremity, than both art and intelligence.

Despite her instinctive sympathy with Cicio, Lawrence does not allow Alvina an easy and obvious choice, nor insist that she has made the right decision by submitting to Cicio. She constantly courts him, though he fails to respond to her on any but the sexual level, and chooses him with all his obvious defects. Alvina is like the woman in Ezekiel 19:5: "When she saw that she had waited, and her hope was lost, then she took another of her whelps, and made him a young lion." But Lawrence does not make Alvina's love for Cicio entirely convincing (" 'and I can hardly bear it that I love you so much,' she said, quavering, across the potatoes") nor persuade us that Cicio, though better than her five unsatisfactory lovers, is the right man for her. The theme of the novel is Alvina's inability to find a man who unites passion with intellect, and her willingness to choose the former if she cannot have both. Lawrence creates three types of male characters: the sensitive intellectual (Paul Morel, Rupert Birkin, Richard Somers), the passionate animal (Annable, Cicio, Mellors), and the strong leader (Rawdon Lilly, Ben Cooley, Ramón Carasco). But the ideal hero, who combines all these qualities, is never realized in his fiction.

Cicio is even more strongly attracted to Italy than Alvina, so that country becomes their goal and destiny. It pulls him away from England, the troupe, and their little playlet, in which he is repeatedly crushed by a bear ("I am tired of being dead, you see"). Both Cicio and Alvina realize that she cannot live in England as the wife of a "dirty Eyetalian" and that in Italy she will legally be his property—helpless even if he beats her.

They travel to Italy soon after their marriage. The novel becomes more lively, intimate, and intense in the last three chapters, when they enter a world more fierce and barbaric than Verga's. It is much more like the threatening Alps of *Twilight in Italy* and *Women in Love* than the romantic promise of Naples and the castles, almond trees, rocks, bays, and glittering water of the classic Mediterranean that Alvina glimpses when they reach Genoa. The actual journey to the Abruzzi, where Lawrence had an introduction to Orazio Cerni (Pancrazio, in the novel), who had been an artist's model for the father of a friend, took place just before he completed the novel in early 1920. Though Lawrence spent only seven days in the Abruzzi and three in Montecassino, Picinisco, like the monastery, provided a shocking inspiration, and these chapters contain some of his greatest travel writing.

"This is what is so attractive about the remote places," Lawrence writes in Sea and Sardinia, "the Abruzzi, for example. Life is so primitive, so pagan, so strangely heathen and half-savage." But both Alvina and Cicio decline in Italy as it changes from a symbolic (as it had been in England) to an actual country. The wild and savage landscape and new mode of life reflect the difficulties of Alvina's marriage and force her to examine her innermost self. The house is crude and filthy (but soon scrubbed in characteristic Lawrentian fashion), the cold is piercing, the sun seems extinguished, the atmosphere is strange and hostile, the people are "watchful, venomous, dangerous," the "fetish-worship" in the church is repulsive, there is a constant threat of war.

Critics of the novel have seen the Abruzzi as an "opposite pole to England"; have stated: "Alvina escapes the frustrations of conventionality, and briefly finds a new 'life' in the underworld" and have insisted: "An Italian man and the Italian landscape emancipate 'the lost girl' from England and set her face toward a new destiny." But this is not true. The great irony of The Lost Girl, like Sea and Sardinia, is that Alvina is profoundly disappointed in the primitive landscape and that Califano, though apparently very different, has the same restrictive features as Woodhouse. Both houses (the largest in the place) are "gloomy miserable holes." In both towns the people are money-grubbing, and Alvina is fearful of gossip and scandal, subject to an almost oriental surveillance, threatened by financial insecurity, and faced with an apparently hopeless future. Both Alvina and Cicio are intensely miserable, as eager to flee from Califano as they were to escape from England. As Gudrun tells Ursula at the end of *Women in Love:* "Isn't it really an illusion to think you can get out of it? After all, a cottage in the Abruzzi, or wherever it may be, isn't a new world."

The one hope is Alvina's pregnancy (thematically related to her maternity nursing), which follows extreme despair, foreshadows the coming of new life in the spring, and symbolizes her love for Cicio: "And even as he turned to look for her, she felt a strange thrilling in her bowels: a sort of trill strangely within her, yet extraneous to her.... She knew how he loved her—almost elementally, without communication. . . . It seemed to her she was with child."

This particular aspect of the novel, in which Lawrence tries to convey a sense of elemental life and primitive emotions (both the pregnant Mrs. Tukes and the amorous Cicio howl with pain), provoked an angry response from the subtle and sensitive Katherine Mansfield, who objected to his visceral mode of expression. She intended to review *The Lost Girl* for the *Athenaeum* in December 1920, and sent the editor her notes on the novel when she became seriously ill:

> Lawrence denies his humanity. He denies the powers of the Imagination. He denies Life—I mean *human* life. His hero and heroine are non-human. They are animals on the prowl. . . . They submit to the physical response and for the rest go veiled—blind—*faceless—mindless*. This is the doctrine of mindlessness. . . .
>
> Take the scene where the hero throws her in the kitchen, possesses her, and she returns singing to the washing-up. It's a *disgrace*. Take the rotten rubbishy scene of the woman in labour asking the Italian into her bedroom. All false. All a pack of lies! . . .
>
> Don't forget where Alvina feels "a trill in her bowels" and discovers herself with child. A TRILL—What does that mean? And why is it so peculiarly offensive from a man? Because it is *not on this plane* that the emotions of others are conveyed to our imagination. It's a kind of sinning against art.

Though Mansfield had formerly praised Lawrence's vital response to life, she now felt that he had descended into a kind of crude mindlessness that degraded women to the level of animals. She herself, who had portrayed the gruesome details of childbirth in her *German Pension* stories, had been through a miscarriage and an abortion that prevented her from having the children she so desperately wanted. She therefore had little tolerance for Lawrence's portrayal of female physiology.

The malicious letter that Alvina receives from Dr. Mitchell (which recalls Ernest Weekley's spiteful missives to the adulterous Frieda), and Cicio's farewell to Geoffrey in the Paris railway station, represent the final break with their life in England and their commitment to each other. Cicio is drawn away from Alvina and forced into military service when Italy enters the war in May 1915. His love must be tested and annealed by the army as hers was by the raw experience of Italy. Though *The Lost Girl* ends with characteristic inconclusiveness, Cicio promises that he will come back to his wife and child, if he survives the war; and both he and Alvina believe America offers the best hope of a new life.

THE LOST GIRL

CHAPTER 1

The Decline of Manchester House

Take a mining townlet like Woodhouse, with a population of ten thousand people, and three generations behind it. This space of three generations argues a certain well-established society. The old 'County' has fled from the sight of so much disembowelled coal, to flourish on mineral rights in regions still idyllic. Remains one great and inaccessible magnate, the local coal-owner: three generations old, and clambering on the bottom step of the 'County', kicking off the mass below. Rule him out.

A well established society in Woodhouse, full of fine shades, ranging from the dark of coal-dust to grit of stonemason and sawdust of timber-merchant, through the lustre of lard and butter and meat, to the perfume of the chemist and the disinfectant of the doctor, on to the serene gold-tarnish of bank-managers, cashiers for the firm, clergymen and such-like, as far as the automobile refulgence of the general-manager of all the collieries. Here the *ne plus ultra*. The general-manager lives in the shrubberied seclusion of the so-called Manor. The genuine Hall, abandoned by the 'County', has been taken over as offices by the firm.

Here we are then: a vast substratum of colliers; a thick sprinkling of tradespeople intermingled with small employers of labour and diversified by elementary schoolmasters and nonconformist clergy; a higher layer of bank-managers, rich millers and well-to-do ironmasters, episcopal clergy and the managers of collieries: then the rich and sticky cherry of the local coal-owner glistening over all.

Such the complicated social system of a small industrial town in the Midlands of England, in this year of grace 1920. But let us go back a little. Such it was in the last calm year of plenty, 1913.

A calm year of plenty. But one chronic and dreary malady: that of the odd women. Why, in the name of all prosperity, should every class but the lowest in such a society hang over-burdened with Dead Sea fruit of odd women, unmarried, unmarriageable women, called old maids? Why it is that every tradesman, every schoolmaster, every bank-manager, and every clergyman produces one, two, three, or more old maids. Do the middle-classes, particularly the lower middle-classes, give birth to more girls than boys? Or do the lower middle-class men assiduously climb up or down, in marriage, thus leaving their true partners stranded? Or are middle-class women very squeamish in their choice of husbands?

However it be, it is a tragedy. Or perhaps it is not.

Perhaps these unmarried women of the middle-classes are the famous sexless-workers of our ant-industrial society, of which we hear so much. Perhaps all they lack is an occupation: in short, a job. But perhaps we might hear their own opinion, before we lay the law down.

In Woodhouse, there was a terrible crop of old maids among the 'nobs', the tradespeople, and the clergy. The whole town of women, colliers' wives and all, held its breath as it saw a chance of one of these daughters of comfort and woe getting off. They flocked to the well-to-do weddings with an intoxication of relief. For let class-jealousy be what it may, a woman hates to see another woman left stately on the shelf, without a chance. They all *wanted* the middle-class girls to find husbands. Everyone wanted it, including the girls themselves. Hence the dismalness.

Now James Houghton had only one child: his daughter Alvina. Surely Alvina Houghton—

But let us retreat to the early eighties, when Alvina

was a baby: or even further back, to the palmy days of James Houghton. In his palmy days, James Houghton was *crème de la crême* of Woodhouse society. The house of Houghton had always been well-to-do: tradespeople, we must admit; but after a few generations of affluence, tradespeople acquire a distinct *cachet*. Now James Houghton, at the age of twenty-eight, inherited a splendid business in Manchester goods, in Woodhouse. He was a tall, thin elegant young man with side-whiskers, genuinely refined, somewhat in the Bulwer style. He had a taste for elegant conversation and elegant literature and elegant Christianity: a tall, thin, brittle young man, rather fluttering in his manner, full of facile ideas, and with a beautiful speaking voice: most beautiful. Withal, of course, a tradesman. He courted a small, dark woman, older than himself, daughter of a Derbyshire squire. He expected to get at least ten thousand pounds with her. In which he was disappointed, for he got only eight hundred. Being of a romantic-commercial nature, he never forgave her, but always treated her with the most elegant courtesy. To see him peel and prepare an apple for her was an exquisite sight. But that peeled and quartered apple was her portion. This elegant Adam of commerce gave Eve her own back, nicely cored, and had no more to do with her. Meanwhile Alvina was born.

Before all this, however, before his marriage, James Houghton had built Manchester House. It was a vast square building—vast, that is, for Woodhouse—standing on the main street and highroad of the small but growing town. The lower front consisted of two fine shops, one for Manchester goods, one for silk and woollens. This was James Houghton's commercial poem.

For James Houghton was a dreamer, and something of a poet: commercial, be it understood. He liked the novels of George Macdonald, and the fantasies of that author, extremely. He wove one continual fantasy for himself, a fantasy of commerce. He dreamed of silks and poplins, luscious in texture and of unforeseen exquisiteness: he dreamed of carriages of the 'County' arrested before his windows, of exquisite women ruffling charmed, entranced, to his counter. And charming, entrancing, he served them his lovely fabrics, which only he and they could sufficiently appreciate. His fame spread, until Alexandra, Princess of Wales, and Elizabeth, Empress of Austria, the two best-dressed women in Europe, floated down from heaven to the shop in Woodhouse, and sallied forth to show what could be done by purchasing from James Houghton.

We cannot say why James Houghton failed to become the Liberty or the Snelgrove of his day. Perhaps he had too much imagination. Be that as it may, in those early days when he brought his wife to her new home, his window on the Manchester side was a foam and a mayblossom of mus-lins and prints, his window on the London side was an au-tumn evening of silks and rich fabrics. What could fail to be dazzled! But she, poor darling, from her stone hall in stony Derbyshire, was a little bit repulsed by the man's dancing in front of his stock, like David before the ark.

The home to which he brought her was a monument. In the great bedroom over the shop he had had his furniture *built:* built of solid mahogany: oh too, too solid. No doubt he hopped or skipped himself with satisfaction into the monstrous matrimonial bed: it could only be mounted by means of a stool and chair. But the poor, secluded little woman, older than he, must have climbed up with a heavy heart, to lie and face the gloomy Bastille of Mahogany, the great cupboard opposite, or to turn wearily sideways to the great cheval mirror, which performed a perpetual and hid-eous bow before her grace. Such furniture! It could never be removed from the room.

The little child was born in the second year. And then James Houghton decamped to a small, half-furnished bed-room at the other end of the house, where he slept on a rough board and played the anchorite for the rest of his days. His wife was left alone with her baby and the built-in furniture. She developed heart disease, as a result of nervous repressions.

But like a butterfly James fluttered over his fabrics. He was a tyrant to his shop-girls. No French marquis in a Dick-ens novel could have been more elegant and *raffiné* and heartless. The girls detested him. And yet, his curious re-finement and enthusiasm bore them away. They submitted to him. The shop attracted much curiosity. But the poor-spirited Woodhouse people were weak buyers. They wearied James Houghton with their demand for common zephyrs, for red flannel which they would scallop with black worsted, for black alpacas and bombazines and merinos. He fluffed out his silk-striped muslins, his India cotton-prints. But the natives shied off as if he had offered them the poisoned robes of Herakles.

There was a sale. These sales contributed a good deal to Mrs Houghton's nervous heart-disease. They brought the first signs of wear and tear into the face of James Houghton. At first, of course, he merely marked down, with discretion, his less-expensive stock of prints and muslins, nuns-veilings and muslin delaines, with a few fancy braidings and trimmings in guimp or bronze to enliven the affair. And Woodhouse bought cautiously.

After the sale, however, James Houghton felt himself at liberty to plunge into an orgy of new stock. He flitted, with a tense look on his face, to Manchester. After which huge bundles, bales, and boxes arrived in Woodhouse, and were dumped on the pavement of the shop. Friday evening came, and with it a revelation in Houghton's window: the first piqués, the first strangely-woven and honeycombed toilet covers and bed quilts, the first frill-caps and aprons for maid-servants: a wonder in white. That was how James advertised it. 'A Wonder in White'. Who knows but that he had been reading Wilkie Collins' famous novel!

As the nine days of the wonder-in-white passed and receded, James disappeared in the direction of London. A few Fridays later he came out with his Winter Touch. Weird and wonderful winter coats, for ladies—everything James handled was for ladies, he scorned the coarser sex—: weird and wonderful winter coats for ladies, of thick, black, pock-marked cloth, stood and flourished their bear-fur cuffs in the background, while tippets, boas, muffs, and winter-fancies coquetted in front of the window-space. Friday-night crowds gathered outside: the gas-lamps shone their brightest: James Houghton hovered in the background like an author on his first night in the theatre. The result was a sensation. Ten villages stared and crushed round the plate glass. It was a sensation: but what sensation! In the breasts of the crowd, wonder, admiration, *fear,* and ridicule. Let us stress the word fear. The inhabitants of Woodhouse were afraid lest James Houghton should impose his standards upon them. His goods were in excellent taste: but his customers were in as bad taste as possible. They stood outside and pointed, giggled, and jeered. Poor James, like an author on his first night, saw his work fall more than flat.

But still, he believed in his own excellence: and quite justly. What he failed to perceive was that the crowd hated excellence. Woodhouse wanted a gently graduated progress in mediocrity, a mediocrity so stale and flat that it fell outside the imagination of any sensitive mortal. Woodhouse wanted a series of vulgar little thrills, as one tawdry mediocrity was imported from Nottingham or Birmingham to take the place of some tawdry mediocrity which Nottingham and Birmingham had already discarded. That Woodhouse, as a very condition of its own being, hated any approach to originality or real taste, this James Houghton could never learn. He thought he had not been clever enough, when he had been far, far too clever already. He always thought that Dame Fortune was a capricious and fastidious dame, a sort of Elizabeth of Austria or Alexandra, Princess of Wales, elegant beyond his grasp. Whereas Dame Fortune, even in London or Vienna, let alone in Woodhouse, was a vulgar woman of the middle and lower middle-class, ready to put her heavy foot on anything that was not vulgar, machine-made, and appropriate to the herd. When he saw his delicate originalities, as well as his faint flourishes of draper's fantasy, squashed flat under the calm and solid foot of vulgar Dame Fortune, he fell into fits of depression bordering on mysticism, and talked to his wife in a vague way of higher influences and the angel Israfel. She, poor lady, was thoroughly scared by Israfel, and completely unhooked by the vagaries of James.

At last—we hurry down the slope of James's misfortunes—the real days of Houghton's Great Sales began. Houghton's Great Bargain Events were really events. After some years of hanging on, he let go splendidly. He marked down his prints, his chintzes, his dimities, and his veilings with a grand and lavish hand. Bang went his blue pencil through 3/11, and nobly he subscribed 1/0¾. Prices fell like nuts. A lofty one-and-eleven rolled down to six-three, 1/6 magically shrunk into 4¾d., whilst good solid prints exposed themselves at 3¾d. per yard.

Now this was really an opportunity. Moreover the goods, having become a little stale during their years of ineffectuality, were beginning to approximate to the public taste. And besides, good sound stuff it was, no matter what the pattern. And so the little Woodhouse girls went to school in petties and drawers made of material which James had destined for fair summer dresses: petties and drawers of which the little Woodhouse girls were ashamed, for all that. For if they should chance to turn up their little skirts, be sure they would raise a chorus among their companions: 'Yah-h-h, yer've got Houghton's threp'ny draws on!'

All this time James Houghton walked on air. He still saw the Fata Morgana snatching his fabrics round her lovely form, and pointing him to wealth untold. True, he became also Superintendent of the Sunday School. But whether this was an act of vanity, or whether it was an attempt to establish an Entente Cordiale with higher powers, who shall judge.

Meanwhile his wife became more and more an invalid; the little Alvina was a pretty, growing child. Woodhouse was really impressed by the sight of Mrs Houghton, small, pale and withheld, taking a walk with her dainty little girl, so fresh in an ermine tippet and a muff. Mrs Houghton in shiny black bear's-fur, the child in the white and spotted ermine, passing silent and shadowy down the street, made an impression which the people did not forget.

But Mrs Houghton had pains at her heart. If, during her walk, she saw two little boys having a scrimmage, she had to run to them with pence and entreaty, leaving them dumbfounded, whilst she leaned blue at the lips against a wall. If she saw a carter crack his whip over the ears of the horse, as the horse laboured uphill, she had to cover her eyes and avert her face, and all her strength left her.

So she stayed more and more in her room, and the child was given to the charge of a governess. Miss Frost was a handsome, vigorous young woman of about thirty years of age, with grey-white hair and gold-rimmed spectacles. The white hair was not at all tragical: it was a family *trait*.

Miss Frost mattered more than anyone else to Alvina Houghton, during the first long twenty-five years of the girl's life. The governess was a strong, generous woman, a musician by nature. She had a sweet voice, and sang in the choir of the chapel, and took the first class of girls in the Sunday School of which James Houghton was Superintendent. She disliked and rather despised James Houghton, saw in him elements of a hypocrite, detested his airy and gracious selfishness, his lack of human feeling, and most of all, his fairy fantasy. As James went further into life, he became a dreamer. Sad indeed that he died before the days of Freud. He enjoyed the most wonderful and fairy-like dreams, which he could describe perfectly, in charming, delicate language. At such times his beautifully modulated voice all but sang, his grey eyes gleamed fiercely under his bushy, hairy eyebrows, his pale face with its side-whiskers had a strange *lueur*, his long thin hands fluttered occasionally. He had become meagre in figure, his skimpy but genteel coat would be buttoned over his breast, as he recounted his dream-adventures, adventures that were half Edgar Allan Poe, half Andersen, with touches of Vathek and Lord Byron and George Macdonald: perhaps more than a touch of the last. Ladies were always struck by these accounts. But Miss Frost never felt so strongly moved to impatience as when she was within hearing.

For twenty years, she and James Houghton treated each other with a courteous distance. Sometimes she broke into open impatience with him, sometimes he answered her tartly: 'Indeed, indeed! Oh, indeed! Well, well, I'm sorry you find it so—' as if the injury consisted in her finding it so. Then he would flit away to the Conservative Club, with a fleet, light, hurried step, as if pressed by fate. At the club he played chess—at which he was excellent—and conversed. Then he flitted back at half-past twelve, to dinner.

The whole morale of the house rested immediately on Miss Frost. She saw her line in the first year. She must defend the little Alvina, whom she loved as her own, and the

nervous, petulant, heart-stricken woman, the mother, from
the vagaries of James. Not that James had any vices. He did
not drink or smoke, was abstemious and clean as an anchorite, and never lowered his fine tone. But still, the two unprotected ones must be sheltered from him. Miss Frost
imperceptibly took into her hands the reins of the domestic
government. Her rule was quiet, strong, and generous. She
was not seeking her own way. She was steering the poor
domestic ship of Manchester House, illuminating its dark
rooms with her own sure, radiant presence: her silver-white
hair, and her pale, heavy, reposeful face seemed to give off
a certain radiance. She seemed to give weight, ballast and
repose to the staggering and bewildered home. She con-
trolled the maid, and suggested the meals—meals which
James ate without knowing what he ate. She brought in
flowers and books, and, very rarely, a visitor. Visitors were
out of place in the dark sombreness of Manchester House.
Her flowers charmed the petulant invalid, her books she
sometimes discussed with the airy James: after which dis-
cussions she was invariably filled with exasperation and impatience, whilst James invariably retired to the shop, and
was heard raising his musical voice, which the work-girls
hated, to one or other of the work-girls.

James certainly had an irritating way of speaking of a
book. He talked of incidents, and effects, and suggestions,
as if the whole thing had just been a sensational-aesthetic
attribute to himself. Not a grain of human feeling in the
man, said Miss Frost, flushing pink with exasperation. She
herself invariably took the human line.

Meanwhile the shops began to take on a hopeless and
frowsty look. After ten years' sales, spring sales, summer
sales, autumn sales, winter sales, James began to give up the
drapery dream. He himself could not bear any more to put
the heavy, pock-holed black cloth coat, with wild bear cuffs
and collar, on to the stand. He had marked it down from
five guineas to one guinea, and then, oh ignoble day, to ten-
and-six. He nearly kissed the gipsy woman with a basket of
tin saucepan-lids, when at last she bought it for five shillings,
at the end of one of his winter sales. But even she, in spite
of the bitter sleety day, would not put the coat on in the

shop. She carried it over her arm down to the Miners' Arms. And later, with a shock that really hurt him, James, peeping bird-like out of his shop door, saw her sitting driving a dirty rag-and-bone cart with a green-white, mouldy pony, and flourishing her arms like some wild and hairy-decorated squaw. For the long bear-fur, wet with sleet, seemed like a *chevaux de frise* of long porcupine quills round her forearms and her neck. Yet such good, such wonderful material! James eyed it for one moment, and then fled like a rabbit to the stove in his back regions.

The higher powers did not seem to fulfil the terms of treaty which James hoped for. He began to back out from the Entente. The Sunday School was a great trial to him. Instead of being carried away by his grace and eloquence, the nasty louts of colliery boys and girls openly banged their feet and made deafening noises when he tried to speak. He said many acid and withering things, as he stood there on the rostrum. But what is the good of saying acid things to those little fiends and gall-bladders, the colliery children? The situation was saved by Miss Frost's sweeping together all the big girls, under her surveillance, and by her organizing that the tall and handsome blacksmith who taught the lower boys should extend his influence over the upper boys. His influence was more than effectual. It consisted in gripping any recalcitrant boy just above the knee, and jesting with him in a jocular manner, in the dialect. The blacksmith's hand was all a blacksmith's hand need be, and his dialect was as broad as could be wished. Between the grip and the homely idiom no boy could endure without squealing. So the Sunday School paid more attention to James, whose prayers were beautiful. But then one of the boys, a protégé of Miss Frost, having been left for half an hour in the obscure room with Mrs Houghton, gave away the secret of the blacksmith's grip, which secret so haunted the poor lady that it marked a stage in the increase of her malady, and made Sunday afternoon a nightmare to her. And then James Houghton resented something in the coarse Scotch manner of the minister of that day. So that the superintendency of the Sunday School came to an end.

At the same time, Solomon had to divide his baby. That

is, he let the London side of his shop to W. H. Johnson, the tailor and haberdasher, a parvenu little fellow whose English would not bear analysis. Bitter as it was, it had to be. Carpenters and joiners appeared, and the premises were completely severed. From her room in the shadows at the back the invalid heard the hammering and sawing, and suffered. W. H. Johnson came out with a spick-and-span window, and had his wife, a shrewd, quiet woman, and his daughter, a handsome, loud girl, to help him on Friday evenings. Men flocked in—even women, buying their husbands a sixpence-halfpenny tie. They could have bought a tie for four-three from James Houghton. But no, they would rather give sixpence-halfpenny for W. H. Johnson's fresh but rubbishy stuff. And James, who had tried to rise to another successful sale, saw the streams pass into the other doorway, and heard the heavy feet on the hollow boards of the other shop: his shop no more.

After this cut at his pride and integrity he lay in retirement for a while, mystically inclined. Probably he would have come to Swedenborg, had not his clipt wings spread for a new flight. He hit on the brilliant idea of working up his derelict fabrics into ready-mades: not men's clothes, oh no: women's, or rather, ladies'. Ladies' Tailoring, said the new announcement.

James Houghton was happy once more. A zigzag wooden stairway was rigged up the high bank of Manchester House. In the great lofts sewing-machines of various patterns and movements were installed. A manageress was advertised for, and work-girls were hired. So a new phase of life started. At half-past six in the morning there was a clatter of feet and of girls' excited tongues along the back-yard and up the wooden stairway outside the back wall. The poor invalid heard every clack and every vibration. She could never get over her nervous apprehension of an invasion. Every morning alike, she felt an invasion of some enemy was breaking in on her. And all day long the low, steady rumble of sewing-machines overhead seemed like the low drumming of a bombardment upon her weak heart. To make matters worse, James Houghton decided that he must have his sewing-machines driven by some extra-human force. He installed another plant of machinery—acetylene or some such contrivance—which was intended to drive all the little machines from one big belt. Hence a further throbbing and shaking in the upper regions, truly terrible to endure. But, fortunately or unfortunately, the acetylene plant was not a success. Girls got their thumbs pierced, and sewing-machines absolutely refused to stop sewing, once they had started, and absolutely refused to start, once they had stopped. So that after a while, one loft was reserved for disused and rusty, but expensive engines.

Dame Fortune, who had refused to be taken by fine fabrics and fancy trimmings, was just as reluctant to be captured by ready-mades. Again the good dame was thoroughly lower middle-class. James Houghton designed 'robes'. Now Robes were the mode. Perhaps it was Alexandra, Princess of Wales, who gave glory to the slim, glove-fitting Princess Robe. Be that as it may, James Houghton designed robes. His work-girls, a race even more callous than shop-girls, proclaimed the fact that James tried on his own inventions upon his own elegant thin person, before the privacy of his own cheval mirror. And even if he did, why not? Miss Frost, hearing this legend, looked sideways at the enthusiast.

Let us remark in time that Miss Frost had already ceased to draw any maintenance from James Houghton. Far from it, she herself contributed to the upkeep of the domestic hearth and board. She had fully decided never to leave her two charges. She knew that a governess was an impossible item in Manchester House, as things went. And so she trudged the country, giving music lessons to the daughters of tradesmen and of colliers who boasted pianofortes. She even taught heavy-handed but dauntless colliers, who were seized with a passion to 'play'. Miles she trudged, on her round from village to village: a white-haired woman with a long, quick stride, a strong figure, and a quick, handsome smile when once her face awoke behind her gold-rimmed glasses. Like many short-sighted people, she had a certain intent look of one who goes her own way.

The miners knew her, and entertained the highest respect and admiration for her. As they streamed in a grimy stream home from pit, they diverged like some magic dark river from off the pavement into the horse-way, to give her room as she approached. And the men who knew her well enough to salute her, by calling her name 'Miss Frost!' giving it the proper intonation of salute, were fussy men indeed. 'She's a lady if ever there was one,' they said. And they meant it. Hearing her name, poor Miss Frost would flash a smile and a nod from behind her spectacles, but whose black face she smiled to she never, or rarely, knew. If she did chance to get an inkling, then gladly she called in reply 'Mr Lamb', or 'Mr Calladine'. In her way she was a proud woman, for she was regarded with cordial respect, touched with veneration, by at least a thousand colliers, and by perhaps as many colliers' wives. That is something, for any woman.

Miss Frost charged fifteen shillings for thirteen weeks' lessons, two lessons a week. And at that she was considered rather dear. She was supposed to be making money. What money she made went chiefly to support the Houghton household. In the meanwhile she drilled Alvina thoroughly in theory and pianoforte practice, for Alvina was naturally musical, and besides this she imparted to the girl the elements of a young lady's education, including the drawing of flowers in water-colour, and the translation of a Lamartine poem.

Now incredible as it may seem, fate threw another prop to the falling house of Houghton, in the person of the manageress of the work-girls, Miss Pinnegar. James Houghton complained of Fortune, yet to what other man would Fortune have sent two such women as Miss Frost and Miss Pinnegar, *gratis*? Yet there they were. And doubtful if James was ever grateful for their presence.

If Miss Frost saved him from heaven knows what domestic débâcle and horror, Miss Pinnegar saved him from the work-house. Let us not mince matters. For a dozen years Miss Frost supported the heart-stricken, nervous invalid, Clariss Houghton: for more than twenty years she cherished, tended and protected the young Alvina, shielding the child alike from a neurotic mother and a father such as James. For nearly twenty years she saw that food was set on the table, and clean sheets were spread on the beds: and all the time remained virtually in the position of an outsider, without one grain of established authority.

And then to find Miss Pinnegar! In her way, Miss Pinnegar was very different from Miss Frost. She was a rather short, stout, mouse-coloured, creepy kind of woman with a high colour in her cheeks and dun, close hair like a cap. It was evident she was not a lady: her grammar was not without reproach. She had pale grey eyes, and a padding step, and a soft voice, and almost purplish cheeks. Mrs Houghton, Miss Frost, and Alvina did not like her. They suffered her unwillingly.

But from the first she had a curious ascendancy over James Houghton. One would have expected his aesthetic eye to be offended. But no doubt it was her voice: her soft, near, sure voice, which seemed almost like a secret touch upon her hearer. Now many of her hearers disliked being secretly touched, as it were beneath their clothing. Miss Frost abhorred it: so did Mrs Houghton. Miss Frost's voice was clear and straight as a bell-note, open as the day. Yet Alvina, though in loyalty she adhered to her beloved Miss Frost, did not really mind the quiet suggestive power of Miss Pinnegar. For Miss Pinnegar was not vulgarly insinuating. On the contrary, the things she said were rather clumsy and downright. It was only that she seemed to weigh what she said, secretly, before she said it, and then she approached as if she would slip it into her hearer's consciousness without his being aware of it. She seemed to slide her speeches unnoticed into one's ears, so that one accepted them without the slightest challenge. That was just her manner of approach. In her own way, she was as loyal and unselfish as Miss Frost. There are such poles of opposition between honesties and loyalties.

Miss Pinnegar had the *second* class of girls in the Sunday School, and she took second, subservient place in Manchester House. By force of nature, Miss Frost took first place. Only when Miss Pinnegar spoke to Mr Houghton—nay, the very way she addressed herself to him—'What do *you* think, Mr Houghton?'—then there seemed to be assumed an immediacy of correspondence between the two, and an unquestioned priority in their unison, his and hers, which was a cruel thorn in Miss Frost's outspoken breast. This sort of secret intimacy and secret exulting in having, *really*, the chief power, was most repugnant to the white-haired woman. Not that there was, in fact, any secrecy, or any form of unwarranted correspondence between James Houghton and Miss Pinnegar. Far from it. Each of them would have found any suggestion of such a possibility repulsive in the extreme. It was simply an implicit correspondence between their two psyches, an immediacy of understanding which preceded all expression, tacit, wireless.

Miss Pinnegar lived in: so that the household consisted of the invalid, who mostly sat, in her black dress with a white lace collar fastened by a twisted gold brooch, in her own dim room, doing nothing, nervous and heart-suffering; then James, and the thin young Alvina, who adhered to her beloved Miss Frost, and then these two strange women. Miss Pinnegar never lifted up her voice in household affairs: she seemed, by her silence, to admit her own inadequacy in culture and intellect, when topics of interest were being discussed, only coming out now and then with defiant platitudes and truisms—for almost defiantly she took the commonplace, vulgarian point of view; yet everything she would turn with her quiet, triumphant assurance to James Houghton, and start on some point of business, soft, assured, ascendant. The others shut their ears.

Now Miss Pinnegar had to get her footing slowly. She had to let James run the gamut of his creations. Each Friday night new wonders, robes and ladies' 'suits'—the phrase was very new—garnished the window of Houghton's shop. It was one of the sights of the place, Houghton's window on Friday night. Young or old, no individual, certainly no female left Woodhouse without spending an excited and usually hilarious ten minutes on the pavement under the window. Muffled shrieks of young damsels who had just got their first view, guffaws of sympathetic youths, continued giggling and expostulation and 'Eh, but what price the umbrella skirt, my girl!' and 'You'd like to marry me in *that*, my boy—what? not half!'—or else 'Eh, now, if you'd seen me in *that* you'd have fallen in love with me at first sight, shouldn't you?'—with a probable answer 'I should have

fallen over myself making haste to get away'—loud guffaws:
—all this was the regular Friday night's entertainment in
Woodhouse. James Houghton's shop was regarded as a
weekly comic issue. His piqué costumes with glass buttons
and sort of steel-trimming collars and cuffs were immortal.

But why, once more, drag it out. Miss Pinnegar served in
the shop on Friday nights. She stood by her man. Sometimes
when the shrieks grew loudest she came to the shop door
and looked with her pale grey eyes at the ridiculous mob of
lasses in tam-o'-shanters and youths half-buried in caps.
And she imposed a silence. They edged away.

Meanwhile Miss Pinnegar pursued the sober and even
tenor of her own way. Whilst James lashed out, to use the
local phrase, in robes and 'suits', Miss Pinnegar steadily
ground away, producing strong, indestructible shirts and
singlets for the colliers, sound, serviceable aprons for the
colliers' wives, good print dresses for servants, and so on.
She executed no flights of fancy. She had her goods made
to suit her people. And so, underneath the foam and froth
of James's creative adventure flowed a slow but steady
stream of output and income. The women of Woodhouse
came at last to *depend* on Miss Pinnegar. Growing lads in
the pit reduce their garments to shreds with amazing expe-
dition. 'I'll go to Miss Pinnegar for thy shirts this time, my
lad,' said the harassed mothers, 'and see if *they'll* stand thee.'
It was almost like a threat. But it served Manchester House.

James bought very little stock in these days; just remnants
and pieces for his immortal robes. It was Miss Pinnegar who
saw the travellers and ordered the unions and calicoes and
grey flannel. James hovered round and said the last word,
of course. But what was his last word but an echo of Miss
Pinnegar's penultimate! He was not interested in unions and
twills.

His own stock remained on hand. Time, like a slow whirl-
pool, churned it over into sight and out of sight, like a mass
of dead sea-weed in a backwash. There was a regular series
of sales fortnightly. The display of 'creations' fell off. The
new entertainment was the Friday-night's sale. James would
attack some portion of his stock, make a wild jumble of it,
spend a delirious Wednesday and Thursday marking down,

and then open on Friday afternoon. In the evening there
was a crush. A good moiré underskirt for one-and-eleven-
three was not to be neglected, and a handsome stringlace
collarette for six-three would iron out and be worth at least
three-and-six. That was how it went: it would nearly all of
it iron out into something really nice, poor James's crum-
pled stock. His fine, semi-transparent face flushed pink, his
eyes flashed as he took in the sixpences and handed back
knots of tape or packets of pins for the notorious farthings.
What matter if the farthing change had originally cost him
a halfpenny! His shop was crowded with women peeping
and pawing and turning things over and commenting in
loud, unfeeling tones. For there were still many comic items.
Once, for example, he suddenly heaped up piles of hats,
trimmed and untrimmed, the weirdest, sauciest, most
screaming shapes. Woodhouse enjoyed itself that night.

And all the time, in her quiet, polite, think-the-more fashion Miss Pinnegar waited on the people, showing them con-
siderable forbearance and just a tinge of contempt. She
became very tired those evenings—her hair under its invisible hair-net became flatter, her cheeks hung down purplish
and mottled. But while James stood she stood. The people
did not like her, yet she influenced them. And the stock
slowly wilted, withered. Some was scrapped. The shop
seemed to have digested some of its indigestible contents.

James accumulated sixpences in a miserly fashion. Luckily
for her work-girls, Miss Pinnegar took her own orders, and
received payments for her own productions. Some of her
regular customers paid her a shilling a week—or less. But it
made a small, steady income. She reserved her own modest
share, paid the expenses of her department, and left the res-
idue to James.

James had accumulated sixpences, and made a little space
in his shop. He had desisted from 'creations'. Time now for
a new flight. He decided it was better to be a manufacturer
than a tradesman. His shop, already only half its original
size, was again too big. It might be split once more. Rents
had risen in Woodhouse. Why not cut off another shop
from his premises?

No sooner said than done. In came the architect, with

whom he had played many a game of chess. Best, said the architect, take off one good-sized shop, rather than halve the premises. James would be left a little cramped, a little tight, with only one-third of his present space. But as we age we dwindle.

More hammering and alterations, and James found himself cooped in a long, long narrow shop, very dark at the back, with a high oblong window and a door that came in at a pinched corner. Next door to him was a cheerful new grocer of the cheap and florid type. The new grocer whistled 'Just Like the Ivy', and shouted boisterously to his shop-boy. In his doorway, protruding on James's sensitive vision, was a pyramid of sixpence-halfpenny tins of salmon, red, shiny tins with a pink halved salmon depicted, and another yellow pyramid of fourpence-halfpenny tins of pineapple. Bacon dangled in pale rolls *almost* over James's doorway, whilst straw and paper, redolent of cheese, lard, and stale eggs filtered through the threshold.

This was coming down in the world, with a vengeance. But what James lost downstairs he tried to recover upstairs. Heaven knows what he would have done, but for Miss Pinnegar. She kept her own work-rooms against him, with a soft, heavy, silent tenacity that would have beaten stronger men than James. But his strength lay in his pliability. He rummaged in the empty lofts, and among the discarded machines, and started an elastic department, making elastic for garters, and for hat-chins.

He was immensely proud of his first cards of elastic, and saw Dame Fortune this time fast in his yielding hands. But, becoming used to disillusionment, he almost welcomed it. Within six months he realized that every inch of elastic cost him exactly sixty per cent more than he could sell it for, and so he scrapped his new department. Luckily, he sold one machine and even gained two pounds on it.

After this, he made one last effort. This was hosiery webbing, which could be cut up and made into as-yet-unheard-of garments. Miss Pinnegar kept her thumb on this enterprise, so that it was not much more than abortive. And then James left her alone.

Meanwhile the shop slowly churned its oddments. Every

Thursday afternoon James sorted out tangles of bits and bobs, antique garments and occasional finds. With these he trimmed his window, so that it looked like a historical museum, rather soiled and scrappy. Indoors he made baskets of assortments: threepenny, sixpenny, ninepenny, and shilling baskets, rather like a bran pie in which everything was a plum. And then, on Friday evening, thin and alert he hovered behind the counter, his coat shabbily buttoned over his narrow chest, his face agitated. He had shaved his side-whiskers, so that they only grew becomingly as low as his ears. His rather large, grey moustache was brushed off his mouth. His hair, gone very thin, was brushed frail and floating over his baldness. But still a gentleman, still courteous, with a charming voice he suggested the possibilities of a pad of green parrots' tail-feathers, or of a few yards of pink-pearl trimming or of old chenille fringe. The women would pinch the thick, exquisite old chenille fringe, delicate and faded, curious to feel its softness. But they wouldn't give threepence for it. Tapes, ribbons, braids, buttons, feathers, jabots, bussels, appliqués, fringes, jet-trimmings, bugle-trimmings, bundles of old coloured machine-lace, many bundles of strange cord, in all colours, for old-fashioned braid-patterning, ribbons with H.M.S. *Birkenhead*, for boys' sailor caps—everything that nobody wanted, did the women turn over and over, till they chanced on a find. And James's quick eyes watched the slow surge of his flotsam, as the pot boiled but did not boil away. Wonderful that he did not think of the days when these bits and bobs were new treasures. But he did not.

And at his side Miss Pinnegar quietly took orders for shirts, discussed and agreed, made measurements and received instalments.

The shop was now only opened on Friday afternoons and evenings, so every day, twice a day, James was seen dithering bareheaded and hastily down the street, as if pressed by fate, to the Conservative Club, and twice a day he was seen as hastily returning, to his meals. He was becoming an old man: his daughter was a young woman: but in his own mind he was just the same, and his daughter was a little child, his wife a young invalid whom he must charm by some few delicate attentions—such as the peeled apple.

At the club he got into more mischief. He met men who wanted to extend a brickfield down by the railway. The brickfield was called Klondyke. James had now a new direction to run in: downhill towards Bagthorpe, to Klondyke. Big penny-daisies grew in tufts on the brink of the yellow clay at Klondyke, yellow eggs-and-bacon spread their midsummer mats of flower. James came home with clay smeared all over him, discoursing brilliantly on grit and paste and presses and kilns and stamps. He carried home a rough and pinkish brick, and gloated over it. It was a *hard* brick, it was a non-porous brick. It was an ugly brick, painfully heavy and parched-looking.

This time he was sure: Dame Fortune would rise like Persephone out of the earth. He was all the more sure, because other men of the town were in with him at this venture: sound, moneyed grocers and plumbers. They were all going to become rich.

Klondyke lasted a year and a half, and was not so bad, for in the end, all things considered, James had lost not more than five per cent of his money. In fact, all things considered, he was about square. And yet he felt Klondyke as the greatest blow of all. Miss Pinnegar would have aided and abetted him in another scheme, if it would but have cheered him. Even Miss Frost was nice with him. But to no purpose. In the year after Klondyke he became an old man, he seemed to have lost all his feathers, he acquired a plucked, tottering look.

Yet he roused up, after a coal-strike. Throttle-Ha'penny put new life into him. During a coal-strike the miners themselves began digging in the fields, just near the houses, for the surface coal. They found a plentiful seam of drossy, yellowish coal behind the Methodist New Connexion chapel. The seam was opened in the side of a bank, and approached by a footrill, a sloping shaft down which the men walked. When the strike was over, two or three miners still remained working the soft, drossy coal, which they sold for eight-and-sixpence a ton—or sixpence a hundredweight. But a mining population scorned such dirt, as they called it.

James Houghton, however, was seized with a desire to work the Connexion Meadow seam, as he called it. He gathered two miner partners—he trotted endlessly up to the field, he talked, as he had never talked before, with innumerable colliers. Everybody he met he stopped, to talk Connexion Meadow.

And so at last he sank a shaft, sixty feet deep, rigged up a corrugated-iron engine-house with a winding-engine, and lowered his men one at a time down the shaft, in a big bucket. The whole affair was rickety, amateurish, and twopenny. The name Connexion Meadow was forgotten within three months. Everybody knew the place as Throttle-Ha'penny. 'What!' said a collier to his wife: 'have we got no coal? You'd better get a bit from Throttle-Ha'penny.' 'Nay,' replied the wife, 'I'm sure I shan't. I'm sure I shan't burn that muck, and smother myself with white ash.'

It was in early Throttle-Ha'penny days that Mrs Houghton died. James Houghton cried, and put a black band on his Sunday silk hat. But he was too feverishly busy at Throttle-Ha'penny, selling his hundredweights of ash-pit fodder, as the natives called it, to realize anything else.

He had three men and two boys working his pit, besides a superannuated old man driving the winding engine. And in spite of all jeering, he flourished. Shabby old coal-carts rambled up behind the New Connexion, and filled from the pit-bank. The coal improved a little in quality: it was cheap and it was handy. James could sell at least fifty or sixty tons a week: for the stuff was easy getting. And now at least he was actually handling money. He saw millions ahead.

This went on for more than a year. A year after the death of Mrs Houghton, Miss Frost became ill and suddenly died. Again James Houghton cried and trembled. But it was Throttle-Ha'penny that made him tremble. He trembled in all his limbs, at the touch of success. He saw himself making noble provision for his only daughter.

But alas—it is wearying to repeat the same thing over and over. First the Board of Trade began to make difficulties. Then there was a fault in the seam. Then the roof of Throttle-Ha'penny was so loose and soft, James could not afford timber to hold it up. In short, when his daughter Alvina was about twenty-seven years old, Throttle-Ha'penny closed down. There was a sale of poor machinery, and James Houghton came home to the dark, gloomy house—to Miss Pinnegar and Alvina.

It was a pinched, dreary house. James seemed down for the last time. But Miss Pinnegar persuaded him to take the shop again on Friday evening. For the rest, faded and peaked, he hurried shadowily down to the club.

CHAPTER 2

The Rise of Alvina Houghton

The heroine of this story is Alvina Houghton. If we leave her out of the first chapter of her own story it is because, during the first twenty-five years of her life, she really was left out of count, or so overshadowed as to be negligible. She and her mother were the phantom passengers in the ship of James Houghton's fortunes.

In Manchester House, every voice lowered its tone. And so from the first Alvina spoke with a quiet, refined, almost convent voice. She was a thin child with delicate limbs and face, and wide, grey-blue, ironic eyes. Even as a small girl she had that odd ironic tilt of the eyelids which gave her a look as if she were hanging back in mockery. If she were, she was quite unaware of it, for under Miss Frost's care she received no education in irony or mockery. Miss Frost was straightforward, good-humoured, and a little earnest. Consequently Alvina, or Vina as she was called, understood only the explicit mode of good-humoured straightforwardness.

It was doubtful which shadow was greater over the child: that of Manchester House, gloomy and a little sinister, or that of Miss Frost, benevolent and protective. Sufficient that the girl herself worshipped Miss Frost: or believed she did.

Alvina never went to school. She had her lessons from her beloved governess, she worked at the piano, she took her

walks, and for social life she went to the Congregational
Chapel, and to the functions connected with the chapel.
While she was little, she went to Sunday School twice and
to chapel once on Sundays. Then occasionally there was a
magic lantern or a penny reading, to which Miss Frost accompanied her. As she grew older, she entered the choir at
chapel, she attended Christian Endeavour and P.S.A., and
the Literary Society on Monday evenings. Chapel provided
her with a whole social activity, in the course of which she
met certain groups of people, made certain friends, found
opportunity for strolls into the country and jaunts to the
local entertainments. Over and above this, every Thursday
evening she went to the subscription library to change the
week's supply of books, and there again she met friends and
acquaintances. It is hard to overestimate the value of church
or chapel—but particularly chapel—as a social institution,
in places like Woodhouse. The Congregational Chapel provided Alvina with a whole outer life, lacking which she
would have been poor indeed. She was not particularly re-
ligious by inclination. Perhaps her father's beautiful prayers
put her off. So she neither questioned nor accepted, but just
let be.

She grew up a slim girl, rather distinguished in appearance, with a slender face, a fine, slightly arched nose, and
beautiful grey-blue eyes over which the lids tilted with a
very odd, sardonic tilt. The sardonic quality was, however,
quite in abeyance. She was ladylike, not vehement at all. In
the street her walk had a delicate, lingering motion, her face
looked still. In conversation she had rather a quick, hurried
manner, with intervals of well-bred repose and attention.
Her voice was like her father's, flexible and curiously attractive.

Sometimes, however, she would have fits of boisterous
hilarity, not quite natural, with a strange note half pathetic,
half jeering. Her father tended to a supercilious, sneering
tone. In Vina it came out in mad bursts of hilarious jeering.
This made Miss Frost uneasy. She would watch the girl's
strange face, that could take on a gargoyle look. She would
see the eyes rolling strangely under the sardonic lids, and
then Miss Frost would feel that never, never had she known

anything so utterly alien and incomprehensible and unsympathetic as her own beloved Vina. For twenty years the strong, protective governess reared and tended her lamb, her dove, only to see the lamb open a wolf's mouth, to hear the dove utter the wild cackle of a daw or a magpie, a strange sound of derision. At such times Miss Frost's heart went cold within her. She dared not realize. And she chid and checked her ward, restored her to the usual impulsive, affectionate demureness. Then she dismissed the whole matter. It was just an accidental aberration on the girl's part from her own true nature. Miss Frost taught Alvina thoroughly the qualities of her own true nature, and Alvina believed what she was taught. She remained for twenty years the demure, refined creature of her governess's desire. But there was an odd, derisive look at the back of her eyes, a look of old knowledge and deliberate derision. She herself was unconscious of it. But it was there. And this it was, perhaps, that scared away the young men.

Alvina reached the age of twenty-three, and it looked as if she were destined to join the ranks of the old maids, so many of whom found cold comfort in the chapel. For she had no suitors. True there were extraordinarily few young men of her class—for whatever her condition, she had certain breeding and inherent culture—in Woodhouse. The young men of the same social standing as herself were in some curious way outsiders to her. Knowing nothing, yet her ancient sapience went deep, deeper than Woodhouse could fathom. The young men did not like her for it. They did not like the tilt of her eyelids.

Miss Frost, with anxious foreseeing, persuaded the girl to take over some pupils, to teach them the piano. The work was distasteful to Alvina. She was not a good teacher. She persevered in an off-hand way, somewhat indifferent, albeit dutiful.

When she was twenty-three years old, Alvina met a man called Graham. He was an Australian, who had been in Edinburgh taking his medical degree. Before going back to Australia, he came to spend some months practising with old Dr Fordham in Woodhouse—Dr Fordham being in some way connected with his mother.

Alexander Graham called to see Mrs Houghton. Mrs Houghton did not like him. She said he was creepy. He was a man of medium height, dark in colouring, with very dark eyes, and a body which seemed to move inside his clothing. He was amiable and polite, laughed often, showing his teeth. It was his teeth which Miss Frost could not stand. She seemed to see a strong mouthful of cruel, compact teeth. She declared he had dark blood in his veins, that he was not a man to be trusted, and that never, never would he make any woman's life happy.

Yet in spite of all, Alvina was attracted by him. The two would stay together in the parlour, laughing and talking by the hour. What they could find to talk about was a mystery. Yet there they were, laughing and chatting, with a running insinuating sound through it all which made Miss Frost pace up and down unable to bear herself.

The man was always running in when Miss Frost was out. He contrived to meet Alvina in the evening, to take a walk with her. He went a long walk with her one night, and wanted to make love to her. But her upbringing was too strong for her.

'Oh no,' she said. 'We are only friends.'

He knew her upbringing was too strong for him also.

'We're more than friends,' he said. 'We're more than friends.'

'I don't think so,' she said.

'Yes we are,' he insisted, trying to put his arm round her waist.

'Oh, don't!' she cried. 'Let us go home.'

And then he burst out with wild and thick protestations of love, which thrilled her and repelled her slightly.

'Anyhow I must tell Miss Frost,' she said.

'Yes, yes,' he answered. 'Yes, yes. Let us be engaged at once.'

As they passed under the lamps he saw her face lifted, the eyes shining, the delicate nostrils dilated, as of one who scents battle and laughs to herself. She seemed to laugh with a certain proud, sinister recklessness. His hands trembled with desire.

So they were engaged. He bought her a ring, an emerald

set in tiny diamonds. Miss Frost looked grave and silent, but would not openly deny her approval.

'You like him, don't you? You don't dislike him?' Alvina insisted.

'I don't dislike him,' replied Miss Frost. 'How can I? He is a perfect stranger to me.'

And with this Alvina subtly contented herself. Her father treated the young man with suave attention, punctuated by fits of jerky hostility and jealousy. Her mother merely sighed, and took sal volatile.

To tell the truth, Alvina herself was a little repelled by the man's love-making. She found him fascinating, but a trifle repulsive. And she was not sure whether she hated the repulsive element, or whether she rather gloried in it. She kept her look of arch, half-derisive recklessness, which was so unbearably painful to Miss Frost, and so exciting to the dark little man. It was a strange look in a refined, really virgin girl—oddly sinister. And her voice had a curious bronze-like resonance that acted straight on the nerves of her hearers: unpleasantly on most English nerves, but like fire on the different susceptibilities of the young man—the darkie, as people called him.

But after all, he had only six weeks in England, before sailing to Sydney. He suggested that he and Alvina should marry before he sailed. Miss Frost would not hear of it. He must see his people first, she said.

So the time passed, and he sailed. Alvina missed him, missed the extreme excitement of him rather than the human being he was. Miss Frost set to work to regain her influence over her ward, to remove that arch, reckless, almost lewd look from the girl's face. It was a question of heart against sensuality. Miss Frost tried and tried to wake again the girl's loving heart—which loving heart was certainly not occupied by *that man*. It was a hard task, an anxious, bitter task Miss Frost had set herself.

But at last she succeeded. Alvina seemed to thaw. The hard shining of her eyes softened again to a sort of demureness and tenderness. The influence of the man was revoked, the girl was left uninhabited, empty and uneasy.

She was due to follow her Alexander in three months'

time, to Sydney. Came letters from him, *en route*—and then
a cablegram from Australia. He had arrived. Alvina should
have been preparing her trousseau, to follow. But owing to
her change of heart, she lingered indecisive.

'*Do* you love him, dear?' said Miss Frost with emphasis,
knitting her thick, passionate, earnest eyebrows. 'Do you
love him sufficiently? *That's* the point.'

The way Miss Frost put the question implied that Alvina
did not and could not love him—because Miss Frost could
not. Alvina lifted her large, blue eyes, confused, half-tender
towards her governess, half shining with unconscious derision.

'I don't really know,' she said, laughing hurriedly. 'I don't
really.'

Miss Frost scrutinized her, and replied with a meaningful:

'Well—!'

To Miss Frost it was clear as daylight. To Alvina not so.
In her periods of lucidity, when she saw as clear as daylight
also, she certainly did not love the little man. She felt him a
terrible outsider, an inferior, to tell the truth. She wondered
how he could have the slightest attraction for her. In fact
she could not understand it at all. She was as free of him as
if he had never existed. The square green emerald on her
finger was almost nonsensical. She was quite, quite sure of
herself.

And then, most irritating, a complete *volte-face* in her
feelings. The clear-as-daylight mood disappeared as daylight
is bound to disappear. She found herself in a night where
the little man loomed large, terribly large, potent and magical, while Miss Frost had dwindled to nothingness. At such
times she wished with all her force that she could travel like
a cablegram to Australia. She felt it was the only way. She
felt the dark, passionate receptivity of Alexander over-
whelmed her, enveloped her even from the Antipodes. She
felt herself going distracted—she felt she was going out of
her mind. For she could not act.

Her mother and Miss Frost were fixed in one line. Her
father said:

'Well, of course, you'll do as you think best. There's a

great risk in going so far—a great risk. You would be entirely unprotected.'

'I don't mind being unprotected,' said Alvina perversely.

'Because you don't understand what it means,' said her father.

He looked at her quickly. Perhaps he understood her better than the others.

'Personally,' said Miss Pinnegar, speaking of Alexander, 'I don't care for him. But everyone has their own taste.'

Alvina felt she was being overborne, and that she was letting herself be overborne. She was half relieved. She seemed to nestle into the well-known surety of Woodhouse. The other unknown had frightened her.

Miss Frost now took a definite line.

'I feel you don't love him, dear. I'm almost sure you don't. So now you have to choose. Your mother dreads your going—she dreads it. I am certain you would never see her again. She says she can't bear it—she can't bear the thought of you out there with Alexander. It makes her shudder. She suffers dreadfully, you know. So you will have to choose, dear. You will have to choose for the best.'

Alvina was made stubborn by pressure. She herself had come fully to believe that she did not love him. She was quite sure she did not love him. But out of a certain perversity, she wanted to go.

Came his letter from Sydney, and one from his parents to her and one to her parents. All seemed straightforward—not *very* cordial, but sufficiently. Over Alexander's letter Miss Frost shed bitter tears. To her it seemed so shallow and heartless, with terms of endearment stuck in like exclamation marks. He seemed to have no thought, no feeling for the girl herself. All he wanted was to hurry her out there. He did not even mention the grief of her parting from her English parents and friends: not a word. Just a rush to get her out there, winding up 'And now, dear, I shall not be myself till I see you here in Sydney—Your ever-loving Alexander.' A selfish, sensual creature, who would forget the dear little Vina in three months, if she did not turn up, and who would neglect her in six months, if she did. Probably Miss Frost was right.

Alvina knew the tears she was costing all round. She went upstairs and looked at his photograph—his dark and impertinent muzzle. Who was *he*, after all? She did not know him. With cold eyes she looked at him, and found him repugnant.

She went across to her governess's room, and found Miss Frost in a strange mood of trepidation.

'Don't trust me, dear, don't trust what I say,' poor Miss Frost ejaculated hurriedly, even wildly. 'Don't notice what I have said. Act for yourself, dear. Act for yourself entirely. I am sure I am wrong in trying to influence you. I know I am wrong. It is wrong and foolish of me. Act just for yourself, dear—the rest doesn't matter. The rest doesn't matter. Don't take *any* notice of what I have said. I know I am wrong.'

For the first time in her life Alvina saw her beloved governess flustered, the beautiful white hair looking a little draggled, the grey, near-sighted eyes, so deep and kind behind the gold-rimmed glasses, now distracted and scared. Alvina immediately burst into tears and flung herself into the arms of Miss Frost. Miss Frost also cried as if her heart would break, catching her indrawn breath with a strange sound of anguish, forlornness, the terrible crying of a woman with a loving heart, whose heart has never been able to relax. Alvina was hushed. In a second, she became the elder of the two. The terrible poignancy of the woman of fifty-two, who now at last had broken down, silenced the girl of twenty-three, and roused all her passionate tenderness. The terrible sound of 'Never now, never now—it is too late,' which seemed to ring in the curious, indrawn cries of the elder woman, filled the girl with a deep wisdom. She knew the same would ring in her mother's dying cry. Married or unmarried, it was the same—the same anguish, realized in all its pain after the age of fifty—the loss in never having been able to relax, to submit.

Alvina felt very strong and rich in the fact of her youth. For her it was not too late. For Miss Frost it was forever too late.

'I don't want to go, dear,' said Alvina to the elder woman. 'I know I don't care for him. He is nothing to me.'

Miss Frost became gradually silent, and turned aside her face. After this there was a hush in the house. Alvina announced her intention of breaking off her engagement. Her mother kissed her, and cried, and said, with the selfishness of an invalid:

'I couldn't have parted with you, I couldn't.' Whilst the father said:

'I think you are wise, Vina. I have thought a lot about it.'

So Alvina packed up his ring and his letters and little presents, and posted them over the seas. She was relieved, really: as if she had escaped some very trying ordeal. For some days she went about happily, in pure relief. She loved everybody. She was charming and sunny and gentle with everybody, particularly with Miss Frost, whom she loved with a deep, tender, rather sore love. Poor Miss Frost seemed to have lost a part of her confidence, to have taken on a new wistfulness, a new silence and remoteness. It was as if she found her busy contact with life a strain now. Perhaps she was getting old. Perhaps her proud heart had given way.

Alvina had kept a little photograph of the man. She would often go and look at it. Love?—no, it was not love! It was something more primitive still. It was curiosity, deep, radical, burning curiosity. How she looked and looked at his dark, impertinent-seeming face. A flicker of derision came into her eyes. Yet still she looked.

In the same manner she would look into the faces of the young men of Woodhouse. But she never found there what she found in her photograph. They all seemed like blank sheets of paper in comparison. There was a curious pale surface-look in the faces of the young men of Woodhouse: or, if there was some underneath suggestive power, it was a little abject or humiliating, inferior, common. They were all either blank or common.

CHAPTER 3

The Maternity Nurse

Of course Alvina made everybody pay for her mood of submission and sweetness. In a month's time she was quite intolerable.

'I can't stay here all my life,' she declared, stretching her eyes in a way that irritated the other inmates of Manchester House extremely. 'I know I can't. I can't bear it. I simply can't bear it, and there's an end of it. I can't, I tell you. I can't bear it. I'm buried alive—simply buried alive. And it's more than I can stand. It is, really.'

There was an odd clang, like a taunt, in her voice. She was trying them all.

'But what do you want, dear?' asked Miss Frost, knitting her dark brows in agitation.

'I want to go away,' said Alvina bluntly.

Miss Frost gave a slight gesture with her right hand, of helpless impatience. It was so characteristic, that Alvina almost laughed.

'But where do you want to go?' asked Miss Frost.

'I don't know. I don't care,' said Alvina. 'Anywhere, if I can get out of Woodhouse.'

'Do you wish you had gone to Australia?' put in Miss Pinnegar.

'No, I don't wish I had gone to Australia,' retorted Alvina

with a rude laugh. 'Australia isn't the only other place besides Woodhouse.'

Miss Pinnegar was naturally offended. But the curious
insolence which sometimes came out in the girl was inherited direct from her father.

'You see, dear,' said Miss Frost, agitated: 'if you knew
what you wanted, it would be easier to see the way.'

'I want to be a nurse,' rapped out Alvina.

Miss Frost stood still, with the stillness of a middle-aged,
disapproving woman, and looked at her charge. She believed
that Alvina was just speaking at random. Yet she dared not
check her, in her present mood.

Alvina was indeed speaking at random. She had never
thought of being a nurse—the idea had never entered her
head. If it had she would certainly never have entertained it.
But she had heard Alexander speak of Nurse This and Sister
That. And so she had rapped out her declaration. And
having rapped it out, she prepared herself to stick to it.
Nothing like leaping before you look.

'A nurse!' repeated Miss Frost. 'But do you feel yourself
fitted to be a nurse? Do you think you could bear it?'

'Yes, I'm sure I could,' retorted Alvina. 'I want to be a
maternity nurse—' She looked strangely, even outrageously,
at her governess. 'I want to be a maternity nurse. Then I
shouldn't have to attend operations.' And she laughed
quickly.

Miss Frost's right hand beat like a wounded bird. It was
reminiscent of the way she beat time, insistently, when she
was giving music lessons, sitting close beside her pupils at
the piano. Now it beat without time or reason. Alvina
smiled brightly and cruelly.

'Whatever put such an idea into your head, Vina?' asked
poor Miss Frost.

'I don't know,' said Alvina, still more archly and brightly.

'Of course you don't mean it, dear,' said Miss Frost,
quailing.

'Yes, I do. Why should I say it if I don't?'

Miss Frost would have done anything to escape the arch,
bright, cruel eyes of her charge.

'Then we must think about it,' said she, numbly. And she went away.

Alvina floated off to her room, and sat by the window looking down on the street. The bright, arch look was still on her face. But her heart was sore. She wanted to cry, and fling herself on the breast of her darling. But she couldn't. No, for her life she couldn't. Some little devil sat in her breast and kept her smiling archly.

Somewhat to her amazement, he sat steadily on for days and days. Every minute she expected him to go. Every minute she expected to break down, to burst into tears and tenderness and reconciliation. But no—she did not break down. She persisted. They all waited for the old loving Vina to be herself again. But the new and recalcitrant Vina still shone hard. She found a copy of *The Lancet*, and saw an advertisement of a home in Islington where maternity nurses would be fully trained and equipped in six months' time. The fee was sixty guineas. Alvina declared her intention of departing to this training home. She had two hundred pounds of her own, bequeathed by her grandfather.

In Manchester House they were all horrified—not moved with grief, this time, but shocked. It seemed such a repulsive and indelicate step to take. Which it was. And which, in her curious perverseness, Alvina must have intended it to be. Mrs Houghton assumed a remote air of silence, as if she did not hear any more, did not belong. She lapsed far away. She was really very weak. Miss Pinnegar said: 'Well really, if she wants to do it, why, she might as well try.' And, as often with Miss Pinnegar, this speech seemed to contain a veiled threat.

'A maternity nurse!' said James Houghton. 'A maternity nurse! What exactly do you mean by a maternity nurse?'

'A trained midwife,' said Miss Pinnegar curtly. 'That's it, isn't it? It is as far as I can see. A trained midwife.'

'Yes, of course,' said Alvina brightly.

'But—!' stammered James Houghton, pushing his spectacles up on to his forehead, and making his long fleece of painfully thin hair uncover his baldness. 'I can't understand that any young girl of any—any upbringing, any upbringing whatever, should want to choose such a—such an—occupation. I can't understand it.'

'Can't you?' said Alvina brightly.

'Oh, well, if she *does*—' said Miss Pinnegar cryptically.

Miss Frost said very little. But she had serious confidential talks with Dr Fordham. Dr Fordham didn't approve, certainly he didn't—but neither did he see any great harm in it. At that time it was rather the thing for young ladies to enter the nursing profession, if their hopes had been blighted or checked in another direction! And so, inquiries were made. Inquiries were made.

The upshot was, that Alvina was to go to Islington for her six months' training. There was a great bustle, preparing her nursing outfit. Instead of a trousseau, nurse's uniforms in fine blue-and-white stripe, with great white aprons. Instead of a wreath of orange blossom, a rather chic nurse's bonnet of blue silk, and for a trailing veil, a blue silk fall.

Well and good! Alvina expected to become frightened, as the time drew near. But no, she wasn't a bit frightened. Miss Frost watched her narrowly. Would there not be a return of the old, tender, sensitive, shrinking Vina—the exquisitely sensitive and nervous, loving girl? No, astonishing as it may seem, there was no return of such a creature. Alvina remained bright and ready, the half-hilarious clang remained in her voice, taunting. She kissed them all good-bye, brightly and sprightly, and off she set. She wasn't nervous.

She came to St Pancras, she got her cab, she drove off to her destination—and as she drove, she looked out of the window. Horrid, vast, stony, dilapidated, crumbly-stuccoed streets and squares of Islington, grey, grey, greyer by far than Woodhouse, and interminable. How exceedingly sordid and disgusting! But instead of being repelled and heartbroken Alvina enjoyed it. She felt her trunk rumble on the top of the cab, and still she looked out on the ghastly dilapidated flat façades of Islington, and still she smiled brightly, as if there were some charm in it all. Perhaps for her there was a charm in it all. Perhaps it acted like a tonic on the little devil in her breast. Perhaps if she had seen tufts of snowdrops—it was February—and yew-hedges and cottage windows, she would have broken down. As it was, she just enjoyed it. She enjoyed glimpsing in through uncurtained windows, into sordid rooms where human beings moved as if sordidly unaware. She enjoyed the smell of a toasted bloater, rather burnt. So common! so indescribably common! And she detested bloaters, because of the hairy feel of the spines in her mouth. But to smell them like this, to know that she was in the region of 'penny beef-steaks', gave her a perverse pleasure.

The cab stopped at a yellow house at the corner of a square where some shabby bare trees were flecked with bits of blown paper, bits of paper and refuse cluttered inside the round railings of each tree. She went up some dirty-yellowish steps, and rang the 'Patients' bell, because she knew she ought not to ring the 'Tradesmen's'. A servant, not exactly dirty, but unattractive, let her into a hall painted a pale drab, and floored with coco-matting, otherwise bare. Then up bare stairs to a room where a stout, pale, common woman with two warts on her face was drinking tea. It was three o'clock. This was the matron. The matron soon deposited her in a bedroom, not very small, but bare and hard and dusty-seeming, and there left her. Alvina sat down on her chair, looked at her box opposite her, looked round the uninviting room, and smiled to herself. Then she rose and went to the window: a very dirty window, looking down into a sort of well of an area, with other wells ranging along, and straight opposite like a reflection another solid range of back premises, with iron stairways and horrid little doors and washing and little W.C.s and people creeping up and down like vermin. Alvina shivered a little, but still smiled. Then slowly she began to take off her hat. She put it down on the drab-painted chest of drawers.

Presently the servant came in with a tray, set it down, lit a naked gas-jet, which roared faintly, and drew down a crackly dark-green blind, which showed a tendency to fly back again alertly to the ceiling.

'Thank you,' said Alvina, and the girl departed.

Then Miss Houghton drank her black tea and ate her bread and margarine.

Surely enough books have been written about heroines in

similar circumstances. There is no need to go into the details of Alvina's six months in Islington.

The food was objectionable—yet Alvina got fat on it. The air was filthy—and yet never had her colour been so warm and fresh, her skin so soft. Her companions were almost without exception vulgar and coarse—yet never had she got on so well with women of her own age—or older than herself. She was ready with a laugh and a word, and though she was unable to venture on indecencies herself, yet she had an amazing faculty for *looking* knowing and indecent beyond words, rolling her eyes and pitching her eyebrows in a certain way—oh, it was quite sufficient for her companions! And yet, if they had ever actually demanded a dirty story or a really open indecency from her, she would have been floored.

But she enjoyed it. Amazing how she enjoyed it. She did not care *how* revolting and indecent these nurses were—she put on a look as if she were in with it all, and it all passed off as easy as winking. She swung her haunches and arched her eyes with the best of them. And they behaved as if she were exactly one of themselves. And yet, with the curious cold tact of women, they left her alone, one and all, in private: just ignored her.

It is truly incredible how Alvina became blooming and bouncing at this time. Nothing shocked her, nothing upset her. She was always ready with her hard, nurse's laugh and her nurse's quips. No one was better than she at *double-entendres*. No one could better give the nurse's leer. She had it all in a fortnight. And never once did she feel anything but exhilarated and in full swing. It seemed to her she had not a moment's time to brood or reflect about things—she was too much in the swing. Every moment, in the swing, living, or active in full swing. When she got into bed she went to sleep. When she awoke, it was morning, and she got up. As soon as she was up and dressed she had somebody to answer, something to say, something to do. Time passed like an express train—and she seemed to have known no other life than this.

Not far away was a lying-in hospital. A dreadful place it was. There she had to go, right off, and help with cases.

There she had to attend lectures and demonstrations. There she met the doctors and students. Well, a pretty lot they were, one way and another. When she had put on flesh and become pink and bouncing she was just their sort; just their very ticket. Her voice had the right twang, her eyes the right roll, her haunches the right swing. She seemed altogether just the ticket. And yet she wasn't.

It would be useless to say she was not shocked. She was profoundly and awfully shocked. Her whole state was perhaps largely the result of shock: a sort of play-acting based on hysteria. But the dreadful things she saw in the lying-in hospital, and afterwards, went deep, and finished her youth and her tutelage for ever. How many infernos deeper than Miss Frost could ever know, did she not travel? the inferno of the human animal, the human organism in its convulsions, the human social beast in its abjection and its degradation.

For in her latter half she had to visit the slum cases. And such cases! A woman lying on a bare, filthy floor, a few old coats thrown over her, and vermin crawling everywhere, in spite of sanitary inspectors. But what did the woman, the sufferer, herself care! She ground her teeth and screamed and yelled with pains. In her calm periods she lay stupid and indifferent—or she cursed a little. But abject, stupid indifference was the bottom of it all: abject, brutal indifference to everything—yes, everything. Just a piece of female functioning, no more.

Alvina was supposed to receive a certain fee for these cases she attended in their homes. A small proportion of her fee she kept for herself, the rest she handed over to the Home. That was the agreement. She received her grudged fee callously, threatened and exacted it when it was not forthcoming. Ha!—if they didn't have to pay you at all, these slum-people, they would treat you with more contempt than if you were one of themselves. It was one of the hardest lessons Alvina had to learn—to bully these people, in their own hovels, into some sort of obedience to her commands, and some sort of respect for her presence. She had to fight tooth and nail for this end. And in a week she was as hard and callous to them as they to her. And so her work was well done. She did not hate them. There they were. They had a certain life, and you had to take them at their own worth in their own way. What else! If one should be gentle, one was gentle. The difficulty did not lie there. The difficulty lay in being sufficiently rough and hard: that was the trouble. It cost a great struggle to be hard and callous enough. Glad she would have been to be allowed to treat them quietly and gently, with consideration. But pah—it was not their line. They wanted to be callous, and if you were not callous to match, they made a fool of you and prevented your doing your work.

Was Alvina her own real self all this time? The mighty question arises upon us, what is one's own real self? It certainly is not what we think we are and ought to be. Alvina had been bred to think of herself as a delicate, tender, chaste creature with unselfish inclinations and a pure, 'high' mind. Well, so she was, in the more-or-less exhausted part of herself. But high-mindedness had really come to an end with James Houghton, had really reached the point, not only of pathetic, but of dry and anti-human, repulsive quixotry. In Alvina high-mindedness was already stretched beyond the breaking point. Being a woman of some flexibility of temper, wrought through generations to a fine, pliant hardness, she flew back. She went right back on high-mindedness. Did she thereby betray it?

We think not. If we turn over the head of the penny and look at the tail, we don't thereby deny or betray the head. We do but adjust it to its own complement. And so with high-mindedness. It is but one side of the medal—the crowned reverse. On the obverse the three legs still go kicking the soft-footed spin of the universe, the dolphin flirts and the crab leers.

So Alvina spun her medal, and her medal came down tails. Heads or tails? Heads for generations. Then tails. See the poetic justice.

Now Alvina decided to accept the decision of her fate. Or rather, being sufficiently a woman, she didn't decide anything. She *was* her own fate. She went through her training experiences like another being. She was not herself, said Everybody. When she came home to Woodhouse at Easter, in her bonnet and cloak, Everybody was simply knocked out. Imagine that this frail, pallid, diffident girl, so ladylike, was now a rather fat, warm-coloured young woman, strapping and strong-looking, and with a certain bounce. Imagine her mother's startled, almost expiring:

'Why, Vina dear!'

Vina laughed. She knew how they were all feeling.

'At least it agrees with your *health*,' said her father, sarcastically, to which Miss Pinnegar answered:

'Well, that's a good deal.'

But Miss Frost said nothing the first day. Only the second day, at breakfast, as Alvina ate rather rapidly and rather well, the white-haired woman said quietly, with a tinge of cold contempt:

'How changed you are, dear!'

'Am I?' laughed Alvina. 'Oh, not really.' And she gave the arch look with her eyes, which made Miss Frost shudder.

Inwardly, Miss Frost shuddered, and abstained from questioning. Alvina was always speaking of the doctors: Doctor Young and Doctor Headley and Doctor James. She spoke of theatres and music-halls with these young men, and the jolly good time she had with them. And her blue-grey eyes seemed to have become harder and greyer, lighter somehow. In her wistfulness and her tender pathos, Alvina's eyes would deepen their blue, so beautiful. And now, in her floridity, they were bright and arch and light-grey. The deep, tender, flowery blue was gone for ever. They were luminous and crystalline, like the eyes of a changeling.

Miss Frost shuddered, and abstained from question. She wanted, she *needed* to ask of her charge: 'Alvina, have you betrayed yourself with any of these young men?' But coldly her heart abstained from asking—or even from seriously thinking. She left the matter untouched for the moment. She was already too much shocked.

Certainly Alvina represented the young doctors as very nice, but rather fast young fellows. 'My word, you have to have your wits about you with them!' Imagine such a speech from a girl tenderly nurtured: a speech uttered in her own home, and accompanied by a florid laugh, which would lead a chaste, generous woman like Miss Frost to imagine—well, she merely abstained from imagining anything. She had that strength of mind. She never for one moment attempted to answer the question to herself, as to whether Alvina had betrayed herself with any of these young doctors, or not. The question remained stated, but completely unanswered—coldly awaiting its answer. Only when Miss Frost kissed Alvina good-bye at the station, tears came to her eyes, and she said hurriedly, in a low voice:

'Remember we are all praying for you, dear!'

'No, don't do that!' cried Alvina involuntarily, without knowing what she said.

And then the train moved out, and she saw her darling standing there on the station, the pale, well-modelled face looking out from behind the gold-rimmed spectacles, wistfully, the strong, rather stout figure standing very still and unchangeable, under its coat and skirt of dark purple, the white hair glistening under the folded dark hat. Alvina threw herself down on the seat of her carriage. She loved her darling. She would love her through eternity. She knew she was right—amply and beautifully right, her darling, her beloved Miss Frost. Eternally and gloriously right.

And yet—and yet—it was a right which was fulfilled. There were other rights. There was another side to the medal. Purity and high-mindedness—the beautiful, but unbearable tyranny. The beautiful, unbearable tyranny of Miss Frost! It was time now for Miss Frost to die. It was time for that perfected flower to be gathered to immortality. A lovely *immortel*. But an obstruction to other, purple and carmine blossoms which were in bud on the stem. A lovely edelweiss—but time it was gathered into eternity. Black-purple and red anemones were due, real Adonis blood, and strange individual orchids, spotted and fantastic. Time for Miss Frost to die. She, Alvina, who loved her as no one else would ever love her, with that love which goes to the core of the universe, knew that it was time for her darling to be folded, oh, so gently and softly, into immortality. Mortality was busy with the day after her day. It was time for Miss Frost to die. As Alvina sat motionless in the train, running from Woodhouse to Tibshelf, it decided itself in her.

She was glad to be back in Islington, among all the horrors

of her confinement cases. The doctors she knew hailed her.
On the whole, these young men had not any too deep respect for the nurses as a whole. Why drag in respect? Human
functions were too obviously established to make any great
fuss about. And so the doctors put their arms round Alvina's
waist, because she was plump, and they kissed her face, because the skin was soft. And she laughed and squirmed a
little, so that they felt all the more her warmth and softness
under their arm's pressure.

'It's no use, you know,' she said, laughing rather breathless, but looking into their eyes with a curious definite look
of unchangeable resistance. This only piqued them.

'What's no use?' they asked.

She shook her head slightly.

'It isn't any use your behaving like that with me,' she said,
with the same challenging definiteness, finality: a flat negative.

'Who're you telling?' they said.

For she did not at all forbid them to 'behave like that'.
Not in the least. She almost encouraged them. She laughed
and arched her eyes and flirted. But her backbone became
only the stronger and firmer. Soft and supple as she was, her
backbone never yielded for an instant. It could not. She had
to confess that she liked the young doctors. They were alert,
their faces were clean and bright-looking. She liked the sort
of intimacy with them, when they kissed her and wrestled
with her in the empty laboratories or corridors—often in
the intervals of most critical and appalling cases. She liked
their arm around her waist, the kisses as she reached back
her face, straining away, the sometimes desperate struggles.
They took unpardonable liberties. Sometimes her blood really came up in the fight, and she felt as if, with her hands,
she could tear any man, any male creature, limb from limb.
A super-human, voltaic force filled her. For a moment she
surged in massive, inhuman, female strength. The men always wilted. And invariably, when they wilted, she touched
them with a sudden gentle touch, pitying. So that she always
remained friends with them. When her curious Amazonic
power left her again, and she was just a mere woman, she

made shy eyes at them once more, and treated them with the inevitable female-to-male homage.

The men liked her. They cocked their eyes at her, when she was not looking, and wondered at her. They wondered over her. They had been beaten by her, every one of them. But they did not openly know it. They looked at her, as if she were Woman itself, some creature not quite personal. What they noticed, all of them, was the way her brown hair looped over her ears. There was something chaste, and noble, and warlike about it. The remote quality which hung about her in the midst of her intimacies and her frequencies, nothing high or lofty, but something given to the struggle and as yet invincible in the struggle, made them seek her out.

They felt safe with her. They knew she would not let them down. She would not intrigue into marriage, or try and make use of them in any way. She didn't care about them. And so, because of her isolate self-sufficiency in the fray, her wild, overweening backbone, they were ready to attend on her and serve her. Headley in particular hoped he might overcome her. He was a well-built fellow with sandy hair and a pugnacious face. The battle-spirit was really roused in him, and he heartily liked the woman. If he could have overcome her he would have been mad to marry her.

With him, she summoned up all her mettle. She had never to be off her guard for a single minute. The treacherous suddenness of his attack—for he was treachery itself—had to be met by the voltaic suddenness of her resistance and counter-attack. It was nothing less than magical the way the soft, slumbering body of the woman could leap in one jet into terrible, overwhelming voltaic force, something strange and massive, at the first treacherous touch of the man's determined hand. His strength was so different from hers—quick, muscular, lambent. But hers was deep and heaving, like the strange heaving of an earthquake, or the heave of a bull as it rises from earth. And by sheer non-human power, electric and paralysing, she could overcome the brawny redheaded fellow.

He was nearly a match for her. But she did not like him. The two were enemies—and good acquaintances. They were more or less matched. But as he found himself continually foiled, he became sulky, like a bear with a sore head. And then she avoided him.

She really liked Young and James much better. James was a quick, slender, dark-haired fellow, a gentleman, who was always trying to catch her out with his quickness. She liked his fine, slim limbs, and his exaggerated generosity. He would ask her out to ridiculously expensive suppers, and send her sweets and flowers, fabulously recherché. He was always immaculately well-dressed.

'Of course, as a lady *and* a nurse,' he said to her, 'you are two sorts of women in one.'

But she was not impressed by his wisdom.

She was most strongly inclined to Young. He was a plump young man of middle height, with those blue eyes of a little boy which are so knowing: particularly of a woman's secrets. It is a strange thing that these childish men have such a deep, half-perverse knowledge of the other sex. Young was certainly innocent as far as acts went. Yet his hair was going thin at the crown already.

He also played with her—being a doctor, and she a nurse who encouraged it. He too touched her and kissed her: and did *not* rouse her to contest. For his touch and his kiss had that nearness of a little boy's, which nearly melted her. She could almost have succumbed to him. If it had not been that with him there was no question of succumbing. She would have had to take him between her hands and caress and cajole him like a cherub, into a fall. And though she would have liked to do so, yet that inflexible stiffness of her backbone prevented her. She could not do as she liked. There was an inflexible fate within her, which shaped her ends.

Sometimes she wondered to herself, over her own virginity. Was it worth much, after all, behaving as she did? Did she care about it, anyhow? Didn't she rather despise it? To sin in thought was as bad as to sin in act. If the thought was the same as the act, how much more was her behaviour equivalent to a whole committal? She wished she were wholly committed. She wished she had gone the whole length.

But sophistry and wishing did her no good. There she

was, still isolate. And still there was that in her which would preserve her intact, sophistry and deliberate intention notwithstanding. Her time was up. She was returning to Woodhouse virgin as she had left it. In a measure she felt herself beaten. Why? Who knows. But so it was, she felt herself beaten, condemned to go back to what she was before. Fate had been too strong for her and her desires: fate which was not an external association of forces, but which was integral in her own nature. Her own inscrutable nature was her fate: sore against her will.

It was August when she came home, in her nurse's uniform. She was beaten by fate, as far as chastity and virginity went. But she came home with high material hopes. Here was James Houghton's own daughter. She had an affluent future ahead of her. A fully-qualified maternity nurse, she was going to bring all the babies of the district easily and triumphantly into the world. She was going to charge the regulation fee of two guineas a case: and even on a modest estimate of ten babies a month, she would have twenty guineas. For well-to-do mothers she would charge from three to five guineas. At this calculation she would make an easy three hundred a year, without slaving either. She would be independent, she could laugh everyone in the face.

She bounced back into Woodhouse to make her fortune.

CHAPTER 4

Two Women Die

It goes without saying that Alvina Houghton did not make her fortune as a maternity nurse. Being her father's daughter, we might almost expect that she did not make a penny. But she did—just a few pence. She had exactly four cases—and then no more.

The reason is obvious. Who in Woodhouse was going to afford a two-guinea nurse, for a confinement? And who was going to engage Alvina Houghton, even if they were ready to stretch their purse-strings? After all, they all knew her as *Miss* Houghton, with a stress on the *Miss*, and they could not conceive of her as Nurse Houghton. Besides, there seemed something positively indecent in technically engaging one who was so much part of themselves. They all preferred either a simple midwife, or a nurse procured out of the unknown by the doctor.

If Alvina wanted to make her fortune—or even her living—she should have gone to a strange town. She was so advised by everyone she knew. But she never for one moment reflected on the advice. She had become a maternity nurse in order to practise in Woodhouse, just as James Houghton had purchased his elegancies to sell in Woodhouse. And father and daughter alike calmly expected

Woodhouse demand to rise to their supply. So both alike were defeated in their expectations.

For a little while Alvina flaunted about in her nurse's uniform. Then she left it off. And as she left it off she lost her bounce, her colour, and her flesh. Gradually she shrank back to the old, slim, reticent pallor, with eyes a little too large for her face. And now it seemed her face was a little too long, a little gaunt. And in her civilian clothes she seemed a little dowdy, shabby. And altogether, she looked older: she looked more than her age, which was only twenty-four years. Here was the old Alvina come back, rather battered and deteriorated, apparently. There was even a tiny touch of the trollop in her dowdiness—so the shrewd-eyed collier-wives decided. But she was a lady still, and unbeaten. Undeniably she was a lady. And that was rather irritating to the well-to-do and florid daughter of W. H. Johnson, next door but one. Undeniably a lady, and undeniably unmastered. This last was irritating to the goodnatured but easy-coming young men in the Chapel Choir, where she resumed her seat. These young men had the good nature of dogs that wag their tails and expect to be patted. And Alvina did not pat them. To be sure, a pat from such a shabbily-black-kid-gloved hand would not have been so flattering—she need not imagine it! The way she hung back and looked at them, the young men, as knowing as if she were a prostitute, and yet with the well-bred indifference of a lady—well, it was almost offensive.

As a matter of fact, Alvina was detached for the time being from her interest in young men. Manchester House had settled down on her like a doom. There was the quartered shop, through which one had to worm one's encumbered way in the gloom—unless one liked to go miles round a back street, to the yard entry. There was James Houghton, faintly powdered with coal-dust, flitting back and forth in a fever of nervous frenzy, to Throttle-Ha'penny—so carried away that he never saw his daughter at all the first time he came in, after her return. And when she reminded him of her presence, with her—'Hello, father!'—he merely glanced hurriedly at her, as if vexed with her interruption, and said:

'Well, Alvina, you're back. You're back to find us busy.'
And he went off into his ecstasy again.

Mrs Houghton was now very weak, and so nervous in
her weakness that she could not bear the slightest sound.
Her greatest horror was lest her husband should come into
the room. On his entry she became blue at the lips immediately, so he had to hurry out again. At last he stayed away,
only hurriedly asking, each time he came into the house,
'How is Mrs Houghton? Ha!' Then off into uninterrupted
Throttle-Ha'penny ecstasy once more.

When Alvina went up to her mother's room, on her return, all the poor invalid could do was to tremble into tears,
and cry faintly:

'Child, you look dreadful. It isn't you.'

This from the pathetic little figure in the bed had struck
Alvina like a blow.

'Why not, mother?' she said.

But for her mother she had to remove her nurse's uniform. And at the same time, she had to constitute herself
nurse. Miss Frost, and a woman who came in, and the servant had been nursing the invalid between them. Miss Frost
was worn and rather heavy: her old buoyancy and brightness was gone. She had become irritable also. She was very
glad that Alvina had returned to take this responsibility of
nursing off her shoulders. For her wonderful energy had
ebbed and oozed away.

Alvina said nothing, but settled down to her task. She was
quiet and technical with her mother. The two loved one
another, with a curious impersonal love which had not a
single word to exchange: an almost after-death love. In these
days Mrs Houghton never talked—unless to fret a little. So
Alvina sat for many hours in the lofty, sombre bedroom,
looking out silently on the street, or hurriedly rising to attend the sick woman. For continually came the fretful
murmur:

'Vina!'

To sit still—who knows the long discipline of it, nowadays, as our mothers and grandmothers knew. To sit still,
for days, months, and years—perforce to sit still, with some
dignity of tranquil bearing. Alvina was old-fashioned. She

had the old, womanly faculty for sitting quiet and collected—not indeed for a life-time, but for long spells together. And so it was during these months nursing her
mother. She attended constantly on the invalid: she did a
good deal of work about the house: she took her walks and
occupied her place in the choir on Sunday mornings. And
yet, from August to January, she seemed to be seated in her
chair in the bedroom, sometimes reading, but mostly quite
still, her hands quietly in her lap, her mind subdued by musing. She did not even think, not even remember. Even such
activity would have made her presence too disturbing in the
room. She sat quite still, with all her activities in abeyance—
except that strange will-to-passivity which was by no means
a relaxation, but a severe, deep, soul-discipline.

For the moment there was a sense of prosperity—or
probable prosperity, in the house. And there was an abundance of Throttle-Ha'penny coal. It was dirty ashy stuff.
The lower bars of the grate were constantly blanked in with
white powdery ash, which it was fatal to try to poke away.
For if you poked and poked, you raised white cumulus
clouds of ash, and you were left at last with a few darkening
and sulphurous embers. But even so, by continuous application, you could keep the room moderately warm, without
feeling you were consuming the house's meat and drink in
the grate. Which was one blessing.

The days, the months darkened past, and Alvina returned
to her old thinness and pallor. Her fore-arms were thin, they
rested very still in her lap, there was a ladylike stillness about
them as she took her walk, in her lingering, yet watchful
fashion. She saw everything. Yet she passed without attract-
ing any attention.

Early in the year her mother died. Her father came and
wept self-conscious tears, Miss Frost cried a little, painfully.
And Alvina cried also: she did not quite know why or
wherefore. Her poor mother! Alvina had the old-fashioned
wisdom to let be, and not to think. After all, it was not for
her to reconstruct her parents' lives. She came after them.
Her day was not their day, their life was not hers. Returning
up-channel to re-discover their course was quite another
matter from flowing down-stream into the unknown, as

they had done thirty years before. This supercilious and impertinent exploration of the generation gone by, by the present generation, is nothing to our credit. As a matter of fact, no generation repeats the mistakes of the generation ahead, any more than any river repeats its course. So the young need not be so proud of their superiority over the old. The young generation glibly makes its own mistakes: and *how* detestable these new mistakes are, why, only the future will be able to tell us. But be sure they are quite as detestable, quite as full of lies and hypocrisy, as any of the mistakes of our parents. There is no such thing as *absolute* wisdom.

Wisdom has reference only to the past. The future remains forever an infinite field for mistakes. You can't know beforehand.

So Alvina refrained from pondering on her mother's life and fate. Whatever the fate of the mother, the fate of the daughter will be otherwise. That is organically inevitable. The business of the daughter is with her own fate, not with her mother's.

Miss Frost, however, meditated bitterly on the fate of the poor dead woman. Bitterly she brooded on the lot of woman. Here was Clariss Houghton, married, and a mother—and dead. What a life! Who was responsible? James Houghton. What ought James Houghton to have done differently? Everything. In short, he should have been somebody else, and not himself. Which is the *reductio ad absurdum* of idealism. The universe should be something else, and not what it is; so the nonsense of idealistic conclusion. The cat should not catch the mouse, the mouse should not nibble holes in the table-cloth, and so on and so on, in the House that Jack Built.

But Miss Frost sat by the dead in grief and despair. This was the end of another woman's life: such an end! Poor Clariss; guilty James.

Yet why? Why was James more guilty than Clariss? Is the only aim and end of a man's life, to make some woman, or parcel of women, happy? Why? Why should anybody expect to be *made happy*, and develop heart-disease if she isn't? Surely Clariss's heart-disease was a more emphatic sign of obstinate self-importance than ever James's shop-windows were. She expected to be *made happy*. Every woman in Europe and America expects it. On her own head then if she is made unhappy: for her expectation is arrogant and impertinent. The be-all and end-all of life doesn't lie in feminine happiness—or in any happiness. Happiness is a sort of soap-tablet—he won't be happy till he gets it, and when he's got it, the precious baby, it'll cost him his eyes and his stomach. Could anything be more puerile than a mankind howling because it isn't happy: like a baby in the bath!

Poor Clariss, however, was dead—and if she had developed heart-disease because she wasn't happy, well, she had died of her own heart-disease, poor thing. Wherein lies every moral that mankind can wish to draw.

Miss Frost wept in anguish, and saw nothing but another woman betrayed to sorrow and a slow death. Sorrow and a slow death, because a man had married her. Miss Frost wept also for herself, for her own sorrow and slow death. Sorrow and slow death, because a man had *not* married her. Wretched man, what is he to do with these exigent and never-to-be-satisfied women? Our mothers pined because our fathers drank and were rakes. Our wives pine because we are virtuous but inadequate. Who is this sphinx, this woman? Where is the Oedipus that will solve her riddle of happiness, and then strangle her?—only to marry his own mother!

In the months that followed her mother's death, Alvina went on the same, in abeyance. She took over the housekeeping, and received one or two overflow pupils from Miss Frost, young girls to whom she gave lessons in the dark drawing-room of Manchester House. She was busy—chiefly with housekeeping. There seemed a great deal to put in order after her mother's death.

She sorted all her mother's clothes—expensive, old-fashioned clothes, hardly worn. What was to be done with them? She gave them away, without consulting anybody. She kept a few private things, she inherited a few pieces of jewellery. Remarkable how little trace her mother left—hardly a trace.

She decided to move into the big, monumental bedroom in front of the house. She liked space, she liked the windows.

She was strictly mistress, too. So she took her place. Her mother's little sitting-room was cold and disused.

Then Alvina went through all the linen. There was still abundance, and it was all sound. James had had such large ideas of setting up house, in the beginning. And now he begrudged the household expenses, begrudged the very soap and candles, and even would have liked to introduce margarine instead of butter. This last degradation the women refused. But James was above food.

The old Alvina seemed completely herself again. She was quiet, dutiful, affectionate. She appealed in her old, childish way to Miss Frost, and Miss Frost called her 'Dear!' with all the old protective gentleness. But there was a difference. Underneath her appearance of appeal, Alvina was almost coldly independent. She did what she thought she would. The old manner of intimacy persisted between her and her darling. And perhaps neither of them knew that the intimacy itself had gone. But it had. There was no spontaneous interchange between them. It was a kind of deadlock. Each knew the great love she felt for the other. But now it was a love static, inoperative. The warm flow did not run any more. Yet each would have died for the other, would have done anything to spare the other hurt.

Miss Frost was becoming tired, dragged looking. She would sink into a chair as if she wished never to rise again—never to make the effort. And Alvina quickly would attend on her, bring her tea and take away her music, try to make everything smooth. And continually the young woman exhorted the elder to work less, to give up her pupils. But Miss Frost answered quickly, nervously:

'When I don't work I shan't live.'

'But why—?' came the long query from Alvina. And in her expostulation there was a touch of mockery for such a creed.

Miss Frost did not answer. Her face took on a greyish tinge.

In these days Alvina struck up an odd friendship with Miss Pinnegar, after so many years of opposition. She felt herself more in sympathy with Miss Pinnegar—it was so easy to get on with her, she left so much unsaid. What was left unsaid mattered more to Alvina now than anything that was expressed. She began to hate outspokenness and direct speaking-forth of the whole mind. It nauseated her. She wanted tacit admission of difference, not open, whole-hearted communication. And Miss Pinnegar made this admission all along. She never made you feel for an instant that she was one with you. She was never even near. She kept quietly on her own ground, and left you on yours. And across the space came her quiet commonplaces—but fraught with space.

With Miss Frost all was openness, explicit and down-right. Not that Miss Frost trespassed. She was far more well-bred than Miss Pinnegar. But her very breeding had that Protestant, northern quality which assumes that we have all the same high standards, really, and all the same divine nature, intrinsically. It is a fine assumption. But willy-nilly, it sickened Alvina at this time.

She preferred Miss Pinnegar, and admired Miss Pinnegar's humble wisdom with a new admiration. The two were talking of Dr Headley, who, they read in the newspaper, had disgraced himself finally.

'I suppose,' said Miss Pinnegar, 'it takes his sort to make all sorts.'

Such bits of homely wisdom were like relief from cramp and pain, to Alvina. 'It takes his sort to make all sorts.' It took her sort too, and it took her father's sort—as well as her mother's and Miss Frost's. It took every sort to make all sorts. Why have standards and a regulation pattern? Why have a human criterion? There's the point! Why, in the name of all the free heavens, have human criteria? Why? Simply for bullying and narrowness.

Alvina felt at her ease with Miss Pinnegar. The two women talked away to one another, in their quiet moments: and slipped apart like conspirators when Miss Frost came in: as if there was something to be ashamed of. If there was, heaven knows what it might have been, for their talk was ordinary enough. But Alvina liked to be with Miss Pinnegar in the kitchen. Miss Pinnegar wasn't competent and masterful like Miss Frost: she was ordinary and uninspired, with quiet, unobserved movements. But she was deep, and there was some secret satisfaction in her very quality of secrecy.

So the days and weeks and months slipped by, and Alvina was hidden like a mole in the dark chambers of Manchester House, busy with cooking and cleaning and arranging, getting the house in her own order, and attending to her pupils. She took her walk in the afternoon. Once and only once she went to Throttle-Ha'penny, and, seized with sudden curiosity, insisted on being wound down in the iron bucket to the little workings underneath. Everything was quite tidy in the short gangways down below, timbered and in sound order. The miners were competent enough. But water dripped dismally in places, and there was a stale feeling in the air.

Her father accompanied her, pointed her to the seam of yellow-flecked coal, the shale and the bind, the direction of the trend. He had already an airy-fairy kind of knowledge of the whole affair, and seemed like some not quite trustworthy conjuror who had conjured it all up by sleight of hand. In the background the miners stood grey and ghostly, in the candle-light, and seemed to listen sardonically. One of them, facile in his subordinate way as James in his authoritative, kept chiming in:

'Ay, that's the road it goes, Miss Huffen—yis, yo'll see th' roof theer bellies down a bit—s' loose. No, you dunna get th' puddin' stones i' this pit—s' not deep enough. Eh, they come down on you plumb, as if th' roof had laid its egg on you. Ay, it runs a bit thin down here—six inches. You see th' bed's soft, it's a sort o' clay-bind, it's not clunch such as you get deeper. Oh, it's easy workin'—you don't have to knock your guts out. There's no need for shots, Miss Huffen—we bring it down—you see here—' And he stooped, pointed to a shallow, shelving excavation which he was making under the coal. The working was low, you must stoop all the time. The roof and the timbered sides of the way seemed to press on you. It was as if she were in her tomb forever, like the dead and everlasting Egyptians. She was frightened, but fascinated. The collier kept on talking to her, stretching his bare, grey-black, hairy arm across her vision, and pointing with his knotted hand. The thick-

wicked tallow candles guttered and smelled. There was a
thickness in the air, a sense of dark, fluid presence in the
thick atmosphere, the dark, fluid, viscous voice of the collier
making a broad-vowelled, clapping sound in her ear. He
seemed to linger near her as if he knew—as if he knew—
what? Something forever unknowable and inadmissible,
something that belonged purely to the underground: to the
slaves who work underground: knowledge humiliated, subjected, but ponderous and inevitable. And still his voice
went on clapping in her ear, and still his presence edged near
her, and seemed to impinge on her—a smallish, semi-
grotesque, grey-obscure figure with a naked brandished
forearm: not human: a creature of the subterranean world,
melted out like a bat, fluid. She felt herself melting out also,
to become a mere vocal ghost, a presence in the thick atmosphere. Her lungs felt thick and slow, her mind dissolved,
she felt she could cling like a bat in the long swoon of the
crannied, underworld darkness. Cling like a bat and sway
forever swooning in the draughts of the darkness—

When she was up on the earth again she blinked and
peered at the world in amazement. What a pretty, luminous
place it was, carved in substantial luminosity. What a strange
and lovely place, bubbling iridescent-golden on the surface
of the underworld. Iridescent-golden—could anything be
more fascinating! Like lovely glancing surface on fluid pitch.
But a velvet surface. A velvet surface of golden light, velvet-
pile of gold and pale luminosity, and strange beautiful ele-
vations of houses and trees, and depressions of fields and
roads, all golden and floating like atmospheric majolica.
Never had the common ugliness of Woodhouse seemed so
entrancing. She thought she had never seen such beauty—a
lovely luminous majolica, living and palpitating, the glossy,
svelte world-surface, the exquisite face of all the darkness.
It was like a vision. Perhaps gnomes and subterranean work-
ers, enslaved in the era of light, see with such eyes. Perhaps
that is why they are absolutely blind to conventional ugliness. For truly nothing could be more hideous than Woodhouse, as the miners had built it and disposed it, and yet,
the very cabbage-stumps and rotten fences of the gardens,
the very backyards were instinct with magic, molten as they

seemed with the bubbling-up of the under-darkness, bubbling up of majolica weight and luminosity, quite ignorant
of the sky, heavy and satisfying.

Slaves of the underworld! She watched the swing of the
grey colliers along the pavement with a new fascination,
hypnotized by a new vision. Slaves—the underground trolls
and iron-workers, magic, mischievous, and enslaved, of the
ancient stories. But tall—the miners seemed to her to loom
tall and grey, in their enslaved magic. Slaves who would
cause the superimposed day-order to fall. Not because, in-
dividually, they wanted to. But because, collectively, something bubbled up in them, the force of darkness which had
no master and no control. It would bubble and stir in them
as earthquakes stir the earth. It would be simply disastrous,
because it had no master. There was no dark master in the
world. The puerile world went on crying out for a new Jesus, another Saviour from the sky, another heavenly super-
man. When what was wanted was a Dark Master from the
underworld.

So they streamed past her, home from work—grey from
head to foot, distorted in shape, cramped, with curious faces
that came out pallid from under their dirt. Their walk was
heavy-footed and slurring, their bearing stiff and grotesque.
A stream they were—yet they seemed to her to loom like
strange, valid figures of fairy-lore, unrealized and as yet
unexperienced. The miners, the iron-workers, those who
fashion the stuff of the underworld.

As it always comes to its children, the nostalgia of the
repulsive, heavy-footed Midlands came over her again, even
whilst she was there in the midst. The curious, dark, inexplicable and yet insatiable craving—as if for an earthquake.
To feel the earth heave and shudder and shatter the world
from beneath. To go down in the débâcle.

And so, in spite of everything, poverty, dowdiness, obscurity, and nothingness, she was content to stay in abeyance at home for the time. True, she was filled with the same
old, slow, dreadful craving of the Midlands: a craving insatiable and inexplicable. But the very craving kept her still.
For at this time she did not translate it into a desire, or need,
for love. At the back of her mind somewhere was the fixed

idea, the fixed intention of finding love, a man. But as yet, at this period, the idea was in abeyance, it did not act. The craving that possessed her as it possesses everybody, in a greater or less degree, in those parts, sustained her darkly and unconsciously.

A hot summer waned into autumn, the long, bewildering days drew in, the transient nights, only a few breaths of shadow between noon and noon, deepened and strengthened. A restlessness came over everybody. There was another short strike among the miners. James Houghton, like an excited beetle, scurried to and fro, feeling he was making his fortune. Never had Woodhouse been so thronged on Fridays with purchasers and money-spenders. The place seemed surcharged with life.

Autumn lasted beautiful till end of October. And then, suddenly, cold rain, endless cold rain, and darkness heavy, wet, ponderous. Through the wind and rain it was a toil to move. Poor Miss Frost, who had seemed almost to blossom again in the long hot days, regaining a free cheerfulness that amounted almost to liveliness, and who even caused a sort of scandal by her intimacy with a rather handsome but common stranger, an insurance agent who had come into the place with a good, unused tenor voice—now she wilted again. She had given the rather florid young man tea in her room, and had laboured away at his fine, metallic voice, correcting him and teaching him and laughing with him and spending really a remarkable number of hours alone with him in her room in Woodhouse—for she had given up tramping the country, and had hired a music-room in a quiet street, where she gave her lessons. And the young man had hung round, and had never wanted to go away. They would prolong their tête-à-tête and their singing on till ten o'clock at night, and Miss Frost would return to Manchester House flushed and handsome and a little shy, while the young man, who was common, took on a new boldness in the streets. He had auburn hair, high colouring, and a rather challenging bearing. He took on a new boldness, his own estimate of himself rose considerably, with Miss Frost and his trained voice to justify him. He was a little insolent and condescending to the natives, who disliked him. For their lives they could not imagine what Miss Frost could find in him. They began even to dislike her, and a pretty scandal was started about the pair, in the pleasant room where Miss Frost had her piano, her books, and her flowers. The scandal was as unjust as most scandals are. Yet truly, all that summer and autumn Miss Frost had a new and slightly aggressive cheerfulness and humour. And Manchester House saw little of her, comparatively.

And then, at the end of September, the young man was removed by his Insurance Company to another district. And at the end of October set in the most abominable and unbearable weather, deluges of rain and north winds, cutting the tender, summer-enfolded people to pieces. Miss Frost wilted at once. A silence came over her. She shuddered when she had to leave the fire. She went in the morning to her room, and stayed there all the day, in a hot, close atmosphere, shuddering when her pupils brought the outside weather with them to her.

She was always subject to bronchitis. In November she had a bad bronchitis cold. Then suddenly one morning she could not get up. Alvina went in and found her semiconscious.

The girl was almost mad. She flew to the rescue. She dispatched her father instantly for the doctor, she heaped the sticks in the bedroom grate and made a bright fire, she brought hot milk and brandy.

'Thank you, dear, thank you. It's a bronchial cold,' whispered Miss Frost hurriedly, trying to sip the milk. She could not. She didn't want it.

'I've sent for the doctor,' said Alvina, in her cool voice, wherein none the less there rang the old hesitancy of sheer love.

Miss Frost lifted her eyes:

'There's no need,' she said, and she smiled winsomely at Alvina.

It was pneumonia. Useless to talk of the distracted anguish of Alvina during the next two days. She was so swift and sensitive in her nursing, she seemed to have second sight. She talked to nobody. In her silence her soul was alone with the soul of her darling. The long semi-consciousness and the tearing pain of pneumonia, the anguished sickness.

But sometimes the grey eyes would open and smile with delicate winsomeness at Alvina, and Alvina smiled back, with a cheery, answering winsomeness. But that costs something.

On the evening of the second day, Miss Frost got her hand from under the bedclothes, and laid it on Alvina's hand. Alvina leaned down to her.

'Everything is for you, my love,' whispered Miss Frost, looking with strange eyes on Alvina's face.

'Don't talk, Miss Frost,' moaned Alvina.

'Everything is for you,' murmured the sick woman—'except—' and she enumerated some tiny legacies which showed her generous, thoughtful nature.

'Yes, I shall remember,' said Alvina, beyond tears now.

Miss Frost smiled with her old bright, wonderful look, that had a touch of queenliness in it.

'Kiss me, dear,' she whispered.

Alvina kissed her, and could not suppress the whimpering of her too-much grief.

The night passed slowly. Sometimes the grey eyes of the sick woman rested dark, dilated, haggard on Alvina's face, with a heavy, almost accusing look, sinister. Then they closed again. And sometimes they looked pathetic, with a mute, stricken appeal. Then again they closed—only to open again tense with pain. Alvina wiped her blood-phlegmed lips.

In the morning she died—lay there haggard, death-smeared, with her lovely white hair smeared also, and disorderly: she who had been so beautiful and clean always.

Alvina knew death—which is untellable. She knew that her darling carried away a portion of her own soul into death.

But she was alone. And the agony of being alone, the agony of grief, passionate, passionate grief for her darling who was torn into death—the agony of self-reproach, regret; the agony of remembrance; the agony of the looks of the dying woman, winsome, and sinisterly accusing, and pathetically, despairingly appealing—probe after probe of mortal agony, which throughout eternity would never lose its power to pierce to the quick!

Alvina seemed to keep strangely calm and aloof all the days after the death. Only when she was alone she suffered till she felt her heart really broke.

'I shall never feel anything any more,' she said in her abrupt way to Miss Frost's friend, another woman of over fifty.

'Nonsense, child!' expostulated Mrs Lawson gently.

'I shan't! I shall never have a heart to feel anything any more,' said Alvina, with a strange, distraught roll of the eyes.

'Not like this, child. But you'll feel other things—'

'I haven't the heart,' persisted Alvina.

'Not yet,' said Mrs Lawson gently. 'You can't expect— But time—time brings back—'

'Oh well—but I don't believe it,' said Alvina.

People thought her rather hard. To one of her gossips Miss Pinnegar confessed:

'I thought she'd have felt it more. She cared more for her than she did for her own mother—and her mother knew it. Mrs Houghton complained bitterly, sometimes, that *she* had no love. They were everything to one another, Miss Frost and Alvina. I should have thought she'd have felt it more. But you never know. A good thing if she doesn't, really.'

Miss Pinnegar herself did not care one little bit that Miss Frost was dead. She did not feel herself implicated.

The nearest relatives came down, and everything was settled. The will was found, just a brief line on a piece of notepaper expressing a wish that Alvina should have everything. Alvina herself told the verbal requests. All was quietly fulfilled.

As it might well be. For there was nothing to leave. Just sixty-three pounds in the bank—no more: then the clothes, piano, books and music. Miss Frost's brother had these latter, at his own request: the books and music, and the piano. Alvina inherited the few simple trinkets, and about forty-five pounds in money.

'Poor Miss Frost,' cried Mrs Lawson, weeping rather bitterly—'she saved nothing for herself. You can see why she never wanted to grow old, so that she couldn't work. You can see. It's a shame, it's a shame, one of the best women that ever trod earth.'

Manchester House settled down to its deeper silence, its darker gloom. Miss Frost was irreparably gone. With her, the reality went out of the house. It seemed to be silently waiting to disappear. And Alvina and Miss Pinnegar might move about and talk in vain. They could never remove the sense of waiting to finish: it was all just waiting to finish. And the three, James and Alvina, and Miss Pinnegar, waited lingering through the months, for the house to come to an end. Dark, empty-feeling, it seemed all the time like a house just before a sale.

CHAPTER 5

The Beau

Throttle-Ha'penny worked fitfully through the winter, and in the spring broke down. By this time James Houghton had a pathetic, childish look which touched the hearts of Alvina and Miss Pinnegar. They began to treat him with a certain feminine indulgence, as he fluttered round, agitated and bewildered. He was like a bird that has flown into a room and is exhausted, enfeebled by its attempts to fly through the false freedom of the window-glass. Sometimes he would sit moping in a corner, with his head under his wing. But Miss Pinnegar chased him forth, like the stealthy cat she was, chased him up to the work-room to consider some detail of work, chased him into the shop to turn over the old débris of the stock. At one time he showed the alarming symptom of brooding over his wife's death. Miss Pinnegar was thoroughly scared. But she was not inventive. It was left to Alvina to suggest: 'Why doesn't father let the shop, and some of the house?'

Let the shop! Let the last inch of frontage on the street! James thought of it. Let the shop! Permit the name of Houghton to disappear from the list of tradesmen? Withdraw? Disappear? Become a nameless nobody, occupying obscure premises?

He thought about it. And thinking about it, became so

indignant at the thought that he pulled his scattered energies together within his frail frame. And then he came out with the most original of all his schemes. Manchester House was to be fitted up as a boarding-house for the better classes, and was to make a fortune catering for the needs of these gentry, who had now nowhere to go. Yes, Manchester House should be fitted up as a sort of quiet family hotel for the better classes. The shop should be turned into an elegant hall-entrance, carpeted, with a hall-porter and a wide plate-glass door, round-arched, in the round arch of which the words: 'Manchester House' should appear large and distinguished, making an arch also, whilst underneath, more refined and smaller, should show the words 'Private Hotel'. James was to be proprietor and secretary, keeping the books and attending to correspondence: Miss Pinnegar was to be manageress, superintending the servants and directing the house, whilst Alvina was to occupy the equivocal position of 'hostess'. She was to play the piano, and she was to nurse the sick. For in the prospectus James would include: 'Trained nurse always on the premises.'

'Why!' cried Miss Pinnegar, for once brutally and angrily hostile to him: 'You'll make it sound like a private lunatic asylum.'

'Will you explain why?' answered James tartly.

For himself, he was enraptured with the scheme. He began to tot up ideas and expenses. There would be the handsome entrance and hall: there would be an extension of the kitchen and scullery: there would be an installing of new hot-water and sanitary arrangements: there would be a light lift-arrangement from the kitchen; there would be a handsome glazed balcony or loggia or terrace on the first floor at the back, over the whole length of the backyard. This loggia would give a wonderful outlook to the south-west and the west. In the immediate foreground, to be sure, would be the yard of the livery-stables and the rather slummy dwellings of the colliers, sloping downhill. But these could be easily overlooked, for the eye would instinctively wander across the green and shallow valley, to the long upslope opposite, showing the Manor set in its clump of trees and farms and haystacks pleasantly dotted, and

moderately far off coal-mines with twinkling headstocks
and narrow railway-lines crossing the arable fields, and
heaps of burning slag. The balcony or covered terrace—
James settled down at last to the word *terrace*—was to be
one of the features of the house: *the* feature. It was to be
fitted up as a sort of elegant lounging restaurant. Elegant
teas, at two-and-six per head, and elegant suppers, at five
shillings without wine, were to be served there.

As a teetotaller and a man of ascetic views, James, in his
first shallow moments, before he thought about it, assumed
that his house should be entirely non-alcoholic. A temperance house! Already he winced. We all know what a provincial Temperance Hotel is. Besides, there is a magic in the
sound of wine. *Wines Served*. The legend attracted him immensely—as a teetotaller, it had a mysterious, hypnotic influence. He must have wines. He knew nothing about them.
But Alfred Swayn, from the Liquor Vaults, would put him
in the running in five minutes.

It was most curious to see Miss Pinnegar turtle up at the
mention of this scheme. When first it was disclosed to her,
her colour came up like a turkey's in a flush of indignant
anger.

'It's ridiculous. It's just ridiculous!' she blurted, bridling
and ducking her head and turning aside, like an indignant
turkey.

'Ridiculous! Why? Will you explain why!' retorted
James, turtling also.

'It's absolutely ridiculous!' she repeated, unable to do
more than splutter.

'Well, we'll see,' said James, rising to superiority.

And again he began to dart absorbedly about, like a bird
building a nest. Miss Pinnegar watched him with a sort of
sullen fury. She went to the shop door to peep out after him.
She saw him slip into the Liquor Vaults, and she came back
to announce to Alvina:

'He's taken to drink!'

'Drink?' said Alvina.

'That's what it is,' said Miss Pinnegar vindictively.
'Drink!'

Alvina sank down and laughed till she was weak. It all seemed really too funny to her—too funny.

'I can't see what it is to laugh at,' said Miss Pinnegar. 'Disgraceful—it's disgraceful! But I'm not going to stop to be made a fool of. I shall be no manageress, I tell you. It's absolutely ridiculous. Who does he think will come to this place? He's out of his mind—and it's drink; that's what it is! Going into the Liquor Vaults at ten o'clock in the morning! That's where he gets his ideas—out of whisky—or brandy! But he's not going to make a fool of me—'

'Oh dear!' sighed Alvina, laughing herself into composure and a little weariness. 'I know it's *perfectly* ridiculous. We shall have to stop him.'

'I've said all I can say,' blurted Miss Pinnegar.

As soon as James came in to a meal, the two women attacked him.

'But father,' said Alvina, 'there'll be nobody to come.'

'Plenty of people—plenty of people,' said her father. 'Look at the Shakespeare's Head, in Knarborough.'

'Knarborough! Is this Knarborough!' blurted Miss Pinnegar. 'Where are the business men here? Where are the foreigners coming here for business, where's *our* lace-trade and our stocking-trade?'

'There *are* business men,' said James. 'And there are ladies.'

'Who,' retorted Miss Pinnegar, 'is going to give half-a-crown for a tea. They expect tea and bread-and-butter for fourpence, and cake for sixpence, and apricots or pineapple for ninepence, and ham-and-tongue for a shilling, and fried ham and eggs and jam and cake as much as they can eat for one-and-two. If they expect a knife-and-fork tea for a shilling, what are you going to give them for half-a-crown?'

'I know what I shall offer,' said James. 'And we may make it two shillings.' Through his mind flitted the idea of 1/11½—but he rejected it. 'You don't realize that I'm catering for a higher class of custom—'

'But there *isn't* any higher class in Woodhouse, father,' said Alvina, unable to restrain a laugh.

'If you create a supply you create a demand,' he retorted.

'But how can you create a supply of better-class people?' asked Alvina mockingly.

James took on his refined, abstracted look, as if he were preoccupied on higher planes. It was the look of an obstinate little boy who poses on the side of the angels—or so the women saw it.

Miss Pinnegar was prepared to combat him now by sheer weight of opposition. She would pitch her dead negative will obstinately against him. She would not speak to him, she would not observe his presence, she was stone deaf and stone blind: there *was* no James. This nettled him. And she miscalculated him. He merely took another circuit, and rose another flight higher on the spiral of his spiritual egotism. He believed himself finely and sacredly in the right, that he was frustrated by lower beings, above whom it was his duty to rise, to soar. So he soared to serene heights, and his Private Hotel seemed a celestial injunction, an erection on a higher plane.

He saw the architect: and then, with his plans and schemes, he saw the builder and contractor. The builder gave an estimate of six or seven hundred—but James had better see the plumber and fitter who was going to instal the new hot-water and sanitary system. James was a little dashed. He had calculated much less. Having only a few hundred pounds in possession after Throttle-Ha'penny, he was prepared to mortgage Manchester House if he could keep in hand a sufficient sum of money for the running of his establishment for a year. He knew he would have to sacrifice Miss Pinnegar's work-room. He knew, and he feared Miss Pinnegar's violent and unmitigated hostility. Still—his obstinate spirit rose—he was quite prepared to risk everything on this last throw.

Miss Allsop, daughter of the builder, called to see Alvina. The Allsops were great Chapel people, and Cassie Allsop was one of the old maids. She was thin and nipped and wistful looking, about forty-two years old. In private, she was tyrannously exacting with the servants, and spiteful, rather mean with her motherless nieces. But in public she had this nipped, wistful look.

Alvina was surprised by this visit. When she found Miss Allsop at the back door, all her inherent hostility awoke.

'Oh, is it you, Miss Allsop! Will you come in.'

They sat in the middle room, the common living-room of the house.

'I called,' said Miss Allsop, coming to the point at once, and speaking in her Sunday-school-teacher voice, 'to ask you if you know about this Private Hotel scheme of your father's?'

'Yes,' said Alvina.

'Oh, you do! Well, we wondered. Mr Houghton came to father about the building alterations yesterday. They'll be awfully expensive.'

'Will they?' said Alvina, making big, mocking eyes.

'Yes, very. What do *you* think of the scheme?'

'I?—well—!' Alvina hesitated, then broke into a laugh. 'To tell the truth I haven't thought much about it at all.'

'Well I think you should,' said Miss Allsop severely. 'Father's sure it won't pay—and it will cost I don't know how much. It is bound to be a dead loss. And your father's getting on. You'll be left stranded in the world without a penny to bless yourself with. I think it's an awful outlook for you.'

'Do you?' said Alvina.

Here she was, with a bang, planked upon the shelf among the old maids.

'Oh, I do. Sincerely! I should do all I could to prevent him, if I were you.'

Miss Allsop took her departure. Alvina felt herself jolted in her mood. An old maid along with Cassie Allsop!—and James Houghton fooling about with the last bit of money, mortgaging Manchester House up to the hilt. Alvina sank in a kind of weary mortification, in which *her* peculiar obstinacy persisted devilishly and spitefully. 'Oh, well, so be it,' said her spirit vindictively. 'Let the meagre, mean, despicable fate fulfil itself.' Her old anger against her father arose again.

Arthur Witham, the plumber, came in with James Houghton to examine the house. Arthur Witham was also one of the Chapel men—as had been his common, interfering, un-

educated father before him. The father had left each of his
sons a fair little sum of money, which Arthur, the eldest,
had already increased ten-fold. He was sly and slow and
uneducated also, and spoke with a broad accent. But he was
not bad-looking, a tight fellow with big blue eyes, who as-
pired to keep his 'h's' in the right place, and would have
been a gentleman if he could.

Against her usual habit, Alvina joined the plumber and
her father in the scullery. Arthur Witham saluted her with
some respect. She liked his blue eyes and tight figure. He
was keen and sly in business, very watchful, and slow to
commit himself. Now he poked and peered and crept under
the sink. Alvina watched him half disappear—she handed
him a candle—and she laughed to herself seeing his tight,
well-shaped hind-quarters protruding out from under the
sink like the wrong end of a dog from a kennel. He was keen
after money, was Arthur—and bossy, creeping slyly after
his own self-importance and power. He wanted power—
and he would creep quietly after it till he got it: as much as
he was capable of. His 'h's' were a barbed-wire fence and
entanglement, preventing his unlimited progress.

He emerged from under the sink, and they went to the
kitchen and afterwards upstairs. Alvina followed them persistently, but a little aloof, and silent. When the tour of inspection was almost over, she said innocently:

'Won't it cost a great deal?'

Arthur Witham slowly shook his head. Then he looked
at her. She smiled rather archly into his eyes.

'It won't be done for nothing,' he said, looking at her
again.

'We can go into that later,' said James, leading off the
plumber.

'Good-morning, Miss Houghton,' said Arthur Witham.

'Good-morning, Mr Witham,' replied Alvina brightly.

But she lingered in the background, and as Arthur
Witham was going she heard him say: 'Well, I'll work it out,
Mr Houghton. I'll work it out, and let you know to-night.
I'll get the figures by to-night.'

The younger man's tone was a little off-hand, just a little

supercilious with her father, she thought. James's star was setting.

In the afternoon, directly after dinner, Alvina went out. She entered the shop, where sheets of lead and tins of paint and putty stood about, varied by sheets of glass and fancy paper. Lottie Witham, Arthur's wife, appeared. She was a woman of thirty-five, a bit of a shrew, with social ambitions and no children.

'Is Mr Witham in?' said Alvina.

Mrs Witham eyed her.

'I'll see,' she answered, and she left the shop.

Presently Arthur entered, in his shirt-sleeves: rather attractive-looking.

'I don't know what you'll think of me, and what I've come for,' said Alvina, with hurried amiability. Arthur lifted his blue eyes to her, and Mrs Witham appeared in the background, in the inner doorway.

'Why, what is it?' said Arthur stolidly.

'Make it as dear as you can for father,' said Alvina, laughing nervously.

Arthur's blue eyes rested on her face. Mrs Witham advanced into the shop.

'Why? What's that for?' asked Lottie Witham shrewdly.

Alvina turned to the woman.

'Don't say anything,' she said. 'But we don't want father to go on with this scheme. It's bound to fail. And Miss Pinnegar and I can't have anything to do with it anyway. I shall go away.'

'It's bound to fail,' said Arthur Witham stolidly.

'And father has no money, I'm sure,' said Alvina.

Lottie Witham eyed the thin, nervous face of Alvina. For some reason, she liked her. And of course, Alvina was considered a lady in Woodhouse. That was what it had come to, with James's declining fortunes: she was merely *considered* a lady. The consideration was no longer indisputable.

'Shall you come in a minute?' said Lottie Witham, lifting the flap of the counter. It was a rare and bold stroke on Mrs Witham's part. Alvina's immediate instinct was to refuse. But she liked Arthur Witham, in his shirt sleeves.

'Well—I must be back in a minute,' she said, as she entered the embrasure of the counter. She felt as if she were really venturing on new ground. She was led into the new drawing-room, done in new peacock-and-bronze brocade furniture, with gilt and brass and white walls. This was the Withams' new house, and Lottie was proud of it. The two women had a short confidential chat. Arthur lingered in the doorway awhile, then went away.

Alvina did not really like Lottie Witham. Yet the other woman was sharp and shrewd in the uptake, and for some reason she fancied Alvina. So she was invited to tea at Manchester House.

After this, so many difficulties rose up in James Houghton's way that he was worried almost out of his life. His two women left him alone. Outside difficulties multiplied on him till he abandoned his scheme—he was simply driven out of it by untoward circumstances.

Lottie Witham came to tea, and was shown over Manchester House. She had no opinion at all of Manchester House—wouldn't hang a cat in such a gloomy hole. *Still,* she was rather impressed by the sense of superiority.

'Oh my goodness!' she exclaimed as she stood in Alvina's bedroom, and looked at the enormous furniture, the lofty tableland of the bed.

'Oh, my goodness! I wouldn't sleep in *that* for a trifle, by myself! Aren't you frightened out of your life? Even if I had Arthur at one side of me, I should be that frightened on the other side I shouldn't know what to do. Do you sleep here by yourself?'

'Yes,' said Alvina laughing. 'I haven't got an Arthur, even for one side.'

'Oh, my word, you'd want a husband on both sides, in that bed,' said Lottie Witham.

Alvina was asked back to tea—on Wednesday afternoon, closing day. Arthur was there to tea—very ill at ease and feeling as if his hands were swollen. Alvina got on better with his wife, who watched closely to learn from her guest the secret of repose. The indefinable repose and inevitability of a lady—even of a lady who is nervous and agitated—this was the problem which occupied Lottie's shrewd and active, but lower-class mind. She even did not resent Alvina's laughing attempts to draw out the clumsy Arthur: because Alvina was a lady, and her tactics must be studied.

Alvina really liked Arthur, and thought a good deal about him—heaven knows why. He and Lottie were quite happy together, and he was absorbed in his petty ambitions. In his limited way, he was invincibly ambitious. He would end by making a sufficient fortune, and by being a town councillor and a J.P. But beyond Woodhouse he did not exist. Why then should Alvina be attracted by him? Perhaps because of his 'closeness', and his secret determinedness.

When she met him in the street she would stop him— though he was always busy—and make him exchange a few words with her. And when she had tea at his house, she would try to arouse his attention. But though he looked at her, steadily, with his blue eyes, from under his long lashes, still, she knew, he looked at her objectively. He never conceived any connection with her whatsoever.

It was Lottie who had a scheming mind. In the family of three brothers there was one—not black sheep, but white. There was one who was climbing out, to be a gentleman. This was Albert, the second brother. He had been a school teacher in Woodhouse: had gone out to South Africa and occupied a post in a sort of Grammar School in one of the cities of Cape Colony. He had accumulated some money, to add to his patrimony. Now he was in England, at Oxford, where he would take his belated degree. When he had got his degree, he would return to South Africa to become head of his school, at seven hundred a year.

Albert was thirty-two years old, and unmarried. Lottie was determined he should take back to the Cape a suitable wife: presumably Alvina. He spent his vacations in Woodhouse—and he was only in his first year at Oxford. Well now, what could be more suitable—a young man at Oxford, a young lady in Woodhouse. Lottie told Alvina all about him, and Alvina was quite excited to meet him. She imagined him a taller, more fascinating, educated Arthur.

For the fear of being an old maid, the fear of her own virginity was really gaining on Alvina. There was a terrible sombre futility, nothingness, in Manchester House. She was twenty-six years old. Her life was utterly barren now Miss

Frost had gone. She was shabby and penniless, a mere household drudge: for James begrudged even a girl to help in the kitchen. She was looking faded and worn. Panic, the terrible and deadly panic which overcomes so many unmarried women at about the age of thirty, was beginning to overcome her. She would not care about marriage, if even she had a lover. But some sort of *terror* hunted her to the search of a lover. She would become loose, she would become a prostitute, she said to herself, rather than die off like Cassie Allsop and the rest, wither slowly and ignominiously and hideously on the tree. She would rather kill herself.

But it needs a certain natural gift to become a loose woman or a prostitute. If you haven't got the qualities which attract loose men, what are you to do? Supposing it isn't in your nature to attract loose and promiscuous men! Why, then you can't be a prostitute, if you try your head off: nor even a loose woman. Since *willing* won't do it. It requires a second party to come to an agreement.

Therefore all Alvina's desperate and profligate schemes and ideas fell to nought before the inexorable in her nature. And the inexorable in her nature was highly exclusive and selective, an inevitable negation of looseness or prostitution. Hence men were afraid of her—of her power, once they had committed themselves. She would involve and lead a man on, she would destroy him rather than not get of him what she wanted. And what she wanted was something serious and risky. Not mere marriage—oh dear no! But a profound and dangerous inter-relationship. As well ask the paddlers in the small surf of passion to plunge themselves into the heaving gulf of mid-ocean. Bah, with their trousers turned up to their knees, it was enough for them to wet their toes in the dangerous sea. They were having nothing to do with such desperate nereids as Alvina.

She had cast her mind on Arthur. Truly ridiculous. But there was something compact and energetic and wilful about him that she magnified tenfold and so obtained, imaginatively, an attractive lover. She brooded her days shabbily away in Manchester House, busy with housework drudgery. Since the collapse of Throttle-Ha'penny, James Houghton had become so stingy that it was like an inflammation in him. A silver sixpence had a pale and celestial radiance which he could not forego, a nebulous whiteness which made him feel he had heaven in his hold. How then could he let it go? Even a brown penny seemed alive and pulsing with mysterious blood, potent, magical. He loved the flock of his busy pennies, in the shop, as if they had been divine bees bringing him sustenance from the infinite. But the pennies he saw dribbling away in household expenses troubled him acutely, as if they were live things leaving his fold. It was a constant struggle to get from him enough money for necessities.

And so the household diet became meagre in the extreme, the coal was eked out inch by inch, and when Alvina must have her boots mended she must draw on her own little stock of money. For James Houghton had the impudence to make her an allowance of two shillings a week. She was very angry. Yet her anger was of that dangerous, half-ironical sort which wears away its subject and has no outward effect. A feeling of half-bitter mockery kept her going. In the ponderous, rather sordid nullity of Manchester House she became shadowy and absorbed, absorbed in nothing in particular, yet absorbed. She was always more or less busy: and certainly there was always something to be done, whether she did it or not.

The shop was opened once a week, on Friday evenings. James Houghton prowled round the warehouses in Knarborough and picked up job lots of stuff, with which he replenished his shabby window. But his heart was not in the business. Mere tenacity made him hover on with it.

In midsummer Albert Witham came to Woodhouse, and Alvina was invited to tea. She was very much excited. All the time imagining Albert a taller, finer Arthur, she had abstained from actually fixing her mind upon this latter little man. Picture her disappointment when she found Albert quite unattractive. He was tall and thin and brittle, with a pale, rather dry, flattish face, and with curious pale eyes. His impression was one of uncanny flatness, something like a lemon sole. Curiously flat and fish-like he was, one might have imagined his backbone to be spread like the backbone

of a sole or a plaice. His teeth were sound, but rather large
and yellowish and flat. A most curious person.

He spoke in a slightly mouthing way, not well bred in
spite of Oxford. There was a distinct Woodhouse twang.
He would never be a gentleman if he lived for ever. Yet he
was not ordinary. Really an odd fish: quite interesting, if
one could get over the feeling that one was looking at him
through the glass wall of an aquarium: that most horrifying
of all boundaries between two worlds. In an aquarium fish
seem to come smiling broadly to the doorway, and there to
stand talking to one, in a mouthing fashion awful to behold.
For one hears no sound from all their mouthing and staring
conversation. Now although Albert Witham had a good
strong voice, which rang like water among rocks in her ear,
still she seemed never to hear a word he was saying. He
smiled down at her and fixed her and swayed his head, and
said quite original things, really. For he was a genuine odd
fish. And yet she seemed to hear no sound, no word from
him: nothing came to her. Perhaps as a matter of fact fish
do actually pronounce streams of watery words, to which
we, with our aerial-resonant ears, are deaf for ever.

The odd thing was that this odd fish seemed from the very
first to imagine she had accepted him as a follower. And he
was quite prepared to follow. Nay, from the very first moment he was smiling on her with a sort of complacent
delight—compassionate, one might almost say—as if there
was a full understanding between them. If only she could
have got into the right state of mind, she would really rather
have liked him. He smiled at her, and said really interesting
things between his big teeth. There was something rather
nice about him. But, we must repeat, it was as if the glass
wall of an aquarium divided them.

Alvina looked at Arthur. Arthur was short and dark-
haired and nicely coloured. But, now his brother was there,
he too seemed to have a dumb, aqueous silence, fish-like
and aloof, about him. He seemed to swim like a fish in his
own little element. Strange it all was, like Alice in Wonder-
land. Alvina understood now Lottie's strained sort of thinness, a haggard, sinewy, sea-weedy look. The poor thing was
all the time swimming for her life.

For Alvina it was a most curious tea-party. She listened and smiled and made vague answers to Albert, who leaned his broad, thin, brittle shoulders towards her. Lottie seemed rather shadowily to preside. But it was Arthur who came out into communication. And now, uttering his rather broad, mouthed speeches, she seemed to hear in him a quieter, subtler edition of his father. His father had been a little, terrifically loud-voiced, hard-skinned man, amazingly uneducated and amazingly bullying, who had tyrannized for many years over the Sunday school children during morning service. He had been an odd-looking creature with round grey whiskers: to Alvina, always a creature, never a man: an atrocious leprechaun from under the Chapel floor. And how he used to dig the children in the back with his horrible iron thumb, if the poor things happened to whisper or nod in chapel!

These were his children—most curious chips off the old block. Who ever would have believed she would have been taking tea with them?

'Why don't you have a bicycle, and go out on it?' Arthur was saying.

'But I can't ride,' said Alvina.

'You'd learn in a couple of lessons. There's nothing in riding a bicycle.'

'I don't believe I ever should,' laughed Alvina.

'You don't mean to say you're nervous?' said Arthur rudely and sneeringly.

'I *am*,' she persisted.

'You needn't be nervous with me,' smiled Albert broadly, with his odd, genuine gallantry. 'I'll hold you on.'

'But I haven't got a bicycle,' said Alvina, feeling she was slowly colouring to a deep, uneasy blush.

'You can have mine to learn on,' said Lottie. 'Albert will look after it.'

'There's your chance,' said Arthur rudely. 'Take it while you've got it.'

Now Alvina did not want to learn to ride a bicycle. The two Miss Carlins, two more old maids, had made themselves ridiculous for ever by becoming twin cycle fiends. And the horrible energetic strain of peddling a bicycle over miles and miles of highway did not attract Alvina at all. She was completely indifferent to sight-seeing and scouring about. She liked taking a walk, in her lingering indifferent fashion. But rushing about in any way was hateful to her. And then, to be taught to ride a bicycle by Albert Witham! Her very soul stood still.

'Yes,' said Albert, beaming down at her from his strange pale eyes. 'Come on. When will you have your first lesson?'

'Oh,' cried Alvina in confusion. 'I can't promise. I haven't time, really.'

'Time!' exclaimed Arthur rudely. 'But what do you do wi' yourself all day?'

'I have to keep house,' she said, looking at him archly.

'House! You can put a chain round its neck, and tie it up,' he retorted.

Albert laughed, showing all his teeth.

'I'm sure you find plenty to do, with everything on your hands,' said Lottie to Alvina.

'I do!' said Alvina. 'By evening I'm quite tired—though you mayn't believe it, since you say I do nothing,' she added, laughing confusedly to Arthur.

But he, hard-headed little fortune-maker, replied:

'You have a girl to help you, don't you!'

Albert, however, was beaming at her sympathetically.

'You have too much to do indoors,' he said. 'It would do you good to get a bit of exercise out of doors. Come down to the Coach Road to-morrow afternoon, and let me give you a lesson. Go on—'

Now the coach-road was a level drive between beautiful park-like grass-stretches, down in the valley. It was a delightful place for learning to ride a bicycle, but open in full view of all the world. Alvina would have died of shame. She began to laugh nervously and hurriedly at the very thought.

'No, I can't. I really can't. Thanks awfully,' she said.

'Can't you really!' said Albert. 'Oh well, we'll say another day, shall we?'

'When I feel I can,' she said.

'Yes, when you feel like it,' replied Albert.

'That's more it,' said Arthur. 'It's not the time. It's the

nervousness.' Again Albert beamed at her sympathetically, and said:

'Oh, I'll hold you. You needn't be afraid.'

'But I'm not afraid,' she said.

'You won't *say* you are,' interposed Arthur. 'Women's faults mustn't be owned up to.'

Alvina was beginning to feel quite dazed. Their mechanical, overbearing way was something she was unaccustomed to. It was like the jaws of a pair of insentient iron pincers. She rose, saying she must go.

Albert rose also, and reached for his straw hat, with its coloured band.

'I'll stroll up with you, if you don't mind,' he said. And he took his place at her side along the Knarborough Road, where everybody turned to look. For, of course, he had a sort of fame in Woodhouse. She went with him laughing and chatting. But she did not feel at all comfortable. He seemed so pleased. Only he was not pleased with *her*. He was pleased with himself on her account: inordinately pleased with himself. In his world, as in a fish's, there was but his own swimming self: and if he chanced to have something swimming alongside and doing him credit, why, so much the more complacently he smiled.

He walked stiff and erect, with his head pressed rather back, so that he always seemed to be advancing from the head and shoulders, in a flat kind of advance, horizontal. He did not seem to be walking with his whole body. His manner was oddly gallant, with a gallantry that completely missed the individual in the woman, circled round her and flew home gratified to his own hive. The way he raised his hat, the way he inclined and smiled flatly, even rather excitedly, as he talked, was all a little discomforting and comical.

He left her at the shop door, saying:

'I shall see you again, I hope.'

'Oh, yes,' she replied, rattling the door anxiously, for it was locked. She heard her father's step at last tripping down the shop.

'Good-evening, Mr Houghton,' said Albert suavely and with a certain confidence, as James peered out.

'Oh, good-evening!' said James, letting Alvina pass, and shutting the door in Albert's face.

'Who was that?' he asked her sharply.

'Albert Witham,' she replied.

'What has *he* got to do with you?' said James shrewishly.

'Nothing, I hope.'

She fled into the obscurity of Manchester House, out of the grey summer evening. The Withams threw her off her pivot, and made her feel she was not herself. She felt she didn't know, she couldn't feel, she was just scattered and decentralized. And she was rather afraid of the Witham brothers. She might be their victim. She intended to avoid them.

The following days she saw Albert, in his Norfolk jacket and flannel trousers and his straw hat, strolling past several times and looking in through the shop door and up at the upper windows. But she hid herself thoroughly. When she went out, it was by the back way. So she avoided him.

But on Sunday evening, there he sat, rather stiff and brittle in the old Withams' pew, his head pressed a little back, so that his face and neck seemed slightly flattened. He wore very low, turn-down starched collars that showed all his neck. And he kept looking up at her during the service—she sat in the choir-loft—gazing up at her with apparently love-lorn eyes and a faint, intimate smile—the sort of *je-sais-tout* look of a private swain. Arthur also occasionally cast a judicious eye on her, as if she were a chimney that needed repairing, and he must estimate the cost, and whether it was worth it.

Sure enough, as she came out through the narrow choir gate into Knarborough Road, there was Albert stepping forward like a policeman, and saluting her and smiling down on her.

'I don't know if I'm presuming—' he said, in a mock deferential way that showed he didn't imagine he *could* presume.

'Oh, not at all,' said Alvina airily. He smiled with assurance.

'You haven't got any engagement, then, for this evening?' he said.

'No,' she replied simply.

'We might take a walk. What do you think?' he said, glancing down the road in either direction.

What, after all, was she to think? All the girls were pairing off with the boys for the after-chapel stroll and spoon.

'I don't mind,' she said. 'But I can't go far. I've got to be in at nine.'

'Which way shall we go?' he said.

He steered off, turned downhill through the common gardens, and proposed to take her the not-very-original walk up Flint's Lane, and along the railway line—the colliery railway, that is—then back up the Marlpool Road: a sort of circle. She agreed.

They did not find a great deal to talk about. She questioned him about his plans, and about the Cape. But save for bare outlines, which he gave readily enough, he was rather close.

'What do you do on Sunday nights as a rule?' he asked her.

'Oh, I have a walk with Lucy Grainger—or I go down to Hallam's—or go home,' she answered.

'You don't go walks with the fellows, then?'

'Father would never have it,' she replied.

'What will he say now?' he asked, with self-satisfaction.

'Goodness knows!' she laughed.

'Goodness usually does,' he answered archly.

When they came to the rather stumbly railway, he said: 'Won't you take my arm?'—offering her the said member.

'Oh, I'm all right,' she said. 'Thanks.'

'Go on,' he said, pressing a little nearer to her, and offering his arm. 'There's nothing against it, is there?'

'Oh, it's not that,' she said.

And feeling in a false position, she took his arm, rather unwillingly. He drew a little nearer to her, and walked with a slight prance.

'We get on better, don't we?' he said, giving her hand the tiniest squeeze with his arm against his side.

'Much!' she replied, with a laugh.

Then he lowered his voice oddly.

'It's many a day since I was on this railroad,' he said.

'Is this one of your old walks?' she asked, malicious.

'Yes, I've been it once or twice—with girls that are all married now.'

'Didn't you want to marry?' she asked.

'Oh, I don't know. I may have done. But it never came off, somehow. I've sometimes thought it never would come off.'

'Why?'

'I don't know, exactly. It didn't seem to, you know. Perhaps neither of us was properly inclined.'

'I should think so,' she said.

'And yet,' he admitted slyly, 'I should *like* to marry—' To this she did not answer.

'Shouldn't you?' he continued.

'When I meet the right man,' she laughed.

'That's it,' he said. 'There, that's just it! And you *haven't* met him?' His voice seemed smiling with a sort of triumph, as if he had caught her out.

'Well—once I thought I had—when I was engaged to Alexander.'

'But you found you were mistaken?' he insisted.

'No. Mother was so ill at the time—'

'There's always something to consider,' he said.

She kept on wondering what she should do if he wanted to kiss her. The mere incongruity of such a desire on his part formed a problem. Luckily, for this evening he formulated no desire, but left her in the shop-door soon after nine, with the request:

'I shall see you in the week, shan't I?'

'I'm not sure. I can't promise now,' she said hurriedly. 'Good-night.'

What she felt chiefly about him was a decentralized perplexity, very much akin to no feeling at all.

'Who do you think took me for a walk, Miss Pinnegar?' she said, laughing, to her confidante.

'I can't imagine,' replied Miss Pinnegar, eyeing her.

'You never would imagine,' said Alvina. 'Albert Witham.'

'Albert Witham!' exclaimed Miss Pinnegar, standing quite motionless.

'It may well take your breath away,' said Alvina.

'No, it's not that!' hurriedly expostulated Miss Pinnegar. 'Well—! Well, I declare!—' and then, on a new note: 'Well, he's very eligible, I think.'

'Most eligible!' replied Alvina.

'Yes, he is,' insisted Miss Pinnegar. 'I think it's very good.'

'What's very good?' asked Alvina.

Miss Pinnegar hesitated. She looked at Alvina. She reconsidered.

'Of course he's not the man I should have imagined for you, but—'

'You think he'll do?' said Alvina.

'Why not?' said Miss Pinnegar. 'Why shouldn't he do—if you like him.'

'Ah—!' cried Alvina, sinking on the sofa with a laugh. 'That's it.'

'Of course you couldn't have anything to do with him if you don't care for him,' pronounced Miss Pinnegar.

Albert continued to hang round. He did not make any direct attack for a few days. Suddenly one evening he appeared at the back door with a bunch of white stocks in his hand. His face lit up with a sudden, odd smile when she opened the door—a broad, pale-gleaming, remarkable smile.

'Lottie wanted to know if you'd come to tea to-morrow,' he said straight out, looking at her with the pale light in his eyes, that smiled palely right into her eyes, but did not see her at all. He was waiting on the doorstep to come in.

'Will you come in?' said Alvina. 'Father is in.'

'Yes, I don't mind,' he said, pleased. He mounted the steps, still holding his bunch of white stocks.

James Houghton screwed round in his chair and peered over his spectacles to see who was coming.

'Father,' said Alvina, 'you know Mr Witham, don't you?'

James Houghton half rose. He still peered over his glasses at the intruder.

'Well—I do by sight. How do you do?'

He held out his frail hand.

Albert held back, with the flowers in his own hand, and giving his broad, pleased, pale-gleaming smile from father to daughter, he said:

'What am I to do with these? Will you accept them, Miss Houghton?' He stared at her with shining, pallid smiling eyes.

'Are they for me?' she said, with false brightness. 'Thank you.'

James Houghton looked over the top of his spectacles, searchingly, at the flowers, as if they had been a bunch of white and sharp-toothed ferrets. Then he looked as suspiciously at the hand which Albert at last extended to him. He shook it slightly, and said:

'Take a seat.'

'I'm afraid I'm disturbing you in your reading,' said Albert, still having the drawn, excited smile on his face.

'Well—' said James Houghton. 'The light is fading.'

Alvina came in with the flowers in a jar. She set them on the table.

'Haven't they a lovely scent?' she said.

'Do you think so?' he replied, again with the excited smile. There was a pause. Albert, rather embarrassed, reached forward, saying:

'May I see what you're reading?' And he turned over the book. 'Tommy and Grizel! Oh yes! What do you think of it?'

'Well,' said James, 'I am only in the beginning.'

'I think it's interesting, myself,' said Albert, 'as a study of a man who can't get away from himself. You meet a lot of people like that. What I wonder is why they find it such a drawback.'

'Find what a drawback?' asked James.

'Not being able to get away from themselves. That self-consciousness. It hampers them, and interferes with their power of action. Now I wonder why self-consciousness should hinder a man in his action? Why does it cause misgiving? I think I'm self-conscious, but I don't think I have so many misgivings. I don't see that they're necessary.'

'Certainly I think Tommy is a weak character. I believe he's a despicable character,' said James.

'No, I don't know so much about that,' said Albert. 'I shouldn't say weak, exactly. He's only weak in one direction. No, what I wonder is why he feels guilty. If you feel self-conscious, there's no need to feel guilty about it, is there?'

He stared with his strange, smiling stare at James.

'I shouldn't say so,' replied James. 'But if a man never knows his own mind, he certainly can't be much of a man.'

'I don't see it,' replied Albert. 'What's the matter is that he feels guilty for not knowing his own mind. That's the unnecessary part. The guilty feeling—'

Albert seemed insistent on this point, which had no particular interest for James.

'Where we've got to make a change,' said Albert, 'is in the feeling that other people have a right to tell us what we ought to feel and do. Nobody knows what another man ought to feel. Every man has his own special feelings, and his own right to them. That's where it is with education. You ought not to want all your children to feel alike. Their natures are all different, and so they should all feel different, about practically everything.'

'There would be no end to the confusion,' said James.

'There needn't be any confusion to speak of. You agree to a number of rules and conventions and laws, for social purposes. But in private you feel just as you do feel, without occasion for trying to feel something else.'

'I don't know,' said James. 'There are certain feelings common to humanity, such as love, and honour, and truth.'

'Would you call them feelings?' said Albert. 'I should say what is common is the idea. The idea is common to humanity, once you've put it into words. But the feeling varies with every man. The same idea represents a different kind of feeling in every different individual. It seems to me that's what we've got to recognize if we're going to do anything with education. We don't want to produce mass feelings. Don't you agree?'

Poor James was too bewildered to know whether to agree or not to agree.

'Shall we have a light, Alvina?' he said to his daughter.

Alvina lit the incandescent gas-jet that hung in the middle of the room. The hard white light showed her somewhat haggard-looking as she reached up to it. But Albert watched her, smiling abstractedly. It seemed as if his words came off him without affecting him at all. He did not think about what he was feeling, and he did not feel what he was thinking about. And therefore she hardly heard what he said. Yet she believed he was clever.

It was evident Albert was quite blissfully happy, in his own way, sitting there at the end of the sofa not far from the fire, and talking animatedly. The uncomfortable thing was that though he talked in the direction of his interlocutor, he did not speak *to* him: merely said his words towards him. James, however, was such an airy feather himself he did not remark this, but only felt a little self-important at sustaining such a subtle conversation with a man from Oxford. Alvina, who never expected to be interested in clever conversations, after a long experience of her father, found her expectation justified again. She was not interested.

The man was quite nicely dressed, in the regulation tweed jacket and flannel trousers and brown shoes. He was even rather smart, judging from his yellow socks and yellow-and-brown tie. Miss Pinnegar eyed him with approval when she came in.

'Good-evening!' she said, just a trifle condescendingly, as she shook hands. 'How do you find Woodhouse, after being away so long?' Her way of speaking was so quiet, as if she hardly spoke aloud.

'Well,' he answered. 'I find it the same in many ways.'

'You wouldn't like to settle here again?'

'I don't think I should. It feels a little cramped, you know, after a new country. But it has its attractions.' Here he smiled, meaningfully.

'Yes,' said Miss Pinnegar. 'I suppose the old connections count for something.'

'They do. Oh decidedly they do. There's no associations like the old ones.' He smiled flatly as he looked towards Alvina.

'You find it so, do you!' returned Miss Pinnegar. 'You don't find that the new connections make up for the old?'

'Not altogether, they don't. There's something missing—' Again he looked towards Alvina. But she did not answer his look.

'Well,' said Miss Pinnegar. 'I'm glad we still count for

something, in spite of the greater attractions. How long have you in England?'

'Another year. Just a year. This time next year I expect I shall be sailing back to the Cape.' He smiled as if in anticipation. Yet it was hard to believe that it mattered to him—or that anything mattered.

'And is Oxford agreeable to you?' she asked.

'Oh, yes. I keep myself busy.'

'What are your subjects?' asked James.

'English and History. But I do mental science for my own interest.'

Alvina had taken up a piece of sewing. She sat under the light, brooding a little. What *had* all this to do with her? The man talked on, and beamed in her direction. And she felt a little important. But moved or touched?—not the least in the world.

She wondered if anyone would ask him to supper—bread and cheese and currant-loaf, and water, was all that offered. No one asked him, and at last he rose.

'Show Mr Witham out through the shop, Alvina,' said Miss Pinnegar.

Alvina piloted the man through the long, dark, encumbered way of the shop. At the door he said:

'You've never said whether you're coming to tea on Thursday.'

'I don't think I can,' said Alvina.

He seemed rather taken aback.

'Why?' he said. 'What stops you?'

'I've so much to do.'

He smiled slowly and satirically.

'Won't it keep?' he said.

'No, really. I can't come on Thursday—thank you so much. Good-night!' She gave him her hand and turned quickly into the shop, closing the door. He remained standing in the porch, staring at the closed door. Then, lifting his lip, he turned away.

'Well,' said Miss Pinnegar decidedly, as Alvina re-entered. 'You can say what you like—but I think he's *very pleasant, very* pleasant.'

'Extremely intelligent,' said James Houghton, shifting in his chair.

'I was awfully bored,' said Alvina.

They both looked at her, irritated.

After this she really did what she could to avoid him. When she saw him sauntering down the street in all his leisure, a sort of anger possessed her. On Sunday, she slipped down from the choir into the chapel, and out through the main entrance, whilst he awaited her at the small exit. And by good luck, when he called one evening in the week, she was out. She returned down the yard. And there, through the uncurtained window, she saw him sitting awaiting her. Without a thought, she turned on her heel and fled away. She did not come in till he had gone.

'How late you are!' said Miss Pinnegar. 'Mr Witham was here till ten minutes ago.'

'Yes,' laughed Alvina. 'I came down the yard and saw him. So I went back till he'd gone.'

Miss Pinnegar looked at her in displeasure:

'I suppose you know your own mind,' she said.

'How do you explain such behaviour?' said her father pettishly.

'I didn't want to meet him,' she said.

The next evening was Saturday. Alvina had inherited Miss Frost's task of attending to the chapel flowers once a quarter. She had been round the gardens of her friends, and gathered the scarlet and hot yellow and purple flowers of August, asters, red stocks, tall Japanese sunflowers, coreopsis, geraniums. With these in her basket she slipped out towards evening, to the chapel. She knew Mr Calladine, the caretaker, would not lock up till she had been.

The moment she got inside the chapel—it was a big, airy, pleasant building—she heard hammering from the organ-loft, and saw the flicker of a candle. Some workman busy before Sunday. She shut the baize door behind her, and hurried across to the vestry, for vases, then out to the tap, for water. All was warm and still.

It was full early evening. The yellow light streamed through the side windows, the big stained-glass window at the end was deep and full of glowing colour, in which the yellows and reds were richest. Above in the organ-loft the hammering continued. She arranged her flowers in many vases, till the communion table was like the window, a tangle of strong yellow, and crimson, and purple, and bronze-green. She tried to keep the effect light and kaleidoscopic, an interplay of tossed pieces of strong, hot colour, vibrating and lightly intermingled. It was very gorgeous, for a communion table. But the day of white lilies was over.

Suddenly there was a terrific crash and bang and tumble, up in the organ-loft, followed by a cursing.

'Are you hurt?' called Alvina, looking up into space. The candle had disappeared.

But there was no reply. Feeling curious, she went out of the chapel to the stairs in the side porch, and ran up to the organ. She went round the side—and there she saw a man in his shirt-sleeves sitting crouched in the obscurity on the floor between the organ and the wall of the back, while a collapsed pair of steps lay between her and him. It was too dark to see who it was.

'That rotten pair of steps came down with me,' said the infuriated voice of Arthur Witham, 'and about broke my leg.'

Alvina advanced towards him, picking her way over the steps. He was sitting nursing his leg.

'Is it bad?' she asked, stooping towards him.

In the shadow he lifted up his face. It was pale, and his eyes were savage with anger. Her face was near his.

'It is bad,' he said, furious because of the shock. The shock had thrown him off his balance.

'Let me see,' she said.

He removed his hands from clasping his shin, some distance above the ankle. She put her fingers over the bone, over his stockings, to feel if there was any fracture. Immediately her fingers were wet with blood. Then he did a curious thing. With both his hands he pressed her hand down over his wounded leg, pressed it with all his might, as if her hand were a plaster. For some moments he sat pressing her hand over his broken shin, completely oblivious, as some people are when they have had a shock and a hurt, intense

on one point of consciousness only, and for the rest unconscious.

Then he began to come to himself. The pain modified
itself. He could not bear the sudden acute hurt to his shin.
That was one of his sensitive, unbearable parts.

'The bone isn't broken,' she said professionally. 'But
you'd better get the stocking out of it.'

Without a thought, he pulled his trouser-leg higher and
rolled down his stocking, extremely gingerly, and sick with
pain.

'Can you show a light?' he said.

She found the candle. And she knew where matches always rested on a little ledge of the organ. So she brought
him a light, whilst he examined his broken shin. The blood
was flowing, but not so much. It was a nasty cut bruise,
swelling and looking very painful. He sat looking at it absorbedly, bent over it in the candle-light.

'It's not so very bad, when the pain goes off,' she said,
noticing the black hairs of his shin. 'We'd better tie it up.
Have you got a handkerchief?'

'It's in my jacket,' he said.

She looked round for his jacket. He annoyed her a little,
by being completely oblivious of her. She got his handkerchief and wiped her fingers on it. Then of her own kerchief
she made a pad for the wound.

'Shall I tie it up, then?' she said.

But he did not answer. He sat still nursing his leg, looking
at his hurt, while the blood slowly trickled down the wet
hairs towards his ankle. There was nothing to do but wait
for him.

'Shall I tie it up, then?' she repeated at length, a little impatient. So he put his leg a little forward.

She looked at the wound, and wiped it a little. Then she
folded the pad of her own handkerchief, and laid it over the
hurt. And again he did the same thing, he took her hand as
if it were a plaster, and applied it to his wound, pressing it
cautiously but firmly down. She was rather angry. He took
no notice of her at all. And she, waiting, seemed to go into
a dream, a sleep, her arm trembled a little, stretched out and
fixed. She seemed to lose count, under the firm compression

he imposed on her. It was as if the pressure on her hand
pressed her into oblivion.

'Tie it up,' he said briskly.

And she, obedient, began to tie the bandage with numb
fingers. He seemed to have taken the use out of her.

When she had finished, he scrambled to his feet, looked
at the organ which he was repairing, and looked at the collapsed pair of steps.

'A rotten pair of things to have, to put a man's life in
danger,' he said, towards the steps. Then stubbornly, he
rigged them up again, and stared again at his interrupted job.

'You won't go on, will you?' she asked.

'It's got to be done, Sunday to-morrow,' he said. 'If you'd
hold them steps a minute! There isn't more than a minute's
fixing to do. It's all done, but for fixing.'

'Hadn't you better leave it?' she said.

'Would you mind holding the steps, so that they don't let
me down again,' he said. Then he took the candle, and hob-
bled stubbornly and angrily up again, with spanner and
hammer. For some minutes he worked, tapping and read-
justing, whilst she held the rickety steps and stared at him
from below, the shapeless bulk of his trousers. Strange the
difference—she could not help thinking it—between the
vulnerable hairy, and somehow childish leg of the real man,
and the shapeless form of these workmen's trousers. The
kernel, the man himself, seemed so tender—the covering so
stiff and insentient.

And was he not going to speak to her—not one human
word of recognition? Men are the most curious and unreal
creatures. After all he had made use of her. Think how he
had pressed her hand gently but firmly down, down over
his bruise, how he had taken the virtue out of her, till she
felt all weak and dim. And after that was he going to relapse
into his tough and ugly workman's hide, and treat her as if
she were a pair of steps, which might let him down or hold
him up, as might be?

As she stood clinging to the steps she felt weak and a little
hysterical. She wanted to summon her strength, to have her
own back from him. After all he had taken the virtue from

her, he might have the grace to say thank you, and treat her as if she were a human being.

At last he left off tinkering, and looked round.

'Have you finished?' she said.

'Yes,' he answered crossly.

And taking the candle he began to clamber down. When he got to the bottom he crouched over his leg and felt the bandage.

'That gives you what for,' he said, as if it were her fault.

'Is the bandage holding?' she said.

'I think so,' he answered churlishly.

'Aren't you going to make sure?' she said.

'Oh, it's all right,' he said, turning aside and taking up his tools. 'I'll make my way home.'

'So will I,' she answered.

She took the candle and went a little in front. He hurried into his coat and gathered his tools, anxious to get away. She faced him, holding the candle.

'Look at my hand,' she said, holding it out. It was smeared with blood, as was the cuff of her dress—a black-and-white striped cotton dress.

'Is it hurt?' he said.

'No, but look at it. Look here!' She showed the blood-stains on her dress.

'It'll wash out,' he said, frightened of her.

'Yes, so it will. But for the present it's there. Don't you think you ought to thank me?'

He recoiled a little.

'Yes,' he said. 'I'm very much obliged.'

'You ought to be more than that,' she said.

He did not answer, but looked her up and down.

'We'll be going down,' he said. 'We s'll have folks talking.'

Suddenly she began to laugh. It seemed so comical. What a position! The candle shook as she laughed. What a man, answering her like a little automaton! Seriously, quite seriously he said it to her—'We s'll have folks talking!' She laughed in a breathless, hurried way, as they tramped downstairs.

At the bottom of the stairs Calladine, the caretaker, met

them. He was a tall thin man with a black moustache—about fifty years old.

'Have you done for to-night, all of you?' he said, grinning in echo to Alvina's still fluttering laughter.

'That's a nice rotten pair of steps you've got up there for a death-trap,' said Arthur angrily. 'Come down on top of me, and I'm lucky I haven't got my leg broken. It *is* near enough.'

'Come down with you, did they?' said Calladine good-humouredly. 'I never knowed 'em come down wi' me.'

'You ought to, then. My leg's as near broke as it can be.'

'What, have you hurt yourself?'

'I should think I have. Look here—' And he began to pull up his trouser leg. But Alvina had given the candle to Calladine, and fled. She had a last view of Arthur stooping over his precious leg, while Calladine stooped his length and held down the candle.

When she got home she took off her dress and washed herself hard and washed the stained sleeve, thoroughly, thoroughly, and threw away the wash water and rinsed the washbowls with fresh water, scrupulously. Then she dressed herself in her black dress once more, did her hair, and went downstairs.

But she could not sew—and she could not settle down. It was Saturday evening, and her father had opened the shop, Miss Pinnegar had gone to Knarborough. She would be back at nine o'clock. Alvina set about to make a mock woodcock, or a mock something or other, with cheese and an egg and bits of toast. Her eyes were dilated and as if amused, mocking, her face quivered a little with irony that was not all enjoyable.

'I'm glad you've come,' said Alvina, as Miss Pinnegar entered. 'The supper's just done. I'll ask father if he'll close the shop.'

Of course James would not close the shop, though he was merely wasting light. He nipped in to eat his supper, and started out again with a mouthful the moment he heard the ping of the bell. He kept his customers chatting as long as he could. His love for conversation had degenerated into a spasmodic passion for chatter.

Alvina looked across at Miss Pinnegar, as the two sat at the meagre super-table. Her eyes were dilated and arched with a mocking, almost satanic look.

'I've made up my mind about Albert Witham,' said Alvina. Miss Pinnegar looked at her.

'Which way?' she asked, demurely, but a little sharp.

'It's all off,' said Alvina, breaking into a nervous laugh.

'Why? What has happened?'

'Nothing has happened. I can't stand him.'

'Why?—suddenly—' said Miss Pinnegar.

'It's not sudden,' laughed Alvina. 'Not at all. I can't stand him. I never could. And I won't try. There! Isn't that plain?' And she went off into her hurried laugh, partly at herself, partly at Arthur, partly at Albert, partly at Miss Pinnegar.

'Oh, well, if you're so sure—' said Miss Pinnegar rather bitingly.

'I *am* quite sure—' said Alvina. 'I'm quite certain.'

'Cock-sure people are often most mistaken,' said Miss Pinnegar.

'I'd rather have my own mistakes than somebody else's rights,' said Alvina.

'Then don't expect anybody to pay for your mistakes,' said Miss Pinnegar.

'It would be all the same if I did,' said Alvina.

When she lay in bed, she stared at the light of the street-lamp on the wall. She was thinking busily: but heaven knows what she was thinking. She had sharpened the edge of her temper. She was waiting till to-morrow. She was waiting till she saw Albert Witham. She wanted to finish off with him. She was keen to cut clean through any correspondence with him. She stared for many hours at the light of the street-lamp, and there was a narrowed look in her eyes.

The next day she did not go to Morning Service, but stayed at home to cook the dinner. In the evening she sat in her place in the choir. In the Withams' pew sat Lottie and Albert—no Arthur. Albert kept glancing up. Alvina could not bear the sight of him—she simply could not bear the sight of him. Yet in her low, sweet voice she sang the alto to the hymns, right to the vesper:

> Lord keep us safe this night
> Secure from all our fears,
> May angels guard us while we sleep
> Till morning light appears—

As she sang her alto, and as the soft and emotional harmony of the vesper swelled luxuriously through the chapel, she was peeping over her folded hands at Lottie's hat. She could not bear Lottie's hats. There was something aggressive and vulgar about them. And she simply detested the look of the back of Albert's head, as he too stooped to the vesper prayer. It looked mean and rather common. She remembered Arthur had the same look bending to prayer. There!—why had she not seen it before! That petty, vulgar little look! How could she have thought twice of Arthur? She had made a fool of herself, as usual. Him and his little leg. She grimaced round the chapel, waiting for people to bob up their heads and take their departure.

At the gate Albert was waiting for her. He came forward lifting his hat with a smiling and familiar 'Good evening!'

'Good evening,' she murmured.

'It's ages since I've seen you,' he said. 'And I've looked out for you everywhere.'

It was raining a little. She put up her umbrella.

'You'll take a little stroll. The rain isn't much,' he said.

'No thank you,' she said. 'I must go home.'

'Why, what's your hurry? Walk as far as Beeby Bridge. Go on.'

'No thank you.'

'How's that? What makes you refuse?'

'I don't want to.'

He paused and looked down at her. The cold and supercilious look of anger, a little spiteful, came into his face.

'Do you mean because of the rain?' he said.

'No. I hope you don't mind. But I don't want to take any more walks. I don't mean anything by them.'

'Oh, as for that,' he said, taking the words out of her mouth. 'Why should you mean anything by them!' He smiled down on her.

She looked him straight in the face.

'But I'd rather not take any more walks, thank you—none at all,' she said, looking him full in the eyes.

'You wouldn't?' he replied stiffening.

'Yes. I'm quite sure,' she said.

'As sure as all that, are you!' he said, with a sneering grimace. He stood eyeing her insolently up and down.

'Good-night,' she said. His sneering made her furious. Putting her umbrella between him and her, she walked off.

'Good-night then,' he replied, unseen by her. But his voice was sneering and impotent.

She went home quivering. But her soul was burning with satisfaction. She had shaken them off.

Later she wondered if she had been unkind to him. But it was done—and done for ever. *Vogue la galère*.

CHAPTER 6

Houghton's Last Endeavour

The trouble with her ship was that it would *not* sail. It rode water-logged in the rotting port of home. All very well to have wild, reckless moods of irony and independence, if you have to pay for them by withering dustily on the shelf.

Alvina fell again into humility and fear: she began to show symptoms of her mother's heart trouble. For day followed day, month followed month, season after season went by, and she grubbed away like a housemaid in Manchester House, she hurried round doing the shopping, she sang in the choir on Sundays, she attended the various chapel events, she went out to visit friends, and laughed and talked and played games. But all the time, what was there actually in her life? Not much. She was withering towards old-maiddom. Already in her twenty-eighth year, she spent her days grubbing in the house, whilst her father became an elderly, frail man still too lively in mind and spirit. Miss Pinnegar began to grow grey and elderly too, money became scarcer and scarcer, there was a black day ahead when her father would die and the home be broken up, and she would have to tackle life as a worker.

There lay the only alternative: in work. She might slave her days away teaching the piano, as Miss Frost had done:

she might find a subordinate post as nurse: she might sit in
the cash-desk of some shop. Some work of some sort would
be found for her. And she would sink into the routine of
her job, as did so many women, and grow old and die, chattering and fluttering. She would have what is called her independence. But, seriously faced with that treasure, and
without the option of refusing it, strange how hideous she
found it.

Work!—a job! More even than she rebelled against the
Withams did she rebel against a job. Albert Witham was
distasteful to her—or rather, he was not exactly distasteful,
he was chiefly incongruous. She could never get over the
feeling that he was mouthing and smiling at her through the
glass wall of an aquarium, he being on the watery side.
Whether she would ever be able to take to his strange and
dishuman element, who knows? Anyhow it would be some
sort of an adventure: better than a job. She rebelled with all
her backbone against the word *job*. Even the substitutes,
employment or *work,* were detestable, unbearable. Emphatically, she did not want to work for a wage. It was too humiliating. Could anything be more *infra dig* than the
performing of a set of special actions day in day out, for a
lifetime, in order to receive some shillings every seventh
day? Shameful! A condition of shame. The most vulgar, sordid and humiliating of all forms of slavery: so mechanical.
Far better be a slave outright, in contact with all the whims
and impulses of a human being, than serve some mechanical
routine of modern work.

She trembled with anger, impotence, and fear. For
months, the thought of Albert was a torment to her. She
might have married him. He would have been strange, a
strange fish. But were it not better to take the strange leap,
over into his element, than to condemn oneself to the routine of a job? He would have been curious and dis-human.
But after all, it would have been an experience. In a way,
she liked him. There was something odd and integral about
him, which she liked. He was not a liar. In his own line, he
was honest and direct. Then he would take her to South
Africa; a whole new *milieu*. And perhaps she would have
children. She shivered a little. No, not his children! He

seemed so curiously cold-blooded. And yet, why not? Why
not his curious, pale, half-cold-blooded children, like little
fishes of her own? Why not? Everything was possible: and
even desirable, once one could see the strangeness of it.
Once she could plunge through the wall of the aquarium!
Once she could kiss him!

Therefore Miss Pinnegar's quiet harping on the string was
unbearable.

'I can't understand that you disliked Mr Witham so
much,' said Miss Pinnegar.

'We never can understand those things,' said Alvina. 'I
can't understand why I dislike tapioca and arrowroot—but
I do.'

'That's different,' said Miss Pinnegar shortly.

'It's no more easy to understand,' said Alvina.

'Because there's no need to understand it,' said Miss Pinnegar.

'And is there need to understand the other?'

'Certainly. I can see nothing wrong with him,' said Miss
Pinnegar.

Alvina went away in silence. This was in the first months
after she had given Albert his dismissal. He was at Oxford
again—would not return to Woodhouse till Christmas. Between her and the Woodhouse Withams there was a decided
coldness. They never looked at her now—nor she at them.

None the less, as Christmas drew near Alvina worked up
her feelings. Perhaps she would be reconciled to him. She
would slip across and smile to him. She would take the
plunge, once and for all—and kiss him and marry him and
bear the little half-fishes, his children. She worked herself
into quite a fever of anticipation.

But when she saw him, the first evening, sitting stiff and
staring flatly in front of him in chapel, staring away from
everything in the world, at heaven knows what—just as
fishes stare—then his dishumanness came over her again like
an arrest, and arrested all her flights of fancy. He stared
flatly in front of him, and flatly set a wall of oblivion between him and her. She trembled and let be.

After Christmas, however, she had nothing at all to think

forward to. And it was then she seemed to shrink: she seemed positively to shrink.

'You never spoke to Mr Witham?' Miss Pinnegar asked.

'He never spoke to me,' replied Alvina.

'He raised his hat to me.'

'*You* ought to have married him, Miss Pinnegar,' said Alvina. 'He would have been right for you.' And she laughed rather mockingly.

'There is no need to make provision for me,' said Miss Pinnegar.

And after this, she was a long time before she forgave Alvina, and was really friendly again. Perhaps she would never have forgiven her if she had not found her weeping rather bitterly in her mother's abandoned sitting-room.

Now so far, the story of Alvina is commonplace enough. It is more or less the story of thousands of girls. They all find work. It is the ordinary solution of everything. And if we were dealing with an ordinary girl we should have to carry on mildly and dully down the long years of employment; or, at the best, marriage with some dull schoolteacher or office-clerk.

But we protest that Alvina is not ordinary. Ordinary people, ordinary fates. But extraordinary people, extraordinary fates. Or else no fate at all. The all-to-one-pattern modern system is too much for most extraordinary individuals. It just kills them off or throws them disused aside.

There have been enough stories about ordinary people. I should think the Duke of Clarence must even have found malmsey nauseating, when he choked and went purple and was really asphyxiated in a butt of it. And ordinary people are no malmsey. Just ordinary tap-water. And we have been drenched and deluged and so nearly drowned in perpetual floods of ordinariness, that tap-water tends to become a really hateful fluid to us. We loathe its out-of-the-tap tastelessness. We detest ordinary people. We are in peril of our lives from them: and in peril of our souls too, for they would damn us one and all to the ordinary. Every individual should, by nature, have his extraordinary points. But nowadays you may look for them with a microscope, they are so worn-down by the regular machine-friction of our average and mechanical days.

There was no hope for Alvina in the ordinary. If help came, it would have to come from the extraordinary. Hence the extreme peril of her case. Hence the bitter fear and humiliation she felt as she drudged shabbily on in Manchester House, hiding herself as much as possible from public view. Men can suck the heady juice of exalted self-importance from the bitter weed of failure—failures are usually the most conceited of men: even as was James Houghton. But to a woman, failure is another matter. For her it means failure to live, failure to establish her own life on the face of the earth. And this is humiliating, the ultimate humiliation.

And so the slow years crept round, and the completed coil of each one was a further heavy, strangling noose. Alvina had passed her twenty-sixth, twenty-seventh, twenty-eighth and even her twenty-ninth year. She was in her thirtieth. It ought to be a laughing matter. But it isn't.

> Ach, schon zwanzig
> Ach, schon zwanzig
> Immer noch durch's Leben tanz'ich
> Jeder, Jeder will mich küssen
> Mir das Leben zu versüssen.
>
> Ach, schon dreissig
> Ach, schon dreissig
> Immer Mädchen, Mädchen heiss' ich.
> In dem Zopf schon graue Härchen
> Ach, wie schnell vergehn die Jährchen.
>
> Ach, schon vierzig
> Ach, schon vierzig
> Und noch immer Keiner find' sich.
> Im Gesicht schon graue Flecken
> Ach, das muss im Spiegel stecken.
>
> Ach, schon fünfzig
> Ach, schon fünfzig
> Und noch immer Keiner will 'mich;
> Soll ich mich mit Bänden zieren

Soll ich einen Schleier führen?
Dann heisstes, die Alte putzt sich,
Sie ist fu'fzig, sie ist fu'fzig.

True enough, in Alvina's pigtail of soft brown the grey hairs were already showing. True enough, she still preferred to be thought of as a girl. And the slow-footed years, so heavy in passing, were so imperceptibly numerous in their accumulation.

But we are not going to follow our song to its fatal and dreary conclusion. Presumably, the *ordinary* old-maid heroine nowadays is destined to die in her fifties, she is not allowed to be the long-liver of the bygone novels. Let the song suffice her.

James Houghton had still another kick in him. He had one last scheme up his sleeve. Looking out on a changing world, it was the popular novelties which had the last fascination for him. The Skating Rink, like another Charybdis, had all but entangled him in its swirl, as he pushed painfully off from the rocks of Throttle-Ha'penny. But he escaped, and for almost three years had lain obscurely in port like a frail and finished bark, selling the last of his bits and bobs, and making little splashes in warehouse-oddments. Miss Pinnegar thought he had really gone quiet.

But alas, at that degenerated and shabby, down-at-heel club he met another tempter: a plump man who had been in the music-hall line as a sort of agent. This man had catered for the little shows of little towns. He had been in America, out West, doing shows there. He had trailed his way back to England, where he had left his wife and daughter. But he did not resume his family life. Wherever he was, his wife was a hundred miles away. Now he found himself more or less stranded in Woodhouse. He had *nearly* fixed himself up with a music-hall in the Potteries—as manager: he had all-but got such another place at Ickley, in Derbyshire: he had forced his way through the industrial and mining townlets, prospecting for any sort of music-hall or show from which he could get a picking. And now, in very low water, he found himself at Woodhouse.

Woodhouse had a cinema already: a famous Empire run-up by Jordan, the sly builder and decorator who had got on so surprisingly. In James's younger days, Jordan was an obscure and illiterate nobody. And now he had a motor car, and looked at the tottering James with sardonic contempt, from under his heavy, heavy-lidded dark eyes. He was rather stout, frail in health, but silent and insuperable, was A. W. Jordan.

'I missed a chance there,' said James, fluttering. 'I missed a rare chance there. I ought to have been first with a cinema.'

He admitted as much to Mr May, the stranger who was looking for some sort of 'managing' job. Mr May, who also was plump and who could hold his tongue, but whose pink, fat face and light-blue eyes had a loud look, for all that, put the speech in his pipe and smoked it. Not that he smoked a pipe: always cigarettes. But he seized on James's admission, as something to be made the most of.

Now Mr May's mind, though quick, was pedestrian, not winged. He had come to Woodhouse not to look at Jordan's 'Empire', but at the temporary wooden structure that stood in the old Cattle Market—'Wright's Cinematograph and Variety Theatre'. Wright's was not a superior show, like the Woodhouse Empire. Yet it was always packed with colliers and work-lasses. But unfortunately there was no chance of Mr May's getting a finger in the Cattle Market pie. Wright's was a family affair. Mr and Mrs Wright and a son and two daughters with their husbands: a tight old lock-up family concern. Yet it was the kind of show that appealed to Mr May: pictures between the turns. The cinematograph was but an item in the programme, amidst the more thrilling incidents—to Mr May—of conjurers, popular songs, five-minute farces, performing birds, and comics. Mr May was too human to believe that a show should consist entirely of the dithering eye-ache of a film.

He was becoming really depressed by his failure to find any opening. He had his family to keep—and though his honesty was of the variety sort, he had a heavy conscience in the direction of his wife and daughter. Having been so long in America, he had acquired American qualities, one of which was this heavy sort of private innocence, coupled with complacent and natural unscrupulousness in 'matters of business'. A man of some odd sensitiveness in material things, he liked to have his clothes neat and spick, his linen immaculate, his face clean-shaven like a cherub. But alas, his clothes were now old-fashioned, so that their rather expensive smartness was detrimental to his chances, in spite of their scrupulous look of having come almost new out of the bandbox that morning. His rather small felt hats still curved jauntily over his full pink face. But his eyes looked lugubrious, as if he felt he had not deserved so much bad luck, and there were bilious lines beneath them.

So Mr May, in his room in the Moon and Stars, which was the best inn in Woodhouse—he must have a good hotel—lugubriously considered his position. Woodhouse offered little or nothing. He must go to Alfreton. And would he find anything there? Ah, where, where in this hateful world was there refuge for a man saddled with responsibilities, who wanted to do his best and was given no opportunity? Mr May had travelled in his Pullman car and gone straight to the best hotel in the town, like any other American with money—in America. He had done it smart, too. And now, in this grubby penny-picking England, he saw his boots being worn-down at the heel, and was afraid of being stranded without cash even for a railway ticket. If he had to clear out without paying his hotel bill—well, that was the world's fault. He had to live. But he must perforce keep enough in hand for a ticket to Birmingham. He always said his wife was in London. And he always walked down to Lumley to post his letters. He was full of evasions.

So again he walked down to Lumley to post his letters. And he looked at Lumley. And he found it a damn godforsaken hell of a hole. It was a long straggle of a dusty road down in the valley, with a pale-grey dust and spatter from the pottery, and big chimneys bellying forth black smoke right by the road. Then there was a short cross-way, up which one saw the iron foundry, a black and rusty place. A little further on was the railway junction, and beyond that, more houses stretching to Hathersedge, where the stocking factories were busy. Compared with Lumley, Woodhouse, whose church could be seen sticking up proudly and vulgarly on an eminence, above trees and meadow-slopes, was an idyllic heaven.

Mr May turned in to the Derby Hotel to have a small whisky. And of course he entered into conversation.

'You seem somewhat quiet at Lumley,' he said, in his odd, refined-showman's voice. 'Have you *nothing at all* in the way of amusement?'

'They all go up to Woodhouse, else to Hathersedge.'

'But couldn't you support some place of your own—some *rival* to Wright's Variety?'

'Ay—'appen—if somebody started it.'

And so it was that James was inoculated with the idea of starting a cinema on the virgin soil of Lumley. To the women he said not a word. But on the very first morning that Mr May broached the subject, he became a new man. He fluttered like a boy, he fluttered as if he had just grown wings.

'Let us go down,' said Mr May, 'and look at a site. You pledge yourself to nothing—you don't compromise yourself. You merely have a site in your mind.'

And so it came to pass that, next morning, this oddly assorted couple went down to Lumley together. James was very shabby, in his black coat and dark grey trousers, and his cheap grey cap. He bent forward as he walked, and still nipped along hurriedly, as if pursued by fate. His face was thin and still handsome. Odd that his cheap cap, by incongruity, made him look more a gentleman. But it did. As he walked he glanced alertly hither and thither, and saluted everybody.

By his side, somewhat tight and tubby, with his chest out and his head back, went the prim figure of Mr May, reminding one of a consequential bird of the smaller species. His plumbago-grey suit fitted exactly—save that it was perhaps a little tight. The jacket and waistcoat were bound with silk braid of exactly the same shade as the cloth. His soft collar, immaculately fresh, had a dark stripe like his shirt. His boots were black, with grey suede uppers: but a *little* down at heel. His dark-grey hat was jaunty. Altogether he looked very spruce, though a *little* behind the fashions: very pink-faced, though his blue eyes were bilious beneath: very much on the spot, although the spot was the wrong one.

They discoursed amiably as they went, James bending forward, Mr May bending back. Mr May took the refined man-of-the-world tone.

'Of course,' he said—he used the two words very often, and pronounced the second, rather mincingly, to rhyme with *sauce:* 'Of course,' said Mr May, 'it's a disgusting place—*disgusting!* I never was in a worse, in all the *cauce* of my travels. But *then*—that isn't the point—' He spread his plump hands from his immaculate shirt-cuffs.

'No, it isn't. Decidedly it isn't. That's beside the point altogether. What we want—' began James.

'Is an audience—of *cauce*—! And we have it—! Virgin soil—!'

'Yes, decidedly. Untouched! An unspoiled market.'

'An unspoiled market!' reiterated Mr May, in full confirmation, though with a faint flicker of a smile. 'How very *fortunate* for us.'

'Properly handled,' said James. 'Properly handled.'

'Why yes—of *cauce*. Why *shouldn't* we handle it properly!'

'Oh, we shall manage that, we shall manage that,' came the quick, slightly husky voice of James.

'Of *cauce* we shall! Why bless my life, if we can't manage an audience in Lumley, what *can* we do.'

'We have a guide in the matter of their taste,' said James. 'We can see what Wright's are doing—and Jordan's—and we can go to Hathersedge and Knarborough and Alfreton—beforehand, that is—'

'Why certainly—if you think it's *necessary*. I'll do all that for you. *And* I'll interview the managers and the performers themselves—as if I were a journalist, don't you see. I've done a fair amount of journalism, and nothing easier than to get cards from various newspapers.'

'Yes, that's a good suggestion,' said James. 'As if you were going to write an account in the newspapers—excellent.'

'And so simple! You pick up just *all* the information you require.'

'Decidedly—decidedly!' said James.

And so behold our two heroes sniffing round the sordid back and wasted meadows and marshy places of Lumley. They found one barren patch where two caravans were standing. A woman was peeling potatoes, sitting on the bottom step of her caravan. A half-caste girl came up with a large pale-blue enamelled jug of water. In the background were two booths covered up with coloured canvas. Hammering was heard inside.

'Good-morning!' said Mr May, stopping before the woman. ' 'Tisn't fair time, is it?'

'No, it's no fair,' said the woman.

'I see. You're just on your own. Getting on all right?'

'Fair,' said the woman.

'Only fair! Sorry. Good-morning.'

Mr May's quick eye, roving round, had seen a negro stoop from under the canvas that covered one booth. The negro was thin, and looked young but rather frail, and limped. His face was very like that of the young negro in Watteau's drawing—pathetic, wistful, north-bitten. In an instant Mr May had taken all in: the man was the woman's husband—they were acclimatized in these regions: the booth where he had been hammering was a Hoop-La. The other would be a coconut-shy. Feeling the instant American dislike for the presence of a negro, Mr May moved off with James.

They found out that the woman was a Lumley woman, that she had two children, that the negro was a most quiet and respectable chap, but that the family kept to itself, and didn't mix up with Lumley.

'I should think so,' said Mr May, a little disgusted even at the suggestion.

Then he proceeded to find out how long they had stood on this ground—three months—how long they would remain—only another week, then they were moving off to Alfreton fair—who was the owner of the pitch—Mr Bows, the butcher. Ah! And what was the ground used for? Oh, it was building land. But the foundation wasn't very good.

'The very thing! Aren't we *fortunate*,' cried Mr May, perking up the moment they were in the street. But this cheerfulness and brisk perkiness was a great strain on him. He missed his eleven o'clock whisky terribly—terribly—his pick-me-up! And he daren't confess it to James, who, he knew, was T-T. So he dragged his weary and hollow way up to Woodhouse, and sank with a long 'Oh!' of nervous exhaustion in the private bar of the Moon and Stars. He wrinkled his short nose. The smell of the place was distasteful to him. The *disgusting* beer that the colliers drank. Oh!— he *was* so tired. He sank back with his whisky and stared blankly, dismally in front of him. Beneath his eyes he looked more bilious still. He felt thoroughly out of luck, and petulant.

None the less he sallied out with all his old bright perkiness, the next time he had to meet James. He hadn't yet broached the question of costs. When would he be able to get an advance from James? He *must* hurry the matter forward. He brushed his crisp, curly brown hair carefully before the mirror. How grey he was at the temples! No wonder, dear me, with such a life! He was in his shirt sleeves. His waistcoat, with its grey satin back, fitted him tightly. He had filled out—but he hadn't developed a corporation. Not at all. He looked at himself sideways, and feared dismally he was thinner. He was one of those men who carry themselves in a birdie fashion, so that their tail sticks out a little behind, jauntily. How wonderfully the satin of his waistcoat had worn! He looked at his shirt-cuffs. They were going. Luckily, when he had had the shirts made he had secured enough material for the renewing of cuffs and neckbands. He put on his coat, from which he had flicked the faintest suspicion of dust, and again settled himself to go out and meet James on the question of an advance. He simply must have an advance.

He didn't get it that day, none the less. The next morning he was ringing for his tea at six o'clock. And before ten he had already flitted to Lumley and back, he had already had a word with Mr Bows, about that pitch, and, overcoming all his repugnance, a word with the quiet, frail, sad negro, about Alfreton fair, and the chance of buying some sort of collapsible building, for his cinematograph.

With all this news he met James—not at the shabby club, but in the deserted reading-room of the so-called Artisans' Hall—where never an artisan entered, but only men of

James's class. Here they took the chess-board and pretended to start a game. But their conversation was rapid and secretive.

Mr May disclosed all his discoveries. And then he said, tentatively:

'Hadn't we better think about the financial part now? If we're going to look round for an erection—' curious that he always called it an erection—'we shall have to know what we are going to spend.'

'Yes—yes. Well—' said James vaguely, nervously, giving a glance at Mr May. Whilst Mr May abstractedly fingered his black knight.

'You see at the moment,' said Mr May, 'I have no funds that I can represent in cash. I have no doubt a little *later*— if we need it—I can find a few hundreds. Many things are *due*—numbers of things. But it is so difficult to *collect* one's dues, particularly from America.' He lifted his blue eyes to James Houghton. 'Of course we can *delay* for some time, until I get my supplies. Or I can act just as your manager— you can *employ* me—'

He watched James's face. James looked down at the chess-board. He was fluttering with excitement. He did not want a partner. He wanted to be in this all by himself. He hated partners.

'You will agree to be manager, at a fixed salary?' said James hurriedly and huskily, his fine fingers slowly rubbing each other, along the sides.

'Why yes, willingly, if you'll give me the option of becoming your partner, upon terms of mutual agreement, later on.'

James did not quite like this.

'What terms are you thinking of?' he asked.

'Well, it doesn't matter for the moment. Suppose for the moment I enter an engagement as your manager, at a salary, let us say, of—of what, do you think?'

'So much a week?' said James pointedly.

'Hadn't we better make it monthly?'

The two men looked at one another.

'With a month's notice on either hand?' continued Mr May.

'How much?' said James, avaricious.

Mr May studied his own nicely kept hands.

'Well, I don't see how I can do it under twenty pounds a month. Of course it's ridiculously low. In America I *never* accepted less than three hundred dollars a month, and that was my poorest and lowest. But of *cauce*, England's not America—more's the pity.'

But James was shaking his head in a vibrating movement.

'Impossible!' he replied shrewdly. 'Impossible! Twenty pounds a month? Impossible. I couldn't do it. I couldn't think of it.'

'Then name a figure. Say what you *can* think of,' retorted Mr May, rather annoyed by this shrewd, shaking head of a doddering provincial, and by his own sudden collapse into mean subordination.

'I can't make it more than ten pounds a month,' said James sharply.

'What!' screamed Mr May. 'What am I to live on? What is my wife to live on?'

'I've got to make it pay,' said James. 'If I've got to make it pay, I must keep down expenses at the beginning.'

'No—on the contrary. You must be prepared to spend something at the beginning. If you go in a pinch-and-scrape fashion in the beginning, you will get nowhere at all. Ten pounds a month! Why, it's impossible! Ten pounds a month! But how am I to *live*?'

James's head still vibrated in a negative fashion. And the two men came to no agreement *that* morning. Mr May went home more sick and weary than ever, and took his whisky more biliously. But James was lit with the light of battle.

Poor Mr May had to gather together his wits and his sprightliness for his next meeting. He had decided he must make a percentage in other ways. He schemed in all known ways. He would accept the ten pounds—but really, did ever you hear of anything so ridiculous in your life, *ten pounds*!—dirty old screw, dirty, screwing old woman! He would accept the ten pounds; but he would get his own back.

He flitted down once more to the negro, to ask him of a certain wooden show-house, with section sides and roof, an old travelling theatre which stood closed on Selverhay Common, and might probably be sold. He pressed across once more to Mr Bows. He wrote various letters and drew up certain notes. And the next morning, by eight o'clock, he was on his way to Selverhay: walking, poor man, the long and uninteresting seven miles on his small and rather tight-shod feet, through country that had been once beautiful but was now scrubbled all over with mining villages, on and on up heavy hills and down others, asking his way from uncouth clowns, till at last he came to the Common, which wasn't a Common at all, but a sort of village more depressing than usual: naked, high, exposed to heaven and to full barren view.

There he saw the theatre-booth. It was old and sordid-looking, painted dark-red and dishevelled with narrow, tattered announcements. The grass was growing high up the wooden sides. If only it wasn't rotten? He crouched and probed and pierced with his pen-knife, till a country-policeman in a high helmet like a jug saw him, got off his bicycle and came stealthily across the grass wheeling the same bicycle, and startled poor Mr May almost into apoplexy by demanding behind him, in a loud voice:

'What're you after?'

Mr May rose up with flushed face and swollen neck-veins, holding his pen-knife in his hand.

'Oh,' he said, 'good-morning.' He settled his waistcoat and glanced over the tall, lanky constable and the glittering bicycle. 'I was taking a look at this old erection, with a view to buying it. I'm afraid it's going rotten from the bottom.'

'Shouldn't wonder,' said the policeman suspiciously, watching Mr May shut the pocket knife.

'I'm afraid that makes it useless for my purpose,' said Mr May.

The policeman did not deign to answer.

'Could you tell me where I can find out about it, anyway?' Mr May used his most affable, man of the world manner. But the policeman continued to stare him up and down, as if he were some marvellous specimen unknown on the normal, honest earth.

'What, find out?' said the constable.

'About being able to buy it,' said Mr May, a little testily. It was with great difficulty he preserved his man-to-man openness and brightness.

'They aren't here,' said the constable.

'Oh, indeed! Where *are* they? And *who* are they?'

The policeman eyed him more suspiciously than ever.

'Cowlard's their name. An' they live in Offerton when they aren't travelling.'

'Cowlard—thank you.' Mr May took out his pocket-book. 'C-o-w-l-a-r-d—is that right? And the address please?'

'I dunno th' street. But you can find out from the Three Bells. That's Missis' sister.'

'The Three Bells—thank you. Offerton did you say?'

'Yes.'

'Offerton!—where's that?'

'About eight mile.'

'Really—and how do you get there?'

'You can walk—or go by train.'

'Oh, there is a station?'

'Station!' The policeman looked at him as if he were either a criminal or a fool.

'Yes. There *is* a station there?'

'Ay—biggest next to Chesterfield—'

Suddenly it dawned on Mr May.

'Oh-h!' he said. 'You mean *Alfreton*—'

'Alfreton, yes.' The policeman was now convinced the man was a wrong-'un. But fortunately he was not a pushing constable, he did not want to rise in the police-scale: thought himself safest at the bottom.

'And which is the way to the station here?' asked Mr May.

'Do yer want Pinxon or Bull'ill?'

'Pinxon or Bull'ill?'

'There's two,' said the policeman.

'For Selverhay?' asked Mr May.

'Yes, them's the two.'

'And which is the best?'

'Depends what trains is runnin'. Sometimes yer have to wait an hour or two—'

'You don't know the trains, do you—?'

'There's one in th' afternoon—but I don't know if it'd be gone by the time you get down.'

'To where?'

'Bull'ill.'

'Oh Bull'ill! Well, perhaps I'll try. Could you tell me the way?'

When, after an hour's painful walk, Mr May came to Bulwell Station and found there was no train till six in the evening, he felt he was earning every penny he would ever get from Mr Houghton.

The first intelligence which Miss Pinnegar and Alvina gathered of the coming adventure was given them when James announced that he had let the shop to Marsden, the grocer next door. Marsden had agreed to take over James's premises at the same rent as that of the premises he already occupied, and moreover to do all alterations and put in all fixtures himself. This was a grand scoop for James: not a penny was it going to cost him, and the rent was clear profit.

'But when?' cried Miss Pinnegar.

'He takes possession on the first of October.'

'Well—it's a good idea. The shop isn't worth while,' said Miss Pinnegar.

'Certainly it isn't,' said James, rubbing his hands: a sign that he was rarely excited and pleased.

'And you'll just retire, and live quietly,' said Miss Pinnegar.

'I shall see,' said James. And with those fatal words he wafted away to find Mr May.

James was now nearly seventy years old. Yet he nipped about like a leaf in the wind. Only, it was a frail leaf.

'Father's got something going,' said Alvina, in a warning voice.

'I believe he has,' said Miss Pinnegar pensively. 'I wonder what it is, now.'

'I can't imagine,' laughed Alvina. 'But I'll bet it's something awful—else he'd have told us.'

'Yes,' said Miss Pinnegar slowly. 'Most likely he would. I wonder what it can be.'

'I haven't an idea,' said Alvina.

Both women were so retired, they had heard nothing of

James's little trips down to Lumley. So they watched like cats for their man's return, at dinner-time.

Miss Pinnegar saw him coming along talking excitedly to Mr May, who, all in grey, with his chest perkily stuck out like a robin, was looking rather pinker than usual. Having come to an agreement, he had ventured on whisky and soda in honour, and James had actually taken a glass of port.

'Alvina!' Miss Pinnegar called discreetly down the shop. 'Alvina! Quick!'

Alvina flew down to peep round the corner of the shop window. There stood the two men, Mr May like a perky, pink-faced grey bird standing cocking his head in attention to James Houghton, and occasionally catching James by the lapel of his coat, in a vain desire to get a word in, whilst James's head nodded and his face simply wagged with excited speech, as he skipped from foot to foot, and shifted round his listener.

'Who *ever* can that common-looking man be?' said Miss Pinnegar, her heart going down to her boots.

'I can't imagine,' said Alvina, laughing at the comic sight.

'Don't you think he's dreadful?' said the poor elderly woman.

'Perfectly impossible. Did ever you see such a pink face?'

'*And* the braid binding!' said Miss Pinnegar in indignation.

'Father might almost have sold him the suit,' said Alvina.

'Let us hope he hasn't sold your father, that's all,' said Miss Pinnegar.

The two men had moved a few steps farther towards home, and the women prepared to flee indoors. Of course it was frightfully wrong to be standing peeping in the high street at all. But who could consider the proprieties now?

'They've stopped again,' said Miss Pinnegar, recalling Alvina.

The two men were having a few more excited words, their voices just audible.

'I do wonder who he can be,' murmured Miss Pinnegar miserably.

'In the theatrical line, I'm sure,' declared Alvina.

'Do you think so?' said Miss Pinnegar. 'Can't be! Can't be!'

'He couldn't be anything else, don't you think?'

'Oh I *can't* believe it, I can't.'

But now Mr May had laid his detaining hand on James's arm. And now he was shaking his employer by the hand. And now James, in his cheap little cap, was smiling a formal farewell. And Mr May, with a graceful wave of his grey-suede-gloved hand, was turning back to the *Moon and Stars,* strutting, whilst James was running home on tip-toe, in his natural hurry.

Alvina hastily retreated, but Miss Pinnegar stood it out. James started as he nipped into the shop entrance, and found her confronting him.

'Oh—Miss Pinnegar!' he said, and made to slip by her.

'Who was that man?' she asked sharply, as if James were a child whom she could endure no more.

'Eh! I beg your pardon?' said James, starting back.

'Who was that man?'

'Eh? Which man?'

James was a little deaf, and a little husky.

'The man—' Miss Pinnegar turned to the door. 'There! That man!'

James also came to the door, and peered out as if he expected to see a sight. The sight of Mr May's tight and perky back, the jaunty little hat and the grey suede hands retreating quite surprised him. He was angry at being introduced to the sight.

'Oh,' he said. 'That's my manager.' And he turned hastily down the shop, asking for his dinner.

Miss Pinnegar stood for some moments in pure oblivion in the shop entrance. Her consciousness left her. When she recovered, she felt she was on the brink of hysteria and collapse. But she hardened herself once more, though the effort cost her a year of her life. She had never collapsed, she had never fallen into hysteria.

She gathered herself together, though bent a little as from a blow, and, closing the shop door, followed James to the living room, like the inevitable. He was eating his dinner, and seemed oblivious of her entry. There was a smell of Irish stew.

'What manager?' said Miss Pinnegar, short, silent, and inevitable in the doorway.

But James was in one of his abstractions, his trances.

'What manager?' persisted Miss Pinnegar.

But he still bent unknowing over his plate and gobbled his Irish stew.

'Mr Houghton!' said Miss Pinnegar, in a sudden changed voice. She had gone a livid yellow colour. And she gave a queer, sharp little rap on the table with her hand.

James started. He looked up bewildered, as one startled out of sleep.

'Eh?' he said, gaping. 'Eh?'

'Answer me,' said Miss Pinnegar. 'What manager?'

'Manager? Eh? Manager? What manager?'

She advanced a little nearer, menacing in her black dress. James shrank.

'What manager?' he re-echoed. 'My manager. The manager of my cinema.'

Miss Pinnegar looked at him, and looked at him, and did not speak. In that moment all the anger which was due to him from all womanhood was silently discharged at him, like a black bolt of silent electricity. But Miss Pinnegar, the engine of wrath, felt she would burst.

'Cinema! Cinema! Do you mean to tell me—' but she was really suffocated, the vessels of her heart and breast were bursting. She had to lean her hand on the table.

It was a terrible moment. She looked ghastly and terrible, with her mask-like face and her stony eyes and her bluish lips. Some fearful thunderbolt seemed to fall. James withered, and was still. There was silence for minutes, a suspension.

And in those minutes, she finished with him. She finished with him for ever. When she had sufficiently recovered, she went to her chair, and sat down before her plate. And in a while she began to eat, as if she were alone.

Poor Alvina, for whom this had been a dreadful and uncalled-for moment, had looked from one to another, and had also dropped her head to her plate. James too, with bent head, had forgotten to eat. Miss Pinnegar ate very slowly, alone.

'Don't you want your dinner, Alvina?' she said at length.

'Not as much as I did,' said Alvina.

'Why not?' said Miss Pinnegar. She sounded short, almost like Miss Frost. Oddly like Miss Frost.

Alvina took up her fork and began to eat automatically.

'I always think,' said Miss Pinnegar, 'Irish stew is more tasty with a bit of swede in it.'

'So do I, really,' said Alvina. 'But swedes aren't come yet.'

'Oh! Didn't we have some on Tuesday?'

'No, they were yellow turnips—but they weren't swedes.'

'Well then, yellow turnip. I like a little yellow turnip,' said Miss Pinnegar.

'I might have put some in, if I'd known,' said Alvina.

'Yes. We will another time,' said Miss Pinnegar.

Not another word about the cinema: not another breath. As soon as James had eaten his plum tart, he ran away.

'What can he have been doing?' said Alvina when he had gone.

'Buying a cinema show—and that man we saw is his manager. It's quite simple.'

'But what are we going to do with a cinema show?' said Alvina.

'It's what is *he* going to do. It doesn't concern me. It's no concern of mine. I shall not lend him anything, I shall not think about it, it will be the same to me as if there *were* no cinema. Which is all I have to say,' announced Miss Pinnegar.

'But he's gone and done it,' said Alvina.

'Then let him go through with it. It's no affair of mine. After all, your father's affairs don't concern me. It would be impertinent of me to introduce myself into them.'

'They don't concern *me* very much,' said Alvina.

'You're different. You're his daughter. He's no connection of mine, I'm glad to say. I pity your mother.'

'Oh, but he was always alike,' said Alvina.

'That's where it is,' said Miss Pinnegar.

There was something fatal about her feelings. Once they

had gone cold, they would never warm up again. As well try to warm up a frozen mouse. It only putrefies.

But poor Miss Pinnegar after this looked older, and seemed to get a little round-backed. And the things she said reminded Alvina so often of Miss Frost.

James fluttered into conversation with his daughter the next evening, after Miss Pinnegar had retired.

'I told you I had bought a cinematograph building,' said James. 'We are negotiating for the machinery now: the dynamo and so on.'

'But where is it to be?' asked Alvina.

'Down at Lumley. I'll take you and show you the site tomorrow. The building—it is a frame-section travelling theatre—will arrive on Thursday—next Thursday.'

'But who is in with you, father?'

'I am quite alone—quite alone,' said James Houghton. 'I have found an excellent manager, who knows the whole business thoroughly—a Mr May. Very nice man. Very nice man.'

'Rather short and dressed in grey?'

'Yes. And I have been thinking—if Miss Pinnegar will take the cash and issue tickets: if she will take over the ticket-office: and you will play the piano: and if Mr May learns the control of the machine—he is having lessons now—: and if I am the indoors attendant, we shan't need any more staff.'

'Miss Pinnegar won't take the cash, father.'

'Why not? Why not?'

'I can't say why not. But she won't do anything—and if I were you I wouldn't ask her.'

There was a pause.

'Oh, well,' said James huffy. 'She isn't indispensable.'

And Alvina was to play the piano! Here was a blow for her! She hurried off to her bedroom to laugh and cry at once. She just saw herself at the piano, banging off the *Merry Widow Waltz*, and, in tender moments, *The Rosary*. Time after time, *The Rosary*. While the pictures flickered and the audience gave shouts and some grubby boy called 'Chot-let, penny a bar! Chot-let, penny a bar! Chot-let, penny a bar!' away she banged at another tune.

What a sight for the gods! She burst out laughing. And at

the same time, she thought of her mother and Miss Frost, and she cried as if her heart would break. And then all kinds of comic and incongruous tunes came into her head. She imagined herself dressing them up with most priceless variations. *Linger Longer Lucy,* for example. She began to spin imaginary harmonies and variations in her head, upon the theme of *Linger Longer Lucy.*

> Linger longer Lucy, linger longer Loo
> How I love to linger longer linger long o'you.
> Listen while I sing, love, promise you'll be true,
> And linger longer longer linger linger longer Loo.

All the tunes that used to make Miss Frost so angry. All the Dream Waltzes and Maiden's Prayers, and the awful songs.

> For in Spooney-ooney Island
> Is there any one cares for me?
> In Spooney-ooney Island
> Why surely there ought to be—

Poor Miss Frost! Alvina imagined herself leading a chorus of collier louts, in a bad atmosphere of 'Woodbines' and oranges, during the intervals when the pictures had collapsed.

> How'd you like to spoon with me?
> How'd you like to spoon with me?
>   (*Why ra-ther!*)
> Underneath the oak-tree nice and shady
> Calling me your tootsey-wootsey lady?
> How'd you like to hug and squeeze
>   (*Just try me!*)
> Dandle me upon your knee,
> Calling me your little lovey-dovey—
> How'd you like to spoon with me?
>   (*Oh-h—Go on!*)

Alvina worked herself into quite a fever, with her imaginings.

In the morning she told Miss Pinnegar.

'Yes,' said Miss Pinnegar, 'you see me issuing tickets, don't you? Yes—well. I'm afraid he will have to do that part himself. And you're going to play the piano. It's a disgrace! It's a disgrace! It's a disgrace! It's a mercy Miss Frost and your mother are dead. He's lost every bit of shame—every bit—if he ever had any—which I doubt very much. Well, all I can say, I'm glad I am not concerned. And I'm sorry for you, for being his daughter. I'm heart sorry for you, I am. Well, well—no sense of shame—no sense of shame—'

And Miss Pinnegar padded out of the room.

Alvina walked down to Lumley and was shown the site and was introduced to Mr May. He bowed to her in his best American fashion, and treated her with admirable American deference.

'Don't you think,' he said to her, 'it's an admirable scheme?'

'Wonderful,' she replied.

'Of cauce,' he said, 'the erection will be a merely temporary one. Of cauce it won't be anything to *look* at: just an old wooden travelling theatre. But *then*—all we need is to make a start.'

'And you are going to work the film?' she asked.

'Yes,' he said with pride, 'I spend every evening with the operator at Marsh's in Knarborough. Very interesting I find it—very interesting indeed. And *you* are going to play the piano?' he said, perking his head on one side and looking at her archly.

'So father says,' she answered.

'But what do *you* say?' queried Mr May.

'I suppose I don't have any say.'

'Oh but *surely*. Surely you won't do it if you don't wish to. That would never do. Can't we hire some young fellow—?' And he turned to Mr Houghton with a note of query.

'Alvina can play as well as anybody in Woodhouse,' said James. 'We mustn't add to our expenses. And wages in particular—'

'But surely Miss Houghton will have her wage. The labourer is worthy of his hire. Surely! Even of *her* hire, to put it in the feminine. And for the same wage you could get some unimportant fellow with strong wrists. I'm afraid it will tire Miss Houghton to death—'

'I don't think so,' said James. 'I don't think so. Many of the turns she will not need to accompany—'

'Well, if it comes to that,' said Mr May, 'I can accompany some of them myself, when I'm not operating the film. I'm not an expert pianist—but I can play a little, you know—' And he trilled his fingers up and down an imaginary keyboard in front of Alvina, cocking his eye at her and smiling a little archly.

'I'm sure,' he continued, 'I can accompany anything except a man juggling dinner-plates—and then I'd be afraid of making him drop the plates. But songs—oh, songs! *Con molto espressione!*'

And again he trilled the imaginary keyboard, and smiled his rather fat cheeks at Alvina.

She began to like him. There was something a little dainty about him, when you knew him better—really rather fastidious. A showman, true enough! Blatant too. But fastidiously so.

He came fairly frequently to Manchester House, after this. Miss Pinnegar was rather stiff with him, and he did not like her. But he was very happy sitting chatting tête-à-tête with Alvina.

'Where is your wife?' said Alvina to him.

'My wife! Oh, don't speak of *her*,' he said comically. 'She's in London.'

'Why not speak of her?' asked Alvina.

'Oh, every reason for not speaking of her. We don't get on at *all* well, she and I.'

'What a pity,' said Alvina.

'Dreadful pity! But what are you to do?' He laughed comically. Then he became grave. 'No,' he said. 'She's an impossible person.'

'I see,' said Alvina.

'I'm sure you *don't* see,' said Mr May. 'Don't—' and here he laid his hand on Alvina's arm—'don't run away with the

idea that she's *immoral*! You'd never make a greater mistake.
Oh dear me, no. Morality's her strongest point. Live on
three lettuce leaves, and give the rest to the char. That's her.
Oh, dreadful times we had in those first years. We only lived
together for three years. But dear *me*! how awful it was!'

'Why?'

'There was no pleasing the woman. She wouldn't eat. If I
said to her "What shall we have for supper, Grace?" as sure
as anything she'd answer "Oh, I shall take a bath when I go
to bed—that will be my supper." She was one of these advanced vegetarian women, don't you know.'

'How extraordinary!' said Alvina.

'Extraordinary! I should think so. Extraordinary hard
lines on *me*. And she wouldn't let *me* eat either. She followed me to the kitchen in a *fury* while I cooked for myself.
Why imagine! I prepared a dish of *champignons*: oh, most
beautiful champignons, beautiful—and I put them on the
stove to fry in butter: beautiful young champignons. I'm
hanged if she didn't go into the kitchen while my back was
turned, and pour a pint of old carrot water into the pan. I
was *furious*. Imagine!—beautiful fresh young champignons—'

'Fresh mushrooms,' said Alvina.

'Mushrooms—most beautiful things in the world. Oh!
don't you think so?' And he rolled his eyes oddly to heaven.

'They *are* good,' said Alvina.

'I should say so. And swamped—*swamped* with her dirty
old carrot water. Oh I was so angry. And all she could say
was, "Well, I didn't want to waste it!" Didn't want to waste
her old carrot water, and so *ruined* my champignons. *Can*
you imagine such a person?'

'It must have been trying.'

'I should think it was. I lost weight. I lost I don't know
how many pounds, the first year I was married to that
woman. She hated me to eat. Why, one of her great accu-
sations against me, at the last, was when she said: "I've
looked round the larder," she said to me, "and seen it was
quite empty, and I thought to myself: *Now* he *can't* cook a
supper! And *then* you did!" There! What do you think of
that? The spite of it! "And *then* you did!" '

'What did she expect you to live on?' asked Alvina.

'Nibble a lettuce leaf with her, and drink water from the tap—and then elevate myself with a Bernard Shaw pamphlet. That was the sort of woman she was. All it gave *me* was gas in the stomach.'

'So overbearing!' said Alvina.

'Oh!' he turned his eyes to heaven, and spread his hands. 'I didn't believe my senses. I didn't know such people existed. And her friends! Oh the dreadful friends she had—these Fabians! Oh, their eugenics. They wanted to examine my private morals, for eugenic reasons. Oh, you can't imagine such a state! Worse than the Spanish Inquisition. And I stood it for three years. *How* I stood it, I don't know—'

'Now don't you see her?'

'Never! I never let her know where I am! But I *support* her, of cauce.'

'And you daughter?'

'Oh, she's the dearest child in the world. I saw her at a friend's when I came back from America. Dearest little thing in the world. But of *cauce* suspicious of me. Treats me as if she didn't *know* me—'

'What a pity!'

'Oh—unbearable!' He spread his plump, manicured hands, on one finger of which was a green intaglio ring.

'How old is your daughter?'

'Fourteen.'

'What is her name?'

'Gemma. She was born in Rome, where I was managing for Miss Maud Callum, the *danseuse*.'

Curious the intimacy Mr May established with Alvina at once. But it was all purely verbal, descriptive. He made no physical advances. On the contrary, he was like a dove-grey, disconsolate bird pecking the crumbs of Alvina's sympathy, and cocking his eye all the time to watch that she did not advance one step towards him. If he had seen the least sign of coming-on-ness in her, he would have fluttered off in a great dither. Nothing *horrified* him more than a woman who was coming-on towards him. It horrified him, it exasperated him, it made him hate the whole tribe of women: horrific two-legged cats without whiskers. If he had been a bird, his innate horror of a cat would have been such. He liked the *angel*, and particularly the angel-mother in woman. Oh!—that he worshipped. But coming-on-ness!

So he never wanted to be seen out-of-doors with Alvina: if he met her in the street he bowed and passed on: bowed very deep and reverential, indeed, but passed on, with his little back a little more strutty and assertive than ever. Decidedly he turned his back on her in public.

But Miss Pinnegar, a regular old, grey, dangerous she-puss, eyed him from the corner of her pale eye, as he turned tail.

'So unmanly!' she murmured. 'In his dress, in his way, in everything—so unmanly.'

'If I was you, Alvina,' she said, 'I shouldn't see so much of Mr May, in the drawing-room. People will talk.'

'I should almost feel flattered,' laughed Alvina.

'What do you mean?' snapped Miss Pinnegar.

None the less, Mr May was dependable in matters of business. He was up at half-past five in the morning, and by seven was well on his way. He sailed like a stiff little ship before a steady breeze, hither and thither, out of Woodhouse and back again, and across from side to side. Sharp and snappy, he was, on the spot. He trussed himself up, when he was angry or displeased, and sharp, snip-snap came his words, rather like scissors.

'But how is it—' he attacked Arthur Witham—'that the gas isn't connected with the main yet? It was to be ready yesterday.'

'We've had to wait for the fixings for them brackets,' said Arthur.

'*Had* to *wait* for *fixings!* But didn't you know a fortnight ago that you'd want the fixings?'

'I thought we should have some as would do.'

'Oh! you thought so! Really! Kind of you to think so. And have you just thought about those that are coming, or have you made sure?'

Arthur looked at him sullenly. He hated him. But Mr May's sharp touch was not to be foiled.

'I hope you'll go further than *thinking*,' said Mr May.

'Thinking seems such a slow process. And when do you expect the fittings—?'

'To-morrow.'

'What! Another day! Another day *still*! But you're strangely indifferent to time, in your line of business. Oh! *To-morrow*! Imagine it! Two days late already, and then *to-morrow*! Well I hope by to-morrow you mean *Wednesday*, and not to-morrow's to-morrow, or some other absurd and fanciful date that you've just *thought about*. But now, *do* have the thing finished by to-morrow—' here he laid his hand cajoling on Arthur's arm. 'You promise me it will be all ready by to-morrow, don't you?'

'Yes, I'll do it if anybody could do it.'

'Don't say "if anybody could do it". Say it shall be done.'

'It shall if I can possibly manage it—'

'Oh—very well then. Mind you manage it—and thank you *very* much. I shall be *most* obliged, if it *is* done.'

Arthur was annoyed, but he was kept to the scratch. And so, early in October the place was ready, and Woodhouse was plastered with placards announcing 'Houghton's Pleasure Palace'. Poor Mr May could not but see an irony in the Palace part of the phrase. 'We can guarantee the *pleasure*,' he said. 'But personally, I feel I can't take the responsibility for the palace.'

But James, to use the vulgar expression, was in his eye-holes.

'Oh, father's in his eye-holes,' said Alvina to Mr May.

'Oh!' said Mr May, puzzled and concerned.

But it merely meant that James was having the time of his life. He was drawing out announcements. First was a batch of vermilion strips, with the mystic script, in big black letters: Houghton's Picture Palace, underneath which, quite small: Opens at Lumley on October 7th, at 6.30 p.m. Everywhere you went, these vermilion and black bars sprang from the wall at you. Then there were other notices, in delicate pale blue and pale red, like a genuine theatre notice, giving full programmes. And beneath these a broad-letter notice announced, in green letters on a yellow ground: 'Final and Ultimate Clearance Sale at Houghton's, Knarborough Road, on Friday, September 30th. Come and Buy Without Price.'

James was in his eye-holes. He collected all his odds and ends from every corner of Manchester House. He sorted them in heaps, and marked the heaps in his own mind. And then he let go. He pasted up notices all over the window and all over the shop: 'Take what you want and Pay what you Like.'

He and Miss Pinnegar kept shop. The women flocked in. They turned things over. It nearly killed James to take the prices they offered. But take them he did. But he exacted that they should buy one article at a time. 'One piece at a time, if you don't mind,' he said, when they came up with their three-a-penny handfuls. It was not till later in the evening that he relaxed this rule.

Well, by eleven o'clock he had cleared out a good deal— really, a very great deal—and many women had bought what they didn't want, at their own figure. Feverish but content, James shut the shop for the last time. Next day, by eleven, he had removed all his belongings, the door that connected the house with the shop was screwed up fast, the grocer strolled in and looked round his bare extension, took the key from James, and immediately set his boy to paste a new notice in the window, tearing down all James's announcements. Poor James had to run round, down Knarborough Road, and down Wellington Street as far as the Livery Stables, then down long narrow passages, before he could get into his own house, from his own shop.

But he did not mind. Every hour brought the first performance of his Pleasure Palace nearer. He was satisfied with Mr May: he had to admit that he was satisfied with Mr May. The Palace stood firm at last—oh, it was so rickety when it arrived!—and it glowed with a new coat, all over, of dark-red paint, like ox-blood. It was titivated up with a touch of lavender and yellow round the door and round the decorated wooden eaving. It had a new wooden slope up to the doors—and inside, a new wooden floor, with red-velvet seats in front, before the curtain, and old chapel-pews behind. The collier youths recognized the pews.

'Hey! These 'ere's th'pews out of the old Primitive Chapel.'

'Sorry ah! We'n come ter hear t' parson.'

Theme for endless jokes. And the Pleasure Palace was christened, in some lucky stroke, Houghton's Endeavour, a reference to that particular Chapel effort called the Christian Endeavour, where Alvina and Miss Pinnegar both figured.

'Wheer art off, Sorry?'

'Lumley.'

'Houghton's Endeavour?'

'Ah.'

'Rotten.'

So, when one laconic young collier accosted another. But we anticipate.

Mr May had worked hard to get a programme for the first week. His pictures were: 'The Human Bird', which turned out to be a ski-ing film from Norway, purely descriptive; 'The Pancake', a humorous film: and then his grand serial: 'The Silent Grip'. And then, for Turns, his first item was Miss Poppy Traherne, a lady in innumerable petticoats, who could whirl herself into anything you like, from an arum lily in green stockings to a rainbow and a Catherine wheel and a cup-and-saucer: marvellous, was Miss Poppy Traherne. The next turn was The Baxter Brothers, who ran up and down each other's backs and up and down each other's front, and stood on each other's heads and on their own heads, and perched for a moment on each other's shoulders, as if each of them was a flight of stairs with a landing, and the three of them were three flights, three storeys up, the top flight continually running down and becoming the bottom flight, while the middle flight collapsed and became a horizontal corridor.

Alvina had to open the performance by playing an overture called 'Welcome All': a ridiculous piece. She was excited and unhappy. On the Monday morning there was a rehearsal, Mr May conducting. She played 'Welcome All', and then took the thumbed sheets which Miss Poppy Traherne carried with her. Miss Poppy was rather exacting. As she whirled her skirts she kept saying: 'A little faster, please'— 'A little slower'—in a rather haughty, official voice that was somewhat muffled by the swim of her drapery. 'Can you give it *expression*?' she cried, as she got the arum lily in full blow, and there was a sound of real ecstasy in her tones. But why she should have called 'Stronger! Stronger!' as she came into being as a cup and saucer, Alvina could not imagine: unless Miss Poppy was fancying herself a strong cup of tea.

However, she subsided into her mere self, panted frantically and then, in a hoarse voice, demanded if she was in the bare front of the show. She scorned to count 'Welcome All'. Mr May said Yes. She was the first item. Whereupon she began to raise a dust. Mr Houghton said, hurriedly interposing, that he meant to make a little opening speech. Miss Poppy eyed him as if he were a cuckoo-clock, and she had to wait till he'd finished cuckooing. Then she said:

'That's not every night. There's six nights to a week.' James was properly snubbed. It ended by Mr May metamorphosing himself into a pug dog: he said he had got the 'costoom' in his bag: and doing a lump-of-sugar scene with one of the Baxter Brothers, as a brief first item. Miss Poppy's professional virginity was thus saved from outrage.

At the back of the stage there was half-a-yard of curtain screening the two dressing-rooms, ladies and gents. In her spare time Alvina sat in the ladies' dressing room, or in its lower doorway, for there was not room right inside. She watched the ladies making up—she gave some slight assistance. She saw the men's feet, in their shabby pumps, on the other side of the curtain, and she heard the men's gruff voices. Often a slangy conversation was carried on through the curtain—for most of the turns were acquainted with each other: very affable before each other's faces, very sniffy behind each other's backs.

Poor Alvina was in a state of bewilderment. She was extremely nice—oh, much too nice with the female turns. They treated her with a sort of off-hand friendliness, and they snubbed and patronized her and were a little spiteful with her because Mr May treated her with attention and deference. She felt bewildered, a little excited, and as if she was not herself.

The first evening actually came. Her father had produced a pink crêpe de chine blouse and a back-comb massed with brilliants—both of which she refused to wear. She stuck to her black blouse and black skirt, and her simple hair-dressing. Mr May said 'Of cauce! She wasn't intended to attract attention to herself.' Miss Pinnegar actually walked down the hill with her, and began to cry when she saw the ox-blood red erection, with its gas-flares in front. It was the first time she had seen it. She went on with Alvina to the little stage door at the back, and up the steps into the scrap of dressing-room. But she fled out again from the sight of Miss Poppy in her yellow hair and green knickers with green-lace frills. Poor Miss Pinnegar! She stood outside on the trodden grass behind the Band of Hope, and really cried. Luckily she had put a veil on.

She went valiantly round to the front entrance, and climbed the steps. The crowd was just coming. There was James's face peeping inside the little ticket-window.

'One!' he said officially, pushing out the ticket. And then he recognized her. 'Oh,' he said, '*You're* not going to pay.'

'Yes I am,' she said, and she left her fourpence, and James's coppery, grimy fingers scooped it in, as the youth behind Miss Pinnegar shoved her forward.

'Arf way down, fourpenny,' said the man at the door, poking her in the direction of Mr May, who wanted to put her in the red velvet. But she marched down one of the pews, and took her seat.

The place was crowded with a whooping, whistling, ex-cited audience. The curtain was down. James had let it out to his fellow tradesmen, and it represented a patchwork of local adverts. There was a fat porker and a fat pork-pie, and the pig was saying: 'You all know where to find me. Inside the crust at Frank Churchill's, Knarborough Road, Wood-house.' Round about the name of W. H. Johnson floated a bowler hat, a collar-and-necktie, a pair of braces and an um-brella. And so on and so on. It all made you feel very homely. But Miss Pinnegar was sadly hot and squeezed in her pew.

Time came, and the colliers began to drum their feet. It was exactly the excited, crowded audience Mr May wanted. He darted out to drive James round in front of the curtain. But James, fascinated by raking in the money so fast, could not be shifted from the pay-box, and the two men nearly had a fight. At last Mr May was seen shooing James, like a scuffled chicken, down the side gangway and on to the stage.

James before the illuminated curtain of local adverts, bowing and beginning and not making a single word audible! The crowd quieted itself, the eloquence flowed on. The crowd was sick of James, and began to shuffle. 'Come down, come down!' hissed Mr May frantically from in front. But James did not move. He would flow on all night. Mr May waved excitedly at Alvina, who sat obscurely at the piano, and darted on to the stage. He raised his voice and drowned James. James ceased to wave his penny-blackened hands, Alvina struck up 'Welcome All' as loudly and emphatically as she could.

And all the time Miss Pinnegar sat like a sphinx—like a sphinx. What she thought she did not know herself. But stolidly she stared at James, and anxiously she glanced sideways at the pounding Alvina. She knew Alvina had to pound until she received the cue that Mr May was fitted in his pug-dog 'Costoom'.

A twitch of the curtain. Alvina wound up her final flourish, the curtain rose, and:

'Well really!' said Miss Pinnegar, out loud.

There was Mr May as a pug dog begging, too lifelike, and too impossible. The audience shouted. Alvina sat with her hands in her lap. The Pug was a great success.

Curtain! A few bars of Toreador—and then Miss Poppy's sheets of music. Soft music. Miss Poppy was on the ground under a green scarf. And so the accumulating dilation, on to the whirling climax of the perfect arum lily. Sudden curtain, and a yell of ecstasy from the colliers. Of all blossoms, the arum, the arum lily is most mystical and portentous.

Now a crash and rumble from Alvina's piano. This is the storm from whence the rainbow emerges. Up goes the curtain—Miss Poppy twirling till her skirts lift as in a breeze, rise up and become a rainbow above her now darkened legs. The footlights are all but extinguished. Miss Poppy is all but extinguished also.

The rainbow is not so moving as the arum lily. But the Catherine wheel, done at the last moment on one leg and

then an amazing leap into the air, backwards, again brings
down the house.

Miss Poppy herself sets all store on her cup and saucer.
But the audience, vulgar as ever, cannot quite see it.

And so, Alvina slips away with Miss Poppy's music-
sheets, while Mr May sits down like a professional at the
piano and makes things fly for the up-and-down-stairs Baxter Bros. Meanwhile, Alvina's pale face hovering like a ghost
in the side darkness, as it were under the stage.

The lamps go out: gurglings and kissings—and then the
dither on the screen: 'The Human Bird', in awful shivery
letters. It's not a very good machine, and Mr May is not a
very good operator. Audience distinctly critical. Lights up—
and 'Chot-let, penny a bar! Chot-let, penny a bar!' even as
in Alvina's dream—and then 'The Pancake'—and so the
first half over. Lights up for the interval.

Miss Pinnegar sighed and folded her hands. She looked
neither to right nor to left. In spite of herself, in spite of
outraged shame and decency, she was excited. But she felt
such excitement was not wholesome. In vain the boy most
pertinently yelled 'Chot-let' at her. She looked neither to
right nor left. But when she saw Alvina nodding to her with
a quick smile from the side gangway under the stage, she
almost burst into tears. It was too much for her, all at once.
And Alvina looked almost indecently excited. As she slipped
across in front of the audience, to the piano, to play the
seductive 'Dream Waltz' she looked almost fussy, like her
father. James, needless to say, flittered and hurried hither
and thither around the audience and the stage, like a wagtail
on the brink of a pool.

The second half consisted of a comic drama, acted by two
Baxter Bros. disguised as women, and Miss Poppy disguised
as a man—with a couple of locals thrown in to do the
guardsman and the Count. This went very well. The winding up was the first instalment of 'The Silent Grip'.

When lights went up and Alvina solemnly struck 'God
Save Our Gracious King', the audience was on its feet and
not very quiet, evidently hissing with excitement like
doughnuts in the pan even when the pan is taken off the

fire. Mr Houghton thanked them for their courtesy and attention, and hoped—And nobody took the slightest notice.

Miss Pinnegar stayed last, waiting for Alvina. And Alvina, in her excitement, waited for Mr May and her father.

Mr May fairly pranced into the empty hall.

'Well!' he said, shutting both his fists and flourishing them in Miss Pinnegar's face. 'How did it go?'

'I think it went very well,' she said.

'Very well! I should think so, indeed. It went like a house on fire. What? Didn't it?' And he laughed a high, excited little laugh.

James was counting pennies for his life, in the cash-place, and dropping them into a Gladstone bag. The others had to wait for him. At last he locked his bag.

'Well,' said Mr May, 'done well?'

'Fairly well,' said James, huskily excited. 'Fairly well.'

'Only fairly? Oh-h!' And Mr May suddenly picked up the bag. James turned as if he would snatch it from him. 'Well! Feel that, for fairly well!' said Mr May, handing the bag to Alvina.

'Goodness!' she cried handing it to Miss Pinnegar.

'Would you believe it?' said Miss Pinnegar, relinquishing it to James. But she spoke coldly, aloof.

Mr May turned off the gas at the meter, came talking through the darkness of the empty theatre, picking his way with a flash-light.

'C'est le premier pas qui coute,' he said, in a sort of American French, as he locked the doors and put the key in his pocket. James tripped silently alongside, bowed under the weight of his Gladstone bag of pennies.

'How much have we taken, father?' asked Alvina gaily.

'I haven't counted,' he snapped.

When he got home he hurried upstairs to his bare chamber. He swept his table clear, and then, in an expert fashion, he seized handfuls of coin and piled them in little columns on his board. There was an army of fat pennies, a dozen to a column, along the back, rows and rows of fat brown rank-and-file. In front of these, rows of slim half-pence, like an advance-guard. And commanding all, a stout column of half-crowns, a few stoutish and important florin-figures, like general and colonels, then quite a file of shillings, like so many captains, and a little cloud of silvery lieutenant sixpences. Right at the end, like a frail drummer boy, a thin stick of threepenny pieces.

There they all were: burly dragoons of stout pennies, heavy and holding their ground, with a screen of halfpenny light infantry, officered by the immovable half-crown general, who in his turn was flanked by all his staff of florin colonels and shilling captains, from whom lightly moved the nimble sixpenny lieutenants, all ignoring the wan, frail Joey of the threepenny-bits.

Time after time James ran his almighty eye over his army. He loved them. He loved to feel that his table was pressed down, that it groaned under their weight. He loved to see the pence, like innumerable pillars of cloud, standing waiting to lead on into wilderness of unopened resource, while the silver, as pillars of light, should guide the way down the long night of fortune. Their weight sank sensually into his muscle, and gave him gratification. The dark redness of bronze, like full-blooded fleas, seemed alive and pulsing, the silver was magic as if winged.

CHAPTER 7

Natcha-Kee-Tawara

M r May and Alvina became almost inseparable, and
Woodhouse buzzed with scandal. Woodhouse
could not believe that Mr May was absolutely final
in his horror of any sort of coming-on-ness in a woman. It
could not believe that he was only *so* fond of Alvina because
she was like a sister to him, poor, lonely, harassed soul that
he was: a pure sister who really hadn't any body. For although Mr May was rather fond, in an epicurean way, of
his own body, yet other people's bodies rather made him
shudder. So that his grand utterance on Alvina was: 'She's
not physical, she's mental.'

He even explained to her one day how it was, in his naïve
fashion.

'There are two kinds of friendships,' he said, 'physical and
mental. The physical is a thing of the moment. Of cauce you
quite *like* the individual, you remain quite nice with them,
and so on—to keep the thing as decent as possible. It *is* quite
decent, so long as you keep it so. But it is a thing of the
moment. Which you know. It may last a week or two, or a
month or two. But you know from the beginning it is going
to end—quite finally—quite soon. You take it for what it
is. But it's *so* different with the mental friendships. *They* are
lasting. They are eternal—if anything human (he said yu-

man) ever is eternal, ever *can* be eternal.' He pressed his hands together in an odd cherubic manner. He was quite sincere: if man ever *can* be quite sincere.

Alvina was quite content to be one of his mental and eternal friends, or rather *friendships*—since she existed *in abstracto* as far as he was concerned. For she did not find him at all physically moving. Physically he was not there: he was oddly an absentee. But his naïveté roused the serpent's tooth of her bitter irony.

'And your wife?' she said to him.

'Oh, my wife! Dreadful thought! *There* I made the great mistake of trying to find the two in one person! And *didn't* I fall between two stools! Oh dear, *didn't* I? Oh, I fell between the two stools beautifully, beautifully! And *then*— she nearly set the stools on top of me. I thought I should never get up again. When I was physical, she was mental— Bernard Shaw and cold baths for supper!—and when I was mental she was physical, and threw her arms round my neck. In the morning, mark you. Always in the morning, when I was on the alert for business. Yes, invariably. What do you think of it? Could the devil himself have invented anything more trying? Oh dear me, don't mention it. Oh, what a time I had! Wonder I'm alive. Yes, really! Although you smile.'

Alvina did more than smile. She laughed outright. And yet she remained good friends with the odd little man.

He bought himself a new, smart overcoat, that fitted his figure, and a new velour hat. And she even noticed, one day when he was curling himself up cosily on the sofa, that he had pale blue silk underwear, and purple silk suspenders. She wondered where he got them, and how he afforded them. But there they were.

James seemed for the time being wrapt in his undertaking—particularly in the takings part of it. He seemed for the time being contented—or nearly so, nearly so. Certainly there was money coming in. But then he had to pay off all he had borrowed to buy his erection and its furnishings, and a bulk of pennies sublimated into a very small £.s.d. account, at the bank.

The Endeavour was successful—yes, it was successful. But not overwhelmingly so. On wet nights Woodhouse did not care to trail down to Lumley. And then Lumley was one of those depressed, negative spots on the face of the earth which have no pull at all. In that region of sharp hills with fine hill-brows, and shallow, rather dreary canal-valleys, it was the places on the hill-brows, like Woodhouse and Hathersedge and Rapton, which flourished, while the dreary places down along the canals existed only for work-places, not for life and pleasure. It was just like James to have planted his endeavour down in the stagnant dust and rust of potteries and foundries, where no illusion could bloom.

He had dreamed of crowded houses every night, and of raised prices. But there was no probability of his being able to raise his prices. He had to figure lower than the Wood-house Empire. He was second-rate from the start. His hope now lay in the tramway which was being built from Knar-borough away through the country—a black country in-deed—through Woodhouse and Lumley and Hathersedge, to Rapton. When once this tramway-system was working, he would have a supply of youths and lasses always on tap, as it were. So he spread his rainbow wings towards the future, and began to say:

'When we've got the trams, I shall buy a new machine and finer lenses, and I shall extend my premises.'

Mr May did not talk business to Alvina. He was terribly secretive with respect to business. But he said to her once, in the early year following their opening:

'Well, how do you think we're doing, Miss Houghton?'

'We're not going any better than we did at first, I think,' she said.

'No,' he answered. 'No! That's true. That's perfectly true. But why? They seem to like the programmes?'

'I think they do,' said Alvina. 'I think they like them when they're there. But isn't it funny, they don't seem to want to come to them. I know they always talk as if we were second-rate. And they only come because they can't get to the Empire, or up to Hathersedge. We're a stop-gap. I know we are.'

Mr May looked down in the mouth. He cocked his blue

eyes at her, miserable and frightened. Failure began to frighten him abjectly.

'Why do you think that is?' he said.

'I don't believe they like the turns,' she said.

'But *look* how they applaud them! *Look* how pleased they are!'

'I know. I know they like them once they're there, and they see them. But they don't come again. They crowd the Empire—and the Empire is only pictures now: and it's much cheaper to run.'

He watched her dismally.

'I can't believe they want nothing but pictures. I can't believe they want everything in the flat,' he said, coaxing and miserable. He himself was not interested in the film. His interest was still the human interest in living performers and their living feats. 'Why,' he continued, 'they are ever so much more excited after a good turn, than after any film.'

'I know they are,' said Alvina. 'But I don't believe they want to be excited in that way.'

'In what way?' asked Mr May plaintively.

'By the things which the *artistes* do. I believe they're jealous.'

'Oh nonsense!' exploded Mr May, starting as if he had been shot. Then he laid his hand on her arm. 'But forgive my rudeness! I don't mean it, of *cauce*! But do you mean to say that these collier louts and factory girls are jealous of the things the *artistes* do, because they could never do them themselves?'

'I'm sure they are,' said Alvina.

'But I *can't* believe it,' said Mr May, pouting up his mouth and smiling at her as if she were a whimsical child. 'What a low opinion you have of human nature!'

'Have I?' laughed Alvina. 'I've never reckoned it up. But I'm sure that these common people here are jealous if anybody does anything or has anything they can't have themselves.'

'I can't believe it,' protested Mr May. 'Could they be so *silly*! And then why aren't they jealous of the extraordinary things which are done on the film?'

'Because they don't see the flesh-and-blood people. I'm

sure that's it. The film is only pictures, like pictures in the *Daily Mirror*. And pictures don't have any feelings apart from their own feelings. I mean the feelings of the people who watch them. Pictures don't have any life except in the people who watch them. And that's why they like them. Because they make them feel that they are everything.'

'The pictures make the colliers and lasses feel that they themselves are everything? But how? They identify themselves with the heroes and heroines on the screen?'

'Yes—they take it all to themselves—and there isn't anything except themselves. I know it's like that. It's because they can spread themselves over a film, and they *can't* over a living performer. They're up against the performer himself. And they hate it.'

Mr May watched her long and dismally.

'I *can't* believe people are like that!—sane people!' he said. 'Why, to me the whole joy is in the living personality, the curious *personality* of the artiste. That's what I enjoy so much.'

'I know. But that's where you're different from them.'

'But *am* I?'

'Yes. You're not as up to the mark as they are.'

'Not up to the mark? What do you mean? Do you mean they are more intelligent?'

'No, but they're more modern. You like things which aren't yourself. But they don't. They hate to admire anything that they can't take to themselves. They hate anything that isn't themselves. And that's why they like pictures. It's all themselves to them, all the time.'

He still puzzled.

'You know I don't follow you,' he said, a little mocking, as if she were making a fool of herself.

'Because you don't know them. You don't know the common people. You don't know how conceited they are.'

He watched her a long time.

'And you think we ought to cut out the variety, and give nothing but pictures, like the Empire?' he said.

'I believe it takes best,' she said.

'And costs less,' he answered. 'But *then*! It's so dull. Oh my *word*, it's so dull. I don't think I could bear it.'

'And our pictures aren't good enough,' she said. 'We should have to get a new machine, and pay for the expensive films. Our pictures do shake, and our films are rather ragged.'

'But then, *surely* they're good enough!' he said.

That was how matters stood. The Endeavour paid its way, and made just a margin of profit—no more. Spring went on to summer, and then there was a very shadowy margin of profit. But James was not at all daunted. He was waiting now for the trams, and building up hopes since he could not build in bricks and mortar.

The navvies were busy in troops along the Knarborough Road, and down Lumley Hill. Alvina became quite used to them. As she went down the hill soon after six o'clock in the evening, she met them trooping home. And some of them she liked. There was an outlawed look about them as they swung along the pavement—some of them; and there was a certain lurking set of the head which rather frightened her because it fascinated her. There was one tall young fellow with a red face and fair hair, who looked as if he had fronted the seas and the arctic sun. He looked at her. They knew each other quite well, in passing. And he would glance at perky Mr May. Alvina tried to fathom what the young fellow's look meant. She wondered what he thought of Mr May.

She was surprised to hear Mr May's opinion of the navvy.

'*He's* a handsome young man, now!' exclaimed her companion one evening as the navvies passed. And all three turned round, to find all three turning round. Alvina laughed, and made eyes. At that moment she would cheerfully have gone along with the navvy. She was getting so tired of Mr May's quiet prance.

On the whole, Alvina enjoyed the cinema and the life it brought her. She accepted it. And she became somewhat vulgarized in her bearing. She was *déclassée:* she had lost her class altogether. The other daughters of respectable tradesmen avoided her now, or spoke to her only from a distance. She was supposed to be 'carrying on' with Mr May.

Alvina did not care. She rather liked it. She liked being *déclassée.* She liked feeling an outsider. At last she seemed to stand on her own ground. She laughed to herself as she went back and forth from Woodhouse to Lumley, between Manchester House and the Pleasure Palace. She laughed when she saw her father's theatre-notices plastered about. She laughed when she saw his thrilling announcements in the *Woodhouse Weekly*. She laughed when she knew that all the Woodhouse youths recognized her, and looked on her as one of their inferior entertainers. She was off the map: and she liked it.

For after all, she got a good deal of fun out of it. There was not only the continual activity. There were the artistes. Every week she met a new set of stars—three or four as a rule. She rehearsed with them on Monday afternoons, and she saw them every evening, and twice a week at matinées. James now gave two performances each evening—and he always had *some* audience. So that Alvina had opportunity to come into contact with all the odd people of the inferior stage. She found they were very much of a type: a little frowsty, a little flea-bitten as a rule, indifferent to ordinary morality, and philosophical even if irritable. They were often very irritable. And they had always a certain fund of callous philosophy. Alvina did not *like* them—you were not supposed, really, to get deeply emotional over them. But she found it amusing to see them all and know them all. It was so different from Woodhouse, where everything was priced and ticketed. These people were nomads. They didn't care a straw who you were or who you weren't. They had a most irritable professional vanity, and that was all. It was most odd to watch them. They weren't very squeamish. If the young gentlemen liked to peep round the curtain when the young lady was in her knickers: oh, well, she rather roundly told them off, perhaps, but nobody minded. The fact that ladies wore knickers and black silk stockings thrilled nobody, any more than grease-paint or false moustaches thrilled. It was all part of the stock-in-trade. As for immorality—well, what did it amount to? Not a great deal. Most of the men cared far more about a drop of whisky than about any more carnal vice, and most of the girls were good pals with each other, men were only there to act with: even if the act was a private love-farce of an improper description.

What's the odds? You couldn't get excited about it: not as a rule.

Mr May usually took rooms for the artistes in a house down in Lumley. When anyone particular was coming, he would go to a rather better-class widow in Woodhouse. He never let Alvina take any part in the making of these arrangements, except with the widow in Woodhouse, who had long ago been a servant at Manchester House, and even now came in to do cleaning.

Odd, eccentric people they were, these entertainers. Most of them had a streak of imagination, and most of them drank. Most of them were middle-aged. Most of them had an abstracted manner; in ordinary life, they seemed left aside, somehow. Odd, extraneous creatures, often a little depressed, feeling life slip away from them. The cinema was killing them.

Alvina had quite a serious flirtation with a man who played a flute and piccolo. He was about fifty years old, still handsome, and growing stout. When sober, he was completely reserved. When rather drunk, he talked charmingly and amusingly—oh, most charmingly. Alvina quite loved him. But alas, *how* he drank! But what a charm he had! He went, and she saw him no more.

The usual rather American-looking, clean-shaven, slightly pasty young man left Alvina quite cold, though he had an amiable and truly chivalrous *galanterie*. He was quite likeable. But so unattractive. Alvina was more fascinated by the odd fish: like the lady who did marvellous things with six ferrets, or the Jap who was tattooed all over, and had the most amazing strong wrists, so that he could throw down any collier, with one turn of the hand. Queer cuts these!— but just a little bit beyond her. She watched them rather from a distance. She wished she could jump across the distance. Particularly with the Jap, who was almost quite naked, but clothed with the most exquisite tattooing. Never would she forget the eagle that flew with terrible spread wings between his shoulders, or the strange mazy pattern that netted the roundness of his buttocks. He was not very large, but nicely shaped, and with no hair on his smooth, tattooed body. He was almost blue in colour—that is, his

tattooing was blue, with pickings of brilliant vermilion: as
for instance round the nipples, and in a strange red serpent's-
jaws over the navel. A serpent went round his loins and
haunches. He told her how many times he had had blood-
poisoning, during the process of his tattooing. He was a
queer, black-eyed creature, with a look of silence and toad-
like lewdness. He frightened her. But when he was dressed
in common clothes, and was just a cheap, shoddy-looking
European Jap, he was more frightening still. For his face—
he was not tattooed above a certain ring low on his neck—
was yellow and flat and basking with one eye open, like
some age-old serpent. She felt he was smiling horribly all
the time: lewd, unthinkable. A strange sight he was in
Woodhouse, on a sunny morning; a shabby-looking bit of
riff-raff of the East, rather down at the heel. Who could have
imagined the terrible eagle of his shoulders, the serpent of
his loins, his supple, magic skin?

The summer passed again, and autumn. Winter was a better time for James Houghton. The trams, moreover, would
begin to run in January.

He wanted to arrange a good programme for the week
when the trams started. A long time ahead, Mr May prepared it. The one item was the Natcha-Kee-Tawara Troupe.
The Natcha-Kee-Tawara Troupe consisted of five persons,
Madame Rochard and four young men. They were strictly
a Red Indian troupe. But one of the young men, the German
Swiss, was a famous yodeller, and another, the French Swiss,
was a good comic with a French accent, whilst Madame and
the German did a screaming two-person farce. Their great
turn, of course, was the Natcha-Kee-Tawara Red Indian
scene.

The Natcha-Kee-Tawaras were due in the third week in
January, arriving from the Potteries on the Sunday evening.
When Alvina came in from chapel that Sunday evening, she
found her widow, Mrs Rollings, seated in the living room
talking with James, who had an anxious look. Since opening
the Pleasure Palace James was less regular at chapel. And
moreover, he was getting old and shaky, and Sunday was
the one evening he might spend in peace. And that on this
particular black Sunday night it was sleeting dismally out-

side, and James had already a bit of a cough, and we shall
see that he did right to stay at home.

Mrs Rollings sat nursing a bottle. She was to go to the
chemist for some cough-cure, because Madame had got a
bad cold. The chemist was gone to chapel—he wouldn't
open till eight.

Madame and the four young men had arrived at about six.
Madame, said Mrs Rollings, was a little fat woman, and she
was complaining all the time that she had got a cold on her
chest, laying her hand on her chest and trying her breathing
and going 'He-e-e-er! Herr!' to see if she could breathe
properly. She, Mrs Rollings, had suggested that Madame
should put her feet in hot mustard and water, but Madame
said she must have something to clear her chest. The four
young men were four nice civil young fellows. They evidently liked Madame. Madame had insisted on cooking the
chops for the young men. She herself had eaten one, but she
laid her hand on her chest when she swallowed. One of the
young men had gone out to get her some brandy, and he
had come back with half-a-dozen large bottles of Bass as
well.

Mr Houghton was very much concerned over Madame's
cold. He asked the same questions again and again, to try
and make sure how bad it was. But Mrs Rollings didn't seem
quite to know. James wrinkled his brow. Supposing Madame could not take her part! He was most anxious.

'Do you think you might go across with Mrs Rollings
and see how this woman is, Alvina!' he said to his daughter.

'I should think you'll never turn Alvina out on such a
night,' said Miss Pinnegar. 'And, besides, it isn't right.
Where is Mr May? It's his business to go.'

'Oh!' returned Alvina. '*I* don't mind going. Wait a minute, I'll see if we haven't got some of those pastilles for burning. If it's very bad, I can make one of those plasters mother
used.'

And she ran upstairs. She was curious to see what Madame and her four young men were like.

With Mrs Rollings she called at the chemist's back door,
and then they hurried through the sleet to the widow's
dwelling. It was not far. As they went up the entry they

heard sound of voices. But in the kitchen all was quiet. The voices came from the front room.

Mrs Rollings tapped.

'Come in!' said a rather sharp voice. Alvina entered on the widow's heels.

'I've brought you the cough stuff,' said the widow. 'And Miss Huff'n's come as well, to see how you was.'

Four young men were sitting round the table in their shirt-sleeves, with bottles of Bass. There was much cigarette smoke. By the fire, which was burning brightly, sat a plump, pale woman with dark bright eyes and finely-drawn eyebrows: she might be any age between forty and fifty. There were grey threads in her tidy black hair. She was neatly dressed in a well-made black dress with a small lace collar. There was a slight look of self-commiseration on her face. She had a cigarette between her drooped fingers.

She rose as if with difficulty, and held out her plump hand, on which four or five rings showed. She had dropped the cigarette unnoticed into the hearth.

'How do you do,' she said. 'I didn't catch your name.' Madame's voice was a little plaintive and plangent now, like a bronze reed mournfully vibrating.

'Alvina Houghton,' said Alvina.

'Daughter of him as owns the thee-etter where you're goin' to act,' interposed the widow.

'Oh yes! Yes! I see. Miss Houghton. I didn't know how it was said. Huffton—yes? Miss Houghton. I've got a bad cold on my chest—' laying her plump hand with the rings on her plump bosom. 'But let me introduce you to my young men—' A wave of the plump hand, whose forefinger was very slightly cigarette-stained, towards the table.

The four young men had risen, and stood looking at Alvina and Madame. The room was small, rather bare, with horsehair and white-crochet antimacassars and a linoleum floor. The table also was covered with a brightly-patterned American oil-cloth, shiny but clean. A naked gas-jet hung over it. For furniture, there were just chairs, arm-chairs, table, and a horse-hair antimacassar-ed sofa. Yet the little room seemed very full—full of people, young men with smart waistcoats and ties, but without coats.

'That is Max,' said Madame. 'I shall tell you only their names, and not their family names, because that is easier for you—'

In the meantime Max had bowed. He was a tall Swiss with almond eyes and a flattish face and a rather stiff, ramrod figure.

'And that is Louis—' Louis bowed gracefully. He was a Swiss Frenchman, moderately tall, with prominent cheek-bones and a wing of glossy black hair falling on his temple.

'And that is Géoffroi—Geoffrey—' Geoffrey made his bow—a broad-shouldered, watchful, taciturn man from Alpine France.

'And that is Francesco—Frank—' Francesco gave a faint curl of his lip, half smile, as he saluted her involuntarily in a military fashion. He was dark, rather tall and loose, with yellow-tawny eyes. He was an Italian from the south. Madame gave another look at him. 'He doesn't like his English name of Frank. You will see, he pulls a face. No, he doesn't like it. We call him Cicio also—' But Cicio was dropping his head sheepishly, with the same faint smile on his face, half grimace, and stooping to his chair, wanting to sit down.

'These are my family of young men,' said Madame. 'We are drawn from three races, though only Cicio is not of our mountains. Will you please to sit down.'

They all took their chairs. There was a pause.

'My young men drink a little beer, after their horrible journey. As a rule, I do not like them to drink. But to-night they have a little beer. I do not take any myself, because I am afraid of inflaming myself.' She laid her hand on her breast, and took long, uneasy breaths. 'I feel it. I feel it *here*.' She patted her breast. 'It makes me afraid for to-morrow. Will you perhaps take a glass of beer? Cicio, ask for another glass—' Cicio, at the end of the table, did not rise, but looked round at Alvina as if he presumed there would be no need for him to move. The odd, supercilious curl of the lip persisted. Madame glared at him. But he turned the hand-some side of his cheek towards her, with the faintest flicker of a sneer.

'No thank you. I never take beer,' said Alvina hurriedly.

'No? Never? Oh!' Madame folded her hands, but her

black eyes still darted venom at Cicio. The rest of the young men fingered their glasses and put their cigarettes to their lips and blew the smoke down their noses, uncomfortably.

Madame closed her eyes and leaned back a moment. Then her face looked transparent and pallid, there were dark rings under her eyes, the beautifully-brushed hair shone dark like black glass above her ears. She was obviously unwell. The young men looked at her, and muttered to one another.

'I'm afraid your cold is rather bad,' said Alvina. 'Will you let me take your temperature?'

Madame started and looked frightened.

'Oh, I don't think you should trouble to do that,' she said.

Max, the tall, highly-coloured Swiss, turned to her, saying:

'Yes, you must have your temperature taken, and then we s'll know, shan't we. I had a hundred and five when we were in Redruth.'

Alvina had taken the thermometer from her pocket. Cicio meanwhile muttered something in French—evidently something rude—meant for Max.

'What shall I do if I can't work to-morrow!' moaned Madame, seeing Alvina hold up the thermometer towards the light. 'Max, what shall we do?'

'You will stay in bed, and we must do the White Prisoner scene,' said Max, rather staccato and official.

Cicio curled his lip and put his head aside. Alvina went across to Madame with the thermometer. Madame lifted her plump hand and fended off Alvina, while she made her last declaration:

'Never—never have I missed my work, for a single day, for ten years. Never. If I am going to lie abandoned, I had better die at once.'

'Lie abandoned!' said Max. 'You know you won't do no such thing. What are you talking about?'

'Take the thermometer,' said Geoffrey roughly, but with feeling.

'To-morrow, see, you will be well. Quite certain!' said Louis. Madame mournfully shook her head, opened her mouth, and sat back with closed eyes and the stump of the thermometer comically protruding from a corner of her lips.

Meanwhile Alvina took her plump white wrist and felt her pulse.

'We can practise—' began Geoffrey.

'Sh!' said Max, holding up his finger and looking anxiously at Alvina and Madame, who still leaned back with the stump of the thermometer jauntily perking up from her pursed mouth, while her face was rather ghastly.

Max and Louis watched anxiously. Geoffrey sat blowing the smoke down his nose, while Cicio callously lit another cigarette, striking a match on his boot-heel and puffing from under the tip of his rather long nose. Then he took the cigarette from his mouth, turning his head, slowly spat on the floor, and rubbed his foot on his spit. Max flapped his eyelids and looked all disdain, murmuring something about *'ein schmutziges italienisches Volk,'* whilst Louis, refusing either to see or to hear, framed the word *'chien'* on his lips.

Then quick as lightning both turned their attention again to Madame.

Her temperature was a hundred and two.

'You'd better go to bed,' said Alvina. 'Have you eaten anything?'

'One little mouthful,' said Madame plaintively.

Max sat looking pale and stricken, Louis had hurried forward to take Madame's hand. He kissed it quickly, then turned aside his head because of the tears in his eyes. Geoffrey gulped beer in large throatfuls, and Cicio, with his head bent, was watching from under his eyebrows.

'I'll run round for the doctor—' said Alvina.

'Don't! Don't do that, my dear! Don't you go and do that! I'm likely to a temperature—'

'Liable to a temperature,' murmured Louis pathetically.

'I'll go to bed,' said Madame, obediently rising.

'Wait a bit. I'll see if there's a fire in the bedroom,' said Alvina.

'Oh, my dear, you are too good. Open the door for her, Cicio—'

Cicio reached across at the door, but was too late. Max had hastened to usher Alvina out. Madame sank back in her chair.

'Never for ten years,' she was wailing. *'Quoi faire, ah,*

quoi faire! Que ferez-vous, mes pauvres, sans votre Kish-wégin. Que vais-je faire, mourir dans un tel pays! La bonne demoiselle—la bonne demoiselle—elle a du cœur. Elle pourrait aussi être belle, s'il y avait un peu plus de chair. Max, liebster, schau ich sehr elend aus? Ach, oh jeh oh jeh!'

'*Ach nein, Madame, ach nein. Nicht, so furchtbar elend,*' said Max.

'*Manca il cuore solamente al Cicio,*' moaned Madame. '*Che natura povera, senza sentimento—niente di bello. Ahimé, che amico, che ragazzo duro, aspero—*'

'*Trova?*' said Cicio, with a curl of the lip. He looked, as he dropped his long, beautiful lashes, as if he might weep for all that, if he were not bound to be misbehaving just now.

So Madame moaned in four languages as she posed pallid in her armchair. Usually she spoke in French only, with her young men. But this was an extra occasion.

'*La pauvre Kishwégin!*' murmured Madame. '*Elle va finir au monde. Elle passe—la pauvre Kishwégin.*'

Kishwégin was Madame's Red Indian name, the name under which she danced her Squaw's fire-dance.

Now that she knew she was ill, Madame seemed to become more ill. Her breath came in little pants. She had a pain in her side. A feverish flush seemed to mount her cheek. The young men were all extremely uncomfortable. Louis did not conceal his tears. Only Cicio kept the thin smile on his lips, and added to Madame's annoyance and pain.

Alvina came down to take her to bed. The young men all rose, and kissed Madame's hand as she went out: her poor jewelled hand, that was faintly perfumed with eau de Cologne. She spoke an appropriate good-night, to each of them.

'Good-night, my faithful Max, I trust myself to you. Good-night, Louis, the tender heart. Good-night valiant Geoffrey. Ah Cicio, do not add to the weight of my heart. Be good *braves*, all, be brothers in one accord. One little prayer for poor Kishwégin. Good-night!'

After which valediction she slowly climbed the stairs, putting her hand on her knee at each step, with the effort.

'No—no,' she said to Max, who would have followed to her assistance. 'Do not come up. No—no!'

Her bedroom was tidy and proper.

'To-night,' she moaned, 'I shan't be able to see that the boys' rooms are well in order. They are not to be trusted, no. They need an overseeing eye: especially Cicio: especially Cicio!'

She sank down by the fire and began to undo her dress.

'You must let me help you,' said Alvina. 'You know I have been a nurse.'

'Ah, you are too kind, dear young lady. I am a lonely old woman. I am not used to attentions. Best leave me.'

'Let me help you,' said Alvina.

'Alas, *ahime*! Who would have thought Kishwégin would need help. I danced last night with the boys in the theatre in Leek: and to-night I am put to bed in—what is the name of this place, dear?—It seems I don't remember it.'

'Woodhouse,' said Alvina.

'Woodhouse! Woodhouse! Is there not something called Woodlouse? I believe. Ugh, horrible! Why is it horrible?'

Alvina quickly undressed the plump, trim little woman. She seemed so soft. Alvina could not imagine how she could be a dancer on the stage, strenuous. But Madame's softness could flash into wild energy, sudden convulsive power, like a cuttle-fish. Alvina brushed out the long black hair, and plaited it lightly. Then she got Madame into bed.

'Ah,' sighed Madame, 'the good bed! The good bed! But cold—it is so cold. Would you hang up my dress, dear, and fold my stockings?'

Alvina quickly folded and put aside the dainty underclothing. Queer, dainty woman, was Madame, even to her wonderful threaded black-and-gold garters.

'My poor boys—no Kishwégin to-morrow! You don't think I need a priest, dear? A priest!' said Madame, her teeth chattering.

'Priest! Oh no! You'll be better when we can get you warm. I think it's only a chill. Mrs Rollings is warming a blanket—'

Alvina ran downstairs. Max opened the sitting-room door and stood watching at the sound of footsteps. His rather bony fists were clenched beneath his loose shirt-cuffs, his eyebrows tragically lifted.

'Is she much ill?' he asked.

'I don't know. But I don't think so. Do you mind heating the blanket while Mrs Rollings makes thin gruel.'

Max and Louis stood heating blankets, Louis's trousers were cut rather tight at the waist, and gave him a female look. Max was straight and stiff. Mrs Rollings asked Geoffrey to fill the coal-scuttles and carry one upstairs. Geoffrey obediently went out with a lantern to the coal-shed. Afterwards he was to carry up the horse-hair armchair.

'I must go home for some things,' said Alvina to Cicio. 'Will you come and carry them for me?'

He started up, and with one movement threw away his cigarette. He did not look at Alvina. His beautiful lashes seemed to screen his eyes. He was fairly tall, but loosely built for an Italian, with slightly sloping shoulders. Alvina noticed the brown, slender Mediterranean hand, as he put his fingers to his lips. It was a hand such as she did not know, prehensile and tender and dusky. With an odd graceful slouch he went into the passage and reached for his coat.

He did not say a word, but held aloof as he walked with Alvina.

'I'm sorry for Madame,' said Alvina, as she hurried rather breathless through the night. 'She does think for you men.'

But Cicio vouchsafed no answer, and walked with his hands in the pockets of his waterproof, wincing from the weather.

'I'm afraid she will never be able to dance to-morrow,' said Alvina.

'You think she won't be able?' he said.

'I'm almost sure she won't.'

After which he said nothing, and Alvina also kept silence till they came to the black dark passage and encumbered yard at the back of the house.

'I don't think you can see at all,' she said. 'It's this way.' She groped for him in the dark, and met his groping hand.

'This way,' she said.

It was curious how light his fingers were in their clasp—

almost like a child's touch. So they came under the light
from the window of the sitting-room.

Alvina hurried indoors, and the young man followed.

'I shall have to stay with Madame to-night,' she explained
hurriedly. 'She's feverish, but she may throw it off if we can
get her into a sweat.' And Alvina ran upstairs collecting
things necessary. Cicio stood back near the door, and answered all Miss Pinnegar's entreaties to come to the fire with
a shake of the head and a slight smile of the lips, bashful and
stupid.

'But do come and warm yourself before you go out again,'
said Miss Pinnegar, looking at the man as he drooped his
head in the distance. He still shook dissent, but opened his
mouth at last.

'It makes it colder after,' he said, showing his teeth in a
slight, stupid smile.

'Oh, well, if you think so,' said Miss Pinnegar, nettled.
She couldn't make head or tail of him, and didn't try.

When they got back, Madame was light-headed, and talking excitedly of her dance, her young men. The three young
men were terrified. They had got the blankets scorching hot.
Alvina smeared the plasters and applied them to Madame's
side, where the pain was. What a white-skinned, soft, plump
child she seemed! Her pain meant a touch of pleurisy, for
sure. The men hovered outside the door. Alvina wrapped
the poor patient in the hot blankets, got a few spoonfuls of
hot gruel and whisky down her throat, fastened her down
in bed, lowered the light and banished the men from the
stairs. Then she sat down to watch. Madame chafed,
moaned, murmured feverishly. Alvina soothed her, and put
her hands in bed. And at last the poor dear became quiet.
Her brow was faintly moist. She fell into a quiet sleep, perspiring freely. Alvina watched her still, soothed her when
she suddenly started and began to break out of the bed-
clothes, quieted her, pressed her gently, firmly down, folded
her tight and made her submit to the perspiration against
which, in convulsive starts, she fought and strove, crying
that she was suffocating, she was too hot, too hot.

'Lie still, lie still,' said Alvina. 'You must keep warm.'

Poor Madame moaned. How she hated seething in the

bath of her own perspiration. Her wilful nature rebelled strongly. She would have thrown aside her coverings and gasped into the cold air, if Alvina had not pressed her down with that soft, inevitable pressure.

So the hours passed, till about one o'clock, when the perspiration became less profuse, and the patient was really better, really quieter. Then Alvina went downstairs for a moment. She saw the light still burning in the front room. Tapping, she entered. There sat Max by the fire, a picture of misery, with Louis opposite him, nodding asleep after his tears. On the sofa Geoffrey snored lightly, while Cicio sat with his head on the table, his arms spread out, dead asleep. Again she noticed the tender, dusky Mediterranean hands, the slender wrists, slender for a man naturally loose and muscular.

'Haven't you gone to bed?' whispered Alvina, 'Why?'

Louis started awake. Max, the only stubborn watcher, shook his head lugubriously.

'But she's better,' whispered Alvina. 'She's perspired. She's better. She's sleeping naturally.'

Max stared with round, sleep-whitened, owlish eyes, pessimistic and sceptical.

'Yes,' persisted Alvina. 'Come and look at her. But don't wake her, whatever you do.'

Max took off his slippers and rose to his tall height. Louis, like a scared chicken, followed. Each man held his slippers in his hand. They noiselessly entered and peeped stealthily over the heaped bedclothes. Madame was lying, looking a little flushed and very girlish, sleeping lightly, with a strand of black hair stuck to her cheek, and her lips lightly parted.

Max watched her for some moments. Then suddenly he straightened himself, pushed back his brown hair that was brushed up in the German fashion, and crossed himself, dropping his knee as before an altar; crossed himself and dropped his knee once more; and then a third time crossed himself and inclined before the altar. Then he straightened himself again, and turned aside.

Louis also crossed himself. His tears burst out. He bowed and took the edge of a blanket to his lips, kissing it reverently. Then he covered his face with his hand.

Meanwhile Madame slept lightly and innocently on.

Alvina turned to go. Max silently followed, leading Louis by the arm. When they got downstairs, Max and Louis threw themselves in each other's arms, and kissed each other on either cheek, gravely, in Continental fashion.

'She is better,' said Max gravely in French.

'Thanks to God,' replied Louis.

Alvina witnessed all this with some amazement. The men did not heed her. Max went over and shook Geoffrey, Louis put his hand on Cicio's shoulder. The sleepers were difficult to wake. The wakers shook the sleeping, but in vain. At last Geoffrey began to stir. But in vain Louis lifted Cicio's shoulders from the table. The head and the hands dropped inert. The long black lashes lay motionless, the rather long, fine Greek nose drew the same light breaths, the mouth remained shut. Strange fine black hair he had, close as fur, animal, and naked, frail-seeming, tawny hands. There was a silver ring on one hand.

Alvina suddenly seized one of the inert hands that slid on the table-cloth as Louis shook the young man's shoulders. Tight she pressed the hand. Cicio opened his tawny-yellowish eyes, that seemed to have been put in with a dirty finger, as the saying goes, owing to the sootiness of the lashes and brows. He was quite drunk with his first sleep, and saw nothing.

'Wake up,' said Alvina, laughing, pressing his hand again.

He lifted his head once more, suddenly clasped her hand, his eyes came to consciousness, his hand relaxed, he recognized her, and he sat back in his chair, turning his face aside and lowering his lashes.

'Get up, great beast,' Louis was saying softly in French, pushing him as ox-drivers sometimes push their oxen. Cicio staggered to his feet.

'She is better,' they told him. 'We are going to bed.'

They took their candles and trooped off upstairs, each one bowing to Alvina as he passed. Max solemnly, Louis gallant, the other two dumb and sleepy. They occupied the two attic chambers.

Alvina carried up the loose bed from the sofa, and slept on the floor before the fire in Madame's room.

Madame slept well and long, rousing and stirring and settling off again. It was eight o'clock before she asked her first
question. Alvina was already up.

'Oh—*alors*—Then I am better, I am quite well. I can
dance to-day.'

'I don't think to-day,' said Alvina. 'But perhaps to-
morrow.'

'No, to-day,' said Madame. 'I can dance to-day, because
I am quite well. I am Kishwégin.'

'You are better. But you must lie still to-day. Yes, really—
you will find you are weak when you try to stand.'

Madame watched Alvina's thin face with sullen eyes.

'You are an Englishwoman, severe and materialist,' she
said.

Alvina started and looked round at her with wide blue
eyes.

'Why?' she said. There was a wan pathetic look about her,
a sort of heroism which Madame detested, but which now
she found touching.

'Come!' said Madame, stretching out her plump jewelled
hand. 'Come, I am an ungrateful woman. Come, they are
not good for you, the people, I see it. Come to me.'

Alvina went slowly to Madame, and took the outstretched hand. Madame kissed her hand, then drew her
down and kissed her on either cheek, gravely, as the young
men had kissed each other.

'You have been good to Kishwégin, and Kishwégin has a
heart that remembers. There, Miss Houghton, I shall do
what you tell me. Kishwégin obeys you.' And Madame patted Alvina's hand and nodded her head savagely.

'Shall I take your temperature?' said Alvina.

'Yes, my dear, you shall. You shall bid me, and I shall
obey.' So Madame lay back on her pillow, submissively
pursing the thermometer between her lips and watching Alvina with black eyes.

'It's all right,' said Alvina, as she looked at the thermometer. 'Normal.'

'Normal!' re-echoed Madame's rather guttural voice.
'Good! Well, then when shall I dance?'

Alvina turned and looked at her.

'I think, truly,' said Alvina, 'it shouldn't be before Thursday or Friday.'

'Thursday!' repeated Madame. 'You say Thursday?' There was a note of strong rebellion in her voice.

'You'll be so weak. You've only just escaped pleurisy. I can only say what I truly think, can't I?'

'Ah, you English women,' said Madame, watching with black eyes. 'I think you like to have your own way. In all things, to have your own way. And over all people. You are so good, to have your own way. Yes, you good English-women. Thursday. Very well, it shall be Thursday. Till Thursday, then, Kishwégin does not exist.'

And she subsided, already rather weak, upon her pillow again. When she had taken her tea and was washed and her room was tidied, she summoned the young men. Alvina had warned Max that she wanted Madame to be kept as quiet as possible this day.

As soon as the first of the four appeared, in his shirt-sleeves and his slippers, in the doorway, Madame said:

'Ah, there you are, my young men! Come in! Come in! It is not Kishwégin addresses you. Kishwégin does not exist till Thursday, as the English demoiselle makes it.' She held out her hand, faintly perfumed with eau de Cologne—the whole room smelled of eau de Cologne—and Max stooped his brittle spine and kissed it. She touched his cheek gently with her other hand.

'My faithful Max, my support.'

Louis came smiling with a bunch of violets and pinky anemones. He laid them down on the bed before her, and took her hand, bowing and kissing it reverently.

'You are better, dear Madame?' he said, smiling long at her.

'Better, yes, gentle Louis. And better for thy flowers, chivalric heart.' She put the violets and anemones to her face with both hands, and then gently laid them aside to extend her hand to Geoffrey.

'The good Geoffrey will do his best, while there is no Kishwégin?' she said as he stooped to her salute.

'*Bien sûr*, Madame.'

'Cicio, a button off thy shirt-cuff. Where is my needle?' She looked round the room as Cicio kissed her hand.

'Did you want anything?' said Alvina, who had not followed the French.

'My needle, to sew on this button. It is there, in the silk bag.'

'I will do it,' said Alvina.

'Thank you.'

While Alvina sewed on the button, Madame spoke to her young men, principally to Max. They were to obey Max, she said, for he was their eldest brother. This afternoon they would practise well the scene of the White Prisoner. Very carefully they must practise, and they must find someone who would play the young squaw—for in this scene she had practically nothing to do, the young squaw, but just sit and stand. Miss Houghton—but ah, Miss Houghton must play the piano, she could not take the part of the young squaw. Some other then.

While the interview was going on, Mr May arrived, full of concern.

'Shan't we have the procession!' he cried.

'Ah! the procession!' cried Madame.

The Natcha-Kee-Tawara Troupe upon request would signalize its entry into any town by a procession. The young men were dressed as Indian *braves*, and headed by Kishwégin they rode on horseback through the main streets. Cicio, who was the crack horseman, having served a very well-known horsey Marchese in an Italian cavalry regiment, did a bit of show riding.

Mr May was very keen on the procession. He had the horses in readiness. The morning was faintly sunny, after the sleet and bad weather. And now he arrived to find Madame in bed and the young men holding council with her.

'How *very* unfortunate!' cried Mr May. 'How *very* unfortunate!'

'Dreadful! Dreadful!' wailed Madame from the bed.

'But can't we do *anything*?'

'Yes—you can do the White Prisoner scene—the young men can do that, if you find a dummy squaw. Ah, I think I must get up after all.'

Alvina saw the look of fret and exhaustion in Madame's face.

'Won't you all go downstairs now?' said Alvina. 'Mr Max knows what you must do.'

And she shooed the five men out of the bedroom.

'I *must* get up. I won't dance. I will be a dummy. But I must be there. It is too dre-eadful, too dre-eadful!' wailed Madame.

'Don't take any notice of them. They can manage by themselves. Men are such babies. Let them carry it through by themselves.'

'Children—they are all children!' wailed Madame. 'All children! And so, what will they do without their old *gouvernante*? My poor *braves*, what will they do without Kishwégin? It is too dreadful, too dre-eadful, yes. The poor Mr May—so *disappointed*.'

'Then let him *be* disappointed,' cried Alvina, as she forcibly tucked up Madame and made her lie still.

'You are hard! You are a hard Englishwoman. All alike. All alike!' Madame subsided fretfully and weakly. Alvina moved softly about. And in a few minutes Madame was sleeping again.

Alvina went downstairs. Mr May was listening to Max, who was telling in German all about the White Prisoner scene. Mr May had spent his boyhood in a German school. He cocked his head on one side, and, laying his hand on Max's arm, entertained him in odd German. The others were silent. Cicio made no pretence of listening, but smoked and stared at his own feet. Louis and Geoffrey half understood, so Louis nodded with a look of deep comprehension, whilst Geoffrey uttered short, snappy, '*Ja!—Ja!—Doch!—Eben!*' rather irrelevant.

'I'll be the squaw,' cried Mr May in English, breaking off and turning round to the company. He perked up his head in an odd, parrot-like fashion. 'I'll be the squaw! What's her name? Kishwégin? I'll be Kishwégin!' And he bridled and beamed self-consciously.

The two tall Swiss looked down on him, faintly smiling. Cicio, sitting with his arms on his knees on the sofa, screwed round his head and watched the phenomenon of Mr May with inscrutable, expressionless attention.

'Let us go,' said Mr May, bubbling with new importance. 'Let us go and rehearse *this morning*, and let us do the procession this afternoon, when the colliers are just coming home. There! What? Isn't that exactly the idea? Well! Will you be ready at once, *now*?'

He looked excitedly at the young men. They nodded with slow gravity, as if they were already *braves*. And they turned to put on their boots. Soon they were all trooping down to Lumley, Mr May prancing like a little circus-pony beside Alvina, the four young men rolling ahead.

'What do you think of it?' cried Mr May. 'We've saved the situation—what? Don't you think so? Don't you think we can congratulate ourselves?'

They found Mr Houghton fussing about in the theatre. He was on tenterhooks of agitation, knowing Madame was ill.

Max gave a brilliant display of yodelling.

'But I must *explain* to them,' cried Mr May. 'I must *explain* to them what yodel means.'

And turning to the empty theatre, he began, stretching forth his hand.

'In the high Alps of Switzerland, where eternal snows and glaciers reign over luscious meadows full of flowers, if you should chance to awaken, as I have done, in some lonely wooden farm amid the mountain pastures, you—er—you— let me see—if you—no—if you should chance to *spend the night* in some lonely wooden farm amid the upland pastures, dawn will awake you with a wild, inhuman song, you will open your eyes to the first gleam of icy, eternal sunbeams, your ears will be ringing with weird singing, that has no words and no meaning, but sounds as if some wild and icy god were warbling to himself as he wandered among the peaks of dawn. You look forth across the flowers to the blue snow, and you see, far off, a small figure of a man moving among the grass. It is a peasant singing his mountain song, warbling like some creature that lifted up its voice on the edge of the eternal snows, before the human race began—'

During this oration James Houghton sat with his chin in

his hand, devoured with bitter jealousy, measuring Mr May's eloquence. And then he started, as Max, tall and handsome now in Tyrolese costume, white shirt and green, square braces, short trousers of chamois leather stitched with green and red, firm-planted naked knees, naked ankles and heavy shoes, warbled his native yodel strains, a piercing and disturbing sound. He was flushed, erect, keen tempered and fierce and mountainous. There was a fierce, icy passion in the man. Alvina began to understand Madame's subjection to him.

Louis and Geoffrey did a farce dialogue, two foreigners at the same moment spying a purse in the street, struggling with each other and protesting they wanted to take it to the policeman, Cicio, who stood solid and ridiculous. Mr Houghton nodded slowly and gravely, as if to give his measured approval.

They all retired to dress for the great scene. Alvina practised the music Madame carried with her. If Madame found a good pianist, she welcomed the accompaniment: if not, she dispensed with it.

'Am I all right?' said a smirking voice.

And there was Kishwégin, dusky, coy, with long black hair and a short chamois dress, gaiters and mocassins and bare arms: *so* coy, and *so* smirking. Alvina burst out laughing.

'But shan't I do?' protested Mr May, hurt.

'Yes, you're wonderful,' said Alvina, choking. 'But I *must* laugh.'

'But why? Tell me why?' asked Mr May anxiously. 'Is it my *appearance* you laugh at, or is it only *me*? If it's me I don't mind. But if it's my appearance, tell me so.'

Here an appalling figure of Cicio in war-paint strolled on to the stage. He was naked to the waist, wore scalp-fringed trousers, was dusky-red-skinned, had long black hair and eagle's feathers—only two feathers—and a face wonderfully and terribly painted with white, red, yellow, and black lines. He was evidently pleased with himself. His curious soft slouch and curious way of lifting his lip from his white teeth, in a sort of smile, was very convincing.

'You haven't got the girdle,' he said, touching Mr May's plump waist—'and some flowers in your hair.'

Mr May here gave a sharp cry and a jump. A bear on its hind legs, slow, shambling, rolling its loose shoulders, was stretching a paw towards him. The bear dropped heavily on four paws again, and a laugh came from its muzzle.

'You won't have to dance,' said Geoffrey out of the bear.

'Come and put in the flowers,' said Mr May anxiously, to Alvina.

In the dressing-room, the dividing-curtain was drawn. Max, in deerskin trousers but with unpainted torso, looked very white and strange as he put the last touches of war-paint on Louis's face. He glanced round at Alvina, then went on with his work. There was a sort of nobility about his erect white form and stiffly-carried head, the semi-luminous brown hair. He seemed curiously superior.

Alvina adjusted the maidenly Mr May. Louis arose, a *brave* like Cicio, in war-paint even more hideous. Max slipped on a tattered hunting-shirt and cartridge belt. His face was a little darkened. He was the white prisoner.

They arranged the scenery, while Alvina watched. It was soon done. A back-cloth of tree-trunks and dark forest: a wigwam, a fire, and a cradle hanging from a pole. As they worked, Alvina tried in vain to dissociate the two *braves* from their war-paint. The lines were drawn so cleverly that the grimace of ferocity was fixed and horrible, so that even in the quiet work of scene-shifting Louis's stiffish, female grace seemed full of latent cruelty, whilst Cicio's more muscular slouch made her feel she would not trust him for one single moment. Awful things men were, savage, cruel, underneath their civilization.

The scene had its beauty. It began with Kishwégin alone at the door of the wigwam, cooking, listening, giving an occasional push to the hanging cradle, and, if only Madame were taking the part, crooning an Indian cradle-song. Enter the *brave* Louis with his white prisoner, Max, who has his hands bound to his side. Kishwégin gravely salutes her husband—the bound prisoner is seated by the fire—Kishwégin serves food, and asks permission to feed the prisoner. The *brave* Louis, hearing a sound, starts up with his bow and

arrow. There is a dumb scene of sympathy between Kishwégin and the prisoner—the prisoner wants his bonds cut.
Re-enter the *brave* Louis—he is angry with Kishwégin—
enter the *brave* Cicio hauling a bear, apparently dead. Kishwégin examines the bear, Cicio examines the prisoner. Cicio
tortures the prisoner, makes him stand, makes him caper
unwillingly. Kishwégin swings the cradle. The prisoner is
tripped up—falls, and cannot rise. He lies near the fallen
bear. Kishwégin carries food to Cicio. The two *braves* con-
verse in dumb show, Kishwégin swings the cradle and
croons. The men rise once more and bend over the prisoner.
As they do so, there is a muffled roar. The bear is sitting up.
Louis swings round, and at the same moment the bear
strikes him down. Cicio springs forward and stabs the bear,
then closes with it. Kishwégin runs and cuts the prisoner's
bonds. He rises, and stands trying to lift his numbed and
powerless arms, while the bear slowly crushes Cicio, and
Kishwégin kneels over her husband. The bear drops Cicio
lifeless, and turns to Kishwégin. At that moment Max man-
ages to kill the bear—he takes Kishwégin by the hand and
kneels with her beside the dead Louis.

It was wonderful how well the men played their different
parts. But Mr May was a little too frisky as Kishwégin.
However, it would do.

Cicio got dressed as soon as possible, to go and look at
the horses hired for the afternoon procession. Alvina accompanied him, Mr May and the others were busy.

'You know I think it's quite wonderful, your scene,' she
said to Cicio.

He turned and looked down at her. His yellow, dusky-
set eyes rested on her good-naturedly, without seeing her,
his lip curled in a self-conscious, contemptuous sort of
smile.

'Not without Madame,' he said, with the slow, half-
sneering, stupid smile. 'Without Madame—' he lifted his
shoulders and spread his hands and tilted his brows—'fool's
play, you know.'

'No,' said Alvina. 'I think Mr May is good, considering.
What does Madame *do?*' she asked a little jealously.

'Do?' He looked down at her with the same long, half-

sardonic look of his yellow eyes, like a cat looking casually
at a bird which flutters past. And again he made his shrugging motion. 'She does it all, really. The others—they are
nothing—what they are Madame has made them. And now
they think they've done it all, you see. You see, that's it.'

'But how has Madame made it all? Thought it out, you
mean?'

'Thought it out, yes. And then *done* it. You should see
her dance—ah! You should see her dance round the bear,
when I bring him in! Ah, a beautiful thing, you know. She
claps her hand—' And Cicio stood still in the street, with
his hat cocked a little on one side, rather common-looking,
and he smiled along his fine nose at Alvina, and he clapped
his hands lightly, and he tilted his eyebrows and his eyelids
as if facially he were imitating a dance, and all the time his
lips smiled stupidly. As he gave a little assertive shake of his
head, finishing, there came a great yell of laughter from the
opposite pavement, where a gang of pottery lasses, in aprons
all spattered with grey clay, and hair and boots and skin
spattered with pallid spots, had stood to watch. The girls
opposite shrieked again, for all the world like a gang of grey
baboons. Cicio turned round and looked at them with a
sneer along his nose. They yelled the louder. And he was
horribly uncomfortable, walking there beside Alvina with
his rather small and effeminately-shod feet.

'How stupid they are,' said Alvina. 'I've got used to
them.'

'They should be—' he lifted his hand with a sharp, vicious
movement—'*smacked!*' he concluded, lowering his hand
again.

'Who is going to do it?' said Alvina.

He gave a Neapolitan grimace, and twiddled the fingers
of one hand outspread in the air, as if to say: 'There you are!
You've got to thank the fools who've failed to do it.'

'Why do you all love Madame so much?' Alvina asked.

'How, love?' he said, making a little grimace. 'We like
her—we love her—as if she was a mother. You say *love*—'
He raised his shoulders slightly, with a shrug. And all the
time he looked down at Alvina from under his dusky eyelashes, as if watching her sideways, and his mouth had the

peculiar, stupid, self-conscious, half-jeering smile. Alvina was a little bit annoyed. But she felt that a great instinctive good-naturedness came out of him, he was self-conscious and constrained, knowing she did not follow his language of gesture. For him, it was not yet quite natural to express himself in speech. Gesture and grimace were instantaneous, and spoke worlds of things, if you would but accept them.

But certainly he was stupid, in her sense of the word. She could hear Mr May's verdict on him: 'Like a child, you know, just as charming and just as tiresome and just as stupid.'

'Where is your home?' she asked him.

'In Italy.' She felt a fool.

'Which part?' she insisted.

'Naples,' he said, looking down at her sideways, searchingly.

'It must be lovely,' she said.

'Ha—!' He threw his head on one side and spread out his hands, as if to say—'What do you want, if you don't find Naples lovely.'

'I should like to see it. But I shouldn't like to die,' she said.

'What?'

'They say "See Naples and die",' she laughed.

He opened his mouth, and understood. Then he smiled at her directly.

'You know what that means?' he said cutely. 'It means see Naples and die afterwards. Don't die *before* you've seen it.'

He smiled with a knowing smile.

'I see! I see!' she cried. 'I never thought of that.'

He was pleased with her surprise and amusement.

'Ah Naples!' he said. 'She is lovely—' He spread his hand across the air in front of him—'The sea—and Posilippo—and Sorrento—and Capri—Ah-h! You've never been out of England?'

'No,' she said. 'I should love to go.'

He looked down into her eyes. It was his instinct to say at once he would take her.

'You've seen nothing—nothing,' he said to her.

'But if Naples is so lovely, how could you leave it?' she asked.

'What?'

She repeated her question. For answer, he looked at her, held out his hand, and rubbing the ball of his thumb across the tips of his fingers, said, with a fine, handsome smile:

'Pennies! Money! You can't earn money in Naples. Ah, Naples is beautiful, but she is poor. You live in the sun, and you earn fourteen, fifteen pence a day—'

'Not enough,' she said.

He put his head on one side and tilted his brows, as if to say 'What are you to do?' And the smile on his mouth was sad, fine, and charming. There was an indefinable air of sadness or wistfulness about him, something so robust and fragile at the same time, that she was drawn in a strange way.

'But you'll go back?' she said.

'Where?'

'To Italy. To Naples.'

'Yes, I shall go back to Italy,' he said, as if unwilling to commit himself. 'But perhaps I shan't go back to Naples.'

'Never?'

'Ah, never! I don't say never. I shall go to Naples, to see my mother's sister. But I shan't go to live—'

'Have you a mother and father?'

'I? No! I have a brother and two sisters—in America. Parents, none. They are dead.'

'And you wander about the world—' she said.

He looked at her, and made a slight sad gesture, indifferent also.

'But you have Madame for a mother,' she said.

He made another gesture this time: pressed down the corners of his mouth as if he didn't like it. Then he turned with the slow, fine smile.

'Does a man want two mothers? Eh?' he said, as if he posed a conundrum.

'I shouldn't think so,' laughed Alvina.

He glanced at her to see what she meant, what she understood.

'My mother is dead, see!' he said. 'Frenchwomen—

Frenchwomen—they have their babies till they are a hundred—'

'What do you mean?' said Alvina, laughing.

'A Frenchman is a little man when he's seven years old—and if his mother comes, he is a little baby boy when he's seventy. Do you know that?'

'I *didn't* know it,' said Alvina.

'But now—you do,' he said, lurching round a corner with her.

They had come to the stables. Three of the horses were there, including the thoroughbred Cicio was going to ride. He stood and examined the beasts critically. Then he spoke to them with strange sounds, patted them, stroked them down, felt them, slid his hand down them, over them, under them, and felt their legs.

Then he looked up from stooping there under the horses, with a long, slow look of his yellow eyes, at Alvina. She felt unconsciously flattered. His long, yellow look lingered, holding her eyes. She wondered what he was thinking. Yet he never spoke. He turned again to the horses. They seemed to understand him, to prick up alert.

'This is mine,' he said, with his hand on the neck of the old thoroughbred. It was a bay with a white blaze.

'I think he's nice,' she said. 'He seems so sensitive.'

'In England,' he answered suddenly, 'horses live a long time, because they *don't* live—never alive—see? In England railway-engines are alive, and horses go on wheels.' He smiled into her eyes as if she understood. She was a trifle nervous as he smiled at her from out of the stable, so yellow-eyed and half-mysterious, derisive. Her impulse was to turn and go away from the stable. But a deeper impulse made her smile into his face, as she said to him:

'They like you to touch them.'

'Who?' His eyes kept hers. Curious how *dark* they seemed, with only a yellow ring of pupil. He was looking right into her, beyond her usual self, impersonal.

'The horses,' she said. She was afraid of his long, cat-like look. Yet she felt convinced of his ultimate good nature. He seemed to her to be the only passionately good-natured man she had ever seen. She watched him vaguely, with strange vague trust, implicit belief in him. In him—in what?

That afternoon the colliers trooping home in the winter afternoon were rejoiced with a spectacle: Kishwégin, in her deerskin, fringed gaiters and fringed frock of deer-skin, her long hair down her back, and with marvellous cloths and trappings on her steed, riding astride on a tall white horse, followed by Max in chieftain's robes and chieftain's long head-dress of dyed feathers, then by the others in war-paint and feathers and brilliant Navajo blankets. They carried bows and spears. Cicio was without his blanket, naked to the waist, in war-paint, and brandishing a long spear. He dashed up from the rear, saluted the chieftain with his arm and his spear on high as he swept past, suddenly drew up his rearing steed, and trotted slowly back again, making his horse perform its paces. He was extraordinarily velvety and alive on horseback.

Crowds of excited, shouting children ran chattering along the pavements. The colliers, as they tramped grey and heavy, in an intermittent stream uphill from the low grey west, stood on the pavement in wonder as the cavalcade approached and passed, jingling the silver bells of its trappings, vibrating the wonderful colours of the barred blankets and saddle cloths, the scarlet wool of the accoutrements, the bright tips of feathers. Women shrieked as Cicio, in his war-paint, wheeled near the pavement. Children screamed and ran. The colliers shouted. Cicio smiled in his terrifying war-paint, brandished his spear and trotted softly like a flower on its stem round to the procession.

Miss Pinnegar and Alvina and James Houghton had come round into Knarborough Road to watch. It was a great moment. Looking along the road they saw all the shopkeepers at their doors, the pavements eager. And then, in the distance, the white horse jingling its trappings of scarlet hair and bells, with the dusky Kishwégin sitting the saddle-blanket of brilliant, lurid stripes, sitting impassive and all dusky above that intermittent flashing of colour: then the chieftain, dark-faced, erect, easy, swathed in a white blanket, with scarlet and black stripes, and all his strange crest of white, tip-dyed feathers swaying down his back: as he came nearer one saw the wolfskin and the brilliant mocassins against the black sides of his horse: Louis and Geoffrey followed, lurid, horrid in the face, wearing blankets with stroke after stroke of blazing colour upon their duskiness, and sitting stern, holding their spears: lastly, Cicio, on his bay horse with a green seat, flickering hither and thither in the rear, his feathers swaying, his horse sweating, his face ghastlily smiling in its war-paint. So they advanced down the grey pallor of Knarborough Road, in the late wintry afternoon. Somewhere the sun was setting, and far overhead was a flush of orange.

'Well I never!' murmured Miss Pinnegar. 'Well I never!'

The strange savageness of the striped Navajo blankets seemed to her unsettling, advancing down Knarborough Road: she examined Kishwégin curiously.

'Can you *believe* that that's Mr May—he's exactly like a girl. Well, well—it makes you wonder what is and what isn't. But *aren't* they good? What? Most striking. Exactly like Indians. You can't believe your eyes. My word, what a terrifying race they—' Here she uttered a scream and ran back clutching the wall as Cicio swept past, brushing her with his horse's tail, and actually swinging his spear so as to touch Alvina and James Houghton lightly with the butt of it. James too started with a cry, the mob at the corner screamed. But Alvina caught the slow, mischievous smile as the painted horror showed his teeth in passing; she was able to flash back an excited laugh. She felt his yellow-tawny eyes linger on her, in that one second, as if negligently.

'I call that too much!' Miss Pinnegar was crying, thoroughly upset. 'Now that was unnecessary! Why, it was enough to scare one to death. Besides, it's dangerous. It ought to be put a stop to. I don't believe in letting these show-people have liberties.'

The cavalcade was slowly passing, with its uneasy horses and its flare of striped colour and its silent riders. Cicio was trotting softly back, on his green saddle-cloth, suave as velvet, his dusky, naked torso beautiful.

'Eh, you'd think he'd get his death,' the women in the crowd were saying.

'A proper savage one, that. Makes your blood run cold—'

'Ay, an' a man for all that, take's painted face for what's worth. A tidy man, *I* say.'

He did not look at Alvina. The faint, mischievous smile uncovered his teeth. He fell in suddenly behind Geoffrey, with a jerk of his steed, calling out to Geoffrey in Italian.

It was becoming cold. The cavalcade fell into a trot, Mr May shaking rather badly. Cicio halted, rested his lance against a lamp-post, switched his green blanket from beneath him, flung it round him as he sat, and darted off. They had all disappeared over the brow of Lumley Hill, descending. He was gone too. In the wintry twilight the crowd began, lingeringly, to turn away. And in some strange way, it manifested its disapproval of the spectacle: as grown-up men and women, they were a little bit insulted by such a show. It was an anachronism. They wanted a direct appeal to the mind. Miss Pinnegar expressed it.

'Well,' she said, when she was safely back in Manchester House, with the gas lighted, and as she was pouring the boiling water into the tea-pot, 'You may say what you like. It's interesting in a way, just to show what savage Red Indians were like. But it's childish. It's only childishness. I can't understand, myself, how people can go on liking shows. Nothing happens. It's not like the cinema, where you see it all and take it all in at once; you *know* everything at a glance. You don't know anything by looking at these people. You know they're only men dressed up, for money. I can't see why you should encourage it. I don't hold with idle show-people, parading round, I don't, myself. I like to go to the cinema once a week. It's instruction, you take it all in at a glance, all you need to know, and it lasts you for a week. You can get to know everything about people's actual lives from the cinema. I don't see why you want people dressing up and showing off.'

They sat down to their tea and toast and marmalade, during this harangue. Miss Pinnegar was always like a douche of cold water to Alvina, bringing her back to consciousness after a delicious excitement. In a minute Madame and Cicio and all seemed to become unreal—the actual unrealities: while the ragged dithering pictures of the film were actual,

real as the day. And Alvina was always put out when this
happened. She really hated Miss Pinnegar. Yet she had nothing to answer. They *were* unreal, Madame and Cicio and the
rest. Cicio was just a fantasy blown in on the wind, to blow
away again. The real, permanent thing was Woodhouse, the
semper idem Knarborough Road, and the unchangeable
grubby gloom of Manchester House, with the stuffy, padding Miss Pinnegar, and her father, whose fingers, whose
very soul seemed dirty with pennies. These were the solid,
permanent fact. These were life itself. And Cicio, splashing
up on his bay horse and green cloth, he was a mountebank
and an extraneous nonentity, a coloured old rag blown
down the Knarborough Road into Limbo. Into Limbo.
Whilst Miss Pinnegar and her father sat frowsily on for ever,
eating their toast and cutting off the crust, and sipping their
third cup of tea. They would never blow away—never,
never. Woodhouse was there to eternity. And the Natcha-
Kee-Tawara Troupe was blowing like a rag of old paper into
Limbo. Nothingness! Poor Madame! Poor gallant histrionic
Madame! The frowsty Miss Pinnegar could crumple her up
and throw her down the utilitarian drain, and have done
with her. Whilst Miss Pinnegar lived on for ever.

This put Alvina into a sharp temper.

'Miss Pinnegar,' she said. 'I do think you go on in the
most unattractive way sometimes. You're a regular spoil-
sport.'

'Well,' said Miss Pinnegar tartly. 'I don't approve of your
way of sport, I'm afraid.'

'You can't disapprove of it as much as I hate your spoil-
sport existence,' said Alvina in a flare.

'Alvina, are you mad!' said her father.

'Wonder I'm not,' said Alvina, 'considering what my life
is.'

CHAPTER 8

Cicio

Madame did not pick up her spirits, after her cold. For two days she lay in bed, attended by Mrs Rollings and Alvina and the young men. But she was most careful never to give any room for scandal. The young men might not approach her save in the presence of some third party. And then it was strictly a visit of ceremony or business.

'Oh, your Woodhouse, how glad I shall be when I have left it,' she said to Alvina. 'I feel it is unlucky for me.'

'Do you?' said Alvina. 'But if you'd had this bad cold in some places, you might have been much worse, don't you think.'

'Oh my dear!' cried Madame. 'Do you think I could confuse you in my dislike of this Woodhouse? Oh no! You are not Woodhouse. On the contrary, I think it is unkind for you also, this place. You look—also—what shall I say—thin, not very happy.'

It was a note of interrogation.

'I'm sure I dislike Woodhouse much more than you can,' replied Alvina.

'I am sure. Yes! I am sure. I see it. Why don't you go away? Why don't you marry?'

'Nobody wants to marry me,' said Alvina.

Madame looked at her searchingly, with shrewd black eyes under her arched eyebrows.

'How!' she exclaimed. 'How don't they? You are not bad looking, only a little too thin—too haggard—'

She watched Alvina. Alvina laughed uncomfortably.

'Is there *nobody*?' persisted Madame.

'Not now,' said Alvina. 'Absolutely nobody.' She looked with a confused laugh into Madame's strict black eyes. 'You see I didn't care for the Woodhouse young men, either. I *couldn't*.'

Madame nodded slowly up and down. A secret satisfaction came over her pallid, waxy countenance, in which her black eyes were like twin swift extraneous creatures: oddly like two bright little dark animals in the snow.

'Sure!' she said, sapient. 'Sure! How could you? But there are other men besides these here—' She waved her hand to the window.

'I don't meet them, do I?' said Alvina.

'No, not often. But sometimes! Sometimes!'

There was a silence between the two women, very pregnant.

'Englishwomen,' said Madame, 'are so practical. Why are they?'

'I suppose they can't help it,' said Alvina. 'But they're not half so practical and clever as *you*, Madame.'

'Oh la—la! I am practical differently. I am practical impractically—' she stumbled over the words. 'But your Sue now, in *Jude the Obscure*—is it not an interesting book? And is she not always too prac-tically prac-tical! If she had been impractically practical she could have been quite happy. Do you know what I mean?—no. But she is ridiculous, Sue: so Anna Karenine. Ridiculous both. Don't you think?'

'Why?' said Alvina.

'Why did they both make everybody unhappy, when they had the man they wanted, and enough money? I think they are both silly. If they had been beaten, they would have lost all their practical ideas and troubles, merely forgot them, and been happy enough. I am a woman who says it. Such ideas they have are not tragical. No, not at all. They are nonsense, you see, nonsense. That is all. Nonsense. Sue and Anna, they are nonsensical. That is all. No tragedy whatsoever. Nonsense. I am a woman. I know men also. And I know nonsense when I see it. Englishwomen are all nonsense: the worst women in the world for nonsense.'

'Well, I am English,' said Alvina.

'Yes, my dear, you are English. But you are not necessarily so nonsensical. Why are you at all?'

'Nonsensical?' laughed Alvina. 'But I don't know what you call my nonsense.'

'Ah,' said Madame wearily. 'They never understand. But I like you, my dear. I am an old woman—'

'Younger than I,' said Alvina.

'Younger than you, because I am practical from the heart, and not only from the head. You are not practical from the heart. And yet you have a heart.'

'But all Englishwomen have good hearts,' protested Alvina.

'No! No!' objected Madame. 'They are all ve-ry kind, and ve-ry practical with their kindness. But they have no heart in all their kindness. It is all head, all head: the kindness of the head.'

'I can't agree with you,' said Alvina.

'No. No. I don't expect it. But I don't mind. You are very kind to me, and I thank you. But it is from the head, you see. And so I thank you from the head. From the heart—no.'

Madame plucked her white fingers together and laid them on her breast with a gesture of repudiation. Her black eyes stared spitefully.

'But Madame,' said Alvina, nettled, 'I should never be half such a good business-woman as you. Isn't that from the head?'

'Ha! of course! Of course you wouldn't be a good business-woman. Because you are kind from the head. I—' she tapped her forehead and shook her head—'I am not kind from the head. From the head I am business-woman, good business-woman. Of course I am a good business-woman—of course! But—' here she changed her expression, widened her eyes, and laid her hand on her breast—'when the heart speaks—then I listen with the heart. I do not listen with the head. The heart hears the heart. The head—that is another thing. But you have blue eyes, you cannot understand. Only dark eyes—' She paused and mused.

'And what about yellow eyes?' asked Alvina laughing.

Madame darted a look at her, her lips curling with a very faint, fine smile of derision. Yet for the first time her black eyes dilated and became warm.

'Yellow eyes like Cicio's?' she said, with her great watchful eyes and her smiling, subtle mouth. 'They are the darkest of all.' And she shook her head roguishly.

'Are they!' said Alvina confusedly, feeling a blush burning up her throat into her face.

'Ha—ha!' laughed Madame. 'Ha-ha! I am an old woman, you see. My heart is old enough to be kind, and my head is old enough to be clever. My heart is kind to few people—very few—especially in this England. My young men know that. But perhaps to you it is kind.'

'Thank you,' said Alvina.

'There! From the head. *Thank you.* It is not well done, you see. You see!'

But Alvina ran away in confusion. She felt Madame was having her on a string.

Mr May enjoyed himself hugely playing Kishwégin. When Madame came downstairs Louis, who was a good satirical mimic, imitated him. Alvina happened to come into their sitting-room in the midst of their burst of laughter. They all stopped and looked at her cautiously.

'*Continuez! Continuez!*' said Madame to Louis. And to Alvina: 'Sit down, my dear, and see what a good actor we have in our Louis.'

Louis glanced round, laid his head a little on one side and drew in his chin, with Mr May's smirk exactly, and wagging his tail slightly, he commenced to play the false Kishwégin. He sidled and bridled and ejaculated with raised hands, and in the dumb show the tall Frenchman made such a ludicrous caricature of Mr Houghton's manager that Madame wept again with laughter, whilst Max leaned back against the wall and giggled continuously like some pot involuntarily boiling, Geoffrey spread his shut fists across the table and shouted with laughter, Cicio threw back his head and showed all his teeth in a loud laugh of delighted derision. Alvina laughed also. But she flushed. There was a certain biting, annihilating quality in Louis's derision of the absentee. And the others enjoyed it so much. At moments Alvina caught her lip between her teeth, it was so screamingly funny, and so annihilating. She laughed in spite of herself. In spite of herself she was shaken into a convulsion of laughter. Louis was masterful—he mastered her psyche. She laughed till her head lay helpless on the chair, she could not move. Helpless, inert she lay, in her orgasm of laughter. The end of Mr May. Yet she was hurt.

And then Madame wiped her own shrewd black eyes, and nodded slow approval. Suddenly Louis started and held up a warning finger. They all at once covered their smiles and pulled themselves together. Only Alvina lay silently laughing.

'Oh, good-morning, Mrs Rollings!' they heard Mr May's voice. 'Your company is lively. Is Miss Houghton here? May I go through?'

They heard his quick little step and his quick little tap.

'Come in,' called Madame.

The Natcha-Kee-Tawaras all sat with straight faces. Only poor Alvina lay back in her chair in a new weak convulsion. Mr May glanced quickly round and advanced to Madame.

'Oh, good-morning, Madame, so glad to see you downstairs,' he said, taking her hand and bowing ceremoniously. 'Excuse my intruding on your mirth!' He looked archly round. Alvina was still incompetent. She lay leaning sideways in her chair, and could not even speak to him.

'It was evidently a good joke,' he said. 'May I hear it too?'

'Oh,' said Madame, drawling. 'It was no joke. It was only Louis making a fool of himself, doing a turn.'

'Must have been a good one,' said Mr May. 'Can't we put it on?'

'No,' drawled Madame, 'it was nothing—just a nonsensical mood of the moment. Won't you sit down? You would like a little whisky?—yes?'

Max poured out whisky and water for Mr May.

Alvina sat with her face averted, quiet, but unable to speak

to Mr May. Max and Louis had become polite. Geoffrey
stared with his big, dark-blue eyes stolidly at the newcomer.
Cicio leaned with his arms on his knees, looking sideways
under his long lashes at the inert Alvina.

'Well,' said Madame, 'and are you satisfied with your
houses?'

'Oh yes,' said Mr May. 'Quite! The two nights have been
excellent. Excellent!'

'Ah—I am glad. And Miss Houghton tells me I should
not dance to-morrow, it is too soon.'

'Miss Houghton *knows*,' said Mr May archly.

'Of course!' said Madame. 'I must do as she tells me.'

'Why yes, since it is for your good, and not hers.'

'Of course! Of course! It is very kind of her.'

'Miss Houghton is *most* kind—to *everyone*,' said Mr
May.

'I am sure,' said Madame. 'And I am very glad you have
been such a good Kishwégin. That is very nice also.'

'Yes,' replied Mr May. 'I begin to wonder if I have mistaken my vocation. I should have been *on* the boards, instead
of behind them.'

'No doubt,' said Madame. 'But it is a little late—'

The eyes of the foreigners, watching him, flattered Mr
May.

'I'm afraid it is,' he said. 'Yes. Popular taste is a mysterious
thing. How do you feel, now? Do you feel they appreciate
your work as much as they did?'

Madame watched him with her black eyes.

'No,' she replied. 'They don't. The pictures are driving us
away. Perhaps we shall last for ten years more. And after
that, we are finished.'

'You think so,' said Mr May, looking serious.

'I am sure,' she said, nodding sagely.

'But why is it?' said Mr May, angry and petulant.

'Why is it? I don't know. I don't know. The pictures are
cheap, and they are easy, and they cost the audience nothing,
no feeling of the heart, no appreciation of the spirit, cost
them nothing of these. And so they like them, and they
don't like us, because they must *feel* the things we do, from
the heart, and appreciate them from the spirit. There?'

'And they don't want to appreciate and to feel?' said Mr
May.

'No. They don't want. They want it all through the eye
and finished—so! Just curiosity, impertinent curiosity
That's all. In all countries, the same. And so—in ten years
time—no more Kishwégin at all.'

'No. Then what future have you?' said Mr May gloomily

'I may be dead—who knows? If not, I shall have my littl
apartment in Lausanne, or in Bellinzona, and I shall be a
bourgeoise once more, and the good Catholic which I am.'

'Which I am also,' said Mr May.

'So! Are you? An American Catholic?'

'Well—English—Irish—American.'

'So?'

Mr May never felt more gloomy in his life than he did
that day. Where, finally, was he to rest his troubled head?

There was not all peace in the Natcha-Kee-Tawara group
either. For Thursday, there was to be a change of programme—'Kishwégin's Wedding' (with the white prisoner
be it said) was to take the place of the previous scene. Max
of course was the director of the rehearsal. Madame would
not come near the theatre when she herself was not to be
acting.

Though very quiet and unobtrusive as a rule, Max could
suddenly assume an air of *hauteur* and overbearing which
was really very annoying. Geoffrey always fumed under it
But Cicio it put into unholy, ungovernable tempers. For
Max, suddenly, would reveal his contempt of the Eyetalian
as he called Cicio, using the Cockney word.

'*Bah! quelle tête de veau,*' said Max, suddenly contemptuous and angry because Cicio, who really was slow at taking in the things said to him, had once more failed to
understand.

'*Comment?*' queried Cicio, in his slow, derisive way.

'*Comment!*' sneered Max, in echo. '*What? What?* Why
what *did* I say? Calf's-head I said. Pig's-head, if that seems
more suitable to you.'

'To whom? To me or to you?' said Cicio, sidling up.

'To you, lout of an Italian.'

Max's colour was up, he held himself erect, his brown hair

seemed to rise erect from his forehead, his blue eyes glared fierce.

'That is to say, to me, from an uncivilized German pig, ah? Ah?'

All this in French. Alvina, as she sat at the piano, saw Max tall and blanched with anger; Cicio with his neck stuck out, oblivious and convulsed with rage, stretching his neck at Max. All were in ordinary dress, but without coats, acting in their shirt-sleeves. Cicio was clutching a property knife.

'Now! None of that! None of that!' said Mr May, peremptory. But Cicio, stretching forward taut and immobile with rage, was quite unconscious. His hand was fast on his stage knife.

'A dirty Eyetalian,' said Max, in English, turning to Mr May. 'They understand nothing.'

But the last word was smothered in Cicio's spring and stab. Max half-started on to his guard, received the blow on his collar-bone, near the pommel of the shoulder, reeled round on top of Mr May, whilst Cicio sprang like a cat down from the stage and bounded across the theatre and out of the door, leaving the knife rattling on the boards behind him. Max recovered and sprang like a demon, white with rage, straight out into the theatre after him.

'Stop—stop—!' cried Mr May.

'*Halte, Max! Max, Max, attends!*' cried Louis and Geoffrey, as Louis sprang down after his friend. Thud went the boards again, with the spring of a man.

Alvina, who had been seated waiting at the piano below, started up and overturned her chair as Cicio rushed past her. Now Max, white, with set blue eyes, was upon her.

'Don't—!' she cried, lifting her hand to stop his progress. He saw her, swerved, and hesitated, turned to leap over the seats and avoid her, when Louis caught him and flung his arms round him.

'*Max—attends, ami! Laisse-le partir. Max, tu sais que je t'aime. Tu le sais, ami. Tu le sais. Laisse-le partir.*'

Max and Louis wrestled together in the gangway, Max looking down with hate on his friend. But Louis was determined also, he wrestled as fiercely as Max, and at last the latter began to yield. He was panting and beside himself. Louis still held him by the hand and by the arm.

'Let him go, brother, he isn't worth it. What does he understand, Max, dear brother, what does he understand? These fellows from the south, they are half children, half animal. They don't know what they are doing. Has he hurt you, dear friend? Has he hurt you? It was a dummy knife, but it was a heavy blow—the dog of an Italian. Let us see.'

So gradually Max was brought to stand still. From under the edge of his waistcoat, on the shoulder, the blood was already staining the shirt.

'Are you cut, brother, brother?' said Louis. 'Let us see.'

Max now moved his arm with pain. They took off his waistcoat and pushed back his shirt. A nasty blackening wound, with the skin broken.

'If the bone isn't broken!' said Louis anxiously. 'If the bone isn't broken! Lift thy arm, frère—lift. It hurts you—so—No—no—it is not broken—no—the bone is not broken.'

'There is no bone broken, I know,' said Max.

'The animal. He hasn't done *that*, at least.'

'Where do you imagine he's gone?' asked Mr May.

The foreigners shrugged their shoulders, and paid no heed. There was no more rehearsal.

'We had best go home and speak to Madame,' said Mr May, who was very frightened for his evening performance.

They locked up the Endeavour. Alvina was thinking of Cicio. He was gone in his shirt-sleeves. She had taken his jacket and hat from the dressing-room at the back, and carried them under her raincoat, which she had on her arm.

Madame was in a state of perturbation. She had heard someone come in at the back, and go upstairs, and go out again. Mrs Rollings had told her it was the Italian, who had come in in his shirt-sleeves and gone out in his black coat and black hat, taking his bicycle, without saying a word. Poor Madame! She was struggling into her shoes, she had her hat on, when the others arrived.

'What is it?' she cried.

She heard a hurried explanation from Louis.

'Ah, the animal, the animal, he wasn't worth all my pains!'

cried poor Madame, sitting with one shoe off and one shoe on. 'Why, Max, why didst thou not remain man enough to control that insulting mountain temper of thine? Have I not said, and said, and said that in the Natcha-Kee-Tawara there was but one nation, the Red Indian, and but one tribe, the tribe of Kishwe? And now thou hast called him a dirty Italian, or a dog of an Italian, and he has behaved like an animal. Too much, too much of an animal, too little *esprit*. But thou, Max, art almost as bad. Thy temper is a devil's, which maybe is worse than an animal's. Ah, this Woodhouse, a curse is on it, I know it is. Would we were away from it. Will the week never pass? We shall have to find Cicio. Without him the company is ruined—until I get a substitute. I must get a substitute. And how?—and where?—in this country?—tell me that. I am tired of Natcha-Kee-Tawara. There is no true tribe of Kishwe—no, never. I have had enough of Natcha-Kee-Tawara. Let us break up, let us part, *mes braves*, let us say adieu here in this *funeste* Woodhouse.'

'Oh, Madame, dear Madame,' said Louis, 'let us hope. Let us swear a closer fidelity, dear Madame, our Kishwégin. Let us never part. Max, thou dost not want to part, brother, well-loved? Thou dost not want to part, brother whom I love? And thou, Geoffrey, thou—'

Madame burst into tears, Louis wept too, even Max turned aside his face, with tears. Alvina stole out of the room, followed by Mr May.

In a while Madame came out to them.

'Oh,' she said. 'You have not gone away! We are wondering which way Cicio will have gone, on to Knarborough or to Marchay. Geoffrey will go on his bicycle to find him. But shall it be to Knarborough or to Marchay?'

'Ask the policeman in the market-place,' said Alvina. 'He's sure to have noticed him, because Cicio's yellow bicycle is so uncommon.'

Mr May tripped out on this errand, while the others discussed among themselves where Cicio might be.

Mr May returned, and said that Cicio had ridden off down the Knarborough Road. It was raining slightly.

'Ah!' said Madame. 'And now how to find him, in that great town. I am afraid he will leave us without pity.'

'Surely he will want to speak to Geoffrey before he goes,' said Louis. 'They always were good friends.'

They all looked at Geoffrey. He shrugged his broad shoulders.

'Always good friends,' he said. 'Yes. He will perhaps wait for me at his cousin's in Battersea. In Knarborough, I don't know.'

'How much money had he?' asked Mr May.

Madame spread her hands and lifted her shoulders.

'Who knows?' she said.

'These Italians,' said Louis, turning to Mr May. 'They have always money. In another country, they will not spend one sou if they can help. They are like this—' And he made the Neapolitan gesture drawing in the air with his fingers.

'But would he abandon you all without a word?' cried Mr May.

'Yes! Yes!' said Madame, with a sort of stoic pathos. '*He* would. He alone would do such a thing. But he would do it.'

'And what point would he make for?'

'What point? You mean where would he go? To Battersea, no doubt, to his cousin—and then to Italy, if he thinks he has saved enough money to buy land, or whatever it is.'

'And so good-bye to him,' said Mr May bitterly.

'Geoffrey ought to know,' said Madame, looking at Geoffrey.

Geoffrey shrugged his shoulders, and would not give his comrade away.

'No,' he said. 'I don't know. He will leave a message at Battersea, I know. But I don't know if he will go to Italy.'

'And you don't know where to find him in Knarborough?' asked Mr May, sharply, very much on the spot.

'No—I don't. Perhaps at the station he will go by train to London.' It was evident Geoffrey was not going to help Mr May.

'*Alors!*' said Madame, cutting through this futility. 'Go thou to Knarborough, Geoffrey, and see—and be back at the theatre for work. Go now. And if thou canst find him, bring him again to us. Tell him to come out of kindness to me. Tell him.'

And she waved the young man away. He departed on his nine-mile ride through the rain to Knarborough.

'They know,' said Madame. 'They know each other's places. It is a little more than a year since we came to Knarborough. But they will remember.'

Geoffrey rode swiftly as possible through the mud. He did not care very much whether he found his friend or not. He liked the Italian, but he never looked on him as a permanency. He knew Cicio was dissatisfied, and wanted a change. He knew that Italy was pulling him away from the troupe, with which he had been associated now for three years or more. And the Swiss from Martigny knew that the Neapolitan would go, breaking all ties, one day suddenly back to Italy. It was so, and Geoffrey was philosophical about it.

He rode into town, and the first thing he did was to seek out the music-hall artistes at their lodgings. He knew a good many of them. They gave him a welcome and a whisky—but none of them had seen Cicio. They sent him off to other artistes, other lodging-houses. He went the round of associates known and unknown, of lodgings strange and familiar, of third-rate possible public houses. Then he went to the Italians down in the Marsh—he knew these people always ask for one another. And then, hurrying, he dashed to the Midland Station, and then to the Great Central Station, asking the porters on the London departure platform if they had seen his pal, a man with a yellow bicycle, and a black bicycle cape. All to no purpose.

Geoffrey hurriedly lit his lamp and swung off in the dark back to Woodhouse. He was a powerfully built, imperturbable fellow. He pressed slowly uphill through the streets, then ran downhill into the darkness of the industrial country. He had continually to cross the new tram-lines, which were awkward, and he had occasionally to dodge the brilliantly-illuminated tram-cars which threaded their way across-country through so much darkness. All the time it rained, and his back wheel slipped under him, in the mud and on the new tram-track.

As he pressed in the long darkness that lay between Slaters Mill and Durbeyhouses, he saw a light ahead—another cy-

clist. He moved to his side of the road. The light approached
very fast. It was a strong acetylene flare. He watched it. A
flash and a splash and he saw the humped back of what was
probably Cicio going by at a great pace on the low racing
machine.

'Hi Cic—! Cicio!' he yelled, dropping off his own bicycle.

'Ha-er-er!' he heard the answering shout, unmistakably
Italian, way down the darkness.

He turned—saw the other cyclist had stopped. The flare
swung round, and Cicio softly rode up. He dropped off
beside Geoffrey.

'*Toi!*' said Cicio.

'*Hé! Où vas-tu?*'

'*Hé!*' ejaculated Cicio.

Their conversation consisted a good deal in noises vari-
ously ejaculated.

'Coming back?' asked Geoffrey.

'Where've you been?' retorted Cicio.

'Knarborough—looking for thee. Where have you—?'

'Buckled my front wheel at Durbeyhouses.'

'Come off?'

'*Hé!*'

'Hurt?'

'Nothing.'

'Max is all right.'

'*Merde!*'

'Come on, come back with me.'

'Nay.' Cicio shook his head.

'Madame's crying. Wants thee to come back.'

Cicio shook his head.

'Come on, Cic'—' said Geoffrey.

Cicio shook his head.

'Never?' said Geoffrey.

'*Basta*—had enough,' said Cicio, with an invisible grimace.

'Come for a bit, and we'll clear together.'

Cicio again shook his head.

'What, is it adieu?'

Cicio did not speak.

'Don't go, comrade,' said Geoffrey.

'*Faut*,' said Cicio, slightly derisive.

'*Eh alors!* I'd like to come with thee. What?'

'Where?'

'Doesn't matter. Thou'rt going to Italy?'

'Who knows!—seems so.'

'I'd like to go back.'

'*Eh alors!*' Cicio half veered round.

'Wait for me a few days,' said Geoffrey.

'Where?'

'See you to-morrow in Knarborough. Go to Mrs Pym's 6 Hampden Street. Gettiventi is there. Right, eh?'

'I'll think about it.'

'Eleven o'clock, eh?'

'I'll think about it.'

'Friends ever—Cicio—eh?' Geoffrey held out his hand.

Cicio slowly took it. The two men leaned to each other and kissed farewell, on either cheek.

'To-morrow, Cic'—'

'*Au revoir, Gigi.*'

Cicio dropped on to his bicycle and was gone in a breath. Geoffrey waited a moment for a tram which was rushing brilliantly up to him in the rain. Then he mounted and rode in the opposite direction. He went straight down to Lumley, and Madame had to remain on tenterhooks till ten o'clock.

She heard the news, and said:

'To-morrow I go to fetch him.' And with this she went to bed.

In the morning she was up betimes, sending a note to Alvina. Alvina appeared at nine o'clock.

'You will come with me?' said Madame. 'Come. Together we will go to Knarborough and bring back the naughty Cicio. Come with me, because I haven't all my strength. Yes, you will? Good! Good! Let us tell the young men, and we will go now, on the tram-car.'

'But I am not properly dressed,' said Alvina.

'Who will see?' said Madame. 'Come, let us go.'

They told Geoffrey they would meet him at the corner of Hampden Street at five minutes to eleven.

'You see,' said Madame to Alvina, 'they are very funny, these young men, particularly Italians. You must never let them think you have caught them. Perhaps he will not let us see him—who knows? Perhaps he will go off to Italy all the same.'

They sat in the bumping tram-car, a long and wearying journey. And then they tramped the dreary, hideous streets of the manufacturing town. At the corner of the street they waited for Geoffrey who rode up muddily on his bicycle.

'Ask Cicio to come out to us, and we will go and drink coffee at the Geisha Restaurant—or tea or something,' said Madame.

Again the two women waited wearily at the street-end. At last Geoffrey returned, shaking his head.

'He won't come?' cried Madame.

'No.'

'He says he is going back to Italy?'

'To London.'

'It is the same. You can never trust them. Is he quite obstinate?'

Geoffrey lifted his shoulders. Madame could see the beginnings of defection in him too. And she was tired and dispirited.

'We shall have to finish the Natcha-Kee-Tawara, that is all,' she said fretfully.

Geoffrey watched her stolidly, impassively.

'Dost thou want to go with him?' she asked suddenly.

Geoffrey smiled sheepishly, and his colour deepened. But he did not speak.

'Go then—' she said. 'Go then! Go with him! But for the sake of my honour, finish this week at Woodhouse. Can I make Miss Houghton's father lose these two nights? Where is your shame? Finish this week, and then go, go—But finish this week. Tell Francesco that. I have finished with him. But let him finish this engagement. Don't put me to shame, don't destroy my honour, and the honour of the Natcha-Kee-Tawara. Tell him that.'

Geoffrey turned again into the house. Madame, in her chic little black hat and spotted veil, and her trim black coat-and-skirt, stood there at the street-corner staring before her, shivering a little with cold, but saying no word of any sort.

Again Geoffrey appeared out of the doorway. His face was impassive.

'He says he doesn't want,' he said.

'Ah!' she cried suddenly in French, 'the ungrateful, the animal! He shall suffer. See if he shall not suffer. The low canaille, without faith or feeling. My Max, thou wert right. Ah, such canaille should be beaten, as dogs are beaten, till they follow at heel. Will no one beat him for me, no one? Yes. Go back. Tell him before he leaves England he shall feel the hand of Kishwégin, and it shall be heavier than the Black Hand. Tell him that, the coward, that causes a woman's word to be broken against her will. Ah, canaille, canaille! Neither faith nor feeling, neither faith nor feeling. Trust them not, dogs of the south.' She took a few agitated steps down the pavement. Then she raised her veil to wipe away her tears of anger and bitter disappointment.

'Wait a bit,' said Alvina. 'I'll go.' She was touched.

'No. Don't you!' cried Madame.

'Yes, I will,' she said. The light of battle was in her eyes. 'You'll come with me to the door,' she said to Geoffrey.

Geoffrey started obediently, and led the way up a long narrow stair, covered with yellow-and-brown oilcloth, rather worn, on to the top of the house.

'Cicio,' he said, outside the door.

'*Oui!*' came the surly voice of Cicio.

Geoffrey opened the door. Cicio was sitting on a narrow bed, in a rather poor attic, under the steep slope of the roof.

'Don't come in,' said Alvina to Geoffrey, looking over her shoulder at him as she entered. Then she closed the door, behind her, and stood with her back to it, facing the Italian. He sat loose on the bed, a cigarette between his fingers, dropping ash on the bare boards between his feet. He looked up curiously at Alvina. She stood watching him with wide, bright blue eyes, smiling slightly, and saying nothing. He looked up at her steadily on his guard, from under his long black lashes.

'Won't you come?' she said, smiling and looking into his eyes. He flicked off the ash of his cigarette with his little finger. She wondered why he wore the nail of his little finger

so long, so very long. Still she smiled at him, and still he
gave no sign.

'Do come!' she urged, never taking her eyes from him.

He made not the slightest movement, but sat with his
hands dropped between his knees, watching her, the cigarette wavering up its blue thread of smoke.

'Won't you?' she said, as she stood with her back to the
door. 'Won't you come?' She smiled strangely and vividly.

Suddenly she took a pace forward, stooped, watching his
face as if timidly, caught his brown hand in her own, and
lifted it towards herself. His hand started, dropped the cigarette, but was not withdrawn.

'You will come, won't you?' she said, smiling gently into
his strange, watchful yellow eyes, that looked fixedly into
hers, the dark pupil opening round and softening. She smiled
into his softening round eyes, the eyes of some animal which
stares in one of its silent, gentler moments. And suddenly
she kissed his hand, kissed it twice, quickly, on the fingers
and the back. He wore a silver ring. Even as she kissed his
fingers with her lips, the silver ring seemed to her a symbol
of his subjection, inferiority. She drew his hand slightly.
And he rose to his feet.

She turned round and took the door-handle, still holding
his fingers in her left hand.

'You are coming, aren't you?' she said, looking over her
shoulder into his eyes. And taking consent from his un-
changing eyes, she let go his hand and slightly opened the
door. He turned slowly, and taking his coat from a nail,
slung it over his shoulders and drew it on. Then he picked
up his hat, and put his foot on his half-smoked cigarette,
which lay smoking still. He followed her out of the room,
walking with his head rather forward, in the half-loutish,
sensual-subjected way of the Italians.

As they entered the street, they saw the trim, French figure of Madame standing alone, as if abandoned. Her face
was very white under her spotted veil, her eyes very black.
She watched Cicio following behind Alvina in his dark,
hang-dog fashion, and she did not move a muscle until he
came to a standstill in front of her. She was watching his
face.

'*Te voilà donc!*' she said without expression. '*Allons boire un café, hé?* Let us go and drink some coffee.' She had now put an inflection of tenderness into her voice. But her eyes were black with anger. Cicio smiled slowly, the slow, fine, stupid smile, and turned to walk alongside.

Madame said nothing as they went. Geoffrey passed on his bicycle, calling out that he would go straight to Woodhouse.

When the three sat with their cups of coffee, Madame pushed up her veil just above her eyes, so that it was a black band above her brows. Her face was pale and full like a child's, but almost stonily expressionless, her eyes were black and inscrutable. She watched both Cicio and Alvina with her black, inscrutable looks.

'Would you like also biscuits with your coffee, the two of you?' she said, with an amiable intonation which her strange black looks belied.

'Yes,' said Alvina. She was a little flushed, as if defiant, while Cicio sat sheepishly, turning aside ducked head, the slow, stupid, yet fine smile on his lips.

'And no more trouble with Max, *hein?*—you Cicio?' said Madame, still with the amiable intonation and the same black, watching eyes. 'No more of these stupid scenes, *bein?* What? Do you answer me.'

'No more from me,' he said, looking up at her with a narrowed, cat-like look in his derisive eyes.

'Ho? No? No more? Good then! It is good! We are glad, aren't we, Miss Houghton, that Cicio has come back and there are to be no more rows?—*bein?*—aren't we?'

'*I'm* awfully glad,' said Alvina.

'Awfully glad—yes—awfully glad! You hear, you Cicio. And you remember another time. What? Don't you? *Hé?*'

He looked up at her, the slow, derisive smile curling his lips.

'Sure,' he said slowly, with subtle intonation.

'Yes. Good! Well then! Well then! We are all friends. We are all friends, aren't we, all the Natcha-Kee-Tawaras? *Hé?* What do you think? What you say?'

'Yes,' said Cicio, again looking up at her with his yellow, glinting eyes.

'All right! All right then! It is all right—forgotten—' Madame sounded quite frank and restored. But the sullen watchfulness in her eyes, and the narrowed look in Cicio's, as he glanced at her, showed another state behind the obviousness of the words. 'And Miss Houghton is one of us! Yes? She has united us once more, and so she has become one of us.' Madame smiled strangely from her blank, round white face.

'I should love to be one of the Natcha-Kee-Tawaras,' said Alvina.

'Yes—well—why not? Why not become one? Why not? What you say, Cicio? You can play the piano, perhaps do other things. Perhaps better than Kishwégin. What you say, Cicio, should she not join us? Is she not one of us?'

He smiled and showed his teeth, but did not answer.

'Well, what is it? Say then? Shall she not?'

'Yes,' said Cicio, unwilling to commit himself.

'Yes, so I say! So I say. Quite a good idea! We will think of it, and speak perhaps to your father, and you shall come! Yes.'

So the two women returned to Woodhouse by the tram-car, while Cicio rode home on his bicycle. It was surprising how little Madame and Alvina found to say to one another.

Madame effected the reunion of her troupe, and all seemed pretty much as before. She had decided to dance the next night, the Saturday night. On Sunday the party would leave for Warsall, about thirty miles away, to fulfil their next engagement.

That evening Cicio, whenever he had a moment to spare, watched Alvina. She knew it. But she could not make out what his watching meant. In the same way he might have watched a serpent, had he found one gliding in the theatre. He looked at her sideways, furtively, but persistently. And yet he did not want to meet her glance. He avoided her, and watched her. As she saw him standing in his negligent, muscular, slouching fashion, with his head dropped forward, and his eyes sideways, sometimes she disliked him. But there was a sort of *finesse* about his face. His skin was delicately tawny and slightly lustrous. The eyes were set in so dark, that one expected them to be black and flashing. And then one met the yellow pupils, sulphurous and remote. It was like meeting a lion. His long, fine nose, his rather long, rounded chin and curling lips seemed refined through ages of forgotten culture. He was waiting: silent there, with something muscular and remote about his very droop, he was waiting. What for? Alvina could not guess. She wanted to meet his eye, to have an open understanding with him. But he would not. When she went up to talk to him, he answered in his stupid fashion, with a smile of the mouth and no change of the eyes, saying nothing at all. Obstinately he held away from her. When he was in his war-paint, for one moment she hated his muscular, handsome, downward-drooping torso: so stupid and full. The fine sharp upright-ness of Max seemed much finer, clearer, more manly. Cicio's velvety sauve heaviness, the very heave of his muscles, so full and softly powerful, sickened her.

She flashed away angrily on her piano. Madame, who was dancing Kishwégin on the last evening, cast sharp glances at her. Alvina had avoided Madame as Cicio had avoided Alvina—elusive and yet conscious, a distance, and yet a connection.

Madame danced beautifully. No denying it, she was an artist. She became something quite different: fresh, virginal, pristine, a magic creature flickering there. She was infinitely delicate and attractive. Her *braves* became glamorous and heroic at once, and magically she cast her spell over them. It was all very well for Alvina to bang the piano crossly. She could not put out the glow which surrounded Kishwégin and her troupe. Cicio was handsome now: without war-paint, and roused, fearless and at the same time suggestive, a dark, mysterious glamour on his face, passionate and re-mote. A stranger—and so beautiful. Alvina flashed at the piano, almost in tears. She hated his beauty. It shut her apart. She had nothing to do with it.

Madame, with her long dark hair hanging in finely-brushed tresses, her cheek burning under its dusky stain, was another creature. How soft she was on her feet. How humble and remote she seemed, as across a chasm from the men. How submissive she was, with an eternity of inacces-sible submission. Her hovering dance round the dead bear

was exquisite: her dark, secretive curiosity, her admiration
of the massive, male strength of the creature, her quivers of
triumph over the dead beast, her cruel exultation, and her
fear that he was not really dead. It was a lovely sight, suggesting the world's morning, before Eve had bitten any
white-fleshed apple, whilst she was still dusky, dark-eyed,
and still. And then her stealthy sympathy with the white
prisoner! Now indeed she was the dusky Eve tempted into
knowledge. Her fascination was ruthless. She kneeled by the
dead *brave,* her husband, as she had knelt by the bear: in
fear and admiration and doubt and exultation. She gave him
the least little push with her foot. Dead meat like the bear!
And a flash of delight went over her, that changed into a
sob of mortal anguish. And then, flickering, wicked, doubtful, she watched Cicio wrestling with the bear.

She was the clue to all the action, was Kishwégin. And
her dark *braves* seemed to become darker, more secret, malevolent, burning with a cruel fire, and at the same time wistful, knowing their end. Cicio laughed in a strange way, as
he wrestled with the bear, as he had never laughed on the
previous evenings. The sound went out into the audience, a
soft, malevolent, derisive sound. And when the bear was
supposed to have crushed him, and he was to have fallen,
he reeled out of the bear's arms and said to Madame, in his
derisive voice:

'*Vivo sempre,* Madame.' And then he fell.

Madame stopped as if shot, hearing his words: 'I am still
alive, Madame.' She remained suspended motionless, suddenly wilted. Then all at once her hand went to her mouth
with a scream:

'The Bear!'

So the scene concluded itself. But instead of the tender,
half-wistful triumph of Kishwégin, a triumph electric as it
should have been when she took the white man's hand and
kissed it, there was a doubt, a hesitancy, a nullity, and Max
did not quite know what to do.

After the performance, neither Madame nor Max dared
say anything to Cicio about his innovation into the play.
Louis felt he had to speak—it was left to him.

'I say, Cic'—' he said, 'why did you change the scene? It

might have spoiled everything if Madame wasn't such a genius. Why did you say that?'

'Why,' said Cicio, answering Louis's French in Italian, 'I am tired of being dead, you see.'

Madame and Max heard in silence.

When Alvina had played *God Save the King* she went round behind the stage. But Cicio and Geoffrey had already packed up the property, and left. Madame was talking to James Houghton. Louis and Max were busy together. Mr May came to Alvina.

'Well,' he said. 'That closes another week. I think we've done very well in face of difficulties, don't you?'

'Wonderfully,' she said.

But poor Mr May spoke and looked pathetically. He seemed to feel forlorn. Alvina was not attending to him. Her eye was roving. She took no notice of him.

Madame came up.

'Well, Miss Houghton,' she said, 'time to say good-bye, I suppose.'

'How do you feel after dancing?' asked Alvina.

'Well—not so strong as usual—but not so bad, you know. I shall be all right—thanks to you. I think your father is more ill than I. To me he looks very ill.'

'Father wears himself away,' said Alvina.

'Yes, and when we are no longer young, there is not so much to wear. Well, I must thank you once more—'

'What time do you leave in the morning?'

'By the train at half-past ten. If it doesn't rain, the young men will cycle—perhaps all of them. Then they will go when they like—'

'I will come round to say good-bye—' said Alvina.

'Oh no—don't disturb yourself—'

'Yes, I want to take home the things—the kettle for the bronchitis, and those things—'

'Oh, thank you very much—but don't trouble yourself. I will send Cicio with them—or one of the others—'

'I should like to say good-bye to you all,' persisted Alvina.

Madame glanced round at Max and Louis.

'Are we not all here? No. The two have gone. No! Well! Well what time will you come?'

'About nine?'

'Very well, and I leave at ten. Very well. Then *au revoir* till the morning. Good-night.'

'Good-night,' said Alvina. Her colour was rather flushed.

She walked up with Mr May, and hardly noticed he was there. After supper, when James Houghton had gone up to count his pennies, Alvina said to Miss Pinnegar:

'Don't you think father looks rather seedy, Miss Pinnegar?'

'I've been thinking so a long time,' said Miss Pinnegar tartly.

'What do you think he ought to do?'

'He's killing himself down there, in all weathers and freezing in that box-office, and then the bad atmosphere. He's killing himself, that's all.'

'What can we do?'

'Nothing so long as there's that place down there. Nothing at all.'

Alvina thought so too. So she went to bed.

She was up in time, and watching the clock. It was a grey morning, but not raining. At five minutes to nine, she hurried off to Mrs Rollins. In the back yard the bicycles were out, glittering and muddy according to their owners. Cicio was crouching mending a tyre, crouching balanced on his toes, near the earth. He turned like a quick-eared animal glancing as she approached, but did not rise.

'Are you getting ready to go?' she said, looking down at him. He screwed his head round to her unwillingly, upside down, his chin tilted up at her. She did not know him thus inverted. Her eyes rested on his face, puzzled. His chin seemed so large, aggressive. He was a little bit repellant and brutal, inverted. Yet she continued:

'Would you help me to carry back the things we brought for Madame?'

He rose to his feet, but did not look at her. He was wearing broken cycling shoes. He stood looking at his bicycle tube.

'Not just yet,' she said. 'I want to say good-bye to Madame. Will you come in half an hour?'

'Yes, I will come,' he said, still watching his bicycle tube, which sprawled nakedly on the floor. The forward drop of his head was curiously beautiful to her, the straight, powerful nape of the neck, the delicate shape of the back of the head, the black hair. The way the neck sprang from the strong, loose shoulders was beautiful. There was something mindless but *intent* about the forward reach of his head. His face seemed colourless, neutral-tinted and expressionless.

She went indoors. The young men were moving about making preparations.

'Come upstairs, Miss Houghton!' called Madame's voice from above. Alvina mounted, to find Madame packing.

'It is an uneasy moment, when we are busy to move,' said Madame, looking up at Alvina as if she were a stranger.

'I'm afraid I'm in the way. But I won't stay a minute.'

'Oh, it is all right. Here are the things you brought—' Madame indicated a little pile—'and thank you *very* much, *very* much. I feel you saved my life. And now let me give you one little token of my gratitude. It is not much, because we are not millionaires in the Natcha-Kee-Tawara. Just a little remembrance of our troublesome visit to Woodhouse.'

She presented Alvina with a pair of exquisite bead mocassins, woven in a weird, lovely pattern, with soft deerskin soles and sides.

'They belong to Kishwégin, so it is Kishwégin who gives them to you, because she is grateful to you for saving her life, or at least from a long illness.'

'Oh—but I don't want to take them—' said Alvina.

'You don't like them? Why?'

'I think they're lovely, lovely! But I don't want to take them from you—'

'If I give them, you do not take them from me. You receive them. *Hé!*' And Madame pressed back the slippers, opening her plump jewelled hands in a gesture of finality.

'But I don't like to take *these,*' said Alvina. 'I feel they belong to Natcha-Kee-Tawara. And I don't want to rob Natcha-Kee-Tawara, do I? Do take them back.'

'No, I have given them. You cannot rob Natcha-Kee-Tawara in taking a pair of shoes—impossible!'

'And I'm sure they are much too small for me.'

'Ha!' exclaimed Madame. 'It is that! Try.'

'I know they are,' said Alvina, laughing confusedly.

She sat down and took off her own shoe. The mocassin was a little too short—just a little. But it was charming on the foot, charming.

'Yes,' said Madame. 'It is too short. Very well. I must find you something else.'

'Please don't,' said Alvina. 'Please don't find me anything. I don't want anything. Please!'

'What?' said Madame, eyeing her closely. 'You don't want? Why? You don't want anything from Natcha-Kee-Tawara, or from Kishwégin? *Hé?* From which?'

'Don't give me anything, please,' said Alvina.

'All right! All right, then. I won't. I won't give you anything. I can't give you anything you want from Natcha-Kee-Tawara.'

And Madame busied herself again with the packing.

'I'm awfully sorry you are going,' said Alvina.

'Sorry? Why? Yes, so am I sorry we shan't see you any more. Yes, so I am. But perhaps we shall see you another time—*Hé?* I shall send you a post-card. Perhaps I shall send one of the young men on his bicycle to bring you something which I shall buy for you. Yes? Shall I?'

'Oh! I should be awfully glad—but don't buy—' Alvina checked herself in time. 'Don't buy anything. Send me a little thing from Natcha-Kee-Tawara. I *love* the slippers—'

'But they are too small,' said Madame, who had been watching her with black eyes that read every motive. Madame too had her avaricious side, and was glad to get back the slippers. 'Very well—very well, I will do that. I will send you some small thing from Natcha-Kee-Tawara, and one of the young men shall bring it. Perhaps Cicio? *Hé?*'

'Thank you *so* much,' said Alvina, holding out her hand. 'Good-bye. I'm so sorry you're going.'

'Well—well! We are not going so very far. Not so very far. Perhaps we shall see each other another day. It may be. Good-bye!'

Madame took Alvina's hand, and smiled at her winsomely all at once, kindly, from her inscrutable black eyes. A sudden unusual kindness. Alvina flushed with surprise and a desire to cry.

'Yes. I am sorry you are not with Natcha-Kee-Tawara.'

Alvina carried down the things she had to remove. Then she went to say good-bye to the young men, who were in various stages of their toilet. Max alone was quite presentable.

Cicio was just putting on the outer cover of his front tyre. She watched his brown thumbs press it into place. He was quick and sure, much more capable, and even masterful, than you would have supposed, seeing his tawny Mediterranean hands. He spun the wheel round, patting it lightly.

'Is it finished?'

'Yes, I think.' He reached his pump and blew up the tyre. She watched his softly-applied force. What physical, muscular force there was in him. Then he swung round the bicycle, and stood it again on its wheels. After which he quickly folded his tools.

'Will you come now?' she said.

He turned, rubbing his hands together, and drying them on an old cloth. He went into the house, pulled on his coat and his cap, and picked up the things from the table.

'Where are you going?' Max asked.

Cicio jerked his head towards Alvina.

'Oh, allow me to carry them, Miss Houghton. He is not fit—' said Max.

True, Cicio had no collar on, and his shoes were burst.

'I don't mind,' said Alvina hastily. 'He knows where they go. He brought them before.'

'But I will carry them. I am dressed. Allow me—' and he began to take the things. 'You get dressed, Cicio.'

Cicio looked at Alvina.

'Do let Cicio take them,' said Alvina to Max. 'Thank you *ever* so much. But let him take them.'

So Alvina marched off through the Sunday morning streets, with the Italian, who was down at heel and encumbered with an armful of sick-room apparatus. She did not know what to say, and he said nothing.

'We will go in this way,' she said, suddenly opening the hall door. She had unlocked it before she went out, for that entrance was hardly ever used. So she showed the Italian into the sombre drawing-room, with its high black bookshelves with rows and rows of calf-bound volumes, its old red and flowered carpet, its grand piano littered with music. Cicio put down the things as she directed, and stood with his cap in his hands, looking aside.

'Thank you so much,' she said, lingering.

He curled his lips in a faint deprecatory smile.

'Nothing,' he murmured.

His eye had wandered uncomfortably up to a portrait on the wall.

'That was my mother,' said Alvina.

He glanced down at her, but did not answer.

'I am sorry you're going away,' she said nervously. She stood looking up at him with wide blue eyes.

The faint smile grew on the lower part of his face, which he kept averted. Then he looked at her.

'We have to move,' he said, with his eyes watching her reservedly, his mouth twisting with a half-bashful smile.

'Do you like continually going away?' she said, her wide blue eyes fixed on his face.

He nodded slightly.

'We have to do it. I like it.'

What he said meant nothing to him. He now watched her fixedly, with a slightly mocking look, and a reserve he would not relinquish.

'Do you think I shall ever see you again?' she said.

'Should you like—?' he answered, with a sly smile and a faint shrug.

'I should like awfully—' a flush grew on her cheek. She heard Miss Pinnegar's scarcely audible step approaching.

He nodded at her slightly, watching her fixedly, turning up the corners of his eyes slyly, his nose seeming slyly to sharpen.

'All right. Next week, eh? In the morning?'

'Do!' cried Alvina, as Miss Pinnegar came through the door. He glanced quickly over his shoulder.

'Oh!' cried Miss Pinnegar. 'I couldn't imagine who it was.' She eyed the young fellow sharply.

'Couldn't you?' said Alvina. 'We brought back these things.'

'Oh yes. Well—you'd better come into the other room, to the fire,' said Miss Pinnegar.

'I shall go along. Good-bye!' said Cicio, and with a slight bow to Alvina, and a still slighter to Miss Pinnegar, he was out of the room and out of the front door, as if turning tail.

'I suppose they're going this morning,' said Miss Pinnegar.

CHAPTER 9

Alvina becomes Allaye

Alvina wept when the Natchas had gone. She loved them so much, she wanted to be with them. Even Cicio she regarded as only one of the Natchas. She looked forward to his coming as to a visit from the troupe.

How dull the theatre was without them! She was tired of the Endeavour. She wished it did not exist. The rehearsal on the Monday morning bored her terribly. Her father was nervous and irritable. The previous week had tried him sorely. He had worked himself into a state of nervous apprehension such as nothing would have justified, unless perhaps, if the wooden walls of the Endeavour had burnt to the ground, with James inside victimized like another Samson. He had developed a nervous horror of all *artistes*. He did not feel safe for one single moment whilst he depended on a single one of them.

'We shall have to convert into all pictures,' he said in a nervous fever to Mr May. 'Don't make any more engagements after the end of next month's.'

'Really!' said Mr May. 'Really! Have you quite decided?'

'Yes quite! Yes quite!' James fluttered. 'I have written about a new machine, and the supply of films from Chanticlers.'

'Really!' said Mr May. 'Oh well then, in that case—' But he was filled with dismay and chagrin.

'Of cauce,' he said later to Alvina, 'I can't *possibly* stop on if we are nothing but a picture show!' And he arched his blanched and dismal eyelids with ghastly finality.

'Why?' cried Alvina.

'Oh—why?' He was rather ironic. 'Well, it's not my line at *all*. I'm not a *film-operator*.' And he put his head on one side with a grimace of contempt and superiority.

'But you are, as well,' said Alvina.

'Yes, *as well*. But not *only*! You *may* wash the dishes in the scullery. But you're not only the *char*, are you?'

'But is it the same?' cried Alvina.

'Of cauce!' cried Mr May. 'Of *cauce* it's the same.'

Alvina laughed, a little heartlessly, into his pallid, stricken eyes.

'But what will you do?' she asked.

'I shall have to look for something else,' said the injured but dauntless little man. 'There's nothing *else*, is there?'

'Wouldn't you stay on?' she asked.

'I wouldn't think of it. I wouldn't think of it.' He turtled like an injured pigeon.

'Well,' she said, looking laconically into his face: 'It's between you and father—'

'Of *cauce*!' he said. 'Naturally! Where else—!' But his tone was a little spiteful, as if he had rested his last hopes on Alvina.

Alvina went away. She mentioned the coming change to Miss Pinnegar.

'Well,' said Miss Pinnegar, judicious but aloof, 'it's a move in the right direction. But I doubt if it'll do any good.'

'Do you?' said Alvina. 'Why?'

'I don't believe in the place, and I never did,' declared Miss Pinnegar. 'I don't believe any good will come of it.'

'But why?' persisted Alvina. 'What makes you feel so sure about it?'

'I don't know. But that's how I feel. And I have from the first. It was wrong from the first. It was wrong to begin it.'

'But why?' insisted Alvina, laughing.

'Your father had no business to be led into it. He'd no

business to touch this show business. It isn't like him. It doesn't belong to him. He's gone against his own nature and his own life.'

'Oh but,' said Alvina, 'father was a showman even in the shop. He always was. Mother said he was like a showman in a booth.'

Miss Pinnegar was taken aback.

'Well!' she said sharply. 'If *that's* what you've seen in him!'—there was a pause. 'And in that case,' she continued tartly, 'I think some of the showman has come out in his daughter! or show-woman!—which doesn't improve it, to my idea.'

'Why is it any worse?' said Alvina. 'I enjoy it—and so does father.'

'No,' cried Miss Pinnegar. 'There you're wrong! There you make a mistake. It's all against his better nature.'

'Really!' said Alvina, in surprise. 'What a new idea! But which is father's better nature?'

'You may not know it,' said Miss Pinnegar coldly, 'and if so I can never tell you. But that doesn't alter it.' She lapsed into dead silence for a moment. Then suddenly she broke out, vicious and cold: 'He'll go on till he's killed himself, and *then* he'll know.'

The little adverb *then* came whistling across the space like a bullet. It made Alvina pause. Was her father going to die? She reflected. Well, all men must die.

She forgot the question in others that occupied her. First, could she bear it, when the Endeavour was turned into another cheap and nasty film-shop? The strange figures of the *artistes* passing under her observation had really entertained her, week by week. Some weeks they had bored her, some weeks she had detested them, but there was always a chance in the coming week. Think of the Natcha-Kee-Tawaras!

She thought too much of the Natcha-Kee-Tawaras. She knew it. And she tried to force her mind to the contemplation of the new state of things, when she banged at the piano to a set of dithering and boring pictures. There would be her father, herself and Mr May—or a new operator, a new manager. The new manager!—she thought of him for a moment—and thought of the mechanical factory-faced persons who *managed* Wright's and the Woodhouse Empire.

But her mind fell away from this barren study. She was obsessed by the Natcha-Kee-Tawaras. They seemed to have fascinated her. Which of them it was, or what it was that had cast the spell over her, she did not know. But she was as if hypnotized. She longed to be with them. Her soul gravitated towards them all the time.

Monday passed, and Cicio did not come: Tuesday passed: and Wednesday. In her soul she was sceptical of their keeping their promise—either Madame or Cicio. Why should they keep their promise? She knew what these nomadic *artistes* were. And her soul was stubborn within her.

On Wednesday night there was another sensation at the Endeavour. Mr May found James Houghton fainting in the box-office, after the performance had begun. What to do? He could not interrupt Alvina, nor the performance. He sent the chocolate-and-orange boy across to the Pear Tree for brandy.

James revived. 'I'm all right,' he said, in a brittle fashion. 'I'm all right. Don't bother.' So he sat with his head on his hand in the box-office, and Mr May had to leave him to operate the film.

When the interval arrived, Mr May hurried to the box-office, a narrow hole that James could just sit in, and there he found the invalid in the same posture, semi-conscious. He gave him more brandy.

'I'm all right, I tell you,' said James, his eyes flaring. 'Leave me alone.' But he looked anything but all right.

Mr May hurried for Alvina. When the daughter entered the ticket place, her father was again in a state of torpor.

'Father,' she said, shaking his shoulder gently. 'What's the matter?'

He murmured something, but was incoherent. She looked at his face. It was grey and blank.

'We shall have to get him home,' she said. 'We shall have to get a cab.'

'Give him a little brandy,' said Mr May.

The boy was sent for the cab, James swallowed a spoonful of brandy. He came to himself irritably.

'What? What?' he said. 'I won't have all this fuss. Go on with the performance, there's no need to bother about me.' His eye was wild.

'You must go home, father,' said Alvina.

'Leave me alone! Will you leave me alone! Hectored by women all my life—hectored by women—first one, then another. I won't stand it—I won't stand it—' He looked at Alvina with a look of frenzy as he lapsed again, fell with his head on his hands on his ticket-board. Alvina looked at Mr May.

'We must get him home,' she said. She covered him up with a coat, and sat by him. The performance went on without music.

At last the cab came. James, unconscious, was driven up to Woodhouse. He had to be carried indoors. Alvina hurried ahead to make a light in the dark passage.

'Father's ill!' she announced to Miss Pinnegar.

'Didn't I say so!' said Miss Pinnegar, starting from her chair.

The two women went out to meet the cab-man, who had James in his arms.

'Can you manage?' cried Alvina, showing a light.

'He doesn't weigh much,' said the man.

'Tu-tu-tu-tu-tu-tu-tu!' went Miss Pinnegar's tongue, in a rapid tut-tut of distress. 'What have I said, now,' she exclaimed. 'What have I said all along?'

James was laid on the sofa. His eye was half shut. They made him drink brandy, the boy was sent for the doctor, Alvina's bed was warmed. The sick man was got to bed. And then started another vigil. Alvina sat up in the sick room. James started and muttered, but did not regain consciousness. Dawn came, and he was the same. Pneumonia and pleurisy and a touch of meningitis. Alvina drank her tea, took a little breakfast, and went to bed at about nine o'clock in the morning, leaving James in charge of Miss Pinnegar. Time was all deranged.

Miss Pinnegar was a nervous nurse. She sat in horror and apprehension, her eyebrows raised, starting and looking at James in terror whenever he made a noise. She hurried to

him and did what she could. But one would have said she
was repulsed, she found her task unconsciously repugnant.

During the course of the morning, Mrs Rollings came up
and said that the Italian from last week had come, and could
he speak to Miss Houghton.

'Tell him she's resting, and Mr Houghton is seriously ill,'
said Miss Pinnegar sharply.

When Alvina came downstairs at about four in the afternoon she found a package; a comb of carved bone, and a
message from Madame: 'To Miss Houghton, with kindest
greetings and most sincere thanks from Kishwégin.'

The comb with its carved, beast-faced serpent was her
portion. Alvina asked if there had been any other message.
None.

Mr May came in, and stayed for a dismal half-hour. Then
Alvina went back to her nursing. The patient was no better,
still unconscious. Miss Pinnegar came down, red-eyed and
sullen looking. The condition of James gave little room for
hope.

In the early morning he died. Alvina called Mrs Rollings,
and they composed the body. It was still only five o'clock,
and not light. Alvina went to lie down in her father's little,
rather chilly chamber at the end of the corridor. She tried
to sleep, but could not. At half-past seven she arose, and
started the business of the new day. The doctor came—she
went to the registrar—and so on.

Mr May came. It was decided to keep open the theatre.
He would find someone else for the piano, someone else to
issue the tickets.

In the afternoon arrived Frederick Houghton, James's
cousin and nearest relative. He was a middle-aged, blond,
florid, church-going draper from Knarborough, well-to-do
and very *bourgeois*. He tried to talk to Alvina in a fatherly
fashion, or a friendly, or a helpful fashion. But Alvina could
not listen to him. He got on her nerves.

Hearing the gate bang, she rose and hurried to the window. She was in the drawing-room with her cousin, to give
the interview its proper air of solemnity. She saw Cicio rearing his yellow bicycle against the wall, and going with his

head forward along the narrow, dark way of the back yard, to the scullery door.

'Excuse me a minute,' she said to her cousin, who looked up irritably as she left the room.

She was just in time to open the door as Cicio tapped. She stood on the doorstep above him. He looked up, with a faint smile, from under his black lashes.

'How nice of you to come,' she said. But her face was blanched and tired, without expression. Only her large eyes looked blue in her tiredness, as she glanced down at Cicio. He seemed to her far away.

'Madame asks how is Mr Houghton,' he said.

'Father! He died this morning,' she said quietly.

'He died!' exclaimed the Italian, a flash of fear and dismay going over his face.

'Yes—this morning.' She had neither tears nor emotion, but just looked down on him abstractedly, from her height on the kitchen step. He dropped his eyes and looked at his feet. Then he lifted his eyes again, and looked at her. She looked back at him, as from across a distance. So they watched each other, as strangers across a wide, abstract distance.

He turned and looked down the dark yard, towards the gate where he could just see the pale grey tyre of his bicycle, and the yellow mudguard. He seemed to be reflecting. If he went now, he went for ever. Involuntarily he turned and lifted his face again towards Alvina, as if studying her curiously. She remained there on the door-step, neutral, blanched, with wide, still, neutral eyes. She did not seem to see him. He studied her with alert, yellow-dusky, inscrutable eyes, until she met his look. And then he gave the faintest gesture with his head, as of summons towards him. Her soul started, and died in her. And again he gave the slight, almost imperceptible jerk of the head, backwards and sideways, as if summoning her towards him. His face too was closed and expressionless. But in his eyes, which kept hers, there was a dark flicker of ascendancy. He was going to triumph over her. She knew it. And her soul sank as if it sank out of her body. It sank away out of her body, left her there powerless, soulless.

And yet as he turned, with his head stretched forward, to move away: as he glanced, slightly over his shoulder: she stepped down from the step, down to his level, to follow him. He went ducking along the dark yard, nearly to the gate. Near the gate, near his bicycle, was a corner made by a shed. Here he turned, lingeringly, to her, and she lingered in front of him.

Her eyes were wide and neutral and submissive, with a new, awful submission as if she had lost her soul. So she looked up at him, like a victim. There was a faint smile in his eyes. He stretched forward over her.

'You love me? Yes?—Yes?' he said, in a voice that seemed like a palpable contact on her.

'Yes,' she whispered involuntarily, soulless, like a victim. He put his arm round her, subtly, and lifted her.

'Yes,' he re-echoed, almost mocking in his triumph. 'Yes. Yes!' And smiling, he kissed her, delicately, with a certain finesse of knowledge. She moaned in spirit, in his arms, felt herself dead, dead. And he kissed her with a finesse, a passionate finesse which seemed like coals of fire on her head.

They heard footsteps. Miss Pinnegar was coming to look for her. Cicio set her down, looking long into her eyes, inscrutably, smiling, and said:

'I come to-morrow.'

With which he ducked and ran out of the yard, picking up his bicycle like a feather, and, taking no notice of Miss Pinnegar, letting the yard-door bang to behind him.

'Alvina!' said Miss Pinnegar.

But Alvina did not answer. She turned, slipped past, ran indoors and upstairs to the little bare bedroom she had made her own. She locked the door and kneeled down on the floor, bowing down her head to her knees in a paroxysm on the floor. In a paroxysm—because she loved him. She doubled herself up in a paroxysm on her knees on the floor—because she loved him. It was far more like pain, like agony, than like joy. She swayed herself to and fro in a paroxysm of unbearable sensation, because she loved him.

Miss Pinnegar came and knocked at the door.

'Alvina! Alvina! Oh, you are there! Whatever are you doing? Aren't you coming down to speak to your cousin?'

'Soon,' said Alvina.

And taking a pillow from the bed, she crushed it against herself and swayed herself unconsciously, in her orgasm of unbearable feeling. Right in her bowels she felt it—the terrible, unbearable feeling. How could she bear it?

She crouched over until she became still. A moment of stillness seemed to cover her like sleep: an eternity of sleep in that one second. Then she roused and got up. She went to the mirror, still, evanescent, and tidied her hair, smoothed her face. She was so still, so remote, she felt that nothing, nothing could ever touch her.

And so she went downstairs, to that horrible cousin of her father's. She seemed so intangible, remote and virginal, that her cousin and Miss Pinnegar both failed to make anything of her. She answered their questions simply, but did not talk. They talked to each other. And at last the cousin went away, with a profound dislike of Miss Alvina.

She did not notice. She was only glad he was gone. And she went about for the rest of the day elusive and vague. She slept deeply that night, without dreams.

The next day was Saturday. It came with a great storm of wind and rain and hail: a fury. Alvina looked out in dismay. She knew Cicio would not be able to come—he could not cycle, and it was impossible to get by train and return the same day. She was almost relieved. She was relieved by the intermission of fate, she was thankful for the day of neutrality.

In the early afternoon came a telegram: Coming both tomorrow morning deepest sympathy Madame. To-morrow was Sunday: and the funeral was in the afternoon. Alvina felt a burning inside her, thinking of Cicio. She winced—and yet she wanted him to come. Terribly she wanted him to come.

She showed the telegram to Miss Pinnegar.

'Good gracious!' said the weary Miss Pinnegar. 'Fancy those people. And I warrant they'll want to be at the funeral. As if he was anything to *them*—'

'I think it's very nice of her,' said Alvina.

'Oh well,' said Miss Pinnegar. 'If you think so. I don't fancy he would have wanted such people following, myself.

And what does she mean by *both*. Who's the other?' Miss Pinnegar looked sharply at Alvina.

'Cicio,' said Alvina.

'The Italian! Why goodness me! What's *he* coming for? I can't make you out. Alvina. Is that his name, Chicho? I never heard such a name. Doesn't sound like a name at all to me. There won't be room for them in the cabs.'

'We'll order another.'

'More expense. I never knew such impertinent people—'

But Alvina did not hear her. On the next morning she dressed herself carefully in her new dress. It was black voile. Carefully she did her hair. Cicio and Madame were coming. The thought of Cicio made her shudder. She hung about, waiting. Luckily none of the funeral guests would arrive till after one o'clock. Alvina sat listless, musing, by the fire in the drawing-room. She left everything now to Miss Pinnegar and Mrs Rollings. Miss Pinnegar, red-eyed and yellow-skinned, was irritable beyond words.

It was nearly mid-day when Alvina heard the gate. She hurried to open the front door. Madame was in her little black hat and her black spotted veil, Cicio in a black overcoat was closing the yard-door behind her.

'Oh, my dear girl!' Madame cried, trotting forward with outstretched black-kid hands, one of which held an umbrella: 'I am so shocked—I am so shocked to hear of your poor father. Am I to believe it?—am I really? No, I can't.'

She lifted her veil, kissed Alvina, and dabbed her eyes. Cicio came up the steps. He took off his hat to Alvina, smiled slightly as he passed her. He looked rather pale, constrained. She closed the door and ushered them into the drawing-room.

Madame looked round like a bird, examining the room and the furniture. She was evidently a little impressed. But all the time she was uttering her condolences.

'Tell me, poor girl, how it happened?'

'There isn't much to tell,' said Alvina, and she gave the brief account of James's illness and death.

'Worn out! Worn out!' Madame said, nodding slowly up and down. Her black veil, pushed up, sagged over her brows like a mourning band. 'You cannot afford to waste the stamina. And will you keep on the theatre—with Mr May—?'

Cicio was sitting looking towards the fire. His presence made Alvina tremble. She noticed how the fine black hair of his head showed no parting at all—it grew like a close cap, and was pushed aside at the forehead. Sometimes he looked at her, as Madame talked, and again looked at her, and looked away.

At last Madame came to a halt. There was a long pause.

'You will stay to the funeral?' said Alvina.

'Oh my dear, we shall be too much—'

'No,' said Alvina. 'I have arranged for you—'

'There! You think of everything. But I will come, not Cicio. He will not trouble you.'

Cicio looked up at Alvina.

'I should like him to come,' said Alvina simply. But a deep flush began to mount her face. She did not know where it came from, she felt so cold. And she wanted to cry.

Madame watched her closely.

'*Siamo di accordo,*' came the voice of Cicio.

Alvina and Madame both looked at him. He sat constrained, with his face averted, his eyes dropped, but smiling.

Madame looked closely at Alvina.

'Is it true what he says?' she asked.

'I don't understand him,' said Alvina. 'I don't understand what he said.'

'That you have agreed with him—'

Madame and Cicio both watched Alvina as she sat in her new black dress. Her eyes involuntarily turned to his.

'I don't know,' she said vaguely. 'Have I—?' and she looked at him.

Madame kept silence for some moments. Then she said gravely:

'Well!—yes!—well!' She looked from one to another. 'Well, there is a lot to consider. But if you have decided—'

Neither of them answered. Madame suddenly rose and went to Alvina. She kissed her on either cheek.

'I shall protect you,' she said.

Then she returned to her seat.

'What have you said to Miss Houghton?' she said suddenly to Cicio, tackling him direct, and speaking coldly.

He looked at Madame with a faint derisive smile. Then he turned to Alvina. She bent her head and blushed.

'Speak then,' said Madame, 'you have a reason.' She seemed mistrustful of him.

But he turned aside his face, and refused to speak, sitting as if he were unaware of Madame's presence.

'Oh well,' said Madame, 'I shall be there, Signorino.'

She spoke with a half-playful threat. Cicio curled his lip.

'You do not know him yet,' she said, turning to Alvina.

'I know that,' said Alvina, offended. Then she added: 'Wouldn't you like to take off your hat?'

'If you truly wish me to stay,' said Madame.

'Yes, please do. And will you hang your coat in the hall?' she said to Cicio.

'Oh!' said Madame roughly. 'He will not stay to eat. He will go out to somewhere.'

Alvina looked at him.

'Would you rather?' she said.

He looked at her with sardonic yellow eyes.

'If you want,' he said, the awkward, derisive smile curling his lips and showing his teeth.

She had a moment of sheer panic. Was he just stupid and bestial? The thought went clean through her. His yellow eyes watched her sardonically. It was the clean modelling of his dark, other-world face that decided her—for it sent the deep spasm across her.

'I'd like you to stay,' she said.

A smile of triumph went over his face. Madame watched him stonily as she stood beside the chair, one hand lightly balanced on her hip. Alvina was reminded of Kishwégin. But even in Madame's stony mistrust there was an element of attraction towards him. He had taken his cigarette case from his pocket.

'*On ne fume pas dans le salon,*' said Madame brutally.

'Will you put your coat in the passage?—and do smoke if you wish,' said Alvina.

He rose to his feet and took off his overcoat. His face was obstinate and mocking. He was rather floridly dressed,

though in black, and wore boots of black patent leather with
tan uppers. Handsome he was—but undeniably in bad taste.
The silver ring was still on his finger—and his close, fine,
unparted hair went badly with smart English clothes. He
looked common—Alvina confessed it. And her heart sank.
But what was she to do? He evidently was not happy. Obstinacy made him stick out the situation.

Alvina and Madame went upstairs. Madame wanted to see
the dead James. She looked at his frail, handsome, ethereal
face, and crossed herself as she wept.

'Un bel homme, cependant,' she whispered. 'Mort en un
jour. C'est trop fort, voyez!' And she sniggered with fear
and sobs.

They went down to Alvina's bare room. Madame glanced
round, as she did in every room she entered.

'This was father's bedroom,' said Alvina. 'The other was
mine. He wouldn't have it anything but like this—bare.'

'Nature of a monk, a hermit,' whispered Madame. 'Who
would have thought it! Ah, the men, the men!'

And she unpinned her hat and patted her hair before the
small mirror, into which she had to peep to see herself. Alvina stood waiting.

'And now—' whispered Madame, suddenly turning:
'What about this Cicio, hein?' It was ridiculous that she
would not raise her voice above a whisper, upstairs there.
But so it was.

She scrutinized Alvina with her eyes of bright black glass.
Alvina looked back at her, but did not know what to say.

'What about him, hein? Will you marry him? Why will
you?'

'I suppose because I like him,' said Alvina flushing.

Madame made a little grimace.

'Oh yes!' she whispered, with a contemptuous mouth.
'Oh yes!—because you like him! But you know nothing of
him—nothing. How can you like him, not knowing him?
He may be a real bad character. How would you like him
then?'

'He isn't, is he?' said Alvina.

'I don't know. I don't know. He may be. Even I, I don't
know him—no, though he has been with me for three years.

What is he?—He is a man of the people, a boatman, a labourer, an artist's model. He sticks to nothing—'

'How old is he?' asked Alvina.

'He is twenty-five—a boy only. And you? You are older.'

'Thirty,' confessed Alvina.

'Thirty! Well now—so much difference! How can you trust him? How can you? Why does he want to marry you—why?'

'I don't know—' said Alvina.

'No, and I don't know. But I know something of these Italian men, who are labourers in every country, just labourers and under-men always, always down, down, down—' And Madame pressed her spread palms downwards. 'And so—when they have a chance to come up—' She raised her hand with a spring—'they are very conceited, and they take their chance. He will want to rise, by you, and you will go down, with him. That is how it is. I have seen it before—yes—more than one time—'

'But,' said Alvina, laughing ruefully. 'He can't rise much because of me, can he?'

'How not? How not? In the first place, you are English, and he thinks to rise by that. Then you are not of the lower class, you are of the higher class, the class of the masters, such as employ Cicio and men like him. How will he not rise in the world by you? Yes, he will rise very much. Or he will draw you down, down—Yes, one or another. And then he thinks that now you have money—now your father is dead—' here Madame glanced apprehensively at the closed door—'and they all like money, yes, very much, all Italians—'

'Do they?' said Alvina, scared. 'I'm sure there won't *be* any money. I'm sure father is in debt.'

'What? You think? Do you? Really? Oh poor Miss Houghton! Well—and will you tell Cicio that? *Eh? Hein?*'

'Yes—certainly—if it matters,' said poor Alvina.

'Of course it matters. Of course it matters very much. It matters to him. Because he will not have much. He saves, saves, saves, as they all do, to go back to Italy and buy a piece of land. And if he has you, it will cost him much more, he cannot continue with Natcha-Kee-Tawara. All will be much more difficult—'

'Oh, I will tell him in time,' said Alvina, pale at the lips.

'You will tell him! Yes. That is better. And then you will see. But he is obstinate—as a mule. And if he still will have you, then you must think. Can you live in England as the wife of a labouring man, a dirty Eyetalian, as they all say? It is serious. It is not pleasant for you, you have not known it. I also have not known it. But I have seen—' Alvina watched with wide, troubled eyes, while Madame darted looks, as from bright, deep black glass.

'Yes,' said Alvina. 'I should hate being a labourer's wife in a nasty little house in a street—'

'In a house?' cried Madame. 'It would not be in a house. They live many together in one house. It would be two rooms, or even one room, in another house with many people not quite clean, you see—'

Alvina shook her head.

'I couldn't stand that,' she said finally.

'No!' Madame nodded approval. 'No! you could not. They live in a bad way, the Italians. They do not know the English home—never. They don't like it. Nor do they know the Swiss clean and proper house. No. They don't understand. They run into their holes to sleep or to shelter, and that is all.'

'The same in Italy?' said Alvina.

'Even more—because there it is sunny very often—'

'And you don't need a house,' said Alvina. 'I should like that.'

'Yes, it is nice—but you don't know the life. And you would be alone with people like animals. And if you go to Italy he will beat you—he will beat you—'

'If I let him,' said Alvina.

'But you can't help it, away there from everybody. Nobody will help you. If you are a wife in Italy, nobody will help you. You are his property, when you marry by Italian law. It is not like England. There is no divorce in Italy. And if he beats you, you are helpless—'

'But why should he beat me?' said Alvina. 'Why should he want to?'

'They do. They are so jealous. And then they go into their ungovernable tempers, horrible tempers—'

'Only when they are provoked,' said Alvina, thinking of Max.

'Yes, but you will not know what provokes him. Who can *say* when he will be provoked? And then he beats you—'

There seemed to be a gathering triumph in Madame's bright black eyes. Alvina looked at her, and turned to the door.

'At any rate I know now,' she said, in rather a flat voice.

'And it is *true*. It is all of it true,' whispered Madame vindictively. Alvina wanted to run from her.

'I *must* go to the kitchen,' she said. 'Shall we go down?'

Alvina did not go into the drawing-room with Madame. She was too much upset, and she had almost a horror of seeing Cicio at that moment.

Miss Pinnegar, her face stained carmine by the fire, was helping Mrs Rollings with the dinner.

'Are they both staying, or only one?' she said tartly.

'Both,' said Alvina, busying herself with the gravy, to hide her distress and confusion.

'The man as well,' said Miss Pinnegar. 'What does the woman want to bring *him* for? I'm sure I don't know what your father would say—a common show-fellow, *looks* what he is—and staying to dinner.'

Miss Pinnegar was thoroughly out of temper as she tried the potatoes. Alvina set the table. Then she went to the drawing-room.

'Will you come to dinner?' she said to her two guests.

Cicio rose, threw his cigarette into the fire, and looked round. Outside was a faint, watery sunshine: but at least it was out of doors. He felt himself imprisoned and out of his element. He had an irresistible impulse to go.

When he got into the hall he laid his hand on his hat. The stupid, constrained smile was on his face.

'I'll go now,' he said.

'We have set the table for you,' said Alvina.

'Stop now, since you have stopped for so long,' said Madame, darting her black looks at him.

But he hurried on his coat, looking stupid. Madame lifted her eyebrows disdainfully.

'This is polite behaviour!' she said sarcastically.

Alvina stood at a loss.

'You return to the funeral?' said Madame coldly.

He shook his head.

'When you are ready to go,' he said.

'At four o'clock,' said Madame, 'when the funeral has come home. Then we shall be in time for the train.'

He nodded, smiled stupidly, opened the door, and went.

'This is just like him, to be so—so—' Madame could not express herself as she walked down to the kitchen.

'Miss Pinnegar, this is Madame,' said Alvina.

'How do you do?' said Miss Pinnegar, a little distant and condescending. Madame eyed her keenly.

'Where is the man? I don't know his name,' said Miss Pinnegar.

'He wouldn't stay,' said Alvina. 'What *is* his name, Madame?'

'Marasca—Francesco. Francesco Marasca—Neapolitan.'

'Marasca!' echoed Alvina.

'It has a bad sound—a sound of a bad augury, bad sign,' said Madame. 'Ma-ra-sca!' She shook her head at the taste of the syllables.

'Why do you think so?' said Alvina. 'Do you think there is a meaning in sounds? goodness and badness?'

'Yes,' said Madame. 'Certainly. Some sounds are good, they are for life, for creating, and some sounds are bad, they are for destroying. Ma-ra-sca! that is bad, like swearing.'

'But what sort of badness? What does it do?' said Alvina.

'What does it do? It sends life down—down—instead of lifting it up.'

'Why should things always go up? Why should life always go up?' said Alvina.

'I don't know,' said Madame, cutting her meat quickly. There was a pause.

'And what about other names,' interrupted Miss Pinnegar, a little lofty. 'What about Houghton, for example?'

Madame put down her fork, but kept her knife in her hand. She looked across the room, not at Miss Pinnegar.

'Houghton—Huff-ton!' she said. 'When it is said, it has a sound *against*: that is, against the neighbour, against humanity. But when it is written *Hough-ton!* then it is different, it is *for*.'

'It is always pronounced *Huff-ton*,' said Miss Pinnegar.

'By us,' said Alvina.

'We ought to know,' said Miss Pinnegar.

Madame turned to look at the unhappy, elderly woman. 'You are a relative of the family?' she said.

'No, not a relative. But I've been here many years,' said Miss Pinnegar.

'Oh yes!' said Madame. Miss Pinnegar was frightfully affronted. The meal, with the three women at table, passed painfully.

Miss Pinnegar rose to go upstairs and weep. She felt very forlorn. Alvina rose to wipe the dishes, hastily, because the funeral guests would all be coming. Madame went into the drawing-room to smoke her sly cigarette.

Mr May was the first to turn up for the lugubrious affair: very tight and tailored, but a little extinguished, all in black. He never wore black, and was very unhappy in it, being almost morbidly sensitive to the impression the colour made on him. He was set to entertain Madame.

She did not pretend distress, but sat black-eyed and watchful, very much her business self.

'What about the theatre?—will it go on?' she asked.

'Well I don't know. I don't know Miss Houghton's intentions,' said Mr May. He was a little stilted to-day.

'It's hers?' said Madame.

'Why, as far as I understand—'

'And if she wants to sell out—?'

Mr May spread his hands, and looked dismal, but distant.

'You should form a company, and carry on—' said Madame.

Mr May looked even more distant, drawing himself up in an odd fashion, so that he looked as if he were trussed. But Madame's shrewd black eyes and busy mind did not let him off.

'Buy Miss Houghton out—' said Madame shrewdly.

'Of cauce,' said Mr May. 'Miss Houghton herself must decide.'

'Oh sure—! You—are you married?'

'Yes.'

'Your wife here?'

'My wife is in London.'

'And children—?'

'A daughter.'

Madame slowly nodded her head up and down, as if she put thousands of two-and-two's together.

'You think there will be much to come to Miss Houghton?' she said.

'Do you mean property? I really can't say. I haven't inquired.'

'No, but you have a good idea, eh?'

'I'm afraid I haven't.'

'No! Well! It won't be much, then?'

'Really, I don't know. I should say, not a *large* fortune—!'

'No—eh?' Madame kept him fixed with her black eyes. 'Do you think the other one will get anything?'

'The *other one*—?' queried Mr May, with an uprising cadence. Madame nodded slightly towards the kitchen.

'The old one—the Miss—Miss Pin—Pinney—what you call her.'

'Miss Pinnegar! The manageress of the work-girls? Really, I don't know at all—' Mr May was most freezing.

'Ha—ha! Ha—ha!' mused Madame quietly. Then she asked: 'Which work-girls do you say?'

And she listened astutely to Mr May's forced account of the work-room upstairs, extorting all the details she desired to gather. Then there was a pause. Madame glanced round the room.

'Nice house!' she said. 'Is it their own?'

'So I *believe*—'

Again Madame nodded sagely.

'Debts perhaps—eh? Mortgage—' and she looked slyly sardonic.

'Really!' said Mr May, bouncing to his feet. 'Do you mind if I go to speak to Mrs Rollings—'

'Oh no—go along,' said Madame, and Mr May skipped out in a temper.

Madame was left alone in her comfortable chair, studying details of the room and making accounts in her own mind, until the actual funeral guests began to arrive. And then she had the satisfaction of sizing them up. Several arrived with wreaths. The coffin had been carried down and laid in the small sitting-room—Mrs Houghton's sitting-room. It was covered with white wreaths and streamers of purple ribbon. There was a crush and a confusion.

And then at last the hearse and the cabs had arrived—the coffin was carried out—Alvina followed, on the arm of her father's cousin, whom she disliked. Miss Pinnegar marshalled the other mourners. It was a wretched business.

But it was a great funeral. There were nine cabs, besides the hearse—Woodhouse had revived its ancient respect for the house of Houghton. A posse of minor tradesmen followed the cabs—all in black and with black gloves. The richer tradesmen sat in the cabs.

Poor Alvina, this was the only day in all her life when she was the centre of public attention. For once, every eye was upon her, every mind was thinking about her. Poor Alvina! said every member of the Woodhouse 'middle class': Poor Alvina Houghton, said every collier's wife. Poor thing, left alone—and hardly a penny to bless herself with. Lucky if she's not left with a pile of debts. James Houghton ran through some money in his day. Ay, if she had her rights she'd be a rich woman. Why, her mother brought three or four thousands with her. Ay, but James sank it all in Throttle-Ha'penny and Klondyke and the Endeavour. Well, he was his own worst enemy. He paid his way. I'm not so sure about that. Look how he served his wife, and now Alvina. I'm not so sure he was his own worst enemy. He was bad enough enemy to his own flesh and blood. Ah well, he'll spend no more money, anyhow. No, he went sudden, didn't he? But he was getting very frail, if you noticed. Oh yes, why he fair seemed to totter down to Lumley. Do you reckon as that place pays its way? What, the Endeavour?— they say it does. They say it makes a nice bit. Well, it's mostly pretty full. Ay, it is. Perhaps it won't be now Mr Houghton's gone. Perhaps not. I wonder if he *will* leave much. I'm sure he won't. Everything he's got's mortgaged up to the hilt. He'll leave debts, you see if he doesn't. What is she going to do then? She'll have to go out of Manchester House—her and Miss Pinnegar. Wonder what she'll do. Perhaps she'll take up that nursing. She never made much of that, did she—and spent a sight of money on her training, they say. She's a bit like her father in the business line—all flukes. Pity some nice young man doesn't turn up and marry her. I don't know, she doesn't seem to hook on, does she? Why, she's never had a proper boy. They made out she was engaged once. Ay, but nobody ever saw him, and it was off as soon as it was on. Can you remember she went with Albert Witham for a bit. Did she? No, I never knew. When was that? Why, when he was at Oxford, you know, learning for his head master's place. Why didn't she marry him then? Perhaps he never asked her. Ay, there's that to it. She'd have looked down her nose at him, times gone by. Ay, but that's all over, my boy. She'd snap at anybody now. Look how she carries on with that manager. Why, *that's* something awful. Haven't you ever watched her in the Cinema? She never lets him alone. And it's anybody alike. Oh, she doesn't respect herself. I don't consider. No girl who respected herself would go on as she does, throwing herself at every feller's head. Does she, though? Ay, any performer or anybody. She's a tidy age, though. She's not much chance of getting off. How old do you reckon she is? Must be well over thirty. You never say. Well, she *looks* it. She does beguy—a dragged old maid. Oh but she sprightles up a bit sometimes. Ay, when she thinks she's hooked on to somebody. I wonder why she never did take? It's funny. Oh, she was too high and mighty before, and now it's too late. Nobody wants her. And she's got no relations to go to either, has she? No, that's her father's cousin who she's walking with. Look, they're coming. He's a fine-looking man, isn't he? You'd have thought they'd have buried Miss Frost beside Mrs Houghton. You would, wouldn't you? I should think Alvina will lie by Miss Frost. They say the grave was made for both of them. Ay, she was a lot more of a mother to her than her own mother. She *was* good to them, Miss Frost was. Alvina thought the world of her. That's her stone—look, down there. Not a very grand one, considering. No, it isn't. Look, there's room for Alvina's name underneath. Sh!—

Alvina had sat back in the cab and watched from her obscurity the many faces on the street: so familiar, so familiar, familiar as her own face. And now she seemed to see them from a great distance, out of her darkness. Her big cousin sat opposite her—how she disliked his presence.

In chapel she cried, thinking of her mother, and Miss Frost, and her father. She felt so desolate—it all seemed so empty. Bitterly she cried, when she bent down during the prayer. And her crying started Miss Pinnegar, who cried almost as bitterly. It was all rather horrible. The afterwards—the horrible afterwards.

There was the slow progress to the cemetery. It was a dull, cold day. Alvina shivered as she stood on the bleak hill-side, by the open grave. Her coat did not seem warm enough, her old black sealskin furs were not much protection. The minister stood on the plank by the grave, and she stood near, watching the white flowers blowing in the cold wind. She had watched them for her mother—and for Miss Frost. She felt a sudden clinging to Miss Pinnegar. Yet they would have to part. Miss Pinnegar had been so fond of her father, in a quaint, reserved way. Poor Miss Pinnegar, that was all life had offered her. Well, after all, it had been a home and a home life. To which home and home life Alvina now clung with a desperate yearning, knowing inevitably she was going to lose it, now her father was gone. Strange, that he was gone. But he was weary, worn very thin and weary. He had lived his day. How different it all was, now, at his death, from the time when Alvina knew him as a little child and thought him such a fine gentleman. You live and learn and lose.

For one moment she looked at Madame, who was shuddering with cold, her face hidden behind her black spotted veil. But Madame seemed immensely remote: so unreal. And Cicio—what was his name? She could not think of it. What was it? She tried to think of Madame's slow enunciation. Marasca—maraschino. Marasca! Maraschino! What was maraschino? Where had she heard it? Cudgelling her brains, she remembered the doctors, and the suppers after the theatre. And maraschino—why, that was the favourite white liqueur of the innocent Dr Young. She could remember even now the way he seemed to smack his lips, saying the word *maraschino*. Yet she didn't think much of it. Hot, bitterish stuff—nothing: not like green Chartreuse, which Dr James gave her. Maraschino! Yes, that was it. Made from cherries. Well, Cicio's name was nearly the same. Ridiculous! But she supposed Italian words were a good deal alike.

Cicio, the marasca, the bitter cherry, was standing on the edge of the crowd, looking on. He had no connection whatever with the proceedings—stood outside, self-conscious, uncomfortable, bitten by the wind, and hating the people who stared at him. He saw the trim, plump figure of Madame, like some trim plump partridge among a flock of barn-yard fowls. And he depended on her presence. Without her, he would have felt too horribly uncomfortable on that raw hillside. She and he were in some way allied. But these others, how alien and uncouth he felt them. Impressed by their fine clothes, the English working-classes were none the less barbarians to him, uncivilized: just as he was to them an uncivilized animal. Uncouth, they seemed to him, all raw angles and harshness, like their own weather. Not that he thought about them. But he felt it in his flesh, the harshness and discomfort of them. And Alvina was one of them. As she stood there by the grave, pale and pinched and reserved looking, she was of a piece with the hideous cold grey discomfort of the whole scene. Never had anything been more uncongenial to him. He was dying to get away—to clear out. That was all he wanted. Only some southern obstinacy made him watch, from the duskiness of his face, the pale, reserved girl at the grave. Perhaps he even disliked her, at that time. But he watched in his dislike.

When the ceremony was over, and the mourners turned away to go back to the cabs, Madame pressed forward to Alvina.

'I shall say good-bye now, Miss Houghton. We must go to the station for the train. And thank you, thank you. Good-bye.'

'But—' Alvina looked round.

'Cicio is there. I see him. We must catch the train.'

'Oh but—won't you drive. Won't you ask Cicio to drive with you in the cab. Where is he?'

Madame pointed him out as he hung back among the graves, his black hat cocked a little on one side. He was watching. Alvina broke away from her cousin, and went to him.

'Madame is going to drive to the station,' she said. 'She wants you to get in with her.'

He looked round at the cabs.

'All right,' he said, and he picked his way across the graves to Madame, following Alvina.

'So, we go together in the cab,' said Madame to him. Then: 'Good-bye, my dear Miss Houghton. Perhaps we shall meet once more. Who knows? My heart is with you, my dear.' She put her arms round Alvina and kissed her, a little theatrically. The cousin looked on, very much aloof. Cicio stood by.

'Come then, Cicio,' said Madame.

'Good-bye,' said Alvina to him. 'You'll come again, won't you?' She looked at him from her strained, pale face.

'All right,' he said, shaking her hand loosely. It sounded hopelessly indefinite.

'You will come, won't you?' she repeated, staring at him with strained, unseeing blue eyes.

'All right,' he said, ducking and turning away.

She stood quite still for a moment, quite lost. Then she went on with her cousin to her cab, home to the funeral tea.

'Good-bye!' Madame fluttered a black-edged handkerchief. But Cicio, most uncomfortable in his four-wheeler, kept hidden.

The funeral tea, with its baked meats and sweets, was a terrible affair. But it came to an end, as everything comes to an end, and Miss Pinnegar and Alvina were left alone in the emptiness of Manchester House.

'If you weren't here, Miss Pinnegar, I should be quite by myself,' said Alvina, blanched and strained.

'Yes. And so should I without you,' said Miss Pinnegar doggedly. They looked at each other. And that night both slept in Miss Pinnegar's bed, out of sheer terror of the empty house.

During the days following the funeral, no one could have been more tiresome than Alvina. James had left everything to his daughter, excepting some rights in the work-shop, which were Miss Pinnegar's. But the question was, how much did 'everything' amount to? There was something less than a hundred pounds in the bank. There was a mortgage on Manchester House. There were substantial bills owing on account of the Endeavour. Alvina had about a hundred pounds left from the insurance money, when all funeral expenses were paid. Of that she was sure, and of nothing else.

For the rest, she was almost driven mad by people coming to talk to her. The lawyer came, the clergyman came, her cousin came, the old, stout, prosperous tradesmen of Woodhouse came, Mr May came, Miss Pinnegar came. And they all had schemes, and they all had advice. The chief plan was that the theatre should be sold up: and that Manchester House should be sold, reserving a lease on the top floor, where Miss Pinnegar's work-rooms were: that Miss Pinnegar and Alvina should move into a small house, Miss Pinnegar keeping the work-room, Alvina giving music-lessons: that the two women should be partners in the work-shop.

There were other plans, of course. There was a faction against the chapel faction, which favoured the plan sketched out above. The theatre faction, including Mr May and some of the more florid tradesmen, favoured the risking of everything in the Endeavour. Alvina was to be the proprietress of the Endeavour, she was to run it on some sort of successful lines, and abandon all other enterprise. Minor plans included the election of Alvina to the post of parish nurse, at six pounds a month; a small private school; a small haberdashery shop; and a position in the office of her cousin's Knarborough business. To one and all Alvina answered with a tantalizing: 'I don't know what I'm going to do. I don't know. I can't say yet. I shall see. I shall see.' Till one and all became angry with her. They were all so benevolent, and all so sure that they were proposing the very best thing she could do. And they were all nettled, even indignant that she did not jump at their proposals. She listened to them all. She even invited their advice. Continually she said: 'Well, what do *you* think of it?' And she repeated the chapel plan to the theatre group, the theatre plan to the chapel party, the nursing to the pianoforte proposers, the haberdashery shop to the private school advocates. 'Tell me what *you* think,' she said repeatedly. And they all told her they thought *their* plan was best. And bit by bit she told every advocate the proposal of every other advocate. 'Well, Lawyer Beeby thinks—' and 'Well now, Mr Clay, the minister, advises—' and so on and so on, till it was all buzzing through thirty benevolent and officious heads. And thirty benevolently-officious wills were striving to plant each one its own particular scheme of benevolence. And Alvina, naïve and pathetic, egged them all on in their strife, without even knowing what she was doing. One thing only was certain. Some obstinate will in her own self absolutely refused to have her mind made up. She would *not* have her mind made up for her, and she would not make it up for herself. And so everybody began to say 'I'm getting tired of her. You talk to her, and you get no forrarder. She slips off to something else. I'm not going to bother with her any more.' In truth, Woodhouse was in a fever, for three weeks or more, arranging Alvina's unarrangeable future for her. Offers of charity were innumerable—for three weeks.

Meanwhile, the lawyer went on with the proving of the will and the drawing up of a final account of James's property; Mr May went on with the Endeavour, though Alvina did not go down to play; Miss Pinnegar went on with the work-girls: and Alvina went on unmaking her mind.

Cicio did not come during the first week. Alvina had a post-card from Madame, from Cheshire: rather far off. But such was the buzz and excitement over her material future, such a fever was worked up round about her that Alvina, the pretty-propertied heroine of the moment, was quite carried away in a storm of schemes and benevolent suggestions. She answered Madame's post-card, but did not give much thought to the Natcha-Kee-Tawaras. As a matter of fact, she was enjoying a real moment of importance, there at the centre of Woodhouse's rather domineering benevolence: a benevolence which she unconsciously, but systematically frustrated. All this scheming for selling out and making res-

ervations and hanging on and fixing prices and getting private bids for Manchester House and for the Endeavour, the
excitement of forming a Limited Company to run the Endeavour, of seeing the lawyer about the sale of Manchester
House and the auctioneer about the sale of the furniture, of
receiving men who wanted to pick up the machines upstairs
cheap, and of keeping everything dangling, deciding nothing, putting everything off till she had seen somebody else,
this for the moment fascinated her, went to her head. It was
not till the second week had passed that her excitement began to merge into irritation, and not until the third week
had gone by that she began to feel herself entangled in an
asphyxiating web of indecision, and her heart began to sink
because Cicio had never turned up. Now she would have
given anything to see the Natcha-Kee-Tawaras again. But
she did not know where they were. Now she began to loathe
the excitement of her property: doubtfully hers, every stick
of it. Now she would give anything to get away from Woodhouse, from the horrible buzz and entanglement of her sordid affairs. Now again her wild recklessness came over her.

She suddenly said she was going away somewhere: she
would not say where. She cashed all the money she could:
a hundred-and-twenty-five pounds. She took the train to
Cheshire, to the last address of the Natcha-Kee-Tawaras:
she followed them to Stockport: and back to Chinley: and
there she was stuck for the night. Next day she dashed back
almost to Woodhouse, and swerved round to Sheffield.
There, in that black town, thank heaven, she saw their announcement on the wall. She took a taxi to their theatre, and
then on to their lodgings. The first thing she saw was Louis,
in his shirt sleeves, on the landing above.

She laughed with excitement and pleasure. She seemed
another woman. Madame looked up, almost annoyed, when
she entered.

'I couldn't keep away from you, Madame,' she cried.

'Evidently,' said Madame.

Madame was darning socks for the young men. She was
a wonderful mother for them, sewed for them, cooked for
them, looked after them most carefully. Not many minutes
was Madame idle.

'Do you mind?' said Alvina.

Madame darned for some moments without answering.

'And how is everything at Woodhouse?' she asked.

'I couldn't bear it any longer. I couldn't bear it. So I collected all the money I could, and ran away. Nobody knows where I am.'

Madame looked up with bright, black, censorious eyes, at the flushed girl opposite. Alvina had a certain strangeness and brightness, which Madame did not know, and a frankness which the Frenchwoman mistrusted, but found disarming.

'And all the business, the will and all?' said Madame.

'They're still fussing about it.'

'And there is some money?'

'I have got a hundred pounds here,' laughed Alvina. 'What there will be when everything is settled, I don't know. But not very much, I'm sure of that.'

'How much do you think? A thousand pounds?'

'Oh, it's just possible, you know. But it's just as likely there won't be another penny—'

Madame nodded slowly, as always when she did her calculations.

'And if there is nothing, what do you intend?' said Madame.

'I don't know,' said Alvina brightly.

'And if there is something?'

'I don't know either. But I thought, if you would let me play for you, I could keep myself for some time with my own money. You said perhaps I might be with the Natcha-Kee-Tawaras. I wish you would let me.'

Madame bent her head so that nothing showed but the bright black folds of her hair. Then she looked up, with a slow, subtle, rather jeering smile.

'Cicio didn't come to see you, *hein*?'

'No,' said Alvina. 'Yet he promised.'

Again Madame smiled sardonically.

'Do you call it a promise?' she said. 'You are easy to be satisfied with a word. A hundred pounds? No more?'

'A hundred and twenty—'

'Where is it?'

'In my bag at the station—in notes. And I've got a little here—' Alvina opened her purse, and took out some little gold and silver.

'At the station!' exclaimed Madame, smiling grimly. 'Then perhaps you have nothing.'

'Oh, I think it's quite safe, don't you—?'

'Yes—maybe—since it is England. And you think a hundred and twenty pounds is enough?'

'What for?'

'To satisfy Cicio.'

'I wasn't thinking of him,' cried Alvina.

'No?' said Madame ironically. 'I can propose it to him. Wait one moment.' She went to the door and called Cicio.

He entered, looking not very good-tempered.

'Be so good, my dear,' said Madame to him, 'to go to the station and fetch Miss Houghton's little bag. You have got the ticket, have you?' Alvina handed the luggage ticket to Madame. 'Midland Railway,' said Madame. 'And Cicio, you are listening—? Mind! There is a hundred and twenty pounds of Miss Houghton's money in the bag. You hear? Mind it is not lost.'

'It's all I have,' said Alvina.

'For the time, for the time—till the will is proved, it is all the cash she has. So mind doubly. You hear?'

'All right,' said Cicio.

'Tell him what sort of a bag, Miss Houghton,' said Madame.

Alvina told him. He ducked and went. Madame listened for his final departure. Then she nodded sagely at Alvina.

'Take off your hat and coat, my dear. Soon we will have tea—when Cic' returns. Let him think, let him think what he likes. So much money is certain, perhaps there will be more. Let him think. It will make all the difference that there is so much cash—yes, so much—'

'But would it *really* make a difference to him?' cried Alvina.

'Oh my dear!' exclaimed Madame. 'Why should it not? We are on earth, where we must eat. We are not in Paradise. If it were a thousand pounds, then he would want very badly to marry you. But a hundred and twenty is better than a blow to the eye, eh? Why sure!'

'It's dreadful, though—!' said Alvina.

'Oh la-la! Dreadful! If it was Max, who is sentimental, then no, the money is nothing. But all the others—why, you see, they are men, and they know which side to butter their bread. Men are like cats, my dear, they don't like their bread without butter. Why should they? Nor do I, nor do I.'

'Can I help with the darning?' said Alvina.

'*Hein*? I shall give you Cicio's socks, yes? He pushes holes in the toes—you see?' Madame poked two fingers through the hole in the toe of a red-and-black sock, and smiled a little maliciously at Alvina.

'I don't mind which sock I darn,' she said.

'No? You don't? Well then, I give you another. But if you like I will speak to him—'

'What to say?' asked Alvina.

'To say that you have so much money, and hope to have more. And that you like him—Yes? Am I right? You like him very much?—*hein*? Is it so?'

'And then what?' said Alvina.

'That he should tell me if he should like to marry you also—quite simply. What? Yes?'

'No,' said Alvina.'Don't say anything—not yet.'

'*Hé*? Not yet? Not yet? All right, not yet then. You will see—'

Alvina sat darning the sock and smiling at her own shamelessness. The point that amused her most of all was the fact that she was not by any means sure she wanted to marry him. There was Madame spinning her web like a plump prolific black spider. There was Cicio, the unrestful fly. And there was herself, who didn't know in the least what she was doing. There sat two of them, Madame and herself, darning socks in a stuffy bedroom with a gas fire, as if they had been born to it. And after all, Woodhouse wasn't fifty miles away.

Madame went downstairs to get tea ready. Wherever she was, she superintended the cooking and the preparation of meals for her young men, scrupulous and quick. She called Alvina downstairs. Cicio came in with the bag.

'See my dear, that your money is safe,' said Madame.

Alvina unfastened her bag and counted the crisp white notes.

'And now,' said Madame. 'I shall lock it in my little bank, yes, where it will be safe. And I shall give you a receipt, which the young men will witness.'

The party sat down to tea, in the stuffy sitting-room.

'Now boys,' said Madame, 'what do you say? Shall Miss Houghton join the Natcha-Kee-Tawaras? Shall she be our pianist?'

The eyes of the four young men rested on Alvina. Max, as being the responsible party, looked business-like. Louis was tender, Geoffrey round-eyed and inquisitive, Cicio furtive.

'With great pleasure,' said Max. 'But can the Natcha-Kee-Tawaras afford to pay a pianist for themselves?'

'No,' said Madame. 'No. I think not. Miss Houghton will come for one month, to prove, and in that time she shall pay for herself. Yes? So she fancies it.'

'Can we pay her expenses?' said Max.

'No,' said Alvina. 'Let me pay everything for myself, for a month. I should like to be with you, awfully—'

She looked across with a look half mischievous, half beseeching, at the erect Max. He bowed as he sat at table.

'I think we shall all be honoured,' he said.

'Certainly,' said Louis, bowing also over his tea-cup.

Geoffrey inclined his head, and Cicio lowered his eyelashes in indication of agreement.

'Now then,' said Madame briskly, 'we are all agreed. To-night we will have a bottle of wine on it. Yes, gentlemen? What d'you say? Chianti—*hein*?'

They all bowed above the table.

'And Miss Houghton shall have her professional name, eh? Because we cannot say Miss Houghton—what?'

'Do call me Alvina,' said Alvina.

'Alvina—Al-vy-na! No, excuse me, my dear, I don't like it. I don't like this 'vy' sound. To-night we shall find a name.'

After tea they inquired for a room for Alvina. There was none in the house. But two doors away was another decent lodging-house, where a bedroom on the top floor was found for her.

'I think you are very well here,' said Madame.

'Quite nice,' said Alvina, looking round the hideous little room, and remembering her other term of probation, as a maternity nurse.

She dressed as attractively as possible, in her new dress of black voile, and imitating Madame, she put four jewelled rings on her fingers. As a rule she only wore the mourning-ring of black enamel and diamond, which had been always on Miss Frost's finger. Now she left off this, and took four diamond rings, and one good sapphire. She looked at herself in her mirror as she had never done before, really interested in the effect she made. And in her dress she pinned a valuable old ruby brooch.

Then she went down to Madame's house. Madame eyed her shrewdly, with just a touch of jealousy: the eternal jealousy that must exist between the plump, pale partridge of a Frenchwoman, whose black hair is so glossy and tidy, whose black eyes are so acute, whose black dress is so neat and chic, and the rather thin Englishwoman in soft voile, with soft, rather loose brown hair and demure, blue-grey eyes.

'Oh—a difference—what a difference! When you have a little more flesh—then—' Madame made a slight click with her tongue. 'What a good brooch, eh?' Madame fingered the brooch. 'Old paste—old paste—antique—'

'No,' said Alvina. 'They are real rubies. It was my great-grandmother's.'

'Do you mean it? Real? Are you sure—'

'I think I'm quite sure.'

Madame scrutinized the jewels with a fine eye.

'Hm!' she said. And Alvina did not know whether she was sceptical, or jealous, or admiring, or really impressed.

'And the diamonds are real?' said Madame, making Alvina hold up her hands.

'I've always understood so,' said Alvina.

Madame scrutinized, and slowly nodded her head. Then she looked into Alvina's eyes, really a little jealous.

'Another four thousand francs there,' she said, nodding sagely.

'Really!' said Alvina.

'For sure. It's enough—it's enough—'

And there was a silence between the two women.

The young men had been out shopping for the supper. Louis, who knew where to find French and German stuff, came in with bundles, Cicio returned with a couple of flasks, Geoffrey with sundry moist papers of edibles. Alvina helped Madame to put the anchovies and sardines and tunny and ham and salami on various plates, she broke off a bit of fern from one of the flower-pots, to stick in the pork-pie, she set the table with its ugly knives and forks and glasses. All the time her rings sparkled, her red brooch sent out beams, she laughed and was gay, she was quick, and she flattered Madame by being very deferential to her. Whether she was herself or not, in the hideous, common, stuffy sitting-room of the lodging-house she did not know or care. But she felt excited and gay. She knew the young men were watching her. Max gave his assistance wherever possible. Geoffrey watched her rings, half spell-bound. But Alvina was concerned only to flatter the plump, white, soft vanity of Madame. She carefully chose for Madame the finest plate, the clearest glass, the whitest-hafted knife, the most delicate fork. All of which Madame saw, with acute eyes.

At the theatre the same: Alvina played for Kishwégin, only for Kishwégin. And Madame had the time of her life.

'You know, my dear,' she said afterwards to Alvina, 'I understand sympathy in music. Music goes straight to the heart.' And she kissed Alvina on both cheeks, throwing her arms round her neck dramatically.

'I'm *so* glad,' said the wily Alvina.

And the young men stirred uneasily, and smiled furtively.

They hurried home to the famous supper. Madame sat at one end of the table, Alvina at the other. Madame had Max and Louis by her side, Alvina had Cicio and Geoffrey. Cicio was on Alvina's right hand: a delicate hint.

They began with hors d'œuvres and tumblers three parts full of Chianti. Alvina wanted to water her wine, but was not allowed to insult the sacred liquid. There was a spirit of great liveliness and conviviality. Madame became paler, her

eyes blacker, with the wine she drank, her voice became a
little raucous.

'To-night,' she said, 'the Natcha-Kee-Tawaras make their
feast of affiliation. The white daughter has entered the tribe
of the Hirondelles, swallows that pass from land to land,
and build their nests between roof and wall. A new swallow,
a new Huron from the tents of the pale-face, from the lodges
of the north, from the tribe of the Yengees.' Madame's black
eyes glared with a kind of wild triumph down the table at
Alvina. 'Nameless, without having a name, comes the
maiden with the red jewels, dark-hearted, with the red
beams. Wine from the pale-face shadows, drunken wine for
Kishwégin, strange wine for the *braves* in their nostrils,
Vaali, *à vous*.'

Madame lifted her glass.

'Vaali, drink to her—*Boire à elle*—' She thrust her glass
forwards in the air. The young men thrust their glasses up
towards Alvina, in a cluster. She could see their mouths all
smiling, their teeth white as they cried in their throats:
'Vaali! Vaali! *Boire à vous*.'

Cicio was near to her. Under the table he laid his hand
on her knee. Quickly she put forward her hand to protect
herself. He took her hand, and looked at her along the glass
as he drank. She saw his throat move as the wine went down
it. He put down his glass, still watching her.

'Vaali!' he said, in his throat. Then across the table '*Hé,
Gigi—Viale! Le Petit Chemin! Comment? Me prends-tu?
L'Allée—*'

There came a great burst of laughter from Louis.

'It is good, it is good!' he cried. 'Oh Madame! Viale, it is
Italian for the little way, the alley. That is too rich.'

Max went off into a high and ribald laugh.

'*L'Allée Italienne!*' he said, and shouted with laughter.

'*Alley* or avenue, what does it matter,' cried Madame in
French, 'so long as it is a good journey.'

Here Geoffrey at last saw the joke. With a strange, determined flourish he filled his glass, cocking up his elbow.

'*A toi, Cic*'—*et bon voyage!*' he said, and then he tilted
up his chin and swallowed in great throatfuls.

'Certainly! Certainly!' cried Madame. 'To thy good journey, my Cicio, for thou art not a great traveller—'

'*Na, pour ça, y'a plus d'une voie,*' said Geoffrey.

During this passage in French Alvina sat with very bright eyes looking from one to another, and not understanding. But she knew it was something improper, on her account. Her eyes had a bright, slightly-bewildered look as she turned from one face to another. Cicio had let go her hand, and was wiping his lips with his fingers. He too was a little self-conscious.

'*Assez de cette éternelle voie italienne,*' said Madame. '*Courage, courage au chemin d' Angleterre.*'

'*Assez de cette éternelle voix rauque,*' said Cicio, looking round. Madame suddenly pulled herself together.

'They will not have my name. They will call you *Allay*!' she said to Alvina. 'It is good? Will it do?'

'Quite,' said Alvina.

And she could not understand why Gigi, and then the others after him, went off into a shout of laughter. She kept looking round with bright, puzzled eyes. Her face was slightly flushed and tender looking, she looked naïve, young.

'Then you will become one of the tribe of Natcha-Kee-Tawara, of the name Allaye? Yes?'

'Yes,' said Alvina.

'And obey the strict rules of the tribe. Do you agree?'

'Yes.'

'Then listen.' Madame primmed and preened herself like a black pigeon, and darted glances out of her black eyes.

'We are one tribe, one nation—say it.'

'We are one tribe, one nation,' repeated Alvina.

'Say all,' cried Madame.

'We are one tribe, one nation—' they shouted, with varying accent.

'Good!' said Madame. 'And no nation do we know but the nation of the Hirondelles—'

'No nation do we know but the nation of the Hirondelles,' came the ragged chant of strong male voices, resonant and gay with mockery.

'Hurons—Hirondelles, means *swallows*,' said Madame.

'Yes, I know,' said Alvina.

'So! you know! Well then! We know no nation but the Hirondelles. WE HAVE NO LAW BUT HURON LAW!'

'We have no law but Huron law!' sang the response, in a deep, sardonic chant.

'WE HAVE NO LAWGIVER EXCEPT KISHWÉGIN.'

'We have no lawgiver except Kishwégin,' they sang sonorous.

'WE HAVE NO HOME BUT THE TENT OF KISHWÉGIN.'

'We have no home but the tent of Kishwégin.'

'THERE IS NO GOOD BUT THE GOOD OF NATCHA-KEE-TAWARA.'

'There is no good but the good of Natcha-Kee-Tawara.'

'WE ARE THE HIRONDELLES.'

'We are the Hirondelles.'

'WE ARE KISHWÉGIN.'

'We are Kishwégin—'

'WE ARE MONDAGUA—'

'We are Mondagua—'

'WE ARE ANTONQUOIS—'

'We are Antonquois—'

'WE ARE PACOHUILA—'

'We are Pacohuila—'

'WE ARE WALGATCHKA—'

'We are Walgatchka—'

'WE ARE ALLAYE—'

'We are Allaye—'

'*La musica*, Pacohuila, *la musica!*' cried Madame, starting to her feet and sounding frenzied.

Cicio got up quickly and took his mandoline from its case.

'A—A—Ai—Aii—eee—ya—' began Madame, with a long, faint wail. And on the wailing mandoline the music started. She began to dance a slight but intense dance. Then she waved for a partner, and set up a tarantella wail. Louis threw off his coat and sprang to tarantella attention, Cicio rang out the peculiar tarantella, and Madame and Louis danced in the tight space.

'Brava—Brava!' cried the others, when Madame sank into her place. And they crowded forward to kiss her hand. One after the other, they kissed her fingers, whilst she laid her left hand languidly on the head of one man after another, as she sat slightly panting. Cicio however did not come up, but sat faintly twanging the mandoline. Nor did Alvina leave her place.

'Pacohuila!' cried Madame, with an imperious gesture.

'Allaye! Come—'

Cicio laid down his mandoline and went to kiss the fingers of Kishwégin. Alvina also went forward. Madame held out her hand. Alvina kissed it. Madame laid her hand on the head of Alvina.

'This is the squaw Allaye, this is the daughter of Kishwégin,' she said, in her Tawara manner.

'And where is the *brave* of Allaye, where is the arm that upholds the daughter of Kishwégin, which of the Swallows spreads his wings over the gentle head of the new one!'

'Pacohuila!' said Louis.

'Pacohuila! Pacohuila! Pacohuila!' said the others.

'Spread soft wings, spread dark-roofed wings, Pacohuila,' said Kishwégin, and Cicio, in his shirt-sleeves, solemnly spread his arms.

'Stoop, stoop, Allaye, beneath the wings of Pacohuila,' said Kishwégin, faintly pressing Alvina on the shoulder.

Alvina stooped and crouched under the right arm of Pacohuila.

'Has the bird flown home?' chanted Kishwégin, to one of the strains of their music.

'The bird is home—' chanted the men.

'Is the nest warm?' chanted Kishwégin.

'The nest is warm.'

'Does the he-bird stoop—?'

'He stoops.'

'Who takes Allaye?'

'Pacohuila.'

Cicio gently stooped and raised Alvina to her feet.

'*C'est ça!*' said Madame, kissing her. 'And now, children, unless the Sheffield policeman will knock at our door, we must retire to our wigwams all—'

Cicio was watching Alvina. Madame made him a secret, imperative gesture that he should accompany the young woman.

'You have your key, Allaye?' she said.

'Did I have a key?' said Alvina.

Madame smiled subtly as she produced a latch-key.

'Kishwégin must open your doors for you all,' she said. Then, with a slight flourish, she presented the key to Cicio. 'I give it to him? Yes?' she added, with her subtle, malicious smile.

Cicio, smiling slightly and keeping his head ducked, took the key. Alvina looked brightly, as if bewildered, from one to another.

'Also the light!' said Madame, producing a pocket flash-light, which she triumphantly handed to Cicio. Alvina watched him. She noticed how he dropped his head forward from his straight, strong shoulders, how beautiful that was, the strong, forward-inclining nape and back of the head. It produced a kind of dazed submission in her, the drugged sense of unknown beauty.

'And so good-night, Allaye—*bonne nuit, fille des Tawara.*' Madame kissed her, and darted black, unaccountable looks at her.

Each *brave* also kissed her hand, with a profound salute. Then the men shook hands warmly with Cicio, murmuring to him.

He did not put on his hat nor his coat, but ran round as he was to the neighbouring house with her, and opened the door. She entered, and he followed, flashing on the light. So she climbed weakly up the dusty, drab stairs, he following. When she came to her door, she turned and looked at him. His face scarcely visible, it seemed, and yet so strange and beautiful. It was the unknown beauty which almost killed her.

'You aren't coming?' she quavered.

He gave an odd, half-gay, half-mocking twitch of his thick dark brows, and began to laugh silently. Then he nodded again, laughing at her boldly, carelessly, triumphantly, like the dark Southerner he was. Her instinct was to defend herself. When suddenly she found herself in the dark.

She gasped. And as she gasped, he quite gently put her inside her room, and closed the door, keeping one arm round her all the time. She felt his heavy, muscular predominance. So he took her in both arms, powerful, mysterious, horrible in the pitch dark. Yet the sense of the unknown beauty of him weighed her down like some force. If for one moment she could have escaped from that black spell of his beauty, she would have been free. If only she could, for one second, have seen him ugly, he would not have killed her and made her his slave as he did. But the spell was on her, of his darkness and unfathomed handsomeness. And he killed her. He simply took her and assassinated her. How she suffered no one can tell. Yet all the time, this lustrous dark beauty, unbearable.

When later she pressed her face on his chest and cried, he held her gently as if she was a child, but took no notice, and she felt in the darkness that he smiled. It was utterly dark, and she knew he smiled, and she began to get hysterical. But he only kissed her, his smiling deepening to a heavy laughter, silent and invisible but sensible, as he carried her away once more. He intended her to be his slave, she knew. And he seemed to throw her down and suffocate her like a wave. And she could have fought, if only the sense of his dark, rich handsomeness had not numbed her like a venom. So she washed, suffocated in his passion.

In the morning when it was light he turned and looked at her from under his long black lashes, a long, steady, cruel, faintly-smiling look from his tawny eyes, searching her as if to see whether she were still alive. And she looked back at him, heavy-eyed and half subjected. He smiled slightly at her, rose, and left her. And she turned her face to the wall, feeling beaten. Yet not quite beaten to death. Save for the fatal numbness of her love for him, she could still have escaped him. But she lay inert, as if envenomed. He wanted to make her his slave.

When she went down to the Natcha-Kee-Tawaras' for breakfast she found them waiting for her. She was rather frail and tender-looking, with wondering eyes that showed she had been crying.

'Come, daughter of the Tawaras,' said Madame brightly to her. 'We have been waiting for you. Good-morning, and all happiness, eh? Look, it is a gift-day for you—'

Madame smilingly led Alvina to her place. Beside her

plate was a bunch of violets, a bunch of carnations, a pair of exquisite bead mocassins, and a pair of fine doeskin gloves delicately decorated with feather-work on the cuffs. The slippers were from Kishwégin, the gloves from Mondagua, the carnations from Antonquois, the violets from Walgatchka—all *To the Daughter of the Tawaras, Allaye,* as it said on the little cards.

'The gift of Pacohuila you know,' said Madame, smiling. 'The brothers of Pacohuila are your brothers.'

One by one they went to her and each one laid the back of her fingers against his forehead, saying in turn:

'I am your brother Mondagua, Allaye!'

'I am your brother Antonquois, Allaye!'

'I am your brother Walgatchka, Allaye, best brother, you know—' So spoke Geoffrey, looking at her with large, almost solemn eyes of affection. Alvina smiled a little wanly, wondering where she was. It was all so solemn. Was it all mockery, play-acting? She felt bitterly inclined to cry.

Meanwhile Madame came in with the coffee, which she always made herself, and the party sat down to breakfast. Cicio sat on Alvina's right, but he seemed to avoid looking at her or speaking to her. All the time he looked across the table, with the half-asserted, knowing look in his eyes, at Gigi; and all the time he addressed himself to Gigi, with the throaty, rich, plangent quality in his voice, that Alvina could not bear, it seemed terrible to her: and he spoke in French: and the two men seemed to be exchanging unspeakable communications. So that Alvina, for all her wistfulness and subjectedness, was at last seriously offended. She rose as soon as possible from table. In her own heart she wanted attention and public recognition from Cicio—none of which she got. She returned to her own house, to her own room, anxious to tidy everything, not wishing to have her landlady in the room. And she half expected Cicio to come to speak to her.

As she was busy washing a garment in the bowl, her landlady knocked and entered. She was a rough and rather beery-looking Yorkshire woman, not attractive.

'Oh, yo'n made yer bed then, han' yer!'

'Yes,' said Alvina. 'I've done everything.'

'I see yer han. Yo'n bin sharp.'

Alvina did not answer.

'Seems yer doin' yersen a bit o' weshin'.'

Still Alvina didn't answer.

'Yo' can 'ing it i' th' back yard.'

'I think it'll dry here,' said Alvina.

'Isna much dryin' up here. Send us howd when 't's ready. Yo'll 'appen be wantin' it. I can dry it off for yer i' t' kitchen. You don't take a drop o' nothink, do yer?'

'No,' said Alvina. 'I don't like it.'

'Summat a bit stronger 'n t' bottle, my sakes alive! Well, yo mun ha'e your fling, like t' rest. But coom na, which on 'em is it? I catched sight on 'im goin' out, but I didna ma'e out then which on 'em it wor. He—eh, it's a pity you don't take a drop of nothink, it's a world's pity. Is it the fairest on 'em, the tallest?'

'No,' said Alvina. 'The darkest one.'

'Oh ay! Well, 's a strappin' anuff feller, for them as goes that road. I thought Madame was partikler. I s'll charge yer a bit more, yer know. I s'll 'ave to make a bit out of it. *I'm* partikler as a rule. I don't like 'em comin' in an' goin' out, you know. Things get said. You look so quiet, you do. Come now, it's worth a hextra quart to me, else I shan't have it, I shan't. You can't make as free as all that with the house, you know, be it what it may—'

She stood red-faced and dour in the doorway. Alvina quietly gave her half-a-sovereign.

'Nay, less,' said the woman, 'if you share niver a drop o' th' lashins, you mun split it. Five shillin's is oceans, ma wench. I'm not down on you—not me. On'y we've got to keep up appearances a bit, you know. Dash my rags, it's a caution!'

'I haven't got five shillings—' said Alvina.

'Yer've not? All right, gi'e 's ha'ef crown to-day, an' t'other termorrer. It'll keep, it'll keep. God bless you for a good wench. A' open 'eart's worth all your bum-righteousness. It is for me. An' a sight more. You're all right, ma wench, you're all right—'

And the rather bleary woman went nodding away.

Alvina ought to have minded. But she didn't. She even

laughed into her rickety mirror. At the back of her thoughts, all she minded was that Cicio did not pay her some attention. She really expected him now to come to speak to her. If she could have imagined how far he was from any such intention.

So she loitered unwillingly at her window high over the grey, hard, cobbled street, and saw her landlady hastening along the black asphalt pavement, her dirty apron thrown discreetly over what was most obviously a quart jug. She followed the squat, intent figure with her eye, to the public-house at the corner. And then she saw Cicio humped over his yellow bicycle, going for a steep and perilous ride with Gigi.

Still she lingered in her sordid room. She could feel Madame was expecting her. But she felt inert, weak, incommunicative. Only a real fear of offending Madame drove her down at last.

Max opened the door to let her in.

'Ah!' he said. 'You've come. We were wondering about you.'

'Thank you,' she said, as she passed into the dirty hall where still two bicycles stood.

'Madame is in the kitchen,' he said.

Alvina found Madame trussed in a large white apron, busy rubbing a yellow-fleshed hen with lemon, previous to boiling.

'Ah!' said Madame. 'So there you are! I have been out and done my shopping, and already begun to prepare the dinner. Yes, you may help me. Can you wash leeks? Yes? Every grain of sand? Shall I trust you then?'

Madame usually had a kitchen to herself, in the morning. She either ousted her landlady, or used her as second cook. For Madame was a gourmet, if not gourmand. If she inclined towards self-indulgence in any direction, it was in the direction of food. She *loved* a good table. And hence the Tawaras saved less money than they might. She was an exacting, tormenting, bullying cook. Alvina, who knew well enough how to prepare a simple dinner, was offended by Madame's exactions. Madame turning back the green leaves of a leek, and hunting a speck of earth down into the white, like a flea in a bed, was too much for Alvina.

'I'm afraid I shall never be particular enough,' she said. 'Can't I do anything else for you?'

'For me? I need nothing to be done for me. But for the young men—yes, I will show you in one minute—'

And she took Alvina upstairs to her room, and gave her a pair of the thin leather trousers fringed with hair, belonging to one of the *braves*. A seam had ripped. Madame gave Alvina a fine awl and some waxed thread.

'The leather is not good in these things of Gigi's,' she said. 'It is badly prepared. See, like this.' And she showed Alvina another place where the garment was repaired. 'Keep on your apron. At the week-end you must fetch more clothes, not spoil this beautiful gown of voile. Where have you left your diamonds? What? In your room? Are they locked? Oh my dear—!' Madame turned pale and darted looks of fire at Alvina. 'If they are stolen—!' she cried. 'Oh! I have become quite weak, hearing you!' She panted and shook her head. 'If they are not stolen, you have the Holy Saints alone to be thankful for keeping them. But run, run!'

And Madame really stamped her foot.

'Bring me everything you've got—every *thing* that is valuable. I shall lock it up. How *can* you—'

Alvina was hustled off to her lodging. Fortunately nothing was gone. She brought all to Madame, and Madame fingered the treasures lovingly.

'Now what you want you must ask me for,' she said.

With what close curiosity Madame examined the ruby brooch.

'You can have that if you like, Madame,' said Alvina.

'You mean—what?'

'I will give you that brooch if you like to take it—'

'Give me this—!' cried Madame, and a flash went over her face. Then she changed into a sort of wheedling. 'No—no. I shan't take it! I shan't take it. You don't want to give away such a thing.'

'I don't mind,' said Alvina. 'Do take it if you like it.'

'Oh no! Oh no! I can't take it. A beautiful thing it is,

really. It would be worth over a thousand francs, because I
believe it is quite genuine.'

'I'm sure it's genuine,' said Alvina. 'Do have it since you
like it.'

'Oh, I can't! I can't!—'

'Yes do—'

'The beautiful red stones!—antique gems, antique
gems—! And do you really give it to me?'

'Yes, I should like to.'

'You are a girl with a noble heart—' Madame threw her
arms round Alvina's neck, and kissed her. Alvina felt very
cool about it. Madame locked up the jewels quickly, after
one last look.

'My fowl,' she said, 'which must not boil too fast.'

At length Alvina was called down to dinner. The young
men were at table, talking as young men do, not very inter-
estingly. After the meal, Cicio sat and twanged his mandoline, making its crying noise vibrate through the house.

'I shall go and look at the town,' said Alvina.

'And who shall go with you?' asked Madame.

'I will go alone,' said Alvina, 'unless you will come Madame.'

'Alas no, I can't. I can't come. Will you really go alone?'

'Yes, I want to go to the women's shops,' said Alvina.

'You want to! All right then! And you will come home
at tea-time, yes?'

As soon as Alvina had gone out Cicio put away his mandoline and lit a cigarette. Then after a while he hailed Geoffrey, and the two young men sallied forth. Alvina, emerging
from a draper's shop in Rotherhampton Broadway, found
them loitering on the pavement outside. And they strolled
along with her. So she went into a shop that sold ladies'
underwear, leaving them on the pavement. She stayed as
long as she could. But there they were when she came out.
They had endless lounging patience.

'I thought you would be gone on,' she said.

'No hurry,' said Cicio, and he took away her parcels from
her, as if he had a right. She wished he wouldn't tilt the flap
of his black hat over one eye, and she wished there wasn't
quite so much waist-line in the cut of his coat, and that he

didn't smoke cigarettes against the end of his nose in the street. But wishing wouldn't alter him. He strayed alongside as if he half belonged, and half didn't—most irritating.

She wasted as much time as possible in the shops, then they took the tram home again. Cicio paid the three fares, laying his hand restraining on Gigi's hand, when Gigi's hand sought pence in his trouser pocket, and throwing his arm over his friend's shoulder, in affectionate but vulgar triumph, when the fares were paid. Alvina was on her high horse.

They tried to talk to her, they tried to ingratiate themselves—but she wasn't having any. She talked with icy pleasantness. And so the tea-time passed, and the time after tea. The performance went rather mechanically, at the theatre, and the supper at home, with bottled beer and boiled ham, was a conventionally cheerful affair. Even Madame was a little afraid of Alvina this evening.

'I am tired, I shall go early to my room,' said Alvina.

'Yes, I think we are all tired,' said Madame.

'Why is it?' said Max metaphysically—'why is it that two merry evenings never follow one behind the other?'

'Max, beer makes thee a *farceur* of a fine quality,' said Madame. Alvina rose.

'Please don't get up,' she said to the others. 'I have my key and can see quite well,' she said. 'Good-night all.'

They rose and bowed their good-nights. But Cicio, with an obstinate and ugly little smile on his face, followed her.

'Please don't come,' she said, turning at the street door. But obstinately he lounged into the street with her. He followed her to her door.

'Did you bring the flash-light?' she said. 'The stair is so dark.'

He looked at her, and turned as if to get the light. Quickly she opened the house-door and slipped inside, shutting it sharply in his face. He stood for some moments looking at the door, and an ugly little look mounted his straight nose. He too turned indoors.

Alvina hurried to bed and slept well. And the next day the same; she was all icy pleasantness. The Natcha-Kee-Tawaras were a little bit put out by her. She was a spoke in their wheel, a scotch to their facility. She made them irritable. And that evening—it was Friday—Cicio did not rise to accompany her to her house. And she knew they were relieved that she had gone.

That did not please her. The next day, which was Saturday, the last and greatest day of the week, she found herself again somewhat of an outsider in the troupe. The tribe had assembled in its old unison. She was the intruder, the interloper. And Cicio never looked at her, only showed her the half-averted side of his cheek, on which was a slightly jeering, ugly look.

'Will you go to Woodhouse to-morrow?' Madame asked her, rather coolly. They none of them called her Allaye any more.

'I'd better fetch some things, hadn't I?' said Alvina.

'Certainly, if you think you will stay with us.'

This was a nasty slap in the face for her. But:

'I want to,' she said.

'Yes! Then you will go to Woodhouse to-morrow, and come to Mansfield on Monday morning? Like that shall it be? You will stay one night at Woodhouse?'

Through Alvina's mind flitted the rapid thought—'They want an evening without me.' Her pride mounted obstinately. She very nearly said—'I may stay in Woodhouse altogether.' But she held her tongue.

After all, they were very common people. They ought to be glad to have her. Look how Madame snapped up that brooch! And look what an uncouth lout Cicio was! After all, she was demeaning herself shamefully staying with them in common, sordid lodgings. After all, she had been bred up differently from that. They had horribly low standards—such low standards—not only of morality, but of life altogether. Really, she had come down in the world, conforming to such standards of life. She evoked the images of her mother and Miss Frost: ladies, and noble women both. Whatever could she be thinking of herself!

However, there was time for her to retrace her steps. She had not given herself away. Except to Cicio. And her heart burned when she thought of him, partly with anger and mortification, partly, alas, with undeniable and unsatisfied love. Let her bridle as she might, her heart burned, and she wanted to look at him, she wanted him to notice her. And instinct told her that he might ignore her forever. She went to her room an unhappy woman, and wept and fretted till morning, chafing between humiliation and yearning.

CHAPTER 10

The Fall of Manchester House

Alvina rose chastened and wistful. As she was doing her hair, she heard the plaintive nasal sound of Cicio's mandoline. She looked down the mixed vista of back-yards and little gardens, and was able to catch sight of a portion of Cicio, who was sitting on a box in the blue-brick yard of his house, bare-headed and in his shirt-sleeves, twitching away at the wailing mandoline. It was not a warm morning, but there was a streak of sunshine. Alvina had noticed that Cicio did not seem to feel the cold, unless it were a wind or a driving rain. He was playing the wildly-yearning Neapolitan songs, of which Alvina knew nothing. But, although she only saw a section of him, the glimpse of his head was enough to rouse in her that overwhelming fascination, which came and went in spells. His remoteness, his southernness, something velvety and dark. So easily she might miss him altogether! Within a hair's-breadth she had let him disappear.

She hurried down. Geoffrey opened the door to her. She smiled at him in a quick, luminous smile, a magic change in her.

'I could hear Cicio playing,' she said.

Geoffrey spread his rather thick lips in a smile, and jerked his head in the direction of the back door, with a deep, in-

timate look into Alvina's eyes, as if to say his friend was
love-sick.

'Shall I go through?' said Alvina.

Geoffrey laid his large hand on her shoulder for a moment, looked into her eyes, and nodded. He was a broad-
shouldered fellow, with a rather flat, handsome face,
well-coloured, and with the look of the Alpine ox about
him, slow, eternal, even a little mysterious. Alvina was startled by the deep, mysterious look in his dark-fringed ox-
eyes. The odd arch of his eyebrows made him suddenly
seem not quite human to her. She smiled to him again, startled. But he only inclined his head, and with his heavy hand
on her shoulder gently impelled her towards Cicio.

When she came out at the back she smiled straight into
Cicio's face, with her sudden, luminous smile. His hand on
the mandoline trembled into silence. He sat looking at her
with an instant re-establishment of knowledge. And yet she
shrank from the long, inscrutable gaze of his black-set,
tawny eyes. She resented him a little. And yet she went forward to him and stood so that her dress touched him. And
still he gazed up at her, with the heavy, unspeaking look,
that seemed to bear her down: he seemed like some creature
that was watching her for his purposes. She looked aside at
the black garden, which had a wiry gooseberry bush.

'You will come with me to Woodhouse?' she said.

He did not answer till she turned to him again. Then, as
she met his eyes.

'To Woodhouse?' he said, watching her, to fix her.

'Yes,' she said, a little pale at the lips.

And she saw his eternal smile of triumph slowly growing
round his mouth. She wanted to cover his mouth with her
hand. She preferred his tawny eyes with their black brows
and lashes. His eyes watched her as a cat watches a bird, but
without the white gleam of ferocity. In his eyes was a deep,
deep, sun-warmth, something fathomless, deepening black
and abysmal, but somehow sweet to her.

'Will you?' she repeated.

But his eyes had already begun to glimmer their consent.
He turned aside his face, as if unwilling to give a straight
answer.

'Yes,' he said.

'Play something to me,' she cried.

He lifted his face to her, and shook his head slightly.

'Yes, do,' she said, looking down on him.

And he bent his head to the mandoline, and suddenly began to sing a Neapolitan song, in a faint, compressed head-voice, looking up at her again as his lips moved, looking straight into her face with a curious mocking caress as the muted *voix blanche* came through his lips at her, amid the louder quavering of the mandoline. The sound penetrated her like a thread of fire, hurting, but delicious, the high thread of his voice. She could see the Adam's apple move in his throat, his brows tilted as he looked along his lashes at her all the time. Here was the strange sphinx singing again, and herself between its paws! She seemed almost to melt into his power.

Madame intervened to save her.

'What, serenade before breakfast! You have strong stomachs, I say. Eggs and ham are more the question, *hein*? Come, you smell them, don't you?'

A flicker of contempt and derision went over Cicio's face as he broke off and looked aside.

'I prefer the serenade,' said Alvina. 'I've had ham and eggs before.'

'You do, *hein*? Well—always, you won't. And now you must eat the ham and eggs, however. Yes? Isn't it so?'

Cicio rose to his feet, and looked at Alvina as he would have looked at Gigi, had Gigi been there. His eyes said unspeakable things about Madame. Alvina flashed a laugh, suddenly. And a good-humoured, half-mocking smile came over his face too.

They turned to follow Madame into the house. And so Alvina went before him, she felt his fingers stroke the nape of her neck, and pass in a soft touch right down her back. She started as if some unseen creature had stroked her with its paw, and she glanced swiftly round, to see the face of Cicio mischievous behind her shoulder.

'Now I think,' said Madame, 'that to-day we all take the same train. We go by the Great Central as far as the junction, together. Then you, Allaye, go on to Knarborough, and we leave you until to-morrow. And now there is not much time.'

'I am going to Woodhouse,' said Cicio in French.

'You also! By the train, or the bicycle?'

'Train,' said Cicio.

'Waste so much money?'

Cicio raised his shoulders slightly.

When breakfast was over, and Alvina had gone to her room, Geoffrey went out in the back yard, where the bicycles stood.

'Cic',' he said, 'I should like to go with thee to Woodhouse. Come on bicycle with me.'

Cicio shook his head.

'I'm going in train with *her*,' he said.

Geoffrey darkened with his heavy anger.

'I would like to see how it is, there, *chez elle*!' he said.

'Ask *her*,' said Cicio.

Geoffrey watched him suddenly.

'Thou forsakest me,' he said. 'I would like to see it, there.'

'Ask *her*,' repeated Cicio. 'Then come on bicycle.'

'You're content to leave me,' muttered Geoffrey.

Cicio touched his friend on his broad cheek, and smiled at him with affection.

'I don't leave thee, Gigi. I asked thy advice. You said, Go. But come. Go and ask her, and then come. Come on bicycle, eh? Ask her! Go on! Go and ask her.'

Alvina was surprised to hear a tap at her door, and Gigi's voice, in his strong foreign accent.

'Mees Houghton, I carry your bag.'

She opened her door in surprise. She was all ready.

'There it is,' she said, smiling at him. But he confronted her like a powerful ox, full of dangerous force. Her smile had reassured him.

'Na, Allaye,' he said, 'tell me something.'

'What?' laughed Alvina.

'Can I come to Woodhouse?'

'When?'

'To-day. Can I come on bicycle, to tea, eh? At your house with you and Cicio? Eh?'

He was smiling with a thick, doubtful, half sullen smile.

'Do!' said Alvina.

He looked at her with his large, dark-blue eyes.

'Really, eh?' he said, holding out his large hand.

She shook hands with him warmly.

'Yes, really!' she said. 'I wish you would.'

'Good,' he said, a broad smile on his thick mouth. And all the time he watched her curiously, from his large eyes.

'Cicio—a good chap, eh?' he said.

'Is he?' laughed Alvina.

'Ha-a—!' Gigi shook his head solemnly. 'The best!' He made such solemn eyes, Alvina laughed. He laughed too, and picked up her bag as if it were a bubble.

'Na Cic'—' he said, as he saw Cicio in the street. '*Sommes d'accord.*'

'*Ben!*' said Cicio, holding out his hand for the bag. '*Donne.*'

'*Né-né,*' said Gigi, shrugging.

Alvina found herself on the new and busy station that Sunday morning, one of the little theatrical company. It was an odd experience. They were so obviously a theatrical company—people apart from the world. Madame was darting her black eyes here and there, behind her spotted veil, and standing with the ostensible self-possession of her profession. Max was circling round with large strides, round a big black box on which the red words Natcha-Kee-Tawara showed mystic, and round the small bunch of stage fittings at the end of the platform. Louis was waiting to get the tickets, Gigi and Cicio were bringing up the bicycles. They were a whole train of departure in themselves, busy, bustling, cheerful—and curiously apart, vagrants.

Alvina strolled away towards the half-open bookstall. Geoffrey was standing monumental between her and the company. She returned to him.

'What time shall we expect you?' she said.

He smiled at her in his broad, friendly fashion.

'Expect me to be there? Why—' he rolled his eyes and proceeded to calculate. 'At four o'clock.'

'Just about the time when we get there,' she said.

He looked at her sagely, and nodded.

They were a good-humoured company in the railway carriage. The men smoked cigarettes and tapped off the ash on the heels of their boots, Madame watched every traveller with professional curiosity. Max scrutinized the newspaper, Lloyds, and pointed out items to Louis, who read them over Max's shoulder, Cicio suddenly smacked Geoffrey on the thigh, and looked laughing into his face. So till they arrived at the junction. And then there was a kissing and a taking of farewells, as if the company were separating for ever. Louis darted into the refreshment bar and returned with little pies and oranges, which he deposited in the carriage, Madame presented Alvina with a packet of chocolate. And it was 'Good-bye, good-bye, Allaye! Good-bye Cicio! *Bon voyage*. Have a good time, both.'

So Alvina sped on in the fast train to Knarborough with Cicio.

'I *do* like them all,' she said.

He opened his mouth slightly and lifted his head up and down. She saw in the movement how affectionate he was, and in his own way, how emotional. He loved them all. She put her hand to his. He gave her hand one sudden squeeze, of physical understanding, then left it as if nothing had happened. There were other people in the carriage with them. She could not help feeling how sudden and lovely that moment's grasp of his hand was: so warm, so whole.

And thus they watched the Sunday morning landscape slip by, as they ran into Knarborough. They went out to a little restaurant to eat. It was one o'clock.

'Isn't it strange, that we are travelling together like this?' she said, as she sat opposite him.

He smiled, looking into her eyes.

'You think it's strange?' he said, showing his teeth slightly.

'Don't you?' she cried.

He gave a slight, laconic laugh.

'And I can hardly bear it that I love you so much,' she said, quavering, across the potatoes.

He glanced furtively round, to see if anyone was listening, if anyone might hear. He would have hated it. But no one was near. Beneath the tiny table, he took her two knees between his knees, and pressed them with a slow, immensely powerful pressure. Helplessly she put her hand across the table to him. He covered it for one moment with his hand, then ignored it. But her knees were still between the powerful, living vice of his knees.

'Eat!' he said to her, smiling, motioning to her plate. And he relaxed her.

They decided to go out to Woodhouse on the tram-car, a long hour's ride. Sitting on the top of the covered car, in the atmosphere of strong tobacco smoke, he seemed self-conscious, withdrawn into his own cover, so obviously a dark-skinned foreigner. And Alvina, as she sat beside him, was reminded of the woman with the negro husband, down in Lumley. She understood the woman's reserve. She herself felt, in the same way, something of an outcast, because of the man at her side. An outcast! And glad to be an outcast. She clung to Cicio's dark, despised foreign nature. She loved it, she worshipped it, she defied all the other world. Dark, he sat beside her, drawn in to himself, overcast by his presumed inferiority among these northern industrial people. And she was with him, on his side, outside the pale of her own people.

There were already acquaintances on the tram. She nodded in answer to their salutation, but so obviously from a distance, that they kept turning round to eye her and Cicio. But they left her alone. The breach between her and them was established for ever—and it was her will which established it.

So up and down the weary hills of the hilly, industrial countryside, till at last they drew near to Woodhouse. They passed the ruins of Throttle-Ha'penny, and Alvina glanced at it indifferent. They ran along the Knarborough Road. A fair number of Woodhouse young people were strolling along the pavements in their Sunday clothes. She knew them all. She knew Lizzie Bates's fox furs, and Fanny Clough's lilac costume, and Mrs Smitham's winged hat. She knew them all. And almost inevitably the old Woodhouse feeling began to steal over her, she was glad they could not see her, she was a little ashamed of Cicio. She wished, for the moment, Cicio were not there. And as the time came to get down, she looked anxiously back and forth to see at which halt she had better descend—where fewer people would notice her. But then she threw her scruples to the wind, and descended into the staring, Sunday afternoon street, attended by Cicio, who carried her bag. She knew she was a marked figure.

They slipped round to Manchester House. Miss Pinnegar expected Alvina, but by the train, which came later. So she had to be knocked up, for she was lying down. She opened the door looking a little patched in her cheeks, because of her curious colouring, and a little forlorn, and a little dumpy, and a little irritable.

'I didn't know there'd be two of you,' was her greeting.

'Didn't you,' said Alvina, kissing her. 'Cicio came to carry my bag.'

'Oh,' said Miss Pinnegar. 'How do you do?' and she thrust out her hand to him. He shook it loosely.

'I had your wire,' said Miss Pinnegar. 'You said the train. Mrs Rollings is coming in at four again—'

'Oh all right—' said Alvina.

The house was silent and afternoon-like. Cicio took off his coat and sat down in Mr Houghton's chair. Alvina told him to smoke. He kept silent and reserved. Miss Pinnegar, a poor, patch-cheeked, rather round-backed figure with grey-brown fringe, stood as if she did not quite know what to say or do.

She followed Alvina upstairs to her room.

'I can't think why you bring *him* here,' snapped Miss Pinnegar. 'I don't know what you're thinking about. The whole place is talking already.'

'I don't care,' said Alvina. 'I like him.'

'Oh—for shame!' cried Miss Pinnegar, lifting her hand with Miss Frost's helpless, involuntary movement. 'What do you think of yourself? And your father a month dead.'

'It doesn't matter. Father *is* dead. And I'm sure the dead don't mind.'

'I never *knew* such things as you say.'

'Why? I mean them.'

Miss Pinnegar stood blank and helpless.

'You're not asking him to stay the night,' she blurted.

'Yes. And I'm going back with him to Madame to-morrow. You know I'm part of the company now, as pianist.'

'And are you going to marry him?'

'I don't know.'

'How *can* you say you don't know! Why it's awful. You make me feel I shall go out of my mind.'

'But I *don't* know,' said Alvina.

'It's incredible! Simply incredible! I believe you're out of your senses. I used to think sometimes there was something wrong with your mother. And that's what it is with you. You're not quite right in your mind. You need to be looked after.'

'Do I, Miss Pinnegar! Ah, well, don't you trouble to look after me, will you?'

'No one will if I don't.'

'I hope no one will.'

There was a pause.

'I'm ashamed to live another day in Woodhouse,' said Miss Pinnegar.

'*I'm* leaving it for ever,' said Alvina.

'I should think so,' said Miss Pinnegar.

Suddenly she sank into a chair, and burst into tears, wailing: 'Your poor father. Your poor father!'

'I'm sure the dead are all right. Why must you pity him?'

'You're a lost girl!' cried Miss Pinnegar.

'Am I really?' laughed Alvina. It sounded funny.

'Yes, you're a lost girl,' sobbed Miss Pinnegar, on a final note of despair.

'I like being lost,' said Alvina.

Miss Pinnegar wept herself into silence. She looked huddled and forlorn. Alvina went to her and laid her hand on her shoulder.

'Don't fret, Miss Pinnegar,' she said. 'Don't be silly. I love to be with Cicio and Madame. Perhaps in the end I shall marry him. But if I don't—' her hand suddenly gripped Miss Pinnegar's heavy arm till it hurt—'I wouldn't lose a minute of him, no, not for anything would I.'

Poor Miss Pinnegar dwindled, convinced.

'You make it hard for *me*, in Woodhouse,' she said, hopeless.

'Never mind,' said Alvina, kissing her. 'Woodhouse isn't heaven and earth.'

'It's been my home for forty years.'

'It's been mine for thirty. That's why I'm glad to leave it.' There was a pause.

'I've been thinking,' said Miss Pinnegar, 'about opening a little business in Tamworth. You know the Watsons are there.'

'I believe you'd be happy,' said Alvina.

Miss Pinnegar pulled herself together. She had energy and courage still.

'I don't want to stay here, anyhow,' she said. 'Woodhouse has nothing for me any more.'

'Of course it hasn't,' said Alvina. 'I think you'd be happier away from it.'

'Yes—probably I should—now!'

None the less, poor Miss Pinnegar was grey-haired, she was almost a dumpy, odd old woman.

They went downstairs. Miss Pinnegar put on the kettle.

'Would you like to see the house?' said Alvina to Cicio.

He nodded. And she took him from room to room. His eyes looked quickly and curiously over everything, noticing things, but without criticism.

'This was my mother's little sitting-room,' she said. 'She sat here for years, in this chair.'

'Always here?' he said, looking into Alvina's face.

'Yes. She was ill with her heart. This is another photograph of her. I'm not like her.'

'Who is *that*?' he asked, pointing to a photograph of the handsome, white-haired Miss Frost.

'That was Miss Frost, my governess. She lived here till she died. I loved her—she meant everything to me.'

'She also dead—?'

'Yes, five years ago.'

They went to the drawing-room. He laid his hand on the keys of the piano, sounding a chord.

'Play,' she said.

He shook his head, smiling slightly. But he wished her to play. She sat and played one of Kishwégin's pieces. He listened, faintly smiling.

'Fine piano—eh?' he said, looking into her face.

'I like the tone,' she said.

'Is it yours?'

'The piano? Yes. I suppose everything is mine—in name at least. I don't know how father's affairs are really.'

He looked at her, and again his eye wandered over the room. He saw a little coloured portrait of a child with a fleece of brownish-gold hair and surprised eyes, in a pale-blue stiff frock with a broad dark-blue sash.

'You?' he said.

'Do you recognize me?' she said. 'Aren't I comical?'

She took him upstairs—first to the monumental bed-room.

'This was mother's room,' she said. 'Now it is mine.'

He looked at her, then at the things in the room, then out of the window, then at her again. She flushed, and hurried to show him his room, and the bathroom. Then she went downstairs.

He kept glancing up at the height of the ceilings, the size of the rooms, taking in the size and proportion of the house, and the quality of the fittings.

'It is a big house,' he said. 'Yours?'

'Mine in name,' said Alvina. 'Father left all to me—and his debts as well, you see.'

'Much debts?'

'Oh yes! I don't quite know how much. But perhaps more debts than there is property. I shall go and see the lawyer in the morning. Perhaps there will be nothing at all left for me, when everything is paid.'

She had stopped on the stairs, telling him this, turning round to him, who was on the step above. He looked down on her, calculating. Then he smiled sourly.

'Bad job, eh, if it is all gone—!' he said.

'I don't mind, really, if I can live,' she said.

He spread his hands, deprecating, not understanding. Then he glanced up the stairs and along the corridor again, and downstairs into the hall.

'A fine big house. Grand if it was yours,' he said.

'I wish it were,' she said rather pathetically, 'if you like it so much.'

He shrugged his shoulders.

'*Hé,*' he said. 'How not like it!'

'I don't like it,' she said. 'I think it's a gloomy miserable hole. I hate it. I've lived here all my life and seen everything bad happen here. I hate it.'

'Why?' he said, with a curious, sarcastic intonation.

'It's a bad job it isn't yours, for certain,' he said, as they entered the living-room, where Miss Pinnegar sat cutting bread and butter.

'What?' said Miss Pinnegar sharply.

'The house,' said Alvina.

'Oh well, we don't know. We'll hope for the best,' replied Miss Pinnegar, arranging the bread and butter on the plate. Then, rather tart, she added: 'It *is* a bad job. And a good many things are a bad job, besides that. If Miss Houghton had what she *ought* to have, things would be very different, I assure you.'

'Oh yes,' said Cicio, to whom this address was directed.

'Very different indeed. If all the money hadn't been— lost—in the way it has, Miss Houghton wouldn't be playing the piano, for one thing, in a cinematograph show.'

'No, perhaps not,' said Cicio.

'Certainly not. It's not the right thing for her to be doing, *at all*!'

'You think not?' said Cicio.

'Do you imagine it is?' said Miss Pinnegar, turning point blank on him as he sat by the fire.

He looked curiously at Miss Pinnegar, grinning slightly.

'*Hé!*' he said. 'How do I know!'

'I should have thought it was obvious,' said Miss Pinnegar.

'*Hé!*' he ejaculated, not fully understanding.

'But of course those that are used to nothing better can't see anything but what they're used to,' she said, rising and shaking the crumbs from her black silk apron, into the fire. He watched her.

Miss Pinnegar went away into the scullery. Alvina was laying a fire in the drawing-room. She came with a dust-pan to take some coal from the fire of the living-room.

'What do you want?' said Cicio, rising. And he took the shovel from her hand.

'Big, hot fires, aren't they?' he said, as he lifted the burning coals from the glowing mass of the grate.

'Enough,' said Alvina. 'Enough! We'll put it in the drawing-room.' He carried the shovel of flaming, smoking coals to the other room, and threw them in the grate on the sticks, watching Alvina put on more pieces of coal.

'Fine, a fire! Quick work, eh? A beautiful thing, a fire! You know what they say in my place: You can live without food, but you can't live without fire.'

'But I thought it was always hot in Naples,' said Alvina.

'No, it isn't. And my village, you know, when I was small boy, that was in the mountains, an hour quick train from Naples. Cold in the winter, hot in the summer—'

'As cold as England?' said Alvina.

'*Hé*—and colder. The wolves come down. You could hear them crying in the night, in the frost—'

'How terrifying—!' said Alvina.

'And they will kill the dogs? Always they kill the dogs. You know, they hate dogs, wolves do.' He made a queer noise, to show how wolves hate dogs. Alvina understood, and laughed.

'So should I, if I was a wolf,' she said.

'Yes—eh?' His eyes gleamed on her for a moment. 'Ah, but, the poor dogs! You find them bitten—carried away among the trees or the stones, hard to find them, poor things, the next day.'

'How frightened they must be—!' said Alvina.

'Frightened—hu!' he made sudden gesticulations and ejaculations, which added volumes to his few words.

'And did you like it, your village?' she said.

He put his head on one side in deprecation.

'No,' he said, 'because, you see—*hé*, there is nothing to do—no money—work—work—work—no life—you see nothing. When I was a small boy my father, he died, and my mother comes with me to Naples. Then I go with the little boats on the sea—fishing, carrying people—' He flourished his hand as if to make her understand all the things that must be wordless. He smiled at her—but there was a faint, poignant sadness and remoteness in him, a beauty of old fatality, and ultimate indifference to fate.

'And were you very poor?'

'Poor?—why yes! Nothing. Rags—no shoes—bread, little fish from the sea—shell-fish—'

His hands flickered, his eyes rested on her with a profound look of knowledge. And it seemed in spite of all, one state was very much the same to him as another, poverty was as much life as affluence. Only he had a sort of jealous idea that it was humiliating to be poor, and so, for vanity's sake, he would have possessions. The countless generations of civilization behind him had left him an instinct of the world's meaninglessness. Only his little modern education made money and independence an *idée fixe*. Old instinct told him the world was nothing. But modern education, so shallow, was much more efficacious than instinct. It drove him to make a show of himself to the world. Alvina watching him, as if hypnotized, saw his old beauty, formed through civilization after civilization; and at the same time she saw his modern vulgarianism, and decadence.

'And when you go back, you will go back to your old village?' she said.

He made a gesture with his head and shoulders, evasive, non-committal.

'I don't know, you see,' he said.

'What is the name of it?'

'Pescocalascio.' He said the word subduedly, unwillingly.

'Tell me again,' said Alvina.

'Pescocalascio.'

She repeated it.

'And tell me how you spell it,' she said.

He fumbled in his pocket for a pencil and a piece of paper. She rose and brought him an old sketch-book. He wrote, slowly but with the beautiful Italian hand, the name of his village.

'And write your name,' she said.

'Marasca Francesco', he wrote.

'And write the name of your father and mother,' she said. He looked at her inquiringly.

'I want to see them,' she said.

'Marasca Giovanni', he wrote, and under that 'Califano Maria'.

She looked at the four names, in the graceful Italian script. And one after the other she read them out. He corrected her, smiling gravely. When she said them properly, he nodded.

'Yes,' he said. 'That's it. You say it well.'

At that moment Miss Pinnegar came in to say Mrs Rollings had seen another of the young men riding down the street.

'That's Gigi! He doesn't know how to come here,' said Cicio, quickly taking his hat and going out to find his friend.

Geoffrey arrived, his broad face hot and perspiring.

'Couldn't you find it?' said Alvina.

'I find the house, but I couldn't find no door,' said Geoffrey.

They all laughed, and sat down to tea. Geoffrey and Cicio talked to each other in French, and kept each other in countenance. Fortunately for them, Madame had seen to their table-manners. But still they were far too free and easy to suit Miss Pinnegar.

'Do you know,' said Cicio in French to Geoffrey, 'what a fine house this is?'

'No,' said Geoffrey, rolling his large eyes round the room, and speaking with his cheek stuffed out with food. 'Is it?'

'Ah—if it was *hers,* you know—'

And so, after tea, Cicio said to Alvina:

'Shall you let Geoffrey see the house?'

The tour commenced again. Geoffrey, with his thick legs planted apart, gazed round the rooms, and made his comments in French to Cicio. When they climbed the stairs, he fingered the big, smooth mahogany bannister-rail. In the bedroom he stared almost dismayed at the colossal bed and cupboard. In the bathroom he turned on the old-fashioned, silvered taps.

'Here is my room—' said Cicio in French.

'*Assez éloigné!*' replied Gigi. Cicio also glanced along the corridor.

'Yes,' he said. 'But an open course—'

'Look, my boy—if you could marry *this*—' meaning the house.

'Ha, she doesn't know if it is hers any more! Perhaps the debts cover every bit of it.'

'Don't say so! *Na*, that's a pity, that's a pity! *La pauvre fille—pauvre demoiselle!*' lamented Geoffrey.

'Isn't it a pity! What dost say?'

'A thousand pities! A thousand pities! Look, my boy, love needs no havings, but marriage does. Love is for all, even the grasshoppers. But marriage means a kitchen. That's how it is. *La pauvre demoiselle; c'est malheur pour elle.*'

'That's true,' said Cicio. '*Et aussi pour moi*. For me as well.'

'For thee as well, *cher*! Perhaps—' said Geoffrey, laying his arm on Cicio's shoulder, and giving him a sudden hug. They smiled to each other.

'Who knows!' said Cicio.

'Who knows, truly, my Cic'.'

As they went downstairs to rejoin Alvina, whom they heard playing on the piano in the drawing-room, Geoffrey peeped once more into the big bedroom.

'*Tu n'es jamais monté si haut, mon beau. Pour moi, ça serait difficile de m'élever. J'aurais bien peur, moi. Tu te trouves aussi un peu ébahi, hein? n'est ce pas?*'

'*Y'a place pour trois*,' said Cicio.

'*Non, je crèverais, là—haut. Pas pour moi!*'

And they went laughing downstairs.

Miss Pinnegar was sitting with Alvina, determined not to go to Chapel this evening. She sat, rather hulked, reading a novel. Alvina flirted with the two men, played the piano to them, and suggested a game of cards.

'Oh Alvina, you will never bring out the cards to-night!' expostulated poor Miss Pinnegar.

'But Miss Pinnegar, it can't possibly hurt anybody.'

'You know what I think—and what your father thought—and your Mother and Miss Frost—'

'You see I think it's only prejudice,' said Alvina.

'Oh very well!' said Miss Pinnegar angrily.

And closing her book, she rose and went to the other room. Alvina brought out the cards and a little box of pence

which remained from Endeavour harvests. At that moment
there was a knock. It was Mr May. Miss Pinnegar brought
him in, in triumph.

'Oh!' he said. 'Company! I heard you'd come, Miss
Houghton, so I *hastened* to pay my compliments. I didn't
know you had *company*. How do you do, Francesco! How
do you do, Geoffrey. *Comment allez-vous, alors?*'

'*Bien!*' said Geoffrey. 'You are going to take a hand?'

'Cards on Sunday evening! Dear me, what a revolution!
Of course, I'm not *bigoted*. If Miss Houghton asks
me—'

Miss Pinnegar looked solemnly at Alvina.

'Yes, do take a hand, Mr May,' said Alvina.

'Thank you, I will then, if I may. Especially as I see those
tempting piles of pennies and ha'pennies. Who is bank, may
I ask? Is Miss Pinnegar going to play too?'

But Miss Pinnegar had turned her poor, bowed back, and
departed.

'I'm afraid she's offended,' said Alvina.

'But why? We don't put *her* soul in danger, do we now?
I'm a good Catholic, you know, I *can't* do with these provincial little creeds. Who deals? Do you, Miss Houghton?
But I'm afraid we shall have a rather *dry* game? What? Isn't
that your opinion?'

The other men laughed.

'If Miss Houghton would just *allow* me to run round and
bring something in. Yes? May I? That would be *so* much
more cheerful. What is your choice, gentlemen?'

'Beer,' said Cicio, and Geoffrey nodded.

'Beer! Oh really! Extraor'nary! I always take a little
whisky myself. What kind of beer? Ale?—or bitter? I'm
afraid I'd better bring bottles. Now how can I secrete them?
You haven't a small travelling case, Miss Houghton? Then
I shall look as if I'd just been taking a *journey*. Which I
have—to the Sun and back: and if *that* isn't far enough, even
for Miss Pinnegar and John Wesley, why, I'm sorry.'

Alvina produced the travelling case.

'Excellent!' he said. 'Excellent! It will hold half-a-dozen
beautifully. Now—' he fell into a whisper—'hadn't I better

sneak out at the front door, and so escape the clutches of the watch-dog?'

Out he went, on tip-toe, the other two men grinning at him. Fortunately there were glasses, the best old glasses, in the side cupboard in the drawing-room. But unfortunately, when Mr May returned, a corkscrew was in request. So Alvina stole to the kitchen. Miss Pinnegar sat dumped by the fire, with her spectacles and her book. She watched like a lynx as Alvina returned. And she saw the tell-tale corkscrew. So she dumped a little deeper in her chair.

'There was a sound of revelry by night!' For Mr May, after a long depression, was in high feather. They shouted, positively shouted over their cards, they roared with excitement, expostulation, and laughter. Miss Pinnegar sat through it all. But at one point she could bear it no longer.

The drawing-room door opened, and the dumpy, hulked, faded woman in a black serge dress stood like a rather squat avenging angel in the doorway.

'What would your *father* say to this?' she said sternly.

The company suspended their laughter and their cards, and looked round. Miss Pinnegar wilted and felt strange under so many eyes.

'Father!' said Alvina. 'But why father?'

'You lost girl!' said Miss Pinnegar, backing out and closing the door.

Mr May laughed so much that he knocked his whisky over.

'There,' he cried helpless, 'look what she's cost me!' And he went off into another paroxysm, swelling like a turkey.

Cicio opened his mouth, laughing silently.

'Lost girl! Lost girl! How lost, when you are at home?' said Geoffrey, making large eyes and looking hither and thither as if *he* had lost something.

'No but, really,' said Mr May, 'drinking and card-playing with strange men in the drawing-room on Sunday evening, of *cauce* it's scandalous! It's *terrible*! I don't know how ever you'll be saved, after such a sin. And in Manchester House, too—!' He went off into another silent, turkey-scarlet burst of mirth, wriggling in his chair and squealing faintly: 'Oh, I love it, I love it! *You lost girl!* Why of *cauce* she's lost! And

Miss Pinnegar has only just found it out. Who *wouldn't* be lost? Why even Miss Pinnegar would be lost if she could. Of *cauce* she would! Quite natch'ral!'

Mr May wiped his eyes with his handkerchief which had unfortunately mopped up his whisky.

So they played on, till Mr May and Geoffrey had won all the pennies, except twopence of Cicio's. Alvina was in debt.

'Well, I think it's been a most agreeable game,' said Mr May. 'Most agreeable? Don't you all?'

The two other men smiled and nodded.

'I'm only sorry to think Miss Houghton has *lost* so steadily all evening. Really quite remarkable. But *then*—you see—I comfort myself with the reflection "Lucky in cards, unlucky in love." I'm certainly *hounded* with misfortune in love. And I'm *sure* Miss Houghton would rather be unlucky in cards than in love. What, isn't it so?'

'Of course,' said Alvina.

'There, you see, *of cauce!* Well, all we can do after that is to wish her success in love. Isn't that so, gentlemen. I'm sure *we* are all quite willing to do our best to contribute to it? Isn't it so, gentlemen? Aren't we all ready to do our best to contribute to Miss Houghton's happiness in love? Well then, let us drink to it.' He lifted his glass, and bowed to Alvina. 'With *every* wish for your success in love, Miss Houghton, and your *devoted* servant—' He bowed and drank.

Geoffrey made large eyes at her as he held up his glass.

'*I* know you'll come out all right in love, *I* know,' he said heavily.

'And you, Cicio? Aren't you drinking?' said Mr May.

Cicio held up his glass, looked at Alvina, made a little mouth at her, comical, and drank his beer.

'Well,' said Mr May, '*beer* must confirm it, since words won't.'

'What time is it?' said Alvina. 'We must have supper.'

It was past nine o'clock. Alvina rose and went to the kitchen, the men trailing after her. Miss Pinnegar was not there. She was not anywhere.

'Has she gone to bed?' said Mr May. And he crept stealthily upstairs on tip-toe, a comical, flush-faced, tubby little man. He was familiar with the house. He returned prancing.

'I heard her cough,' he said. 'There's a light under her door. She's gone to bed. Now haven't I always said she was a good soul? I shall drink her health. Miss Pinnegar—' and he bowed stiffly in the direction of the stairs—'your health, and a *good night's rest.*'

After which, giggling gaily, he seated himself at the head of the table and began to carve the cold mutton.

'And where are the Natcha-Kee-Tawaras this week?' he asked. They told him.

'Oh? And you two are cycling back to the camp of Kish-wégin to-night? We mustn't prolong our cheerfulness *too* far.'

'Cicio is staying to help me with my bag to-morrow,' said Alvina. 'You know I've joined the Tawaras permanently—as pianist.'

'No, I didn't know that! Oh really! Really! Oh! Well! I see! Permanently! Yes, I am surprised! As pianist? And if I might ask, what is your share of the tribal income?'

'That isn't settled yet,' said Alvina.

'No! Exactly! Exactly! It *wouldn't* be settled yet. And you say it is a permanent engagement? Of *cauce*, at such a figure.'

'Yes, it is a permanent engagement,' said Alvina.

'Really! What a blow you give me! You won't come back to the Endeavour? What? Not at all?'

'No,' said Alvina. 'I shall sell out of the Endeavour.'

'Really! You've decided, have you? Oh! This is news to me. And is *this* quite final, too?'

'Quite,' said Alvina.

'I see! Putting two and two together, if I may say so—' and he glanced from her to the young men—'I *see*. Most decidedly, most one-sidedly, if I may use the vulgarism, I *see—e—e*! Oh! but what a blow you give me! What a blow you give me!'

'Why?' said Alvina.

'What's to become of the Endeavour? and consequently, of poor me?'

'Can't you keep it going?—form a company?'

'I'm afraid I can't. I've done my best. But I'm afraid, you know, you've landed me.'

'I'm so sorry,' said Alvina. 'I hope not.'

'Thank you for the *hope*!' said Mr May sarcastically. 'They say hope is sweet. *I* begin to find it a little *bitter*!'

Poor man, he had already gone quite yellow in the face. Cicio and Geoffrey watched him with dark-seeing eyes.

'And when are you going to let this fatal decision take effect?' asked Mr May.

'I'm going to see the lawyer to-morrow, and I'm going to tell him to sell everything and clear up as soon as possible,' said Alvina.

'Sell everything! This house, and all it contains?'

'Yes,' said Alvina. 'Everything.'

'Really!' Mr May seemed smitten quite dumb. 'I feel as if the world had suddenly come to an end,' he said.

'But hasn't your world often come to an end before?' said Alvina.

'Well—I suppose, once or twice. But *never* quite on top of me, you see, before—'

There was a silence.

'And have you told Miss Pinnegar?' said Mr May.

'Not finally. But she has decided to open a little business in Tamworth, where she has relations.'

'Has she! And are you *really* going to *tour* with these young people—?' he indicated Cicio and Gigi. 'And at *no* salary!' His voice rose. 'Why! It's almost *White Slave Traffic*, on Madame's part. Upon my word!'

'I don't think so,' said Alvina. 'Don't you see that's insulting.'

'*Insulting!* Well, I don't know. I think it's the *truth*—'

'Not to be said to me, for all that,' said Alvina quivering with anger.

'Oh!' perked Mr May, yellow with strange rage. 'Oh! I mustn't say what I think! Oh!'

'Not if you think those things—' said Alvina.

'Oh really! The difficulty is, you see, I'm afraid I *do* think them—' Alvina watched him with big, heavy eyes.

'Go away,' she said. 'Go away! I won't be insulted by you.'

'No *indeed*!' cried Mr May, starting to his feet, his eyes
almost bolting from his head. 'No *indeed*! I wouldn't *think*
of insulting you in the presence of these *two* young gentlemen.'

Cicio slowly rose also, and with a slow, repeated motion
of the head, indicated the door.

'*Allez!*' he said.

'*Certainement!*' cried Mr May, flying at Cicio, verbally,
like an enraged hen yellow at the gills. '*Certainement! Je
m'en vais. Cette compagnie n'est pas de ma choix.*'

'*Allez!*' said Cicio, more loudly.

And Mr May strutted out of the room like a bird bursting
with its own rage. Cicio stood with his hands leaning on the
table, listening. They heard Mr May slam the front door.

'Gone!' said Geoffrey.

Cicio smiled sneeringly.

'*Voyez! un cochon de lait,*' said Gigi amply and calmly.

Cicio sat down in his chair and Geoffrey poured out some
beer for him, saying:

'Drink, my Cic', the bubble has burst, prfff!' And Gigi
knocked in his own puffed cheek with his fist. 'Allaye, my
dear, your health! We are the Tawaras. We are Allaye! We
are Pacohuila! We are Walgatchka! *Allons!* The milk-pig is
stewed and eaten. *Voilà!*' He drank, smiling broadly.

'One by one,' said Geoffrey, who was a little drunk: 'One
by one we put them out of the field, they are *hors de combat*.
Who remains? Pacohuila, Walgatchka, Allaye—'

He smiled very broadly. Alvina was sitting sunk in
thought and torpor after her sudden anger.

'Allaye, what do you think about? You are the bride of
Tawara,' said Geoffrey.

Alvina looked at him, smiling rather wanly.

'And who is Tawara?' she asked.

He raised his shoulders and spread his hands and swayed
his head from side to side, for all the world like a comic
mandarin.

'There!' he cried. 'The question! Who is Tawara? Who?
Tell me! Cicio is he—and I am he—and Max and Louis—'
he spread his hand to the distant members of the tribe.

'I can't be the bride of all four of you,' said Alvina, laughing.

'No—no! No—no! Such a thing does not come into my mind. But you are the Bride of Tawara. You dwell in the tent of Pacohuila. And comes the day, should it ever be so, there is no room for you in the tent of Pacohuila, then the lodge of Walgatchka the bear is open for you. Open, yes, wide open—' He spread his arms from his ample chest, at the end of the table. 'Open, and when Allaye enters, it is the lodge of Allaye, Walgatchka is the bear that serves Allaye. By the law of the Pale Face, by the law of the Yenghees, by the law of the Fransayes, Walgatchka shall be husband-bear of Allaye, that day she lifts the door-curtain of his tent—'

He rolled his eyes and looked around. Alvina watched him.

'But I might be afraid of a husband-bear,' she said.

Geoffrey got on to his feet.

'By the Manitou,' he said, 'the head of the bear Walgatchka is humble—' here Geoffrey bowed his head—'his teeth are as soft as lilies—' here he opened his mouth and put his finger on his small close teeth—'his hands are as soft as bees that stroke a flower—' here he spread his hands and went and suddenly flopped on his knees beside Alvina showing his hands and his teeth and rolling his eyes. 'Allaye can have no fear at all of the bear Walgatchka,' he said, looking up at her comically.

Cicio who had been watching and slightly grinning, here rose to his feet and took Geoffrey by the shoulder, pulling him up.

'*Basta!*' he said. '*Tu es saoul.* You are drunk, my Gigi. Get up. How are you going to ride to Mansfield, *hein*?—great beast.'

'Cicio,' said Geoffrey solemnly. 'I love thee, I love thee as a brother, and also more. I love thee as a brother, my Cicio, as thou knowest. But—' and he puffed fiercely—'I am the slave of Allaye, I am the tame bear of Allaye.'

'Get up,' said Cicio, 'get up! *Per bacco!* She doesn't want a tame bear.' He smiled down on his friend.

Geoffrey rose to his feet and flung his arms round Cicio.

'Cic',' he besought him. 'Cic'—I love thee as a brother.

But let me be the tame bear of Allaye, let me be the gentle bear of Allaye.'

'All right,' said Cicio. 'Thou art the tame bear of Allaye.'

Geoffrey strained Cicio to his breast.

'Thank you! Thank you! Salute me, my own friend.'

And Cicio kissed him on either cheek. Whereupon Geoffrey immediately flopped on his knees again before Alvina, and presented her his broad, rich-coloured cheek.

'Salute your bear, Allaye,' he cried. 'Salute your slave, the tame bear Walgatchka, who is a wild bear for all except Allaye and his brother Pacohuila the Puma.' Geoffrey growled realistically as a wild bear as he kneeled before Alvina, presenting his cheek.

Alvina looked at Cicio, who stood above, watching. Then she lightly kissed him on the cheek, and said:

'Won't you go to bed, and sleep.'

Geoffrey staggered to his feet, shaking his head.

'No—no—' he said. 'No—no! Walgatchka must travel to the tent of Kishwégin, to the Camp of the Tawaras.'

'Not to-night, *mon brave*,' said Cicio. 'To-night we stay here, *hein*. Why separate, *hein*?—*frére*?'

Geoffrey again clasped Cicio in his arms.

'Pacohuila and Walgatchka are blood-brothers, two bodies, one blood. One blood, in two bodies: one stream, in two valleys: one lake, between two mountains.'

Here Geoffrey gazed with large, heavy eyes on Cicio. Alvina brought a candle and lighted it.

'You will manage in the one room?' she said. 'I will give you another pillow.'

She led the way upstairs. Geoffrey followed, heavily. Then Cicio. On the landing Alvina gave them the pillow and the candle, smiled, bade them good-night in a whisper, and went downstairs again. She cleared away the supper and carried away all glasses and bottles from the drawing-room. Then she washed up, removing all traces of the feast. The cards she restored to their old mahogany box. Manchester House looked itself again.

She turned off the gas at the meter, and went upstairs to bed. From the far room she could hear the gentle, but profound vibration of Geoffrey's snoring. She was tired after her day: too tired to trouble about anything any more.

But in the morning she was first downstairs. She heard Miss Pinnegar, and hurried. Hastily she opened the windows and doors to drive away the smell of beer and smoke. She heard the men rumbling in the bathroom. And quickly she prepared breakfast and made a fire. Mrs Rollings would not appear till later in the day. At a quarter to seven Miss Pinnegar came down, and went into the scullery to make her tea.

'Did both the men stay?' she asked.

'Yes, they both slept in the end room,' said Alvina.

Miss Pinnegar said no more, but padded with her tea and her boiled egg into the living-room. In the morning she was wordless.

Cicio came down, in his shirt-sleeves as usual, but wearing a collar. He greeted Miss Pinnegar politely.

'Good-morning!' she said, and went on with her tea.

Geoffrey appeared. Miss Pinnegar glanced once at him, sullenly, and briefly answered his good-morning. Then she went on with her egg, slow and persistent in her movements, mum.

The men went out to attend to Geoffrey's bicycle. The morning was slow and grey, obscure. As they pumped up the tyres, they heard someone padding behind. Miss Pinnegar came and unbolted the yard door, but ignored their presence. Then they saw her return and slowly mount the outer stair-ladder, which went up to the top floor. Two minutes afterwards they were startled by the irruption of the work-girls. As for the work-girls, they gave quite loud, startled squeals, suddenly seeing the two men on their right hand, in the obscure morning. And they lingered on the stairway to gaze in rapt curiosity, poking and whispering, until Miss Pinnegar appeared overhead, and sharply rang a bell which hung beside the entrance door of the workrooms.

After which excitements Geoffrey and Cicio went in to breakfast which Alvina had prepared.

'You have done it all, eh?' said Cicio, glancing round.

'Yes, I've made breakfast for years, now,' said Alvina.

'Not many more times here, eh?' he said, smiling significantly.

'I hope not,' said Alvina.

Cicio sat down almost like a husband—as if it were his right.

Geoffrey was very quiet this morning. He ate his breakfast, and rose to go.

'I shall see you soon,' he said, smiling sheepishly and bowing to Alvina. Cicio accompanied him to the street.

When Cicio returned, Alvina was once more washing dishes.

'What time shall we go?' he said.

'We'll catch the one train. I must see the lawyer this morning.'

'And what shall you say to him?'

'I shall tell him to sell everything—'

'And marry me?'

She started, and looked at him.

'You don't want to marry, do you?' she said.

'Yes, I do.'

'Wouldn't you rather wait, and see—'

'What?' he said.

'See if there is any money.'

He watched her steadily, and his brow darkened.

'Why?' he said.

She began to tremble.

'You'd like it better if there was money.'

A slow, sinister smile came on his mouth. His eyes never smiled, except to Geoffrey, when a flood of warm, laughing light sometimes suffused them.

'You think I should!'

'Yes. It's true, isn't it? You would!'

He turned his eyes aside, and looked at her hands as she washed the forks. They trembled slightly. Then he looked back at her eyes again, that were watching him large and wistful and a little accusing.

His impudent laugh came on his face.

'Yes,' he said, 'it is always better if there is money.' He put his hand on her, and she winced. 'But I marry you for

love, you know. You know what love is—' And he put his
arms around her, and laughed down into her face.

She strained away.

'But you can have love without marriage,' she said. 'You
know that.'

'All right! All right! Give me love, eh? I want that.'

She struggled against him.

'But not now,' she said.

She saw the light in his eyes fix determinedly, and he nodded.

'Now!' he said. 'Now!'

His yellow-tawny eyes looked down into hers, alien and
overbearing.

'I can't,' she struggled. 'I can't now.'

He laughed in a sinister way: yet with a certain warm-
heartedness.

'Come to that big room—' he said.

Her face flew fixed into opposition.

'I can't now, really,' she said, grimly.

His eyes looked down at hers. Her eyes looked back at
him, hard and cold and determined. They remained motionless for some seconds. Then, a stray wisp of hair catching his attention, desire filled his heart, warm and full,
obliterating his anger in the combat. For a moment he softened. He saw her hardness becoming more assertive, and he
wavered in sudden dislike, and almost dropped her. Then
again the desire flushed his heart, his smile became reckless
of her, and he picked her right up.

'Yes,' he said. 'Now.'

For a second, she struggled frenziedly. But almost instantly she recognized how much stronger he was, and she
was still mute and motionless with anger. White, and mute,
and motionless, she let be. She let herself go down the unknown dark flood of his will, borne from her old footing
forever.

There comes a moment when fate sweeps us away. Now
Alvina felt herself swept—she knew not whither—but into
a dusky region where men had dark faces and translucent
yellow eyes, where all speech was foreign, and life was not
her life. It was as if she had fallen from her own world on

to another, darker star, where meanings were all changed. She was alone, and she did not mind being alone. It was what she wanted. In all the passion of her lover she had found a loneliness, beautiful, cool, like a shadow she wrapped round herself and which gave her a sweetness of perfection. It was a moment of stillness and completeness.

Noises went on, in the street, overhead in the workroom. But theirs was a complete silence.

At last he rose and looked at her.

'Love is a fine thing, Allaye,' he said.

She remained watching him, his strange, smiling face, which she seemed to have known, half-known, before, in some far-off, forbidden existence. He approached and laid his hand on her breast, and kissed her.

'Love?' he said, enigmatical, a little wistful.

But she could not answer, she remained still. He looked down into her eyes, far off, and yet imminent. Then he went away.

She remained in her perfect and beautiful solitude, perfected in being alone. But soon she wanted to find him. She went upstairs and looked in the mirror at herself and at her clothes, adjusted her hair, tied on her apron, and went downstairs once more. She could not find Cicio: he had gone out. A stray cat darted from the scullery, and broke a plate in her leap. Alvina found her washing-up water cold. She put on more, and began to dry her dishes.

Cicio returned shortly, and stood in the doorway looking at her. She turned to him, unexpectedly laughing.

'What do you think of yourself?' she laughed.

'Well,' he said, with a little nod, and a furtive look of triumph about him, evasive. He went past her and into the room. Her inside burned with love for him: so elusive, so beautiful, in his silent passing out of her sight. She wiped her dishes happily. Why was she so absurdly happy, she asked herself? And why did she still fight so hard against the sense of his dark, unseizable beauty? Unseizable, forever unseizable! That made her almost his slave. She fought against her own desire to fall at his feet. Ridiculous to be so happy.

She sang to herself as she went about her work downstairs. Then she went upstairs, to do the bedrooms and pack her bag. At ten o'clock she was to go to the family lawyer.

She lingered over her possessions: what to take, and what not to take. And so doing she wasted her time. It was already ten o'clock when she hurried downstairs. He was sitting quite still, waiting. He looked up at her.

'Now I must hurry,' she said. 'I don't think I shall be more than an hour.'

He put on his hat and went out with her.

'I shall tell the lawyer I am engaged to you. Shall I?' she asked.

'Yes,' he said. 'Tell him what you like.' He was indifferent.

'Because,' said Alvina gaily, 'we can please ourselves what we do, whatever we say. I shall say we think of getting married in the summer, when we know each other better, and going to Italy.'

'Why shall you say all that?' said Cicio.

'Because I shall *have* to give some account of myself, or they'll make me do something I don't want to do. You might come to the lawyer's with me, will you? He's an awfully nice old man. Then he'd believe in you.'

But Cicio shook his head.

'No,' he said. 'I shan't go. He doesn't want to see *me*.'

'Well, if you don't want to. But I remember your name, Francesco Marasca, and I remember Pesocalascio.'

Cicio heard in silence, as they walked the half-empty, Monday-morning street of Woodhouse. People kept nodding to Alvina. Some hurried inquisitively across to speak to her and look at Cicio. Cicio however stood aside and turned his back.

'Oh yes,' Alvina said. 'I am staying with friends, here and there, for a few weeks. No, I don't know when I shall be back. Good-bye!'

'You're looking well, Alvina,' people said to her. 'I think you're looking wonderful. A change does you good.'

'It does, doesn't it,' said Alvina brightly. And she was pleased she was looking well.

'Well, good-bye for a minute,' she said, glancing smiling into his eyes and nodding to him, as she left him at the gate of the lawyer's house, by the ivy-covered wall.

The lawyer was a little man, all grey. Alvina had known him since she was a child: but rather as an official than an individual. She arrived all smiling in his room. He sat down and scrutinized her sharply, officially, before beginning.

'Well, Miss Houghton, and what news have you?'

'I don't think I've any, Mr Beeby. I came to you for news.'

'Ah!' said the lawyer, and he fingered a paper-weight that covered a pile of papers. 'I'm afraid there is nothing very pleasant, unfortunately. And nothing very unpleasant either, for that matter.'

He gave her a shrewd little smile.

'Is the will proved?'

'Not yet. But I expect it will be through in a few days' time.'

'And are all the claims in?'

'Yes. I *think* so! I think so!' And again he laid his hand on the pile of papers under the paper-weight, and ran through the edges with the tips of his fingers.

'All those?' said Alvina.

'Yes,' he said quietly. It sounded ominous.

'Many!' said Alvina.

'A fair amount! A fair amount! Let me show you a statement.'

He rose and brought her a paper. She made out, with the lawyer's help, that the claims against her father's property exceeded the gross estimate of his property by some seven hundred pounds.

'Does it mean we owe seven hundred pounds?' she asked.

'That is only on the *estimate* of the property. It might, of course, realize much more, when sold—or it might realize less.'

'How awful!' said Alvina, her courage sinking.

'Unfortunate! Unfortunate! However, I don't think the realization of the property would amount to less than the estimate. I don't think so.'

'But even then,' said Alvina. 'There is sure to be something owing—'

She saw herself saddled with her father's debts.

'I'm afraid so,' said the lawyer.

'And then what?' said Alvina.

'Oh—the creditors will have to be satisfied with a little less than they claim, I suppose. Not a very great deal, you see. I don't expect they will complain a great deal, In fact, some of them will be less badly off than they feared. No, on that score we need not trouble further. Useless if we do, anyhow. But now, about yourself. Would you like me to try to compound with the creditors, so that you could have some sort of provision? They are mostly people who know you, know your condition: and I might try—'

'Try what?' said Alvina.

'To make some sort of compound. Perhaps you might retain a lease of Miss Pinnegar's work-rooms. Perhaps even something might be done about the cinematograph. What would you like—?'

Alvina sat still in her chair, looking through the window at the ivy sprays, and the leaf buds on the lilac. She felt she could not, she could not cut off every resource. In her own heart she had confidently expected a few hundred pounds: even a thousand or more. And that would make her *something* of a catch, to people who had nothing. But now!—nothing!—nothing at the back of her but her hundred pounds. When that was gone—!

In her dilemma she looked at the lawyer.

'You didn't expect it would be quite so bad?' he said.

'I think I didn't,' she said.

'No. Well—it might have been worse.'

Again he waited. And again she looked at him vacantly.

'What do you think?' he said.

For answer, she only looked at him with wide eyes.

'Perhaps you would rather decide later.'

'No,' she said. 'No. It's no use deciding later.'

The lawyer watched her with curious eyes, his hand beat a little impatiently.

'I will do my best,' he said, 'to get what I can for you.'

'Oh well!' she said. 'Better let everything go. I don't *want* to hang on. Don't bother about me at all. I shall go away, anyhow.'

'You will go away?' said the lawyer, and he studied his finger-nails.

'Yes, I shan't stay here.'

'Oh! And may I ask if you have any definite idea, where you will go?'

'I've got an engagement as pianist, with a travelling theatrical company.'

'Oh indeed!' said the lawyer, scrutinizing her sharply. She stared away vacantly out of the window. He took to the attentive study of his finger-nails once more. 'And at a sufficient salary?'

'Quite sufficient, thank you,' said Alvina.

'Oh! Well! Well now!—' He fidgeted a little. 'You see, we are all old neighbours and connected with your father for many years. We—that is the persons interested, and myself—would not like to think that you were driven out of Woodhouse—er—er—destitute. If—er—we could come to some composition—make some arrangement that would be agreeable to you, and would, in some measures, secure you a means of livelihood—'

He watched Alvina with sharp blue eyes. Alvina looked back at him, still vacantly.

'No—thanks awfully!' she said. 'But don't bother. I'm going away.'

'With the travelling theatrical company!'

'Yes.'

The lawyer studied his finger-nails intensely.

'Well,' he said, feeling with a finger-tip an imaginary roughness of one nail-edge. 'Well, in that case—In that case—Supposing you have made an irrevocable decision—'

He looked up at her sharply. She nodded slowly, like a porcelain mandarin.

'In that case,' he said, 'we must proceed with the valuation and the preparation for the sale.'

'Yes,' she said faintly.

'You realize,' he said, 'that everything in Manchester House, except your private personal property, and that of Miss Pinnegar, belongs to the claimants, your father's creditors, and may not be removed from the house.'

'Yes,' she said.

'And it will be necessary to make an account of everything in the house. So if you and Miss Pinnegar will put your possessions strictly apart—But I shall see Miss Pinnegar during the course of the day. Would you ask her to call about seven—I think she is free then—'

Alvina sat trembling.

'I shall pack my things to-day,' she said.

'Of course,' said the lawyer, 'any little things to which you may be attached the claimants would no doubt wish you to regard as your own. For anything of greater value— your piano, for example—I should have to make a personal request—'

'Oh, I don't want anything—' said Alvina.

'No? Well! You will see. You will be here a few days?'

'No,' said Alvina. 'I'm going away to-day.'

'To-day! Is that also irrevocable?'

'Yes. I must go this afternoon.'

'On account of your engagement? May I ask where your company is performing this week? Far away?'

'Mansfield.'

'Oh! Well then, in case I particularly wished to see you, you could come over?'

'If necessary,' said Alvina. 'But I don't want to come to Woodhouse unless it *is* necessary. Can't we write?'

'Yes—certainly! Certainly!—most things! Certainly! And now—'

He went into certain technical matters, and Alvina signed some documents. At last she was free to go. She had been almost an hour in the room.

'Well, good-morning, Miss Houghton. You will hear from me, and I from you. I wish you a pleasant experience in your new occupation. You are not leaving Woodhouse for ever.'

'Good-bye!' she said. And she hurried to the road.

Try as she might, she felt as if she had had a blow which knocked her down. She felt she had had a blow.

At the lawyer's gate she stood a minute. There, across a little hollow, rose the cemetery hill. There were her graves: her mother's, Miss Frost's, her father's. Looking, she made out the white cross at Miss Frost's grave, the grey stone at her parents'. Then she turned slowly, under the church wall, back to Manchester House.

She felt humiliated. She felt she did not want to see anybody at all. She did not want to see Miss Pinnegar, nor the Natcha-Kee-Tawaras: and least of all, Cicio. She felt strange in Woodhouse, almost as if the ground had risen from under her feet and hit her over the mouth. The fact that Manchester House and its very furniture was under seal to be sold on behalf of her father's creditors made her feel as if all her Woodhouse life had suddenly gone smash. She loathed the thought of Manchester House. She loathed staying another minute in it.

And yet she did not want to go to the Natcha-Kee-Tawaras either. The church clock above her clanged eleven. She ought to take the twelve-forty train to Mansfield. Yet instead of going home she turned off down the alley towards the fields and the brook.

How many times had she gone that road! How many times had she seen Miss Frost bravely striding home that way, from her music-pupils. How many years had she noticed a particular wild cherry-tree come into blossom, a particular bit of blackthorn scatter its whiteness in among the pleached twigs of a hawthorn hedge. How often, how many springs had Miss Frost come home with a bit of this blackthorn in her hand!

Alvina did *not* want to go to Mansfield that afternoon. She felt insulted. She knew she would be much cheaper in Madame's eyes. She knew her own position with the troupe would be humiliating. It would be openly a little humiliating. But it would be much more maddeningly humiliating to stay in Woodhouse and experience the full flavour of Woodhouse's calculated benevolence. She hardly knew which was worse: the cool look of insolent half-contempt, half-satisfaction with which Madame would receive the news of her financial downfall, or the officious patronage which she would meet from the Woodhouse magnates. She knew exactly how Madame's black eyes would shine, how her mouth would curl with a sneering, slightly triumphant smile, as she heard the news. And she could hear the bullying tone in which Henry Wagstaff would dictate the Woodhouse benevolence to her. She wanted to go away from them all—from them all—for ever.

Even from Cicio. For she felt he insulted her too. Subtly,

they all did it. They had regard for her possibilities as an heiress. Five hundred, even two hundred pounds would have made all the difference. Useless to deny it. Even to Cicio. Cicio would have had a lifelong respect for her, if she had come with even so paltry a sum as two hundred pounds. Now she had nothing, he would coolly withhold this respect. She felt he might jeer at her. And she could not get away from this feeling.

Mercifully she had the bit of ready money. And she had a few trinkets which might be sold. Nothing else. Mercifully, for the mere moment, she was independent.

Whatever else she did, she must go back and pack. She must pack her two boxes, and leave them ready. For she felt that once she had left, she could never come back to Woodhouse again. If England had cliffs all round—why, when there was nowhere else to go, and no getting beyond, she could walk over one of the cliffs. Meanwhile, she had her short run before her. She banked hard on her independence.

So she turned back to the town. She would not be able to take the twelve-forty train, for it was already mid-day. But she was glad. She wanted some time to herself. She would send Cicio on. Slowly she climbed the familiar hill—slowly—and rather bitterly. She felt her native place insulted her: and she felt the Natchas insulted her. In the midst of the insult she remained isolated upon herself, and she wished to be alone.

She found Cicio waiting at the end of the yard: eternally waiting, it seemed. He was impatient.

'You've been a long time,' he said.

'Yes,' she answered.

'We shall have to make haste to catch the train.'

'I can't go by this train. I shall have to come on later. You can just eat a mouthful of lunch, and go now.'

They went indoors. Miss Pinnegar had not yet come down. Mrs Rollings was busily peeling potatoes.

'Mr Marasca is going by the train, he'll have to have a little cold meat,' said Alvina. 'Would you mind putting it ready while I go upstairs?'

'Sharpses and Fullbankses sent them bills,' said Mrs Rollings. Alvina opened them, and turned pale. It was thirty pounds, the total funeral expenses. She had completely forgotten them.

'And Mr Atterwell want to know what you'd like put on th' headstone for your father—if you'd write it down.'

'All right.'

Mrs Rollings popped on the potatoes for Miss Pinnegar's dinner, and spread the cloth for Cicio. When he was eating, Miss Pinnegar came in. She inquired for Alvina—and went upstairs.

'Have you had your dinner?' she said. For there was Alvina sitting writing a letter.

'I'm going by a later train,' said Alvina.

'Both of you?'

'No. He's going now.'

Miss Pinnegar came downstairs again, and went through to the scullery. When Alvina came down, she returned to the living-room.

'Give this letter to Madame,' Alvina said to Cicio. 'I shall be at the hall by seven to-night. I shall go straight there.'

'Why can't you come now?' said Cicio.

'I can't possibly,' said Alvina. 'The lawyer has just told me father's debts come to much more than everything is worth. Nothing is ours—not even the plate you're eating from. Everything is under seal to be sold to pay off what is owing. So I've got to get my own clothes and boots together, or they'll be sold with the rest. Mr Beeby wants you to go round at seven this evening, Miss Pinnegar—before I forget.'

'Really!' gasped Miss Pinnegar. 'Really! The house and the furniture and everything got to be sold up? Then we're on the streets! I can't believe it.'

'So he told me,' said Alvina.

'But how positively awful,' said Miss Pinnegar, sinking motionless into a chair.

'It's not more than I expected,' said Alvina. 'I'm putting my things into my two trunks, and I shall just ask Mrs Slaney to store them for me. Then I've the bag I shall travel with.'

'Really!' gasped Miss Pinnegar. 'I can't believe it! And when have we got to get out?'

'Oh, I don't think there's a desperate hurry. They'll take

an inventory of all the things, and we can live on here till they're actually ready for the sale.'

'And when will that be?'

'I don't know. A week or two.'

'And is the cinematograph to be sold the same?'

'Yes—everything! The piano—even mother's portrait—'

'It's impossible to believe it,' said Miss Pinnegar. 'It's impossible. He can never have left things so bad.'

'Cicio,' said Alvina. 'You'll really have to go if you are to catch the train. You'll give Madame my letter, won't you? I should hate you to miss the train. I know she can't bear me already, for all the fuss and upset I cause.'

Cicio rose slowly, wiping his mouth.

'You'll be there at seven o'clock?' he said.

'At the theatre,' she replied.

And without more ado, he left.

Mrs Rollings came in.

'You've heard?' said Miss Pinnegar dramatically.

'I heard somethink,' said Mrs Rollings.

'Sold up! Everything to be sold up. Every stick and rag! I never thought I should live to see the day,' said Miss Pinnegar.

'You might almost have expected it,' said Mrs Rollings. 'But you're all right, yourself, Miss Pinnegar. Your money isn't with his, is it?'

'No,' said Miss Pinnegar. 'What little I have put by is safe. But it's not enough to live on. It's not enough to keep me, even supposing I only live another ten years. If I only spend a pound a week, it costs fifty-two pounds a year. And for ten years, look at it, it's five hundred and twenty pounds. And you couldn't say less. And I haven't half that amount. I never had more than a wage, you know. Why, Miss Frost earned a good deal more than I do. And *she* didn't leave much more than fifty. Where's the money to come from—?'

'But if you've enough to start a little business—' said Alvina.

'Yes, it's what I shall *have* to do. It's what I shall have to do. And then what about you? What about you?'

'Oh, don't bother about me,' said Alvina.

'Yes, it's all very well, don't bother. But when you come to my age, you know you've *got* to bother, and bother a great deal, if you're not going to find yourself in a position you'd be sorry for. You *have* to bother. And *you'll* have to bother before you've done.'

'Sufficient unto the day is the evil thereof,' said Alvina.

'Ha, sufficient for a good many days, it seems to me.'

Miss Pinnegar was in a real temper. To Alvina this seemed an odd way of taking it. The three women sat down to an uncomfortable dinner of cold meat and hot potatoes and warmed-up pudding.

'But whatever you do,' pronounced Miss Pinnegar, 'whatever you do, and however you strive, in this life, you're knocked down in the end. You're always knocked down.'

'It doesn't matter,' said Alvina, 'if it's only in the end. It doesn't matter if you've had your life.'

'You've never had your life, till you're dead,' said Miss Pinnegar. 'And if you work and strive, you've a right to the fruits of your work.'

'It doesn't matter,' said Alvina laconically, 'so long as you've enjoyed working and striving.'

But Miss Pinnegar was too angry to be philosophic. Alvina knew it was useless to be either angry or otherwise emotional. None the less, she also felt as if she had been knocked down. And she almost envied poor Miss Pinnegar the prospect of a little, day-by-day haberdashery shop in Tamworth. Her own problem seemed so much more menacing. 'Answer or die,' said the Sphinx of fate. Miss Pinnegar could answer her own fate according to its question. She could say 'haberdashery shop', and her sphinx would recognize this answer as true to nature, and would be satisfied. But every individual has his own, or her own fate, and her own sphinx. Alvina's sphinx was an old, deep thoroughbred, she would take no mongrel answers. And her thoroughbred teeth were long and sharp. To Alvina, the last of the fantastic but pure-bred race of Houghton, the problem of her fate was terribly abstruse.

The only thing to do was not to solve it: to stay on, and answer fate with whatever came into one's head. No good striving with fate. Trust to a lucky shot, or take the consequences.

'Miss Pinnegar,' said Alvina. 'Have we any money in hand?'

'There is about twenty pounds in the bank. It's all shown in my books,' said Miss Pinnegar.

'We couldn't take it, could we?'

'Every penny shows in the books.'

Alvina pondered again.

'Are there more bills to come in?' she asked. 'I mean my bills. Do I owe anything?'

'I don't think you do,' said Miss Pinnegar.

'I'm going to keep the insurance money, anyway. They can say what they like. I've got it, and I'm going to keep it.'

'Well,' said Miss Pinnegar, 'it's not my business. But there's Sharps and Fullbanks to pay.'

'I'll pay those,' said Alvina. 'You tell Atterwell what to put on father's stone. How much does it cost?'

'Five shillings a letter, you remember.'

'Well, we'll just put the name and the date. How much will that be? James Houghton. Born 17th January—'

'You'll have to put "Also of",' said Miss Pinnegar.

'Also of—' said Alvina. 'One—two—three—four—five—six—Six letters—thirty shillings. Seems an awful lot for *Also of*—'

'But you can't leave it out,' said Miss Pinnegar. 'You can't economize over that.'

'I begrudge it,' said Alvina.

CHAPTER 11

Honourable Engagement

For days, after joining the Natcha-Kee-Tawaras, Alvina was very quiet, subdued, and rather remote, sensible of her humiliating position as a hanger-on. They none of them took much notice of her. They drifted on, rather disjointedly. The cordiality, the *joie de vivre* did not revive. Madame was a little irritable, and very exacting, and inclined to be spiteful. Cicio went his way with Geoffrey.

In the second week, Madame found out that a man had been surreptitiously inquiring about them at their lodgings, from the landlady and the landlady's blowsy daughter. It must have been a detective—some shoddy detective. Madame waited. Then she sent Max over to Mansfield, on some fictitious errand. Yes, the lousy-looking dogs of detectives had been there too, making the most minute inquiries as to the behaviour of the Natcha-Kee-Tawaras, what they did, how their sleeping was arranged, how Madame addressed the men, what attitude the men took towards Alvina.

Madame waited again. And again, when they moved to Doncaster, the same two mongrel-looking fellows were lurking in the street, and plying the inmates of their lodging-house with questions. All the Natchas caught sight of the men. And Madame cleverly wormed out of the righteous and respectable landlady what the men had asked. Once more it was about the sleeping accommodation—whether the landlady heard anything in the night—whether she noticed anything.

No doubt about it, the Natcha-Kee-Tawaras were under suspicion. They were being followed, and watched. What for? Madame made a shrewd guess. 'They want to say we are immoral foreigners,' she said.

'But what have our personal morals got to do with them?' said Max angrily.

'Yes—but the English! They are so pure,' said Madame.

'You know,' said Louis, 'somebody must have put them up to it—'

'Perhaps,' said Madame, 'somebody on account of Allaye.'

Alvina went white.

'Yes,' cried Geoffrey. 'White Slave Traffic! Mr May said it.'

Madame slowly nodded.

'Mr May!' she said. 'Mr May! It is he. He knows all about morals—and immorals. Yes, I know. Yes—yes—yes! He suspects all our immoral doings, *mes braves*.'

'But there aren't any, except mine,' cried Alvina, pale to the lips.

'You! You! There you are!' Madame smiled archly, and rather mockingly.

'What are we to do?' said Max, pale on the cheek-bones.

'Curse them! Curse them!' Louis was muttering, in his rolling accent.

'Wait,' said Madame. 'Wait. They will not do anything to us. You are only dirty foreigners, *mes braves*. At the most they will ask us only to leave their pure country.'

'We don't interfere with none of them,' cried Max.

'Curse them,' muttered Louis.

'Never mind, *mon cher*. You are in a pure country. Let us wait.'

'If you think it's me,' said Alvina, 'I can go away.'

'Oh, my dear, you are only the excuse,' said Madame, smiling indulgently at her. 'Let us wait, and see.'

She took it smilingly. But her cheeks were white as paper, and her eyes black as drops of ink, with anger.

'Wait and see!' she chanted ironically. 'Wait and see! If we must leave the dear country—then *adieu*!' And she gravely bowed to an imaginary England.

'I feel it's my fault. I feel I ought to go away,' cried Alvina, who was terribly distressed, seeing Madame's glitter and pallor, and the black brows of the men. Never had Cicio's brow looked so ominously black. And Alvina felt it was all her fault. Never had she experienced such a horrible feeling: as if something repulsive were creeping on her from behind. Every minute of these weeks was a horror to her: the sense of the low-down dogs of detectives hanging round, sliding behind them, trying to get hold of some clear proof of immorality on their part. And then—the unknown vengeance of the authorities! All the repulsive secrecy, and all the absolute power of the police authorities. The sense of a great malevolent power which had them all the time in its grip, and was watching, feeling, waiting to strike the morbid blow: the sense of the utter helplessness of individuals who were not even accused, only watched and enmeshed! the feeling that they, the Natcha-Kee-Tawaras, herself included, must be monsters of hideous vice, to have provoked all this: and yet the sane knowledge that they, none of them, *were* monsters of vice: this was quite killing. The sight of a policeman would send up Alvina's heart in a flame of fear, agony; yet she knew she had nothing legally to be afraid of. Every knock at the door was horrible.

She simply could not understand it. Yet there it was: they were watched, followed. Of that there was no question. And all she could imagine was that the troupe was secretly accused of White Slave Traffic by somebody in Woodhouse. Probably Mr May had gone the round of the benevolent magnates of Woodhouse, concerning himself with her virtue, and currying favour with his concern. Of this she became convinced, that it was concern for her virtue which had started the whole business: and that the first instigator was Mr May, who had got round some vulgar magistrate or County Councillor.

Madame did not consider Alvina's view very seriously. She thought it was some personal malevolence against the

Tawaras themselves, probably put up by some other professionals, with whom Madame was not popular.

Be that as it may, for some weeks they went about in the shadow of this repulsive finger which was following after them, to touch them and destroy them with the black smear of shame. The men were silent and inclined to be sulky. They seemed to hold together. They seemed to be united into a strong, four-square silence and tension. They kept to themselves—and Alvina kept to herself—and Madame kept to herself. So they went about.

And slowly the cloud melted. It never broke. Alvina felt that the very force of the sullen, silent fearlessness and fury in the Tawaras had prevented its bursting. Once there had been a weakening, a cringing, they would all have been lost. But their hearts hardened with black, indomitable anger. And the cloud melted, it passed away. There was no sign.

Early summer was now at hand. Alvina no longer felt at home with the Natchas. While the trouble was hanging over, they seemed to ignore her altogether. The men hardly spoke to her, they hardly spoke to Madame, for that matter. They kept within the four-square enclosure of themselves.

But Alvina felt herself particularly excluded, left out. And when the trouble of the detectives began to pass off, and the men became more cheerful again, wanted her to jest and be familiar with them, she responded verbally, but in her heart there was no response.

Madame had been quite generous with her. She allowed her to pay for her room, and the expense of travelling. But she had her food with the rest. Wherever she was, Madame bought the food for the party, and cooked it herself. And Alvina came in with the rest: she paid no board.

She waited, however, for Madame to suggest a small salary—or at least, that the troupe should pay her living expenses. But Madame did not make such a suggestion. So Alvina knew that she was not very badly wanted. And she guarded her money, and watched for some other opportunity.

It became her habit to go every morning to the public library of the town in which she found herself, to look through the advertisements: advertisements for maternity-nurses, for nursery governesses, pianists, travelling companions, even ladies' maids. For some weeks she found nothing, though she wrote several letters.

One morning Cicio, who had begun to hang around her again, accompanied her as she set out to the library. But her heart was closed against him.

'Why are you going to the library?' he asked her. It was in Lancaster.

'To look at the papers and magazines.'

'Ha-a! To find a job, eh?'

His acuteness startled her for a moment.

'If I found one I should take it,' she said.

'*Hé!* I know that,' he said.

It so happened that that very morning she saw on the notice-board of the library an announcement that the Borough Council wished to engage the services of an experienced maternity nurse, applications to be made to the medical board. Alvina wrote down the directions. Cicio watched her.

'What is a maternity nurse?' he said.

'An *accoucheuse*!' she said. 'The nurse who attends when babies are born.'

'Do you know how to do that!' he said, incredulous, and jeering slightly.

'I was trained to do it,' she said.

He said no more, but walked by her side as she returned to the lodgings. As they drew near the lodgings, he said:

'You don't want to stop with us any more?'

'I can't,' she said.

He made a slight, mocking gesture.

'I can't,' he repeated. 'Why do you always say you can't?'

'Because I can't,' she said.

'Pff—!' he went, with a whistling sound of contempt.

But she went indoors to her room. Fortunately, when she had finally cleared her things from Manchester House, she had brought with her her nurse's certificate, and recommendations from doctors. She wrote out her application, took the tram to the Town Hall and dropped it in the letter-box there. Then she wired home to her doctor for another reference. After which she went to the library and got out a book on her subject. If summoned, she would have to go before the medical board on Monday. She had a week. She read and pondered hard, recalling all her previous experience and knowledge.

She wondered if she ought to appear before the board in uniform. Her nurse's dresses were packed in her trunk at Mrs Stanley's, in Woodhouse. It was now May. The whole business at Woodhouse was finished. Manchester House and all the furniture was sold to some boot-and-shoe people: at least the boot-and-shoe people had the house. They had given four thousand pounds for it—which was above the lawyer's estimate. On the other hand, the theatre was sold for almost nothing. It all worked out that some thirty-three pounds, which the creditors made up to fifty pounds, remained for Alvina. She insisted on Miss Pinnegar's having half of this. And so that was all over. Miss Pinnegar was already in Tamworth, and her little shop would be opened next week. She wrote happily and excitedly about it.

Sometimes fate acts swiftly and without a hitch. On Thursday Alvina received her notice that she was to appear before the Board on the following Monday. And yet she could not bring herself to speak of it to Madame till the Saturday evening. When they were all at supper, she said:

'Madame, I applied for a post of maternity nurse, to the Borough of Lancaster.'

Madame raised her eyebrows. Cicio had said nothing.

'Oh really! You never told me.'

'I thought it would be no use if it all came to nothing. They want me to go and see them on Monday, and then they will decide—'

'Really! Do they! On Monday? And then if you get this work you will stay here? Yes?'

'Yes, of course.'

'Of course! Of course! Yes! H'm! And if not?'

The two women looked at each other.

'What?' said Alvina.

'If you *don't* get it—! You are not *sure*?'

'No,' said Alvina. 'I am not a bit sure.'

'Well then—! Now! And if you don't get it—?'

'What shall I do, you mean?'

'Yes, what shall you do?'

'I don't know.'

'How! you don't know! Shall you come back to us, then?'

'I will if you like—'

'If I like? If *I* like! Come, it is not a question of if *I* like. It is what you want to do yourself.'

'I feel you don't want me very badly,' said Alvina.

'Why? Why do you feel? Who makes you? Which of us makes you feel so? Tell me.'

'Nobody in particular. But I feel it.'

'Oh we-ell! If nobody makes you, and yet you feel it, it must be in yourself, don't you see? Eh? Isn't it so?'

'Perhaps it is,' admitted Alvina.

'We-ell then! We-ell!—' So Madame gave her her *congé*. 'But if you like to come back—if you *laike*—then—' Madame shrugged her shoulders—'you must come, I suppose.'

'Thank you,' said Alvina.

The young men were watching. They seemed indifferent. Cicio turned aside, with his faint, stupid smile.

In the morning Madame gave Alvina all her belongings, from the little safe she called her bank.

'There is the money—so—and so—and so—that is correct. Please count it once more!—' Alvina counted it and kept it clutched in her hand. 'And there are your rings, and your chain, and your locket—see—all—everything—! But not the brooch. Where is the brooch? Here! Shall I give it back, *hein?*'

'I gave it to you,' said Alvina, offended. She looked into Madame's black eyes. Madame dropped her eyes.

'Yes, you gave it. But I thought, you see, as you have now not much mo-oney, perhaps you would like to take it again—'

'No thank you,' said Alvina, and she went away, leaving Madame with the red brooch in her plump hand.

'Thank goodness I've given her something valuable,' thought Alvina to herself, as she went trembling to her room.

She too had packed her bag. She had to find new rooms. She bade good-bye to the Natcha-Kee-Tawaras. Her face was cold and distant, but she smiled slightly as she bade them good-bye.

'And perhaps,' said Madame, 'per-haps you will come to Wigan to-morrow afternoon—or evening? Yes?'

'Thank you,' said Alvina.

She went out and found a little hotel, where she took her room for the night explaining the cause of her visit to Lancaster. Her heart was hard and burning. A deep, burning, silent anger against everything possessed her, and a profound indifference to mankind.

And therefore, the next day, everything went as if by magic. She had decided that at the least sign of indifference from the medical board people she would walk away, take her bag, and go to Windermere. She had never been to the Lakes. And Windermere was not far off. She would not endure one single hint of contumely from anyone else. She would go straight to Windermere, to see the big lake. Why not do as she wished! She could be quite happy by herself among the lakes. And she would be absolutely free, absolutely free. She rather looked forward to leaving the Town Hall, hurrying to take her bag and off to the station and freedom. Hadn't she still got about a hundred pounds? Why bother for one moment? To be quite alone in the whole world—and quite, quite free, with her hundred pounds— the prospect attracted her sincerely.

And therefore, everything went charmingly at the Town Hall. The medical board were charming to her—charming. There was no hesitation at all. From the first moment she was engaged. And she was given a pleasant room in a hospital in a garden, and the matron was charming to her, and the doctors most courteous.

When could she undertake to commence her duties? When did they want her? The very *moment* she could come. She could begin to-morrow—but she had no uniform. Oh, the matron would lend her uniform and aprons, till her box arrived.

So there she was—by afternoon installed in her pleasant little room looking on the garden, and dressed in a nurse's uniform. It was all sudden like magic. She had wired to Madame, she had wired for her box. She was another person.

Needless to say, she was glad. Needless to say that, in the morning, when she had thoroughly bathed, and dressed in clean clothes, and put on the white dress, the white apron, and the white cap, she felt another person. So clean, she felt, so thankful! Her skin seemed caressed and live with cleanliness and whiteness, luminous she felt. It was so different from being with the Natchas.

In the garden the snowballs, guelder-roses, swayed softly among green foliage, there was pink may-blossom, and single scarlet may-blossom, and underneath the young green of the trees, irises rearing purple and moth-white. A young gardener was working—and a convalescent slowly trailed a few paces.

Having ten minutes still, Alvina sat down and wrote to Cicio: 'I am glad I have got this post as nurse here. Everyone is most kind, and I feel at home already. I feel quite happy here. I shall think of my days with the Natcha-Kee-Tawaras, and of you, who were such a stranger to me. Good-bye.— A. H.'

This she addressed and posted. No doubt Madame would find occasion to read it. But let her.

Alvina now settled down to her new work. There was of course a great deal to do, for she had work both in the hospital and out in the town, though chiefly out in the town. She went rapidly from case to case, as she was summoned. And she was summoned at all hours. So that it was tiring work, which left her no time to herself, except just in snatches.

She had no serious acquaintance with anybody, she was too busy. The matron and sisters and doctors and patients were all part of her day's work, and she regarded them as such. The men she chiefly ignored: she felt much more friendly with the matron. She had many a cup of tea and many a chat in the matron's room, in the quiet, sunny afternoons when the work was not pressing. Alvina took her quiet moments when she could: for she never knew when she would be rung up by one or other of the doctors in the town.

And so, from the matron, she learned to crochet. It was work she had never taken to. But now she had her ball of cotton and her hook, and she worked away as she chatted. She was in good health, and she was getting fatter again. With the Natcha-Kee-Tawaras, she had improved a good deal, her colour and her strength had returned. But undoubtedly the nursing life, arduous as it was, suited her best. She became a handsome, reposeful woman, jolly with the other nurses, really happy with her friend the matron, who was well-bred and wise, and never over-intimate.

The doctor with whom Alvina had most to do was a Dr Mitchell, a Scotchman. He had a large practice among the poor, and was an energetic man. He was about fifty-four years old, tall, largely-built, with a good figure, but with extraordinarily large feet and hands. His face was red and clean-shaven, his eyes blue, his teeth very good. He laughed and talked rather mouthingly. Alvina, who knew what the nurses told her, knew that he had come as a poor boy and bottle-washer to Dr Robertson, a fellow-Scotchman, and that he had made his way up gradually till he became a doctor himself, and had an independent practice. Now he was quite rich—and a bachelor. But the nurses did not set their bonnets at him very much because he was rather mouthy and overbearing.

In the houses of the poor he was a great autocrat.

'What is that stuff you've got there?' he inquired largely, seeing a bottle of somebody's Soothing Syrup by a poor woman's bedside. 'Take it and throw it down the sink, and the next time you want a soothing syrup put a little boot-blacking in hot water. It'll do you just as much good.'

Imagine the slow, pompous, large-mouthed way in which the red-faced, handsomely-built man pronounced these words, and you realize why the poor set such store by him.

He was eagle-eyed. Wherever he went there was a scuffle directly his foot was heard on the stairs. And he knew they were hiding something. He sniffed the air: he glanced round with a sharp eye: and during the course of his visit picked up a blue mug which was pushed behind the looking-glass. He peered inside—and smelled it.

'Stout?' he said in a tone of indignant inquiry: God-Almighty would presumably take on just such a tone, finding the core of an apple flung away among the dead-nettle

of paradise: 'Stout! Have you been drinking stout?' This as
he gazed down on the wan mother in the bed.

'They gave me a drop, doctor. I felt that low.'

The doctor marched out of the room, still holding the
mug in his hand. The sick woman watched him with
haunted eyes. The attendant women threw up their hands
and looked at one another. Was he going for ever? There
came a sudden smash. The doctor had flung the blue mug
downstairs. He returned with a solemn stride.

'There!' he said. 'And the next person that gives you stout
will be thrown down along with the mug.'

'Oh doctor, the bit o'comfort!' wailed the sick woman.
'It 'ud never do me no harm.'

'Harm! Harm! With a stomach as weak as yours. Harm!
Do you know better than I do? What have I come here for?
To be told by *you* what will do you harm and what won't?
It appears to me you need no doctor here, you know every-
thing already—'

'Oh no, doctor. It's not like that. But when you feel as if
you'd sink through the bed, an' you don't know what to do
with yourself—'

'Take a little beef-tea, or a little rice pudding. Take *nourishment,* don't take that muck. Do you hear—' charging
upon the attendant woman, who shrank against the wall—
'she's to have nothing alcoholic at all, and don't let me catch
you giving it her.'

'They say there's nobbut fower per cent i' stout,' retorted
the daring female.

'Fower per cent,' mimicked the doctor brutally. 'Why
what does an ignorant creature like *you* know about fower
per cent?'

The woman muttered a little under her breath.

'What? Speak out! Let me hear what you've got to say,
my woman. I've no doubt it's something for my benefit—'

But the affronted woman rushed out of the room, and burst
into tears on the landing. After which Dr Mitchell, mollified,
largely told the patient how she was to behave, concluding:

'Nourishment! Nourishment is what you want. Nonsense, don't tell me you can't take it. Push it down if it won't
go down by itself—'

'Oh doctor—'

'Don't say *oh doctor* to me. Do as I tell you. That's *your* business.' After which he marched out, and the rattle of his motor-car was shortly heard.

Alvina got used to scenes like these. She wondered why the people stood it. But soon she realized that they loved it—particularly the women.

'Oh, nurse, stop till Dr Mitchell's been. I'm scared to death of him, for fear he's going to shout at me.'

'Why does everybody put up with him?' asked innocent Alvina.

'Oh, he's good-hearted, nurse, he *does* feel for you.'

And everywhere it was the same: 'Oh, he's got a heart, you know. He's rough, but he's got a heart. I'd rather have him than your smarmy slormin sort. Oh, you feel safe with Dr Mitchell, I don't care what you say.'

But to Alvina this peculiar form of blustering, bullying heart which had all the women scurrying like chickens was not particularly attractive.

The men did not like Dr Mitchell, and would not have him if possible. Yet since he was club doctor and panel doctor, they had to submit. The first thing he said to a sick or injured labourer, invariably, was:

'And keep off the beer.'

'Oh ay!'

'Keep off the beer, or I shan't set foot in this house again.'

'Tha's got a red enough face on thee, tha nedna shout.'

'My face is red with exposure to all weathers, attending ignorant people like you. I never touch alcohol in any form.'

'No, an' I dunna. I drink a drop o' beer, if that's what you ca' touchin' alcohol. An' I'm none th' wuss for it, tha sees.'

'You've heard what I've told you.'

'Ah, I have.'

'And if you go on with the beer, you may go on with curing yourself. *I* shan't attend you. You know I mean what I say, Mrs Larrick'—this to the wife.

'I do, doctor. And I know it's true what you say. An' I'm at him night an' day about it—'

'Oh well, if he will hear no reason, he must suffer for it.

He mustn't think *I'm* going to be running after him, if he disobeys my orders.' And the doctor stalked off, and the woman began to complain.

None the less the women had their complaints against Dr Mitchell. If ever Alvina entered a clean house on a wet day, she was sure to hear the housewife chuntering.

'Oh my lawk, come in nurse! What a day! Doctor's not been yet. And he's bound to come now I've just cleaned up, trapesin' wi' his gret feet. He's got the biggest understandin's of any man i' Lancaster. My husband says they're the best pair o' pasties i' th' kingdom. An' he does make such a mess, for he never stops to wipe his feet on th' mat, marches straight up your clean stairs—'

'Why don't you tell him to wipe his feet?' said Alvina.

'Oh my word! Fancy me telling him! He'd jump down my throat with both feet afore I'd opened my mouth. He's not to be spoken to, he isn't. He's my-lord, he is. You mustn't look, or you're done for.'

Alvina laughed. She knew they all liked him for browbeating them, and having a heart over and above.

Sometimes he was given a good hit—though nearly always by a man. It happened he was in a workman's house when the man was at dinner.

'Canna yer gi'e a man summat better nor this 'ere pap, Missis?' said the hairy husband, turning up his nose at the rice pudding.

'Oh go on,' cried the wife. 'I hadna time for owt else.' Dr Mitchell was just stooping his handsome figure in the doorway.

'Rice pudding!' he exclaimed largely. 'You couldn't have anything more wholesome and nourishing. I have a rice pudding every day of my life—every day of my life, I do.'

The man was eating his pudding and pearling his big moustache copiously with it. He did not answer.

'Do you doctor!' cried the woman. 'And never no different.'

'Never,' said the doctor.

'Fancy that! You're that fond of them?'

'I find they agree with me. They are light and digestible. And my stomach is as weak as a baby's.'

The labourer wiped his big moustache on his sleeve.

'Mine *isna*, the sees,' he said, 'so pap's no use. 'S watter ter me. I want ter feel as I've had summat: a bit o' suetty dumplin' an' a pint o' hale, summat ter fill th' hole up. An' tha'd be th' same if tha did my work.'

'If I did your work,' sneered the doctor. 'Why I do ten times the work that any one of you does. It's just the work that has ruined my digestion, the never getting a quiet meal, and never a whole night's rest. When do you think *I* can sit at table and digest my dinner? I have to be off looking after people like you—'

'Eh, tha can ta'e th' titty-bottle wi' thee,' said the labourer.

But Dr Mitchell was furious for weeks over this. It put him in a black rage to have his great manliness insulted. Alvina was quietly amused.

The doctor began by being rather lordly and condescending with her. But luckily she felt she knew her work at least as well as he knew it. She smiled and let him condescend. Certainly she neither feared nor even admired him. To tell the truth, she rather disliked him: the great, red-faced bachelor of fifty-three, with his bald spot and his stomach as weak as a baby's, and his mouthing imperiousness and his good heart which was as selfish as it could be. Nothing can be more cock-suredly selfish than a good heart which believes in its own beneficence. He was a little too much the teetotaller on the one hand to be so largely manly on the other. Alvina preferred the labourers with their awful long moustaches that got full of food. And he was a little too loud-mouthedly lordly to be in human good taste.

As a matter of fact, he was conscious of the fact that he had risen to be a gentleman. Now if a man is conscious of being *a gentleman* he is bound to be a little less than a *man*. But if he is gnawed with anxiety lest he may *not* be a gentleman, he is only pitiable. There is a third case, however. If a man must loftily, by his manner, assert that he is *now* a gentleman, he shows himself a clown. For Alvina, poor Dr Mitchell fell into this third category, of clowns. She tolerated him good-humouredly, as women so often tolerate ninnies and *poseurs*. She smiled to herself when she saw his large

and important presence on the board. She smiled when she
saw him at a sale, buying the grandest pieces of antique furniture. She smiled when he talked of going up to Scotland,
for grouse shooting, or of snatching an hour on Sunday
morning, for golf. And she talked him over, with quiet, delicate malice, with the matron. He was no favourite at the
hospital.

Gradually Dr Mitchell's manner changed towards her.
From his imperious condescension he took to a tone of uneasy equality. This did not suit him. Dr Mitchell had no
equals: he had only the vast stratum of inferiors, towards
whom he exercised his quite profitable beneficence—it
brought him in about two thousand a year: and then his
superiors, people who had been born with money. It was
the tradesmen and professionals who had started at the bottom and clambered to the motor-car footing, who distressed
him. And therefore, whilst he treated Alvina on this uneasy
tradesman footing, he felt himself in a false position.

She kept her attitude of quiet amusement, and little by
little he sank. From being a lofty creature soaring over her
head, he was now like a big fish poking its nose above water
and making eyes at her. He treated her with rather presuming deference.

'You look tired this morning,' he barked at her one hot
day.

'I think it's thunder,' she said.

'Thunder! Work, you mean,' and he gave a slight smile.
'I'm going to drive you back.'

'Oh no, thanks, don't trouble! I've got to call on the way.'

'Where have you got to call?'

She told him.

'Very well. That takes you no more than five minutes. I'll
wait for you. Now take your cloak.'

She was surprised. Yet, like other women, she submitted.

As they drove he saw a man with a barrow of cucumbers.
He stopped the car and leaned towards the man.

'Take that barrow-load of poison and *bury* it!' he shouted,
in his strong voice. The busy street hesitated.

'What's that, mister?' replied the mystified hawker.

Dr Mitchell pointed to the green pile of cucumbers.

'Take that barrow-load of poison, and bury it,' he called, 'before you do anybody any more harm with it.'

'What barrow-load of poison's that?' asked the hawker, approaching. A crowd began to gather.

'What barrow-load of poison is that!' repeated the doctor. 'Why your barrow-load of cucumbers.'

'Oh,' said the man, scrutinizing his cucumbers carefully. To be sure, some were a little yellow at the end. 'How's that? Cumbers is right enough: fresh from market this morning.'

'Fresh or not fresh,' said the doctor, mouthing his words distinctly, ' you might as well put poison into your stomach, as those things. Cucumbers are the worst thing you can eat.'

'Oh!' said the man, stuttering. 'That's 'appen for them as doesn't like them. I niver knowed a cumber do *me* no harm, an' I eat 'em like a happle.' Whereupon the hawker took a 'cumber' from his barrow, bit off the end, and chewed it till the sap squirted. 'What's wrong with that?' he said, holding up the bitten cucumber.

'I'm not talking about what's wrong with that,' said the doctor. 'My business is what's wrong with the stomach it goes into. I'm a doctor. And I know that those things cause me half my work. They cause half the internal troubles people suffer from in summertime.'

'Oh ay! That's no loss to you, is it? Me an' you's partners. More cumbers I sell, more graft for you, 'cordin' to that. What's wrong then. *Cum-berrs! Fine fresh Cumberrrs! All fresh and juisty! All cheap and tasty—!* yelled the man.

'I am a doctor not only to cure illness, but to prevent it where I can. And cucumbers are poison to everybody.'

'*Cum-berrs! Cum-berrs! Fresh cumbers!*' yelled the man. Dr Mitchell started his car.

'When will they learn intelligence?' he said to Alvina, smiling and showing his white even teeth.

'I don't care, you know, myself,' she said. 'I should always let people do what they wanted—'

'Even if you knew it would do them harm?' he queried, smiling with amiable condescension.

'Yes, why not! It's their own affair. And they'll do themselves harm one way or another.'

'And you wouldn't try to prevent it?'

'You might as well try to stop the sea with your fingers.'

'You think so?' smiled the doctor. 'I see, you are a pessimist. You are a pessimist with regard to human nature.'

'Am I?' smiled Alvina, thinking the rose would smell as sweet. It seemed to please the doctor to find that Alvina was a pessimist with regard to human nature. It seemed to give her an air of distinction. In his eyes, she *seemed* distinguished. He was in a fair way to dote on her.

She, of course, when he began to admire her, liked him much better, and even saw graceful, boyish attraction in him. There was really something childish about him. And this something childish, since it looked up to her as if she were the saving grace, naturally flattered her and made her feel gentler towards him.

He got in the habit of picking her up in his car, when he could. And he would tap at the matron's door, smiling and showing all his beautiful teeth, just about tea-time.

'May I come in?' His voice sounded almost flirty.

'Certainly.'

'I see you're having tea! Very nice, a cup of tea at this hour!'

'Have one too, doctor.'

'I will with pleasure.' And he sat down wreathed with smiles. Alvina rose to get a cup. 'I didn't intend to disturb you, nurse,' he said. 'Men are always intruders,' he smiled to the matron.

'Sometimes,' said the matron, 'women are charmed to be intruded upon.'

'Oh really!' his eyes sparkled. 'Perhaps *you* wouldn't say so, nurse?' he said, turning to Alvina. Alvina was just reaching at the cupboard. Very charming she looked, in her fresh dress and cap and soft brown hair, very attractive her figure, with its full, soft loins. She turned round to him.

'Oh yes,' she said. 'I quite agree with the matron.'

'Oh, you do!' He did not quite know how to take it. 'But you mind being disturbed at your tea, I am sure.'

'No,' said Alvina. 'We are so used to being disturbed.'

'Rather weak, doctor?' said the matron, pouring the tea.

'Very weak, please.'

The doctor was a little laboured in his gallantry, but unmistakably gallant. When he was gone, the matron looked demure, and Alvina confused. Each waited for the other to speak.

'Don't you think Dr Mitchell is quite coming out?' said Alvina.

'Quite! *Quite* the ladies' man! I wonder who it is can be *bringing* him out? A very praiseworthy work, I am sure.' She looked wickedly at Alvina.

'No, don't look at me,' laughed Alvina, '*I* know nothing about it.'

'Do you think it may be *me*!' said the matron, mischievous.

'I'm sure it is, matron! He begins to show some taste at last.'

'There now!' said the matron. 'I shall put my cap straight.' And she went to the mirror, fluffing her hair and settling her cap.

'There!' she said, bobbing a little curtsey to Alvina.

They both laughed, and went off to work.

But there was no mistake, Dr Mitchell was beginning to expand. With Alvina he quite unbent, and seemed even to sun himself when she was near, to attract her attention. He smiled and smirked and became oddly self-conscious: rather uncomfortable. He liked to hang over her chair, and he made a great event of offering her a cigarette whenever they met, although he himself never smoked. He had a gold cigarette case.

One day he asked her in to see his garden. He had a pleasant old square house with a big walled garden. He showed her his flowers and his wall-fruit, and asked her to eat his strawberries. He bade her admire his asparagus. And then he gave her tea in the drawing-room, with strawberries and cream and cakes, of all of which he ate nothing. But he smiled expansively all the time. He was a made man: and now he was really letting himself go, luxuriating in everything; above all, in Alvina, who poured tea gracefully from the old Georgian tea-pot, and smiled so pleasantly above the Queen Anne tea-cups.

And she, wicked that she was, admired every detail of his

drawing-room. It was a pleasant room indeed, with roses outside the French door, and a lawn in sunshine beyond, with bright red flowers in beds. But indoors, it was insistently antique. Alvina admired the Jacobean sideboard and the Jacobean arm-chairs and the Hepplewhite wall-chairs and the Sheraton settee and the Chippendale stands and the Ax-minster carpet and the bronze clock with Shakespeare and Ariosto reclining on it—yes, she even admired Shakespeare on the clock—and the ormolu cabinet and the bead-work foot-stools and the dreadful Sèvres dish with a cherub in it and—but why enumerate. She admired *everything*! And Dr Mitchell's heart expanded in his bosom till he felt it would burst, unless he either fell at her feet or did something extraordinary. He had never even imagined what it was to be so expanded: what a delicious feeling. He could have kissed her feet in an ecstasy of wild expansion. But habit, so far, prevented his doing more than beam.

Another day he said to her, when they were talking of age:

'You are as young as you feel. Why, when I was twenty I felt I had all the cares and responsibility of the world on my shoulders. And now I am middle-aged more or less, I feel as light as if I were just beginning life.' He beamed down at her.

'Perhaps you *are* only just beginning your *own* life,' she said. 'You have lived for your work till now.'

'It may be that,' he said. 'It may be that up till now I have lived for others, for my patients. And now perhaps I may be allowed to live a little more for myself.' He beamed with real luxury, saw the real luxury of life begin.

'Why shouldn't you?' said Alvina.

'Oh yes, I intend to,' he said, with confidence.

He really, by degrees, made up his mind to marry now, and to retire in part from his work. That is, he would hire another assistant, and give himself a fair amount of leisure. He was inordinately proud of his house. And now he looked forward to the treat of his life: hanging round the woman he had made his wife, following her about, feeling proud of her and his house, talking to her from morning till night, really finding himself in her. When he had to go his rounds she would go with him in the car: he made up his mind she would be willing to accompany him. He would teach her to drive, and they would sit side by side, she driving him and waiting for him. And he would run out of the houses of his patients, and find her sitting there, and he would get in beside her and feel so snug and so sure and so happy as she drove him off to the next case, he informing her about his work.

And if ever she did not go out with him, she would be there on the doorstep waiting for him the moment she heard the car. And they would have long, cosy evenings together in the drawing-room, as he luxuriated in her very presence. She would sit on his knee, and they would be snug for hours, before they went warmly and deliciously to bed. And in the morning he need not rush off. He would loiter about with her, they would loiter down the garden looking at every new flower and every new fruit, she would wear fresh flowery dresses and no cap on her hair, he would never be able to tear himself away from her. Every morning it would be unbearable to have to tear himself away from her, and every hour he would be rushing back to her. They would be simply everything to one another. And how he would enjoy it! Ah!

He pondered as to whether he would have children. A child would take her away from him. That was his first thought. But then—! Ah well, he would have to leave it till the time. Love's young dream is never so delicious as at the virgin age of fifty-three.

But he was quite cautious. He made no definite advances till he had put a plain question. It was August Bank Holiday, that forever black day of the declaration of war, when his question was put. For this year of our story is the fatal year 1914.

There was quite a stir in the town over the declaration of war. But most people felt that the news was only intended to give an extra thrill to the all-important event of Bank Holiday. Half the world had gone to Blackpool or Southport, the other half had gone to the Lakes or into the country. Lancaster was busy with a sort of fête, nothwithstanding. And as the weather was decent, everybody was in a real holiday mood.

So that Dr Mitchell, who had contrived to pick up Alvina at the Hospital, contrived to bring her to his house at half-past three, for tea.

'What do you think of this new war?' said Alvina.

'Oh, it will be over in six weeks,' said the doctor easily. And there they left it. Only, with a fleeting thought, Alvina wondered if it would affect the Natacha-Kee-Tawaras. She had never heard any more of them.

'Where would you have liked to go to-day?' said the doctor, turning to smile at her as he drove the car.

'I think to Windermere—into the Lakes,' she said.

'We might make a tour of the Lakes before long,' he said. She was not thinking, so she took no particular notice of the speech.

'How nice!' she said vaguely.

'We could go in the car, and take them as we chose,' said the doctor.

'Yes,' she said, wondering at him now.

When they had had tea, quietly and gallantly tête-à-tête in his drawing-room, he asked her if she would like to see the other rooms of the house. She thanked him, and he showed her the substantial oak dining-room, and the little room with medical works and a revolving chair, which he called his study; then the kitchen and the pantry, the house-keeper looking askance; then upstairs to his bedroom, which was very fine with old mahogany tall-boys and silver candlesticks on the dressing-table, and brushes with green ivory backs, and a hygienic white bed and straw mats: then the visitors' bedroom corresponding, with its old satinwood furniture and cream-coloured chairs with large, pale-blue cushions, and a pale carpet with reddish wreaths. Very nice, lovely, awfully nice, I do like that, isn't that beautiful, I've never seen anything like that! came the gratifying fireworks of admiration from Alvina. And he smiled and gloated. But in her mind she was thinking of Manchester House, and how dark and horrible it was, how she hated it, but how it had impressed Cicio and Geoffrey, how they would have loved to feel themselves masters of it, and how done in the

eye they were. She smiled to herself rather grimly. For this
afternoon she was feeling unaccountably uneasy and wistful,
yearning into the distance again: a trick she thought she had
happily lost.

The doctor dragged her up even to the slanting attics. He
was a big man, and he always wore navy-blue suits, well-
tailored and immaculate. Unconsciously she felt that big
men in good navy-blue suits, especially if they had reddish
faces and rather big feet and if their hair was wearing thin,
were a special type all to themselves, solid and rather
namby-pamby and tiresome.

'What very nice attics! I think, the many angles which the
roof makes, the different slants, you know, are so attractive.
Oh, and the fascinating little window!' She crouched in the
hollow of the small dormer window. 'Fascinating! See the
town and the hills! I know I should want this room for my
own.'

'Then have it,' he said. 'Have it for *one* of your own.'

She crept out of the window recess and looked up at him.
He was leaning forward to her, smiling, self-conscious, ten-
tative, and eager. She thought it best to laugh it off.

'I was only talking like a child, from the imagination,' she
said.

'I quite understand that,' he replied deliberately. 'But I
am speaking what I *mean*—'

She did not answer, but looked at him reproachfully. He
was smiling and smirking broadly at her.

'Won't you marry me, and come and have this garret for
your own?' He spoke as if he were offering her a chocolate.
He smiled with curious uncertainty.

'I don't know,' she said vaguely.

His smile broadened.

'Well now,' he said, 'make up your mind. I'm not good
at *talking* about love, you know. But I think I'm pretty good
at *feeling* it, you know. I want you to come here and be
happy: with me.' He added the two last words as a sort of
sly post-scriptum, and as if to commit himself finally.

'But I've never thought about it,' she said, rapidly cogi-
tating.

'I know you haven't. But think about it now—' He began

to be hugely pleased with himself. 'Think about it now. And tell me if you could put up with *me*, as well as the garret.' He beamed and put his head a little on one side—rather like Mr May, for one second. But he was much more dangerous than Mr May. He was overbearing, and had the devil's own temper if he was thwarted. This she knew. He was a big man in a navy-blue suit, with very white teeth.

Again she thought she had better laugh it off.

'It's you I *am* thinking about,' she laughed, flirting still. 'It's you I *am* wondering about.'

'Well,' he said, rather pleased with himself, 'you wonder about me till you've made up your mind—'

'I will—' she said, seizing the opportunity. 'I'll wonder about you till I've made up my mind—shall I?'

'Yes,' he said. 'That's what I wish you to do. And the next time I ask you, you'll let me know. That's it, isn't it?' He smiled indulgently down on her: thought her face young and charming, charming.

'Yes,' she said. 'But don't ask me too soon, will you?'

'How, too soon—' he smiled delightedly.

'You'll give me time to wonder about you, won't you? You won't ask me again this month, will you?'

'This month?' His eyes beamed with pleasure. He enjoyed the procrastination as much as she did. 'But the month's only just begun! However! Yes, you shall have your way. I won't ask you again this month.'

'And I'll promise to wonder about you all the month,' she laughed.

'That's a bargain,' he said.

They went downstairs, and Alvina returned to her duties. She was very much excited, very much excited indeed. A big, well-to-do man in a navy-blue suit, of handsome appearance, aged fifty-three, with white teeth and a delicate stomach: it *was* exciting. A sure position, a very nice home and lovely things in it, once they were dragged about a bit. And of course he'd adore her. That went without saying. She was as fussy as if someone had given her a lovely new pair of boots. She was really fussy and pleased with herself: and *quite* decided she'd take it all on. That was how it put itself to her: she would take it all on.

Of course there was the man himself to consider. But he was quite presentable. There was nothing at all against it: nothing at all. If he had pressed her during the first half of the month of August, he would almost certainly have got her. But he only beamed in anticipation.

Meanwhile the stir and restlessness of the war had begun, and was making itself felt even in Lancaster. And the excitement and the unease began to wear through Alvina's rather glamorous fussiness. Some of her old fretfulness came back on her. Her spirit, which had been as if asleep these months, now woke rather irritably, and chafed against its collar. Who was this elderly man, that she should marry him? Who was he, that she should be kissed by him? Actually kissed and fondled by him! Repulsive. She avoided him like the plague. Fancy reposing against his broad, navy-blue waistcoat! She started as if she had been stung. Fancy seeing his red, smiling face just above hers, coming down to embrace her! She pushed it away with her open hand. And she ran away, to avoid the thought.

And yet! And yet! She would be so comfortable, she would be so well-off for the rest of her life. The hateful problem of material circumstance would be solved for ever. And she knew well how hateful material circumstances can make life.

Therefore, she could not decide in a hurry. But she bore poor Dr Mitchell a deep grudge, that he could not grant her all the advantages of his offer, and excuse her the acceptance of him himself. She dared not decide in a hurry. And this very fear, like a yoke on her, made her resent the man who drove her to decision.

Sometimes she rebelled. Sometimes she laughed unpleasantly in the man's face: though she dared not go *too* far: for she was a little afraid of him and his rapid temper, also. In her moments of sullen rebellion she thought of Natcha-Kee-Tawara. She thought of them deeply. She wondered where they were, what they were doing, how the war had affected them. Poor Geoffrey was a Frenchman—he would have to go to France to fight. Max and Louis were Swiss, it would not affect them: nor Cicio, who was Italian. She wondered if the troupe was in England: if they would continue to-

gether when Geoffrey was gone. She wondered if they
thought of her. She felt they did. She felt they did not forget
her. She felt there was a connection.

In fact, during the latter part of August she wondered a
good deal more about the Natchas than about Dr Mitchell.
But wondering about the Natchas would not help her. She
felt, if she knew where they were, she would fly to them.
But then she knew she wouldn't.

When she was at the station she saw crowds and bustle.
People were seeing their young men off. Beer was flowing:
sailors on the train were tipsy: women were holding young
men by the lapel of the coat. And when the train drew away,
the young men waving, the women cried aloud and sobbed
after them.

A chill ran down Alvina's spine. This was another matter,
apart from her Dr Mitchell. It made him feel very unreal,
trivial. She did not know what she was going to do. She
realized she must do something—take some part in the wild
dislocation of life. She knew that she would put off Dr
Mitchell again.

She talked the matter over with the matron. The matron
advised her to procrastinate. Why not volunteer for war-
service? True, she was a maternity nurse, and this was hardly
the qualification needed for the nursing of soldiers. But still,
she *was* a nurse.

Alvina felt this was the thing to do. Everywhere was a stir
and a seethe of excitement. Men were active, women were
needed too. She put down her name on the list of volunteers
for active service. This was on the last day of August.

On the first of September Dr Mitchell was round at the
hospital early, when Alvina was just beginning her morning
duties there. He went into the matron's room, and asked for
Nurse Houghton. The matron left them together.

The doctor was excited. He smiled broadly, but with a
tension of nervous excitement. Alvina was troubled. Her
heart beat fast.

'Now!' said Dr Mitchell. 'What have you to say to me?'

She looked up at him with confused eyes. He smiled excitedly and meaningful at her, and came a little nearer.

'To-day is the day when you answer, isn't it?' he said. 'Now then, let me hear what you have to say.'

But she only watched him with large, troubled eyes, and did not speak. He came still nearer to her.

'Well, then,' he said, 'I am to take it that silence gives consent.' And he laughed nervously, with nervous anticipation, as he tried to put his arm round her. But she stepped suddenly back.

'No, not yet,' she said.

'Why?' he asked.

'I haven't given my answer,' she said.

'Give it then,' he said, testily.

'I've volunteered for active service,' she stammered. 'I felt I ought to do something.'

'Why?' he asked. He could put a nasty intonation into that monosyllable. 'I should have thought you would answer *me* first.'

She did not answer, but watched him. She did not like him.

'I only signed yesterday,' she said.

'Why didn't you leave it till to-morrow? It would have looked better.' He was angry. But he saw a half-frightened, half-guilty look on her face, and during the weeks of anticipation he had worked himself up.

'But put that aside,' he smiled again, a little dangerously. 'You have still to answer my question. Having volunteered for war service doesn't prevent your being engaged to me, does it?'

Alvina watched him with large eyes. And again he came very near to her, so that his blue-serge waistcoat seemed to impinge on her, and his purplish red face was above her.

'I'd rather not be engaged, under the circumstances,' she said.

'Why?' came the nasty monosyllable. 'What have the circumstances got to do with it?'

'Everything is so uncertain,' she said. 'I'd rather wait.'

' "Wait!" Haven't you waited long enough? There's nothing at all to prevent your getting engaged to me now. Nothing whatsoever! Come now. I'm old enough not to be played with. And I'm much too much in love with you to let you go on indefinitely like this. Come now!' He smiled imminent, and held out his large hand for her hand. 'Let me put the ring on your finger. It will be the proudest day of my life when I make you my wife. Give me your hand—'

Alvina was wavering. For one thing, mere curiosity made her want to see the ring. She half lifted her hand. And but for the knowledge that he would kiss her, she would have given it. But he would kiss her—and against that she obstinately set her will. She put her hand behind her back, and looked obstinately into his eyes.

'Don't play a game with me,' he said dangerously.

But she only continued to look mockingly and obstinately into his eyes.

'Come,' he said, beckoning for her to give her hand.

With a barely perceptible shake of the head, she refused, staring at him all the time. His ungovernable temper got the better of him. He saw red, and without knowing, seized her by the shoulder, swung her back and thrust her, pressed her against the wall as if he would push her through it. His face was blind with anger, like a hot, red sun. Suddenly, almost instantaneously, he came to himself again and drew back his hands, shaking his right hand as if some rat had bitten it.

'I'm sorry!' he shouted, beside himself. 'I'm sorry. I didn't mean it. I'm sorry.' He dithered before her.

She recovered her equilibrium, and, pale to the lips, looked at him with sombre eyes.

'I'm sorry!' he continued loudly, in his strange frenzy like a small boy. 'Don't remember! Don't remember! Don't think I did it.'

His face was a kind of blank, and unconsciously he wrung the hand that had gripped her, as if it pained him. She watched him, and wondered why on earth all this frenzy. She was left rather cold, she did not at all feel the strong feelings he seemed to expect of her. There was nothing so very unnatural, after all, in being bumped up suddenly against the wall. Certainly her shoulder hurt where he had gripped it. But there were plenty of worse hurts in the world. She watched him with wide, distant eyes.

And he fell on his knees before her, as she backed against the bookcase, and he caught hold of the edge of her dress-bottom, drawing it to him. Which made her rather abashed, and much more uncomfortable.

'Forgive me!' he said. 'Don't remember! Forgive me! Love me! Love me! Forgive me and love me! Forgive me and love me!'

As Alvina was looking down dismayed on the great, red-faced, elderly man, who in his crying-out showed his white teeth like a child, and as she was gently trying to draw her skirt from his clutch, the door opened, and there stood the matron, in her big frilled cap. Alvina glanced at her, flushed crimson, and looked down to the man. She touched his face with her hand.

'Never mind,' she said. 'It's nothing. Don't think about it.'

He caught her hand and clung to it.

'Love me! Love me! Love me!' he cried.

The matron softly closed the door again, withdrawing.

'Love me! Love me!'

Alvina was absolutely dumbfounded by this scene. She had no idea men did such things. It did not touch her, it dumbfounded her.

The doctor, clinging to her hand, struggled to his feet and flung his arms round her, clasping her wildly to him.

'You love me! You love me, don't you?' he said, vibrating and beside himself as he pressed her to his breast and hid his face against her hair. At such a moment, what was the good of saying she didn't. But she didn't. Pity for his shame, however, kept her silent, motionless and silent in his arms, smothered against the blue-serge waistcoat of his broad breast.

He was beginning to come to himself. He became silent. But he still strained her fast, he had no idea of letting her go.

'You will take my ring, won't you?' he said at last, still in the strange lamentable voice. 'You will take my ring.'

'Yes,' she said coldly. Anything for a quiet emergence from this scene.

He fumbled feverishly in his pocket with one hand, holding her still fast by the other arm. And with his one hand he managed to extract the ring from its case, letting the case roll away on the floor. It was a diamond solitaire.

'Which finger? Which finger is it?' he asked, beginning to smile rather weakly. She extricated her hand, and held out her engagement finger. Upon it was the mourning-ring Miss Frost had always worn. The doctor slipped the diamond solitaire above the mourning ring, and folded Alvina to his breast again.

'Now,' he said, almost in his normal voice. 'Now I know you love me.' The pleased self-satisfaction in his voice made her angry. She managed to extricate herself.

'You will come along with me now?' he said.

'I can't,' she answered. 'I must get back to my work here.'

'Nurse Allen can do that.'

'I'd rather not.'

'Where are you going to-day?'

She told him her cases.

'Well, you will come and have tea with me. I shall expect you to have tea with me every day.'

But Alvina was straightening her crushed cap before the mirror, and did not answer.

'We can see as much as we like of each other now we're engaged,' he said, smiling with satisfaction.

'I wonder where the matron is,' said Alvina, suddenly going into the cool white corridor. He followed her. And they met the matron just coming out of the ward.

'Matron!' said Dr Mitchell, with a return of his old mouthing importance. 'You may congratulate Nurse Houghton and me on our engagement—' He smiled largely.

'I may congratulate *you*, you mean,' said the matron.

'Yes, of course. And both of us, since we are now one,' he replied.

'Not quite, yet,' said the matron gravely.

And at length she managed to get rid of him.

At once she went to look for Alvina, who had gone to her duties.

'Well, I *suppose* it is all right,' said the matron gravely.

'No, it isn't,' said Alvina. 'I shall *never* marry him.'

'Ah, never is a long while! Did he hear me come in?'

'No, I'm sure he didn't.'

'Thank goodness for that.'

'Yes indeed! It was perfectly horrible. Following me round on his knees and shouting for me to love him! Perfectly horrible!'

'Well,' said the matron. 'You never know what men will do till you've known them. And then you need be surprised at nothing, *nothing*. I'm surprised at nothing they do—'

'I must say,' said Alvina, 'I was surprised. Very unpleasantly.'

'But you accepted him—'

'Anything to quieten him—like a hysterical child.'

'Yes, but I'm not sure you haven't taken a very risky way of quietening him, giving him what he wanted—'

'I think,' said Alvina, 'I can look after myself. I may be moved any day now.'

'Well—!' said the matron. 'He may prevent your getting moved, you know. He's on the board. And if he says you are indispensable—'

This was a new idea for Alvina to cogitate. She had counted on a speedy escape. She put his ring in her apron pocket, and there she forgot it until he pounced on her in the afternoon, in the house of one of her patients. He waited for her, to take her off.

'Where is your ring?' he said.

And she realized that it lay in the pocket of a soiled, discarded apron—perhaps lost forever.

'I shan't wear it on duty,' she said. 'You know that.'

She had to go to tea with him. She avoided his love-making, by telling him any sort of spooniness revolted her. And he was too much an old bachelor to take easily to a fondling habit—before marriage, at least. So he mercifully left her alone: he was on the whole devoutly thankful she wanted to be left alone. But he wanted her to be there. That was his greatest craving. He wanted her to be always there. And so he craved for marriage: to possess her entirely, and to have her always there with him, so that he was never alone. Alone and apart from all the world: but by her side, always by her side.

'Now when shall we fix the marriage?' he said. 'It is no

good putting it back. We both know what we are doing. And now the engagement is announced—'

He looked at her anxiously. She could see the hysterical little boy under the great, authoritative man.

'Oh, not till after Christmas!' she said.

'After Christmas!' he started as if he had been bitten. 'Nonsense! It's nonsense to wait so long. Next month, at the latest.'

'Oh no,' she said. 'I don't think so soon.'

'Why not? The sooner the better. You had better send in your resignation at once, so that you're free.'

'Oh, but is there any need? I may be transferred for war service.'

'That's not likely. You're our only maternity nurse—'

And so the days went by. She had tea with him practically every afternoon, and she got used to him. They discussed the furnishing—she could not help suggesting a few alterations, a few arrangements according to *her* idea. And he drew up a plan of a wedding tour in Scotland. Yet she was quite certain she would not marry him. The matron laughed at her certainty. 'You will drift into it,' she said. 'He is tying you down by too many little threads.'

'Ah, well, you'll see!' said Alvina.

'Yes,' said the matron. 'I *shall* see.'

And it was true that Alvina's will was indeterminate, at this time. She was *resolved* not to marry. But her will, like a spring that is hitched somehow, did not fly direct against the doctor. She had sent in her resignation, as he suggested. But not that she might be free to marry him, but that she might be at liberty to flee him. So she told herself. Yet she worked into his hands.

One day she sat with the doctor in the car near the station—it was towards the end of September—held up by a squad of soldiers in khaki, who were marching off with their band wildly playing, to embark on the special troop train that was coming down from the north. The town was in great excitement. War-fever was spreading everywhere. Men were rushing to enlist—and being constantly rejected, for it was still the day of regular standards.

As the crowds surged on the pavement, as the soldiers tramped to the station, as the traffic waited, there came a certain flow in the opposite direction. The 4.15 train had come in. People were struggling along with luggage, children were running with spades and buckets, cabs were crawling along with families: it was the seaside people coming home. Alvina watched the two crowds mingle.

And as she watched she saw two men, one carrying a mandoline case and a suit-case which she knew. It was Cicio. She did not know the other man: some theatrical individual. The two men halted almost near the car, to watch the band go by. Alvina saw Cicio quite near to her. She would have liked to squirt water down his brown, handsome, oblivious neck. She felt she hated him. He stood there, watching the music, his lips curling in his faintly-derisive Italian manner, as he talked to the other man. His eyelashes were as long and dark as ever, his eyes had still the attractive look of being set in with a smutty finger. He had got the same brownish suit on, which she disliked, the same black hat set slightly, jauntily over one eye. He looked common: and yet with that peculiar southern aloofness which gave him a certain beauty and distinction in her eyes. She felt she hated him, rather. She felt she had been let down by him.

The band had passed. A child ran against the wheel of the standing car. Alvina suddenly reached forward and made a loud, screeching flourish on the hooter. Everyone looked round, including the laden, tramping soldiers.

'We can't move yet,' said Dr Mitchell.

But Alvina was looking at Cicio at that moment. He had turned with the rest, looking inquiringly at the car. And his quick eyes, the whites of which showed so white against his duskiness, the yellow pupils so non-human, met hers with a quick flash of recognition. His mouth began to curl in a smile of greeting. But she stared at him without moving a muscle, just blankly stared, abstracting every scrap of feeling, even of animosity or coldness, out of her gaze. She saw the smile die on his lips, his eyes glance sideways, and again sideways, with that curious animal shyness which characterized him. It was as if he did not want to see her looking at him, and ran from side to side like a caged weasel, avoiding her blank, glaucous look.

She turned pleasantly to Dr Mitchell . . .

'What did you say?' she asked sweetly.

CHAPTER 12

Allaye is also Engaged

A lvina found it pleasant to be respected as she was respected in Lancaster. It is not only the prophet who hath honour *save* in his own country: it is everyone with individuality. In this northern town Alvina found that her individuality really told. Already she belonged to the revered caste of medicine-men. And into the bargain she was a personality, a person.

Well and good. She was not going to cheapen herself. She felt that even in the eyes of the natives—the well-to-do part, at least—she lost a *little* of her distinction when she was engaged to Dr Mitchell. The engagement had been announced in *The Times,* the *Morning Post,* the *Manchester Guardian,* and the local *News.* No fear about its being known. And it cast a slight slur of vulgar familiarity over her. In Woodhouse, she knew, it elevated her in the common esteem tremendously. But she was no longer in Woodhouse. She was in Lancaster. And in Lancaster her engagement pigeon-holed her. Apart from Dr Mitchell she had a magic potentiality. Connected with him, she was a known and labelled quantity.

This she gathered from her contact with the local gentry. The matron was a woman of family, who somehow managed, in her big, white, frilled cap, to be distinguished like an abbess of old. The really toney women of the place came to take tea in her room, and these little teas in the hospital were like a little elegant female conspiracy. There was a slight flavour of art and literature about. The matron had known Walter Pater, in the somewhat remote past.

Alvina was admitted to these teas with the few women who formed the toney intellectual élite of this northern town. There was a certain freemasonry in the matron's room. The matron, a lady-doctor, a clergyman's daughter, and the wives of two industrial magnates of the place, these five, and then Alvina, formed the little group. They did not meet a great deal outside the hospital. But they always met with that curious female freemasonry which can form a law unto itself even among most conventional women. They talked as they would never talk before men, or before feminine outsiders. They threw aside the whole vestment of convention. They discussed plainly the things they thought about—even the most secret—and they were quite calm about the things they did—even the most impossible. Alvina felt that her transgression was a very mild affair, and that her engagement was really *infra dig*.

'And are you going to marry him?' asked Mrs Tuke, with a long, cool look.

'I can't *imagine* myself—' said Alvina.

'Oh, but so many things happen outside one's imagination. That's where your body has you. I can't *imagine* that I'm going to have a child—' She lowered her eyelids wearily and sardonically over her large eyes.

Mrs Tuke was the wife of the son of a local manufacturer. She was about twenty-eight years old, pale, with great dark-grey eyes and an arched nose and black hair, very like a head on one of the lovely Syracusan coins. The old look of a smile which wasn't a smile, at the corners of the mouth, the arched nose, and the slowness of the big, full, classic eyes gave her the dangerous Greek look of the Syracusan women of the past: the dangerous, heavily-civilized women of old Sicily: those who laughed about the latomia.

'But do you think you can have a child without wanting it *at all*?' asked Alvina.

'Oh, but there isn't *one bit* of me wants it, not *one bit*.

My *flesh* doesn't want it. And my mind doesn't—yet there it is!' She spread her fine hands with a flicker of inevitability.

'Something must want it,' said Alvina.

'Oh!' said Mrs Tuke. 'The universe is one big machine, and we're just part of it.' She flicked out her grey silk handkerchief, and dabbed her nose, watching with big, blackgrey eyes the fresh face of Alvina.

'There's not *one bit* of me concerned in having this child,' she persisted to Alvina. 'My flesh isn't concerned, and my mind isn't. And *yet!*—*le voilà!*—I'm just *planté*. I can't *imagine* why I married Tommy. And yet—I did—!' She shook her head as if it was all just beyond her, and the pseudo-smile at the corners of her ageless mouth deepened.

Alvina was to nurse Mrs Tuke. The baby was expected at the end of August. But already the middle of September was here, and the baby had not arrived.

The Tukes were not very rich—the young ones, that is. Tommy wanted to compose music, so he lived on what his father gave him. His father gave him a little house outside the town, a house furnished with expensive bits of old furniture, in a way that the townspeople thought insane. But there you are—Effie would insist on dabbing a rare bit of yellow brocade on the wall, instead of a picture, and in painting apple-green shelves in the recess of the whitewashed wall of the dining-room. Then she enamelled the hall-furniture yellow, and decorated it with curious green and lavender lines and flowers, and had unearthly cushions and Sardinian pottery with unspeakable peaked griffins.

What were you to make of such a woman! Alvina slept in her house these days, instead of at the hospital. For Effie was a very bad sleeper. She would sit up in bed, the two glossy black plaits hanging beside her white, arch face, wrapping loosely round her her dressing-gown of a sort of plumbago-coloured, dark-grey silk lined with fine silk of metallic blue, and there, ivory and jet-black and grey like black-lead, she would sit in the white bed-clothes flicking her handkerchief and revealing a flicker of kingfisher-blue silk and white silk nightdress, complaining of her neuritis nerve and her own impossible condition, and begging Alvina to stay with her another half-hour, and suddenly studying the big, blood-red stone on her finger as if she was reading something in it.

'I believe I shall be like the woman in the *Cent Nouvelles* and carry my child for five years. Do you know that story? She said that eating a parsley leaf on which bits of snow were sticking started the child in her. It might just as well—'

Alvina would laugh and get tired. There was about her a kind of half-bitter sanity and nonchalance which the nervous woman liked.

One night as they were sitting thus in the bedroom, at nearly eleven o'clock, they started and listened. Dogs in the distance had also started to yelp. A mandoline was wailing its vibration in the night outside, rapidly, delicately quivering. Alvina went pale. She knew it was Cicio. She had seen him lurking in the streets of the town, but had never spoken to him.

'What's this?' cried Mrs Tuke, cocking her head on one side. 'Music! A mandoline! How extraordinary! Do you think it's a serenade?—' and she lifted her brows archly.

'I should think it is,' said Alvina.

'How extraordinary! What a moment to choose to serenade the lady! *Isn't* it like life—! I *must* look at it—'

She got out of bed with some difficulty, wrapped her dressing-gown round her, pushed her feet into slippers, and went to the window. She opened the sash. It was a lovely moonlight night of September. Below lay the little front garden, with its short drive and its iron gates that closed on the high-road. From the shadow of the high-road came the noise of the mandoline.

'Hello Tommy!' called Mrs Tuke to her husband, whom she saw on the drive below her. 'How's your musical ear—?'

'All right. Doesn't it disturb you?' came the man's voice from the moonlight below.

'Not a bit. I like it. I'm waiting for the voice. "*O Richard! ô mon roi*"—'

But the music had stopped.

'There!' cried Mrs Tuke. 'You've frightened him off! And we're dying to be serenaded, aren't we, nurse?' She turned to Alvina. 'Do give me my fur, will you? Thanks so much. Won't you open the other window and look out there—'

Alvina went to the second window. She stood looking out.

'Do play again!' Mrs Tuke called into the night. 'Do sing something.' And with her white arm she reached for a glory rose that hung in the moonlight from the wall, and with a flash of her white arm she flung it towards the garden wall—ineffectually, of course.

'Won't you play again?' she called into the night, to the unseen. 'Tommy, go indoors, the bird won't sing when you're about.'

'It's an Italian by the sound of him. Nothing I hate more than emotional Italian music. Perfectly nauseating.'

'Never mind, dear. I know it sounds as if all their inside were coming out of their mouth. But we want to be serenaded, don't we, nurse?—'

Alvina stood at her window, but did not answer.

'Ah-h?' came the odd query from Mrs Tuke. 'Don't you like it?'

'Yes,' said Alvina. 'Very much.'

'And aren't you dying for the song?'

'Quite.'

'There!' cried Mrs Tuke, into the moonlight. '*Una canzone bella-bella—molta bella*'—

She pronounced her syllables one by one, calling into the night. It sounded comical. There came a rude laugh from the drive below.

'Go indoors, Tommy! He won't sing if you're there. Nothing will sing if you're there,' called the young woman.

They heard a footstep on the gravel, and then the slam of the hall door.

'Now!' cried Mrs Tuke.

They waited. And sure enough, came the fine tinkle of the mandoline, and after a few moments, the song. It was one of the well-known Neapolitan songs, and Cicio sang it as it should be sung.

Mrs Tuke went across to Alvina.

'Doesn't he put his *bowels* into it—?' she said, laying her hand on her own full figure, and rolling her eyes mockingly. 'I'm *sure* it's more effective than senna-pods.'

Then she returned to her own window, huddled her furs over her breast, and rested her white elbows in the moonlight.

> Torn'a Surrientu
> Fammi campar—

The song suddenly ended, in a clamorous, animal sort of yearning. Mrs Tuke was quite still, resting her chin on her fingers. Alvina also was still. Then Mrs Tuke slowly reached for the rose-buds on the old wall.

'*Molta bella!*' she cried half ironically. '*Molta bella! Je vous envoie une rose*—' And she threw the roses out on to the drive. A man's figure was seen hovering outside the gate, on the high-road. '*Entrez!*' called Mrs Tuke. '*Entrez! Prenez votre rose.* Come in and take your rose.'

The man's voice called something from the distance.

'What?' cried Mrs Tuke.

'*Je ne peux pas entrer.*'

'*Vous ne pouvez pas entrer? Pourquoi alors! La porte n'est pas fermée à clef. Entrez donc!*'

'*Non. On n'entre pas*—' called the well-known voice of Cicio.

'*Quoi faire, alors!* Alvina, take him the rose to the gate, will you? Yes do! Their singing is horrible, I think. I can't go down to him. But do take him the roses, and see what he looks like. Yes do!' Mrs Tuke's eyes were arched and excited. Alvina looked at her slowly. Alvina also was smiling to herself.

She went slowly down the stairs and out of the front door. From a bush at the side she pulled two sweet-smelling roses. Then in the drive she picked up Effie's flowers. Cicio was standing outside the gate.

'Allaye!' he said, in a soft, yearning voice.

'Mrs Tuke sent you these roses,' said Alvina, putting the flowers through the bars of the gate.

'Allaye!' he said, caressing her hand, kissing it with a soft, passionate, yearning mouth. Alvina shivered. Quickly he opened the gate and drew her through. He drew her into the shadow of the wall, and put his arms round her, lifting her from her feet with passionate yearning.

'Allaye!' he said. 'I love you, Allaye, my beautiful, Allaye. I love you, Allaye!' He held her fast to his breast and began to walk away with her. His throbbing, muscular power seemed completely to envelop her. He was just walking away with her down the road, clinging fast to her, enveloping her.

'Nurse! Nurse! I can't see you! Nurse!—' came the long call of Mrs Tuke through the night. Dogs began to bark.

'Put me down,' murmured Alvina. 'Put me down, Cicio.'

'Come with me to Italy. Come with me to Italy, Allaye, I can't go to Italy by myself, Allaye. Come with me, be married to me—Allaye, Allaye—'

His voice was a strange, hoarse whisper just above her face, he still held her in his throbbing, heavy embrace.

'Yes—yes!' she whispered. 'Yes—yes! But put me down, Cicio. Put me down.'

'Come to Italy with me, Allaye. Come with me,' he still reiterated, in a voice hoarse with pain and yearning.

'Nurse! Nurse! Wherever are you? Nurse! I want you,' sang the uneasy, querulous voice of Mrs Tuke.

'Do put me down!' murmured Alvina, stirring in his arms.

He slowly relaxed his clasp, and she slid down like rain to earth. But still he clung to her.

'Come with me, Allaye! Come with me to Italy!' he said.

She saw his face, beautiful, non-human in the moonlight, and she shuddered slightly.

'Yes!' she said. 'I will come. But let me go now. Where is your mandoline?'

He turned round and looked up the road.

'Nurse! You absolutely *must* come. I can't bear it,' cried the strange voice of Mrs Tuke.

Alvina slipped from the man, who was a little bewildered, and through the gate into the drive.

'You must come!' came the voice in pain from the upper window.

Alvina ran upstairs. She found Mrs Tuke crouched in a chair, with a drawn, horrified, terrified face. As her pains suddenly gripped her, she uttered an exclamation, and pressed her clenched fists hard on her face.

'The pains have begun,' said Alvina, hurrying to her.

'Oh, it's horrible! It's horrible! I don't want it!' cried the woman in travail. Alvina comforted her and reassured her as best she could. And from outside, once more, came the despairing howl of the Neapolitan song, animal and inhuman on the night.

> E tu dic' Io part', addio!
> T'alluntare di sta core,
> Nel paese del amore
> Tien' o cor' di non turnar'
> —Ma nun me lasciar'—

It was almost unendurable. But suddenly Mrs Tuke became quite still, and sat with her fists clenched on her knees, her two jet-black plaits dropping on either side of her ivory face, her big eyes fixed staring into space. At the line—

> Ma nun me lasciar'—

she began to murmur softly to herself—'Yes, it's dreadful! It's horrible! I can't understand it. What does it mean, that noise? It's as bad as these pains. What does it mean? What does he say? I can understand a little Italian—' She paused. And again came the sudden complaint:

> Ma nun me lasciar'—

'*Ma nun me lasciar'*—!' she murmured, repeating the music. 'That means—Don't leave me! Don't leave me! But why? Why shouldn't one human being go away from another? What does it mean? That *awful* noise! Isn't love the most horrible thing! I think it's horrible. It just does one in, and turns one into a sort of howling animal. I'm howling with one sort of pain, he's howling with another. Two hellish animals howling through the night! I'm not myself, he's not himself. Oh, I think it's horrible. What does he look like, Nurse? Is he beautiful? Is he a great hefty brute?'

She looked with big, slow, enigmatic eyes at Alvina.

'He's a man I knew before,' said Alvina.

Mrs Tuke's face woke from its half-trance.

'Really! Oh! A man you knew before! Where?'

'It's a long story,' said Alvina. 'In a travelling music-hall troupe.'

'In a travelling music-hall troupe! How extraordinary! Why, how did you come across such an individual—?'

Alvina explained as briefly as possible. Mrs Tuke watched her. 'Really!' she said. 'You've done all those things!' And she scrutinized Alvina's face. 'You've had some effect on him, that's evident,' she said. Then she shuddered, and dabbed her nose with her handkerchief. 'Oh, the flesh is a *beastly* thing!' she cried. 'To make a man howl outside there like that, because you're here. And to make me howl because I've got a child inside me. It's unbearable! What does he look like, really?'

'I don't know,' said Alvina. 'Not extraordinary. Rather a hefty brute—'

Mrs Tuke glanced at her, to detect the irony.

'I should like to see him,' she said. 'Do you think I might?'

'I don't know,' said Alvina, non-committal.

'Do you think he might come up? Ask him. Do let me see him.'

'Do you really want to?' said Alvina.

'Of course—' Mrs Tuke watched Alvina with big, dark, slow eyes. Then she dragged herself to her feet. Alvina helped her into bed.

'Do ask him to come up for a minute,' Effie said. 'We'll give him a glass of Tommy's famous port. Do let me see him. Yes do!' She stretched out her long white arm to Alvina, with sudden imploring.

Alvina laughed, and turned doubtfully away.

The night was silent outside. But she found Cicio leaning against a gate-pillar. He stared up.

'Allaye!' he said.

'Will you come in for a moment? I can't leave Mrs Tuke.'

Cicio obediently followed Alvina into the house and up the stairs, without a word. He was ushered into the bedroom. He drew back when he saw Effie in the bed, sitting with her long plaits and her dark eyes, and the subtle-seeming smile at the corners of her mouth.

'Do come in!' she said. 'I wanted to thank you for the music. Nurse says it was for her, but I enjoyed it also. Would you tell me the words? I think it's a wonderful song.'

Cicio hung back against the door, his head dropped, and the shy, suspicious, faintly malicious smile on his face.

'Have a glass of port, do!' said Effie. 'Nurse, give us all one. I should like one too. And a biscuit.' Again she stretched out her long white arm from the sudden blue lining of her wrap, suddenly, as if taken with the desire. Cicio shifted on his feet, watching Alvina pour out the port.

He swallowed his in one swallow, and put aside his glass.

'Have some more!' said Effie, watching over the top of her glass.

He smiled faintly, stupidly, and shook his head.

'Won't you? Now tell me the words of the song—'

He looked at her from out of the dusky hollows of his brow, and did not answer. The faint, stupid half-smile, half-sneer was on his lips.

'Won't you tell them me? I understand one line—'

Cicio smiled more pronouncedly as he watched her, but did not speak.

'I understood one line,' said Effie, making big eyes at him. '*Ma non me lasciare—Don't leave me!* There, isn't that it?'

He smiled, stirred on his feet, and nodded.

'Don't leave me! There. I knew it was that. Why don't you want Nurse to leave you? Do you want her to be with you *every minute*?'

He smiled a little contemptuously, awkwardly, and turned aside his face, glancing at Alvina. Effie's watchful eyes caught the glance. It was swift, and full of the terrible yearning which so horrified her.

At the same moment a spasm crossed her face, her expression went blank.

'Shall we go down?' said Alvina to Cicio.

He turned immediately, with his cap in his hand, and followed. In the hall he pricked up his ears as he took the mandoline from the chest. He could hear the stifled cries and exclamations from Mrs Tuke. At the same moment the door of the study opened, and the musician, a burly fellow with troubled hair, came out.

'Is that Mrs Tuke?' he snapped anxiously.

'Yes. The pains have begun,' said Alvina.

'Oh God! And have you left her?' He was quite irascible.

'Only for a minute,' said Alvina.

But with a *Pf!* of angry indignation, he was climbing the stairs.

'She is going to have a child,' said Alvina to Cicio. 'I shall have to go back to her.' And she held out her hand.

He did not take her hand, but looked down into her face with the same slightly distorted look of overwhelming yearning, yearning heavy and unbearable, in which he was carried towards her as on a flood.

'Allaye!' he said, with a faint lift of the lip that showed his teeth, like a pained animal: a curious sort of smile. He could not go away.

'I shall have to go back to her,' she said.

'Shall you come with me to Italy, Allaye?'

'Yes. Where is Madame?'

'Gone! Gigi—all gone.'

'Gone where?'

'Gone back to France—called up.'

'And Madame and Louis and Max?'

'Switzerland.'

He stood helplessly looking at her.

'Well, I must go,' she said.

He watched her with his yellow eyes, from under his long black lashes, like some chained animal, haunted by doom. She turned and left him standing.

She found Mrs Tuke wildly clutching the edge of the sheets, and crying: 'No, Tommy dear. I'm awfully fond of you, you know I am. But go away. Oh God, go away. And put a space between us. Put a space between us!' she almost shrieked.

He pushed up his hair. He had been working on a big choral work which he was composing, and by this time he was almost demented.

'Can't you stand my presence!' he shouted, and dashed downstairs.

'Nurse!' cried Effie. 'It's *no use* trying to get a grip on life. You're just at the mercy of *Forces*!' she shrieked angrily.

'Why not?' said Alvina. 'There are good life-forces. Even the will of God is a life-force.'

'You don't understand! I want to be *myself*. And I'm *not* myself. I'm just torn to pieces by *Forces*. It's horrible—'

'Well, it's not my fault. I didn't make the universe,' said Alvina. 'If you have to be torn to pieces by forces, well, you have. Other forces will put you together again.'

'I don't want them to. I want to be myself. I don't want to be nailed together like a chair, with a hammer. I want to be myself.'

'You won't be nailed together like a chair. You should have faith in life.'

'But I hate life. It's nothing but a mass of forces. *I* am intelligent. Life isn't intelligent. Look at it at this moment. Do you call this intelligent? Oh—Oh! It's horrible! Oh—!' She was wild and sweating with her pains. Tommy flounced out downstairs, beside himself. He was heard talking to someone in the moonlight. To Cicio. He had already telephoned wildly for the doctor. But the doctor had replied that Nurse would ring him up.

The moment Mrs Tuke recovered her breath she began again.

'I hate life, and faith, and such things. Faith is only fear. And life is a mass of unintelligent forces to which intelligent beings are submitted. Prostituted. Oh—oh!!—prostituted—'

'Perhaps life itself is something bigger than intelligence,' said Alvina.

'Bigger than intelligence!' shrieked Effie. '*Nothing* is bigger than intelligence. Your man is a hefty brute. His yellow eyes *aren't* intelligent. They're *animal*—'

'No,' said Alvina. 'Something else. I wish he didn't attract me—'

'There! Because you're not content to be at the mercy of *Forces*!' cried Effie. 'I'm not. I'm not. I want to be myself. And so forces tear me to pieces! Tear me to pie—see— Oh-h-h! No!—'

Downstairs Tommy had walked Cicio back into the house again, and the two men were drinking port in the study, discussing Italy, for which Tommy had a great sentimental affection, though he hated all Italian music after the younger Scarlatti. They drank port all through the night, Tommy being strictly forbidden to interfere upstairs, or even to fetch the doctor. They drank three and a half bottles of port, and were discovered in the morning by Alvina fast asleep in the study, with the electric light still burning. Tommy slept with his fair and ruffled head hanging over the edge of the couch like some great loose fruit, Cicio was on the floor, face downwards, his face in his folded arms.

Alvina had a great difficulty in waking the inert Cicio. In the end, she had to leave him and rouse Tommy first: who in rousing fell off the sofa with a crash which woke him disagreeably. So that he turned on Alvina in a fury, and asked her what the hell she thought she was doing. In answer to which Alvina held up a finger warningly, and Tommy, suddenly remembering, fell back as if he had been struck.

'She is sleeping now,' said Alvina.

'Is it a boy or a girl?' he cried.

'It isn't born yet,' she said.

'Oh God, it's an accursed fugue!' cried the bemused Tommy. After which they proceeded to wake Cicio, who was like the dead doll in Petrushka, all loose and floppy. When he was awake, however, he smiled at Alvina, and said: 'Allaye!'

The dark, waking smile upset her badly.

CHAPTER 13

The Wedded Wife

The upshot of it all was that Alvina ran away to Scarborough without telling anybody. It was in the first week in October. She asked for a week-end, to make some arrangements for her marriage. The marriage was presumably with Dr Mitchell—though she had given him no definite word. However, her month's notice was up, so she was legally free. And therefore she packed a rather large bag with all her ordinary things, and set off in her everyday dress, leaving the nursing paraphernalia behind.

She knew Scarborough quite well: and quite quickly found rooms which she had occupied before, in a boarding-house where she had stayed with Miss Frost long ago. Having recovered from her journey, she went out on to the cliffs on the north side. It was evening, and the sea was before her. What was she to do?

She had run away from both men—from Cicio as well as from Mitchell. She had spent the last fortnight more or less avoiding the pair of them. Now she had a moment to herself. She was even free from Mrs Tuke, who in her own way was more exacting than the men. Mrs Tuke had a baby daughter, and was getting well. Cicio was living with the Tukes. Tommy had taken a fancy to him, and had half-engaged him as a sort of personal attendant: the sort of thing Tommy would do, not having paid his butcher's bills.

So Alvina sat on the cliffs in a mood of exasperation. She was sick of being badgered about. She didn't really want to marry anybody. Why should she? She was thankful beyond measure to be by herself. How sick she was of other people and their importunities! What was she to do? She decided to offer herself again, in a little while, for war service—in a new town this time. Meanwhile she wanted to be by herself.

She made excursions, she walked on the moors, in the brief but lovely days of early October. For three days it was all so sweet and lovely—perfect liberty, pure, almost paradisal.

The fourth day it rained: simply rained all day long, and was cold, dismal, disheartening beyond words. There she sat, stranded in the dismalness, and knew no way out. She went to bed at nine o'clock, having decided in a jerk to go to London and find work in the war-hospitals at once: not to leave off until she had found it.

But in the night she dreamed that Alexander, her first fiancé, was with her on the quay of some harbour, and was reproaching her bitterly, even reviling her, for having come too late, so that they had missed their ship. They were there to catch the boat—and she, for dilatoriness, was an hour late and she could see the broad stern of the steamer not far off. Just an hour late. She showed Alexander her watch—exactly ten o'clock, instead of nine. And he was more angry than ever, because her watch was slow. He pointed to the harbour clock—it was ten minutes past ten.

When she woke up she was thinking of Alexander. It was such a long time since she had thought of him. She wondered if he had a right to be angry with her.

The day was still grey, with sweepy rain-clouds on the sea—gruesome, objectionable. It was a prolongation of yesterday. Well, despair was no good, and being miserable was no good either. She got no satisfaction out of either mood. The only thing to do was to act: seize hold of life and wring its neck.

She took the time-table that hung in the hall: the time-table, that magic carpet of to-day. When in doubt, *move*. This was the maxim. Move. Where to?

Another click of a resolution. She would wire to Cicio and meet him—where? York—Leeds—Halifax—? She looked up the places in the time-table, and decided on Leeds. She wrote out a telegram, that she would be at Leeds that evening. Would he get it in time? Chance it.

She hurried off and sent the telegram. Then she took a little luggage, told the people of her house she would be back next day, and set off. She did not like whirling in the direction of Lancaster. But no matter.

She waited a long time for the train from the north to come in. The first person she saw was Tommy. He waved to her and jumped from the moving train.

'I say!' he said. 'So glad to see you! Cicio is with me. Effie insisted on my coming to see you.'

There was Cicio climbing down with the bag. A sort of servant! This was too much for her.

'So you came with your valet?' she said, as Cicio stood with the bag.

'Not a bit,' said Tommy, laying his hand on the other man's shoulder. 'We're the best of friends. I don't carry bags because my heart is rather groggy. I say, nurse, excuse me, but I like you better in uniform. Black doesn't suit you. You don't *mind*—'

'Yes, I do. But I've only got black clothes, except uniforms.'

'Well look here now—! You're not going on anywhere to-night, are you?'

'It is too late.'

'Well now, let's turn into the hotel and have a talk. I'm acting under Effie's orders, as you may gather—'

At the hotel Tommy gave her a letter from his wife: to the tune of—don't marry this Italian, you'll put yourself in a wretched hole, and one wants to avoid getting into holes. *I know*—concluded Effie, on a sinister note.

Tommy sang another tune. Cicio was a lovely chap, a rare chap, a treat. He, Tommy, could quite understand any woman's wanting to marry him—didn't agree a bit with Effie. But marriage, you know, was so final. And then with this war on: you never knew how things might turn out: a foreigner and all that. And then—you won't mind what I say—? We won't talk about class and that rot. If the man's good enough, he's good enough by himself. But is he your intellectual equal, Nurse? After all, it's a big point. You don't want to marry a man you can't talk to. Cicio's a treat to be with, because he's so natural. But it isn't a *mental* treat—'

Alvina thought of Mrs Tuke, who complained that Tommy talked music and pseudo-philosophy *by the hour* when he was wound up. She saw Effie's long, outstretched arm of repudiation and weariness.

'Of course!'—another of Mrs Tuke's exclamations. 'Why not *be* atavistic if you *can* be, and follow at a man's heel just because he's a man. Be like barbarous women, a slave.'

During all this, Cicio stayed out of the room, as bidden. It was not till Alvina sat before her mirror that he opened her door softly, and entered.

'I come in,' he said, and he closed the door.

Alvina remained with her hair-brush suspended, watching him. He came to her, smiling softly, to take her in his arms. But she put the chair between them.

'Why did you bring Mr Tuke?' she said.

He lifted his shoulders.

'I haven't brought him,' he said, watching her.

'Why did you show him the telegram?'

'It was Mrs Tuke took it.'

'Why did you give it her?'

'It was she gave it me, in her room. She kept it in her room till I came and took it.'

'All right,' said Alvina. 'Go back to the Tukes.' And she began again to brush her hair.

Cicio watched her with narrowing eyes.

'What you mean?' he said. 'I shan't go, Allaye. You come with me.'

'Ha!' she sniffed scornfully. 'I shall go where I like.'

But slowly he shook his head.

'You'll come, Allaye,' he said. 'You come with me, with Cicio.'

She shuddered at the soft, plaintive entreaty.

'How can I go with you? How can I depend on you at all?'

Again he shook his head. His eyes had a curious yellow fire, beseeching, plaintive, with a demon quality of yearning compulsion.

'Yes, you come with me, Allaye. You come with me, to Italy. You don't go to that other man. He is too old, not healthy. You come with me to Italy. Why do you send a telegram?'

Alvina sat down and covered her face, trembling.

'I can't! I can't! I can't!' she moaned. 'I can't do it.'

'Yes, you come with me. I have money. You come with me, to my place in the mountains, to my uncle's house. Fine house, you like it. Come with me, Allaye.'

She could not look at him.

'Why do you want me?' she said.

'Why I want you?' He gave a curious laugh, almost of ridicule. 'I don't know that. You ask me another, eh?'

She was sitting silent, sitting looking downwards.

'I can't, I think,' she said abstractedly, looking up at him.

He smiled, a fine, subtle smile, like a demon's, but inexpressibly gentle. He made her shiver as if she was mesmerized. And he was reaching forward to her as a snake reaches, nor could she recoil.

'You come, Allaye,' he said softly, with his foreign intonation. 'You come. You come to Italy with me. Yes?' He put his hand on her, and she started as if she had been struck. But his hands, with the soft, powerful clasp, only closed her faster.

'Yes?' he said. 'Yes? All right, eh? All right!'—he had a strange mesmeric power over her, as if he possessed the sensual secrets, and she was to be subjected.

'I can't,' she moaned, trying to struggle. But she was powerless.

Dark and insidious he was: he had no regard for her. How could a man's movements be so soft and gentle, and yet so inhumanly regardless! He had no regard for her. Why didn't she revolt? Why couldn't she? She was as if bewitched. She couldn't fight against her bewitchment. Why? Because he seemed to her beautiful, so beautiful. And this left her numb, submissive. Why must she see him beautiful? Why was she will-less? She felt herself like one of the old sacred prostitutes: a sacred prostitute.

In the morning, very early, they left for Scarborough, leaving a letter for the sleeping Tommy. In Scarborough they went to the registrar's office: they could be married in a fortnight's time. And so the fortnight passed, and she was under his spell. Only she knew it. She felt extinguished. Cicio talked to her: but only ordinary things. There was no wonderful intimacy of speech, such as she had always imagined, and always craved for. No. He loved her—but it was in a dark, mesmeric way, which did not let her be herself. His love did not stimulate her or excite her. It extinguished her. She had to be the quiescent, obscure woman: she felt as if she were veiled. Her thoughts were dim, in the dim back regions of consciousness—yet, somewhere, she almost exulted. Atavism! Mrs Tuke's word would play in her mind. Was it atavism, this sinking into extinction under the spell of Cicio? Was it atavism, this strange, sleep-like submission to his being? Perhaps it was. Perhaps it was. But it was also heavy and sweet and rich. Somewhere, she was content. Somewhere even she was vastly proud of the dark veiled eternal loneliness she felt, under his shadow.

And so it had to be. She shuddered when she touched him, because he was so beautiful, and she was so submitted. She quivered when he moved as if she were his shadow. Yet her mind remained distinctly clear. She could criticize him, find fault with him, the things he did. But *ultimately,* she could find no fault with him. She had lost the power. She didn't care. She had lost the power to care about his faults. Strange, sweet, poisonous indifference! She was drugged. And she knew it. Would she ever wake out of her dark, warm coma? She shuddered, and hoped not. Mrs Tuke would say atavism. Atavism! The word recurred curiously.

But under all her questionings she felt well; a nonchalance deep as sleep, a passivity and indifference so dark and sweet she felt it must be evil. Evil! She was evil. And yet she had no power to be otherwise. They were legally married. And she was glad. She was relieved by knowing she could not escape. She was Mrs Marasca. What was the good of trying to be Miss Houghton any longer? Marasca, the bitter cherry. Some dark poison fruit she had eaten. How glad she was she had eaten it! How beautiful he was! And no one saw it but herself. For her it was so potent it made her tremble when she noticed him. His beauty, his dark shadow. Cicio really was much handsomer since his marriage. He seemed to emerge. Before, he had seemed to make himself invisible in the streets, in England, altogether. But now something unfolded in him, he was a potent, glamorous presence, people turned to watch him. There was a certain dark, leopard-like pride in the air about him, something that the English people watched.

He wanted to go to Italy. And now it was *his* will which counted. Alvina, as his wife, must submit. He took her to London the day after the marriage. He wanted to get away to Italy. He did not like being in England, a foreigner, amid the beginnings of the spy craze.

In London they stayed at his cousin's house. His cousin kept a restaurant in Battersea, and was a flourishing London Italian, a real London product with all the good English virtues of cleanliness and honesty added to an Italian shrewdness. His name was Guiseppe Califano, and he was pale, and he had four children of whom he was very proud. He received Alvina with an affable respect, as if she were an asset in the family, but as if he were a little uneasy and dis-approving. She had *come down* in marrying Cicio. She had lost her caste. He rather seemed to exult over her degrada-tion. For he was a northernized Italian, he had accepted En-glish standards. His children were English brats. He almost patronized Alvina.

But then a long, slow look from her remote blue eyes brought him up sharp, and he envied Cicio suddenly, he was almost in love with her himself. She disturbed him. She dis-turbed him in his new English aplomb of a London *restau-rateur,* and she disturbed in him the old Italian dark soul, to which he was renegade. He tried treating her as an English lady. But the slow, remote look in her eyes made this fall flat. He had to be Italian.

And he was jealous of Cicio. In Cicio's face was a lurking smile, and round his fine nose there seemed a subtle, semi-defiant triumph. After all, he had triumphed over his well-to-do, Anglicized cousin. With a stealthy, leopard-like pride Cicio went through the streets of London in those wild early days of war. He was the one victor, arching stealthily over the vanquished north.

Alvina saw nothing of all these complexities. For the time being, she was all dark and potent. Things were curious to her. It was curious to be in Battersea, in the English-Italian household, where the children spoke English more readily than Italian. It was strange to be high over the restaurant, to see the trees of the park, to hear the clang of trams. It was strange to walk out and come to the river. It was strange to feel the seethe of war and dread in the air. But she did not question. She seemed steeped in the passional influence of the man, as in some narcotic. She even forgot Mrs Tuke's atavism. Vague and unquestioning she went through the days, she accompanied Cicio into town, she went with him to make purchases, or she sat by his side in the music-hall, or she stayed in her room and sewed, or she sat at meals with the Califanos, a vague brightness on her face. And Mrs Califano was very nice to her, very gentle, though with a suspicion of malicious triumph, mockery, beneath her gentleness. Still, she was nice and womanly, hovering as she was between her English emancipation and her Italian subordination. She half pitied Alvina, and was more than half jealous of her.

Alvina was aware of nothing—only of the presence of Cicio. It was his physical presence which cast a spell over her. She lived within his aura. And she submitted to him as if he had extended his dark nature over her. She knew nothing about him. She lived mindlessly within his presence, quivering within his influence, as if his blood beat in her. She *knew* she was subjected. One tiny corner of her knew, and watched.

He was very happy, and his face had a real beauty. His eyes glowed with lustrous secrecy, like the eyes of some victorious, happy wild creature seen remote under a bush. And he was very good to her. His tenderness made her quiver into a swoon of complete self-forgetfulness, as if the flood-gates of her depths opened. The depth of his warm, mindless, enveloping love was immeasurable. She felt she could sink forever into his warm, pulsating embrace.

Afterwards, later on, when she was inclined to criticize him, she would remember the moment when she saw his face at the Italian Consulate in London. There were many people at the Consulate, clamouring for passports—a wild and ill-regulated crowd. They had waited their turn and got inside—Cicio was not good at pushing his way. And inside a courteous tall old man with a white beard had lifted the flap for Alvina to go inside the office and sit down to fill in the form. She thanked the old man, who bowed as if he had a reputation to keep up.

Cicio followed, and it was he who had to sit down and fill up the form, because she did not understand the Italian questions. She stood at his side, watching the excited, laughing, noisy, east-end Italians at the desk. The whole place had a certain free-and-easy confusion, a human, unofficial, muddling liveliness which was not quite like England, even though it was in the middle of London.

'What was your mother's name?' Cicio was asking her. She turned to him. He sat with the pen perched flourishingly at the end of his fingers, suspended in the serious and artistic business of filling in a form. And his face had a dark luminousness, like a dark transparence which was shut and has now expanded. She quivered, as if it was more than she could bear. For his face was open like a flower right to the depths of his soul, a dark, lovely translucency, vulnerable to the deep quick of his soul. The lovely, rich darkness of his southern nature, so different from her own, exposing itself now in its passional vulnerability, made her go white with a kind of fear. For an instant, her face seemed drawn and old as she looked down at him, answering his question. Then her eyes became sightless with tears, she stooped as if to look at his writing, and quickly kissed his fingers that held the pen, there in the midst of the crowded, vulgar Consulate.

He stayed suspended, again looking up at her with the bright, unfolded eyes of a wild creature which plays and is not seen. A faint smile, very beautiful to her, was on his face. What did he see when he looked at her? She did not know, she did not know. And she would never know. For an instant, she swore inside herself that God Himself should not take her away from this man. She would commit herself to him through every eternity. And then the vagueness came over her again, she turned aside, photographically seeing the crowd in the Consulate, but really unconscious. His movement as he rose seemed to move her in her sleep, she turned to him at once.

It was early in November before they could leave for Italy, and her dim, lustrous state lasted all the time. She found herself at Charing Cross in the early morning, in all the bustle of catching the Continental train. Giuseppe was there, and Gemma his wife, and two of the children, besides three other Italian friends of Cicio. They all crowded up the platform. Giuseppe had insisted that Cicio should take second-class tickets. They were very early. Alvina and Cicio were installed in a second-class compartment, with all their packages. Cicio was pale, yellowish under his tawny skin, and nervous. He stood excitedly on the platform talking in Italian—or rather, in his own dialect—whilst Alvina sat quite still in her corner. Sometimes one of the women or one of the children came to say a few words to her, or Giuseppe hurried to her with illustrated papers. They treated her as if she were some sort of invalid, or angel, now she was leaving. But most of their attention they gave to Cicio, talking at him rapidly at once, whilst he answered, and glanced in this way and that, under his fine lashes, and smiled his old, nervous, meaningless smile. He was curiously upset.

Time came to shut the doors. The women and children kissed Alvina, saying:

'You'll be all right, eh? Going to Italy—!' And then profound and meaningless nods, which she could not interpret, but which were fraught surely with good-fellowship.

Then they all kissed Cicio. The men took him in their arms and kissed him on either cheek, the children lifted their faces in eager anticipation of the double kiss. Strange, how eager they were for this embrace—how they all kept taking Cicio's hand, one after the other, whilst he smiled constrainedly and nervously.

CHAPTER 14

The Journey Across

The train began to move. Giuseppe ran alongside, holding Cicio's hand still; the women and children were crying and waving their handkerchiefs, the other men were shouting messages, making strange, eager gestures. And Alvina sat quite still, wonderingly. And so the big, heavy train drew out, leaving the others small and dim on the platform. It was foggy, the river was a sea of yellow beneath the ponderous iron bridge. The morning was dim and dank.

The train was very full. Next to Alvina sat a trim French-woman reading *L'Aiglon*. There was a terrible encumbrance of packages and luggage everywhere. Opposite her sat Cicio, his black overcoat open over his pale-grey suit, his black hat a little over his left eye. He glanced at her from time to time, smiling constrainedly. She remained very still. They ran through Bromley and out into the open country. It was grey, with shivers of grey sunshine. On the downs there was thin snow. The air in the train was hot, heavy with the crowd and tense with excitement and uneasiness. The train seemed to rush ponderously, massively, across the Weald.

And so, through Folkestone to the sea. There was sun in the sky now, and white clouds, in the sort of hollow sky-dome above the grey earth with its horizon walls of fog. The air was still. The sea heaved with a sucking noise inside the dock. Alvina and Cicio sat aft on the second-class deck, their bags near them. He put a white muffler round himself, Alvina hugged herself in her beaver scarf and muff. She looked tender and beautiful in her still vagueness, and Cicio, hovering about her, was beautiful too, his estrangement gave him a certain wistful nobility which for the moment put him beyond all class inferiority. The passengers glanced at them across the magic of estrangement.

The sea was very still. The sun was fairly high in the open sky, where white cloud-tops showed against the pale, wintry blue. Across the sea came a silver sun-track. And Alvina and Cicio looked at the sun, which stood a little to the right of the ship's course.

'The sun!' said Cicio, nodding towards the orb and smiling to her.

'I love it,' she said.

He smiled again, silently. He was strangely moved: she did not know why.

The wind was cold over the wintry sea, though the sun's beams were warm. They rose, walked round the cabins. Other ships were at sea—destroyers and battleships, grey, low, and sinister on the water. Then a tall bright schooner glimmered far down the channel. Some brown fishing smacks kept together. All was very still in the wintry sunshine of the Channel.

So they turned to walk to the stern of the boat. And Alvina's heart suddenly contracted. She caught Cicio's arm, as the boat rolled gently. For there behind, behind all the sunshine, was England. England, beyond the water, rising with ash-grey, corpse-grey cliffs, and streaks of snow on the downs above. England, like a long, ash-grey coffin slowly submerging. She watched it, fascinated and terrified. It seemed to repudiate the sunshine, to remain unilluminated, long and ash-grey and dead, with streaks of snow like cerements. That was England! Her thoughts flew to Woodhouse, the grey centre of it all. Home!

Her heart died within her. Never had she felt so utterly strange and far-off. Cicio at her side was as nothing, as spellbound she watched, away off, behind all the sunshine and the sea, the grey, snow-streaked substance of England slowly receding and sinking, submerging. She felt she could not believe it. It was like looking at something else. What? It was like a long, ash-grey coffin, winter, slowly submerging in the sea. England?

She turned again to the sun. But clouds and veils were already weaving in the sky. The cold was beginning to soak in, moreover. She sat very still for a long time, almost an eternity. And when she looked round again there was only a bank of mist behind, beyond the sea: a bank of mist, and a few grey, stalking ships. She must watch for the coast of France.

And there it was already, looming up grey and amorphous, patched with snow. It had a grey, heaped, sordid look in the November light. She had imagined Boulogne gay and brilliant. Whereas it was more grey and dismal than England. But not that magical, mystic, phantom look.

The ship slowly put about, and backed into the harbour. She watched the quay approach. Cicio was gathering up the luggage. Then came the first cry one ever hears: 'Porteur! Porteur! Want a porteur!' A porter in a blouse strung the luggage on his strap, and Cicio and Alvina entered the crush for the exit and the passport inspection. There was a tense, eager, frightened crowd, and officials shouting directions in French and English. Alvina found herself at last before a table where bearded men in uniforms were splashing open the big pink sheets of the English passports: she felt strange and uneasy, that her passport was unimpressive and Italian. The official scrutinized her, and asked questions of Cicio. Nobody asked her anything—she might have been Cicio's shadow. So they went through to the vast, crowded cavern of a Customs house, where they found their porter waving to them in the mob. Cicio fought in the mob while the porter whisked off Alvina to get seats in the big train. And at last she was planted once more in a seat, with Cicio's place reserved beside her. And there she sat, looking across the railway lines at the harbour, in the last burst of grey sunshine. Men looked at her, officials stared at her, soldiers made remarks about her. And at last, after an eternity, Cicio came along the platform, the porter trotting behind.

They sat and ate the food they had brought, and drank wine and tea. After weary hours the train set off through snow-patched country to Paris. Everywhere was crowded, the train was stuffy without being warm. Next to Alvina sat a large, fat, youngish Frenchman who overflowed over her in a hot fashion. Darkness began to fall. The train was very late. There were strange and frightening delays. Strange lights appeared in the sky, everybody seemed to be listening for strange noises. It was all such a whirl and confusion that Alvina lost count, relapsed into a sort of stupidity. Gleams, flashes, noises and then at last the frenzy of Paris.

It was night, a black city, and snow falling, and no train that night across to the Gare de Lyon. In a state of semi-stupefaction after all the questionings and examinings and blusterings, they were finally allowed to go straight across Paris. But this meant another wild tussle with a Paris taxi-driver, in the filtering snow. So they were deposited in the Gare de Lyon.

And the first person who rushed upon them was Geoffrey, in a rather grimy private's uniform. He had already seen some hard service, and had a wild, bewildered look. He kissed Cicio and burst into tears on his shoulder, there in the great turmoil of the entrance hall of the Gare de Lyon. People looked, but nobody seemed surprised. Geoffrey sobbed, and the tears came silently down Cicio's cheeks.

'I've waited for you since five o'clock, and I've got to go back now. Cicio! Cicio! I wanted so badly to see you. I shall never see thee again, brother, my brother!' cried Gigi, and a sob shook him.

'*Gigi! Mon Gigi! Tu as donc reçu ma lettre?*'

'Yesterday. O Cicio, Cicio, I shall die without thee!'

'But no, Gigi, *frère*. You won't die.'

'Yes, Cicio, I shall. I know I shall.'

'I say *no*, brother,' said Cicio. But a spasm suddenly took him, he pulled off his hat and put it over his face and sobbed into it.

'*Adieu, ami! Adieu!*' cried Gigi, clutching the other man's arm. Cicio took his hat from his tear-stained face and put it on his head. Then the two men embraced.

'*Toujours à toi!*' said Geoffrey, with a strange, solemn sa-

lute in front of Cicio and Alvina. Then he turned on his heel
and marched rapidly out of the station, his soiled soldier's
overcoat flapping in the wind at the door. Cicio watched
him go. Then he turned and looked with haunted eyes into
the eyes of Alvina. And then they hurried down the desolate
platform in the darkness. Many people, Italians largely, were
camped waiting there, while bits of snow wavered down.
Cicio bought food and hired cushions. The train backed in.
There was a horrible fight for seats, men scrambling through
windows. Alvina got a place—but Cicio had to stay in the
corridor.

Then the long night journey through France, slow and
blind. The train was now so hot that the iron plate on the
floor burnt Alvina's feet. Outside she saw glimpses of snow.
A fat Italian hotel-keeper put on a smoking cap, covered the
light, and spread himself before Alvina. In the next carriage
a child was screaming. It screamed all the night—all the way
from Paris to Chambéry it screamed. The train came to sudden halts and stood still in the snow. The hotel-keeper
snored. Alvina became almost comatose, in the burning heat
of the carriage. And again the train rumbled on. And again
she saw glimpses of stations, glimpses of snow, through the
chinks in the curtained windows. And again there was a jerk
and a sudden halt, a drowsy mutter from the sleepers, somebody uncovering the light, and somebody covering it again,
somebody looking out, somebody tramping down the corridor, the child screaming.

The child belonged to two poor Italians—Milanese—a
shred of a thin little man, and a rather loose woman. They
had five tiny children, all boys: and the four who could stand
on their feet all wore scarlet caps. The fifth was a baby.
Alvina had seen a French official yelling at the poor shred
of a young father on the platform.

When morning came, and the bleary people pulled the
curtains, it was a clear dawn, and they were in the south of
France. There was no sign of snow. The landscape was half
southern, half Alpine. White houses with brownish tiles
stood among almond trees and cactus. It was beautiful, and
Alvina felt she had known it all before, in a happier life. The

morning was graceful almost as spring. She went out in the corridor to talk to Cicio.

He was on his feet with his back to the inner window, rolling slightly to the motion of the train. His face was pale, he had that sombre, haunted, unhappy look. Alvina, thrilled by the southern country, was smiling excitedly.

'This is my first morning abroad,' she said.

'Yes,' he answered.

'I love it here,' she said. 'Isn't this like Italy?'

He looked darkly out of the window, and shook his head.

But the sombre look remained on his face. She watched him. And her heart sank as she had never known it sink before.

'Are you thinking of Gigi?' she said.

He looked at her, with a faint, unhappy, bitter smile, but he said nothing. He seemed far off from her. A wild unhappiness beat inside her breast. She went down the corridor, away from him, to avoid this new agony, which after all was not her agony. She listened to the chatter of French and Italian in the corridor. She felt the excitement and terror of France, inside the railway carriage: and outside she saw white oxen slowly ploughing, beneath the lingering yellow poplars of the sub-Alps, she saw peasants looking up, she saw a woman holding a baby to her breast, watching the train, she saw the excited, yeasty crowds at the station. And they passed a river, and a great lake. And it all seemed bigger, nobler than England. She felt vaster influences spreading around, the Past was greater, more magnificent in these regions. For the first time the nostalgia of the vast Roman and classic world took possession of her. And she found it splendid. For the first time she opened her eyes on a continent, the Alpine core of a continent. And for the first time she realized what it was to escape from the smallish perfection of England, into the grander imperfection of a great continent.

Near Chambéry they went down for breakfast to the restaurant car. And secretly she was very happy. Cicio's distress made her uneasy. But underneath she was extraordinarily relieved and glad. Cicio did not trouble her very much. The sense of the bigness of the lands about her, the excitement of travelling with Continental people, the pleasantness of her coffee and rolls and honey, the feeling that vast events were taking place—all this stimulated her. She had brushed, as it were, the fringe of the terror of the war and the invasion. Fear was seething around her. And yet she was excited and glad. The vast world was in one of its convulsions, and she was moving amongst it. Somewhere, she believed in the convulsion, the event elated her.

The train began to climb up to Modane. How wonderful the Alps were!—what a bigness, an unbreakable power was in the mountains! Up and up the train crept, and she looked at the rocky slopes, the glistening peaks of snow in the blue heaven, the hollow valleys with fir trees and low-roofed houses. There were quarries near the railway, and men working. There was a strange mountain town, dirty-looking. And still the train climbed up and up, in the hot morning sunshine, creeping slowly round the mountain loops so that a little brown dog from one of the cottages ran alongside the train for a long way, barking at Alvina, even running ahead of the creeping, snorting train, and barking at the people ahead. Alvina, looking out, saw the two unfamiliar engines snorting out their smoke round the bend ahead. And the morning wore away to midday.

Cicio became excited as they neared Modane, the frontier station. His eye lit up again, he pulled himself together for the entrance into Italy. Slowly the train rolled in to the dismal station. And then a confusion indescribable, of porters and masses of luggage, the unspeakable crush and crowd at the customs barriers, the more intense crowd through the passport office, all like a madness.

They were out on the platform again, they had secured their places. Cicio wanted to have luncheon in the station restaurant. They went through the passages. And there in the dirty station gangways and big corridors dozens of Italians were lying on the ground, men, women, children, camping with their bundles and packages in heaps. They were either emigrants or refugees. Alvina had never seen people herd about like cattle, dumb, brute cattle. It impressed her. She could not grasp that an Italian labourer would lie down just where he was tired, in the street, on a station, in any corner, like a dog.

In the afternoon they were slipping down the Alps towards Turin. And everywhere was snow—deep, white, wonderful snow, beautiful and fresh, glistening in the afternoon light all down the mountain slopes, on the railway track, almost seeming to touch the train. And twilight was falling. And at the station people crowded in once more.

It had been dark a long time when they reached Turin. Many people alighted from the train, many surged to get in. But Cicio and Alvina had seats side by side. They were becoming tired now. But they were in Italy. Once more they went down for a meal. And then the train set off again in the night for Alessandria and Genoa, Pisa, and Rome.

It was night, the train ran better, there was a more easy sense in Italy. Cicio talked a little with other travelling companions. And Alvina settled her cushion, and slept more or less till Genoa. After the long wait at Genoa she dozed off again. She woke to see the sea in the moonlight beneath her—a lovely silvery sea, coming right to the carriage. The train seemed to be tripping on the edge of the Mediterranean, round bays and between dark rocks and under castles, a night-time fairy-land, for hours. She watched spell-bound: spell-bound by the magic of the world itself. And she thought to herself: 'Whatever life may be, and whatever horror men have made of it, the world is a lovely place, a magic place, something to marvel over. The world is an amazing place.'

This thought dozed her off again. Yet she had a consciousness of tunnels and hills and of broad marshes pallid under a moon and a coming dawn. And in the dawn there was Pisa. She watched the word hanging in the station in the dimness: 'Pisa'. Cicio told her people were changing for Florence. It all seemed wonderful to her—wonderful. She sat and watched the black station—then she heard the sound of the child's trumpet. And it did not occur to her to connect the train's moving on with the sound of the trumpet.

But she saw the golden dawn, a golden sun coming out of level country. She loved it. She loved being in Italy. She loved the lounging carelessness of the train, she liked having

Italian money, hearing the Italians round her—though they
were neither as beautiful nor as melodious as she expected.
She loved watching the glowing antique landscape. She read
and read again: '*E pericoloso sporgersi*', and '*E vietato fu-
mare*' and other little magical notices on the carriages. Cicio
told her what they meant, and how to say them. And sympathetic Italians opposite at once asked him if they were
married and who and what his bride was, and they gazed at
her with bright, approving eyes, though she felt terribly be-
draggled and travel-worn.

'You come from England? Yes! Nice contry!' said a man
in a corner, leaning forward to make this display of his lin-
guistic capacity.

'Not so nice as this,' said Alvina.

'Eh?'

Alvina repeated herself.

'Not so nice? Oh? No! Fog, eh!' The fat man whisked
his fingers in the air, to indicate fog in the atmosphere. 'But
nice contry! Very—*convenient*.'

He sat up in triumph, having achieved this word. And the
conversation once more became a spatter of Italian. The
women were very interested. They looked at Alvina, at
every atom of her. And she divined that they were wondering if she was already with child. Sure enough, they were
asking Cicio in Italian if she was 'making him a baby'. But
he shook his head and did not know, just a bit constrained.
So they ate slices of sausages and bread and fried rice-balls,
with wonderfully greasy fingers, and they drank red wine
in big throatfuls out of bottles, and they offered their fare
to Cicio and Alvina, and were charmed when she said to
Cicio she *would* have some bread and sausage. He picked
the strips off the sausage for her with his fingers, and made
her a sandwich with a roll. The women watched her bite it,
and bright-eyed and pleased they said, nodding their
heads—

'*Buono? Buono?*'

And she, who knew this word, understood, and replied:

'Yes, good! *Buono!*' nodding her head likewise. Which
caused immense satisfaction. The women showed the whole
paper of sausage slices, and nodded and beamed and said:

'*Se vuole ancora—!*'

And Alvina bit her wide sandwich, and smiled, and said: 'Yes, awfully nice!'

And the women looked at each other and said something, and Cicio interposed, shaking his head. But one woman ostentatiously wiped a bottle mouth with a clean handkerchief, and offered the bottle to Alvina, saying:

'*Vin buono. Vecchio! Vecchio!*' nodding violently and indicating that she should drink. She looked at Cicio, and he looked back at her, doubtfully.

'Shall I drink some?' she said.

'If you like,' he replied, making an Italian gesture of indifference.

So she drank some of the wine, and it dribbled on to her chin. She was not good at managing a bottle. But she liked the feeling of warmth it gave her. She was very tired.

'*Si piace! piace!*'

'Do you like it,' interpreted Cicio.

'Yes, very much. What is very much?' she asked of Cicio. '*Molto.*'

'*Si, molto.* Of course, I knew *molto,* from music,' she added.

The women made noises, and smiled and nodded, and so the train pulsed on again till they came to Rome. There was again the wild scramble with luggage, a general leave-taking, and then the masses of people on the station at Rome. *Roma! Roma!* What was it to Alvina but a name, and a crowded, excited station, and Cicio running after the luggage, and the pair of them eating in a station restaurant?

Almost immediately after eating, they were in the train once more, with new fellow travellers, running south this time towards Naples. In a daze of increasing weariness Alvina watched the dreary, to her sordid-seeming, Campagna that skirts the railway, the broken aqueduct trailing in the near distance over the stricken plain. She saw a tram-car, far out from everywhere, running up to cross the railway. She saw it go to Frascati.

And slowly the hills approached—they passed the vines of the foothills, the reeds, and were among the mountains. Wonderful little towns perched fortified on rocks and peaks, mountains rose straight up off the level plain, like old topographical prints, rivers wandered in the wild, rocky places, it all seemed ancient and shaggy, savage still, under all its remote civilization, this region of the Alban Mountains south of Rome. So the train clambered up and down, and went round corners.

They had not far to go now. Alvina was almost too tired to care what it would be like. They were going to Cicio's native village. They were to stay in the house of his uncle, his mother's brother. This uncle had been a model in London. He had built a house on the land left by Cicio's grandfather. He lived alone now, for his wife was dead and his children were abroad. Giuseppe was his son: Giuseppe of Battersea, in whose house Alvina had stayed.

This much Alvina knew. She knew that a portion of the land down at Pescocalascio belonged to Cicio: a bit of half-savage, ancient earth that had been left to his mother by old Francesco Califano, her hard-grinding peasant father. This land remained integral in the property, and was worked by Cicio's two uncles, Pancrazio and Giovanni. Pancrazio was the well-to-do uncle, who had been a model and had built the 'villa'. Giovanni was not much good. That was how Cicio put it.

They expected Pancrazio to meet them at the station. Cicio collected his bundles and put his hat straight and peered out of the window into the steep mountains of the afternoon. There was a town in the opening between steep hills, a town on a flat plain that ran into the mountains like a gulf. The train drew up. They had arrived.

Alvina was so tired she could hardly climb down to the platform. It was about four o'clock. Cicio looked up and down for Pancrazio, but could not see him. So he put his luggage into a pile on the platform, and told Alvina to stand by it, whilst he went off for the registered boxes. A porter came and asked her questions, of which she understood nothing. Then at last came Cicio, shouldering one small trunk, whilst a porter followed, shouldering another. Out they trotted, leaving Alvina abandoned with the pile of hand luggage. She waited. The train drew out. Cicio and the porter came bustling back. They took her out through the tiny gate, to where, in the flat desert space behind the railway, stood two great drab motor-omnibuses, and a rank of open carriages. Cicio was handing up the handbags to the roof of one of the big post-omnibuses. When it was finished the man on the roof came down, and Cicio gave him and the station porter each sixpence. The station-porter immediately threw his coin on the ground with a gesture of indignant contempt, spread his arms wide and expostulated violently. Cicio expostulated back again, and they pecked at each other, verbally, like two birds. It ended by the rolling up of the burly, black-moustached driver of the omnibus. Whereupon Cicio quite amicably gave the porter two nickel twopences in addition to the sixpence, whereupon the porter quite lovingly wished him '*buon' viaggio*'.

So Alvina was stowed into the body of the omnibus, with Cicio at her side. They were no sooner seated than a voice was heard, in beautifully-modulated English:

'You are here! Why, how have I missed you?'

It was Pancrazio, a smallish, rather battered-looking, shabby Italian of sixty or more, with a big moustache and reddish-rimmed eyes and a deeply-lined face. He was presented to Alvina.

'How have I missed you?' he said. 'I was on the station when the train came, and I did not see you.'

But it was evident he had taken wine. He had no further opportunity to talk. The compartment was full of large mountain-peasants with black hats and big cloaks and overcoats. They found Pancrazio a seat at the far end, and there he sat, with his deeply-lined, impassive face and slightly glazed eyes. He had yellow-brown eyes like Cicio. But in the uncle the eyelids dropped in a curious, heavy way, the eyes looked dulled like those of some old, rakish tom-cat, they were slightly rimmed with red. A curious person! And his English, though slow, was beautifully pronounced. He glanced at Alvina with slow, impersonal glances, not at all a stare. And he sat for the most part impassive and abstract as a Red Indian.

At the last moment a large black priest was crammed in, and the door shut behind him. Every available seat was let down and occupied. The second great post-omnibus rolled away, and then the one for Mola followed, rolling Alvina and Cicio over the next stage of their journey.

The sun was already slanting to the mountain tops, shadows were falling on the gulf of the plain. The omnibus charged at a great speed along a straight white road, which cut through the cultivated level straight towards the core of the mountains. By the road-side, peasant men in cloaks, peasant women in full-gathered dresses with white bodices or blouses having great full sleeves, tramped in the ridge of grass, driving cows or goats, or leading heavily-laden asses. The women had coloured kerchiefs on their heads, like the women Alvina remembered at the Sunday-School treats, who used to tell fortunes with green little love-birds. And they all tramped along towards the blue shadow of the closing-in mountains, leaving the peaks of the town behind on the left.

At a branch-road the bus suddenly stopped, and there it sat calmly in the road beside an icy brook, in the falling twilight. Great moth-white oxen waved past, drawing a long, low load of wood; the peasants left behind began to come up again, in picturesque groups. The icy brook tinkled, goats, pigs and cows wandered and shook their bells along the grassy borders of the road and the flat, unbroken fields, being driven slowly home. Peasants jumped out of the omnibus on to the road, to chat—and a sharp air came in. High overhead, as the sun went down, was the curious icy radiance of snow mountains, and a pinkness, while shadow deepened in the valley.

At last, after about half an hour, the youth who was conductor of the omnibus came running down the wild side-road, everybody clambered in, and away the vehicle charged, into the neck of the plain. With a growl and a rush it swooped up the first loop of the ascent. Great precipices rose on the right, the ruddiness of sunset above them. The road wound and swirled, trying to get up the pass. The omnibus pegged slowly up, then charged round a corner, swirled into another loop, and pegged heavily once more. It seemed dark between the closing-in mountains. The rocks rose very high, the road looped and swerved from one side of the wide defile to the other, the vehicle pulsed and persisted. Sometimes there was a house, sometimes a wood of oak-trees, sometimes the glimpse of a ravine, then the tall white glisten of snow above the earthy blackness. And still they went on and on, up the darkness.

Peering ahead, Alvina thought she saw the hollow between the peaks, which was the top of the pass. And every time the omnibus took a new turn, she thought it was coming out on the top of this hollow between the heights. But no—the road coiled right away again.

A wild little village came in sight. This was the destination. Again no. Only the tall, handsome mountain youth who had sat across from her, descended grumbling because the bus had brought him past his road, the driver having refused to pull up. Everybody expostulated with him, and he dropped into the shadow. The big priest squeezed into his place. The bus wound on and on, and always towards that hollow sky-line between the high peaks.

At last they ran up between buildings nipped between high rock-faces, and out into a little market-place, the crown of the pass. The luggage was got out and lifted down. Alvina descended. There she was, in a wild centre of an old, unfinished little mountain town. The façade of a church rose from a small eminence. A white road ran to the right, where a great open valley showed faintly beyond and beneath. Low, squalid sort of buildings stood around—with some high buildings. And there were bare little trees. The stars were in the sky, the air was icy. People stood darkly, excitedly about, women with an odd, shell-pattern head-dress of goffered linen, something like a parlour-maid's cap, came and stared hard. They were hard-faced mountain women.

Pancrazio was talking to Cicio in dialect.

'I couldn't get a cart to come down,' he said in English. 'But I shall find one here. Now what will you do? Put the luggage in Grazia's place while you wait?—'

They went across the open place to a sort of shop called the Post Restaurant. It was a little hole with an earthen floor and a smell of cats. Three crones were sitting over a low brass brazier, in which charcoal and ashes smouldered. Men were drinking. Cicio ordered coffee with rum—and the hard-faced Grazia, in her unfresh head-dress, dabbled the little dirty coffee-cups in dirty water, took the coffee-pot out of the ashes, poured in the old black boiling coffee three parts full, and slopped the cup over with rum. Then she dashed in a spoonful of sugar, to add to the pool in the saucer, and her customers were served.

However, Cicio drank up, so Alvina did likewise, burning her lips smartly. Cicio paid and ducked his way out.

'Now what will you buy?' asked Pancrazio.

'Buy?' said Cicio.

'Food,' said Pancrazio. 'Have you brought food?'

'No,' said Cicio.

So they trailed up stony dark ways to a butcher, and got a big red slice of meat; to a baker, and got enormous flat loaves. Sugar and coffee they bought. And Pancrazio lamented in his elegant English that no butter was to be obtained. Everywhere the hard-faced women came and stared into Alvina's face, asking questions. And both Cicio and Pancrazio answered rather coldly, with some *hauteur*. There was evidently not too much intimacy between the people of Pescocalascio and these semi-townsfolk of Ossona. Alvina felt as if she were in a strange, hostile country, in the darkness of the savage little mountain town.

At last they were ready. They mounted into a two-wheeled cart, Alvina and Cicio behind, Pancrazio and the driver in front, the luggage promiscuous. The bigger things were left for the morrow. It was icy cold, with a flashing darkness. The moon would not rise till later.

And so, without any light but that of the stars, the cart went spanking and rattling downhill, down the pale road which wound down the head of the valley to the gulf of darkness below. Down in the darkness into the darkness they rattled, wildly, and without heed, the young driver making strange noises to his dim horse, cracking a whip and asking endless questions of Pancrazio.

Alvina sat close to Cicio. He remained almost impassive. The wind was cold, the stars flashed. And they rattled down the rough, broad road under the rocks, down and down in the darkness. Cicio sat crouching forwards, staring ahead. Alvina was aware of mountains, rocks, and stars.

'I didn't know it was so *wild*!' she said.

'It is not much,' he said. There was a sad, plangent note in his voice. He put his hand upon her.

'You don't like it?' he said.

'I think it's lovely—wonderful,' she said, dazed.

He held her passionately. But she did not feel she needed protecting. It was all wonderful and amazing to her. She could not understand why he seemed upset and in a sort of despair. To her there was magnificence in the lustrous stars and the steepnesses, magic, rather terrible and grand.

They came down to the level valley bed, and went rolling along. There was a house, and a lurid red fire burning outside against the wall, and dark figures about it.

'What is that?' she said. 'What are they doing?'

'I don't know,' said Cicio. '*Cosa fanno li*—eh?'

'*Ka*—? *Fanno il buga*—' said the driver.

'They are doing some washing,' said Pancrazio, explanatory.

'Washing!' said Alvina.

'Boiling the clothes,' said Cicio.

On the cart rattled and bumped, in the cold night, down the highway in the valley. Alvina could make out the darkness of the slopes. Overhead she saw the brilliance of Orion. She felt she was quite, quite lost. She had gone out of the world, over the border, into some place of mystery. She was lost to Woodhouse, to Lancaster, to England—all lost.

They passed through a darkness of woods, with a swift sound of cold water. And then suddenly the cart pulled up. Someone came out of a lighted doorway in the darkness.

'We must get down here—the cart doesn't go any further,' said Pancrazio.

'Are we there?' said Alvina.

'No, it is about a mile. But we must leave the cart.'

Cicio asked questions in Italian. Alvina climbed down.

'Good-evening! Are you cold?' came a loud, raucous, American-Italian female voice. It was another relation of Cicio's. Alvina started and looked at the handsome, sinister, raucous-voiced young woman who stood in the light of the doorway.

'Rather cold,' she said.

'Come in, and warm yourself,' said the young woman.

'My sister's husband lives here,' explained Pancrazio.

Alvina went through the doorway into the room. It was a sort of inn. On the earthen floor glowed a great round pan of charcoal, which looked like a flat pool of fire. Men in hats and cloaks sat at a table playing cards by the light of a small lamp, a man was pouring wine. The room seemed like a cave.

'Warm yourself,' said the young woman, pointing to the flat disc of fire on the floor. She put a chair up to it, and Alvina sat down. The men in the room stared, but went on noisily with their cards. Cicio came in with luggage. Men got up and greeted him effusively, watching Alvina between whiles as if she were some alien creature. Words of American sounded among the Italian dialect.

There seemed to be a confab of some sort, aside. Cicio came and said to her:

'They want to know if we will stay the night here.'

'I would rather go on home,' she said.

He averted his face at the word home.

'You see,' said Pancrazio, 'I think you might be more comfortable here, than in my poor house. You see I have no woman to care for it—'

Alvina glanced round the cave of a room, at the rough fellows in their black hats. She was thinking how she would be 'more comfortable' here.

'I would rather go on,' she said.

'Then we will get the donkey,' said Pancrazio stoically. And Alvina followed him out on to the high-road.

From a shed issued a smallish, brigand-looking fellow carrying a lantern. He had his cloak over his nose and his hat over his eyes. His legs were bundled with white rag, crossed and crossed with hide straps, and he was shod in silent skin sandals.

'This is my brother Giovanni,' said Pancrazio. 'He is not quite sensible.' Then he broke into a loud flood of dialect.

Giovanni touched his hat to Alvina, and gave the lantern to Pancrazio. Then he disappeared, returning in a few moments with the ass. Cicio came out with the baggage, and by the light of the lantern the things were slung on either side of the ass, in a rather precarious heap. Pancrazio tested the rope again.

'There! Go on, and I shall come in a minute.'

'Ay-er-er!' cried Giovanni at the ass, striking the flank of the beast. Then he took the leading rope and led on up the dark highway, stalking with his dingy white legs under his muffled cloak, leading the ass. Alvina noticed the shuffle of his skin-sandalled feet, the quiet step of the ass.

She walked with Cicio near the side of the road. He carried the lantern. The ass with its load plodded a few steps ahead. There were trees on the roadside, and a small channel of invisible but noisy water. Big rocks jutted sometimes. It was freezing, the mountain high-road was congealed. High stars flashed overhead.

'How strange it is!' said Alvina to Cicio. 'Are you glad you have come home?'

'It isn't my home,' he replied, as if the word fretted him. 'Yes, I like to see it again. But it isn't the place for young people to live in. You will see how you like it.'

She wondered at his uneasiness. It was the same in Pancrazio. The latter now came running to catch them up.

'I think you will be tired,' he said. 'You ought to have stayed at my relation's house down there.'

'No, I'm not tired,' said Alvina. 'But I'm hungry.'

'Well, we shall eat something when we come to my house.'

They plodded in the darkness of the valley high-road. Pancrazio took the lantern and went to examine the load, hitching the ropes. A great flat loaf fell out, and rolled away, and smack came a little valise. Pancrazio broke into a flood of dialect to Giovanni, handing him the lantern. Cicio picked up the bread and put it under his arm.

'Break me a little piece,' said Alvina.

And in the darkness they both chewed bread.

After a while, Pancrazio halted with the ass just ahead, and took the lantern from Giovanni.

'We must leave the road here,' he said.

And with the lantern he carefully, courteously showed Alvina a small track descending in the side of the bank, between bushes. Alvina ventured down the steep descent, Pancrazio following showing a light. In the rear was Giovanni, making noises at the ass. They all picked their way down into the great white-bouldered bed of a mountain river. It was a wide, strange bed of dry boulders, pallid under the stars. There was a sound of a rushing river, glacial-sounding. The place seemed wild and desolate. In the distance was a darkness of bushes, along the far shore.

Pancrazio swinging the lantern, they threaded their way through the uneven boulders till they came to the river itself—not very wide, but rushing fast. A long, slender, drooping plank crossed over. Alvina crossed rather tremulous, followed by Pancrazio with the light, and Cicio with the bread and the valise. They could hear the click of the ass and the ejaculations of Giovanni.

Pancrazio went back over the stream with the light. Alvina saw the dim ass come up, wander uneasily to the stream, plant his fore legs, and sniff the water, his nose right down.

'Er! Err!' cried Pancrazio, striking the beast on the flank. But it only lifted its nose and turned aside. It would not take the stream. Pancrazio seized the leading rope angrily and turned up stream.

'Why were donkeys made! They are beasts without sense,' his voice floated angrily across the chill darkness.

Cicio laughed. He and Alvina stood in the wide, stony river-bed, in the strong starlight, watching the dim figures of the ass and the men crawl upstream with the lantern.

Again the same performance, the white muzzle of the ass stooping down to sniff the water suspiciously, his hind-quarters tilted up with the load. Again the angry yells and blows from Pancrazio. And the ass seemed to be taking the water. But no! After a long deliberation he drew back. Angry language sounded through the crystal air. The group with the lantern moved again upstream, becoming smaller.

Alvina and Cicio stood and watched. The lantern looked small up the distance. But there—a clucking, shouting, splashing sound.

'He is going over,' said Cicio.

Pancrazio came hurrying back to the plank with the lantern.

'Oh the stupid beast! I could kill him!' cried he.

'Isn't he used to the water?' said Alvina.

'Yes, he is. But he won't go except where he thinks he will go. You might kill him before he should go.'

They picked their way across the river-bed, to the wild scrub and bushes of the farther side. There they waited for the ass, which came up clicking over the boulders, led by the patient Giovanni. And then they took a difficult, rocky track ascending between banks. Alvina felt the uneven scramble a great effort. But she got up. Again they waited for the ass. And then again they struck off to the right, under some trees.

A house appeared dimly.

'Is that it?' said Alvina.

'No. It belongs to me. But that is not my house. A few steps further. Now we are on my land.'

They were treading a rough sort of grass-land—and still climbing. It ended in a sudden little scramble between big stones, and suddenly they were on the threshold of a quite important-looking house: but it was all dark.

'Oh!' exclaimed Pancrazio, 'they have done nothing that I told them.' He made queer noises of exasperation.

'What?' said Alvina.

'Neither made a fire nor anything. Wait a minute—'

The ass came up. Cicio, Alvina, Giovanni and the ass waited in the frosty starlight under the wild house. Pancrazio disappeared round the back. Cicio talked to Giovanni. He seemed uneasy, as if he felt depressed.

Pancrazio returned with the lantern, and opened the big door. Alvina followed him into a stone-floored, wide passage, where stood farm implements, where a litter of straw and beans lay in a corner, and whence rose bare wooden stairs. So much she saw in the glimpse of lantern-light, as Pancrazio pulled the string and entered the kitchen: a dim-walled room with a vaulted roof and a great dark, open hearth, fireless: a bare room with a little rough dark furniture: an unswept stone floor: iron-barred windows, rather small, in the deep thickness of the wall, one-half shut with a drab shutter. It was rather like a room on the stage, gloomy, not meant to be lived in.

'I will make a light,' said Pancrazio, taking a lamp from the mantelpiece, and proceeding to wind it up.

Cicio stood behind Alvina, silent. He had put down the bread and valise on a wooden chest. She turned to him.

'It's a beautiful room,' she said.

Which, with its high, vaulted roof, its dirty whitewash, its great black chimney, it really was. But Cicio did not understand. He smiled gloomily.

The lamp was lighted. Alvina looked round in wonder.

'Now I will make a fire. You, Cicio, will help Giovanni with the donkey,' said Pancrazio, scuttling with the lantern.

Alvina looked at the room. There was a wooden settle in front of the hearth, stretching its back to the room. There was a little table under a square, recessed window, on whose sloping ledge were newspapers, scattered letters, nails and a hammer. On the table were dried beans and two maize cobs. In a corner were shelves, with two chipped enamel plates, and a small table underneath, on which stood a bucket of water with a dipper. Then there was a wooden chest, two little chairs, and a litter of faggots, cane, vine-twigs, bare maize-hubs, oak-twigs filling the corner by the hearth.

Pancrazio came scrambling in with fresh faggots.

'They have not done what I told them, the tiresome people!' he said. 'I told them to make a fire and prepare the house. You will be uncomfortable in my poor home. I have no woman, nothing, everything is wrong—'

He broke the pieces of cane and kindled them in the hearth. Soon there was a good blaze. Cicio came in with the bags and the food.

'I had better go upstairs and take my things off,' said Alvina. 'I am so hungry.'

'You had better keep your coat on,' said Pancrazio. 'The room is cold.' Which it was, ice-cold. She shuddered a little. She took off her hat and fur.

'Shall we fry some meat?' said Pancrazio.

He took a frying-pan, found lard in the wooden chest— it was the food-chest—and proceeded to fry pieces of meat in a frying-pan over the fire. Alvina wanted to lay the table. But there was no cloth.

'We will sit here, as I do, to eat,' said Pancrazio. He produced two enamel plates and one soup-plate, three penny iron forks and two old knives, and a little grey, coarse salt in a wooden bowl. These he placed on the seat of the settle in front of the fire. Cicio was silent.

The settle was dark and greasy, Alvina feared for her clothes. But she sat with her enamel plate and her impossible fork, a piece of meat and a chunk of bread, and ate. It was difficult—but the food was good, and the fire blazed. Only there was a film of wood-smoke in the room, rather smarting. Cicio sat on the settle beside her, and ate in large mouthfuls.

'I think it's fun,' said Alvina.

He looked at her with dark, haunted, gloomy eyes. She wondered what was the matter with him.

'Don't you think it's fun?' she said, smiling.

He smiled slowly.

'You won't like it,' he said.

'Why not?' she cried, in panic lest he prophesied truly.

Pancrazio scuttled in and out with the lantern. He brought wrinkled pears, and green, round grapes, and walnuts, on a white cloth, and presented them.

'I think my pears are still good,' he said. 'You must eat them, and excuse my uncomfortable house.'

Giovanni came in with a big bowl of soup and a bottle of milk. There was room only for three on the settle before the hearth. He pushed his chair among the litter of fire-kindling, and sat down. He had bright, bluish eyes, and a flattish face—was a man of about fifty, but had a simple, kindly, slightly imbecile face. All the men kept their hats on.

The soup was from Giovanni's cottage. It was for Pancrazio and him. But there was only one spoon. So Pancrazio ate a dozen spoonfuls, and handed the bowl to Giovanni—who protested and tried to refuse—but accepted, and ate ten spoonfuls, then handed the bowl back to his brother, with the spoon. So they finished the bowl between them. Then Pancrazio found wine—a whitish wine, not very good, for which he apologized. And he invited Alvina to coffee. Which she accepted gladly.

For though the fire was warm in front, behind was very cold. Pancrazio stuck a long pointed stick down the handle of a saucepan, and gave this utensil to Cicio, to hold over the fire and scald the milk, whilst he put the tin coffee-pot in the ashes. He took a long iron tube or blow-pipe, which rested on two little feet at the far end. This he gave to Giovanni to blow the fire.

Giovanni was a fire-worshipper. His eyes sparkled as he took the blowing tube. He put fresh faggots behind the fire—though Pancrazio forbade him. He arranged the burning faggots. And then softly he blew a red-hot fire for the coffee.

'*Basta! Basta!*' said Cicio. But Giovanni blew on, his eyes sparkling, looking to Alvina. He was making the fire beautiful for her.

There was one cup, one enamelled mug, one little bowl. This was the coffee-service. Pancrazio noisily ground the coffee. He seemed to do everything, old, stooping as he was.

At last Giovanni took his leave—the kettle which hung on the hook over the fire was boiling over. Cicio burnt his hand lifting it off. And at last, at last Alvina could go to bed.

Pancrazio went first with the candle—then Cicio with the black kettle—then Alvina. The men still had their hats on. Their boots tramped noisily on the bare stairs.

The bedroom was very cold. It was a fair-sized room with a concrete floor and white walls, and window-door opening on a little balcony. There were two high white beds on opposite sides of the room. The wash-stand was a little tripod thing.

The air was very cold, freezing, the stone floor was dead cold to the feet. Cicio sat down on a chair and began to take off his boots. She went to the window. The moon had risen. There was a flood of light on dazzling white snow tops, glimmering and marvellous in the evanescent night. She went out for a moment on to the balcony. It was a wonder-world: the moon over the snow heights, the pallid valley-bed away below; the river hoarse, and round about her, scrubby, blue-dark foot-hills with twiggy trees. Magical it all was—but so cold.

'You had better shut the door,' said Cicio.

She came indoors. She was dead tired, and stunned with cold, and hopelessly dirty after that journey. Cicio had gone to bed without washing.

'Why does the bed rustle?' she asked him.

It was stuffed with dry maize-leaves, the dry sheaths from the cobs—stuffed enormously high. He rustled like a snake among dead foliage.

Alvina washed her hands. There was nothing to do with the water but throw it out of the door. Then she washed her face, thoroughly, in good hot water. What a blessed relief! She sighed as she dried herself.

'It does one good!' she sighed.

Cicio watched her as she quickly brushed her hair. She was almost stupefied with weariness and the cold, bruising air. Blindly she crept into the high, rustling bed. But it was made high in the middle. And it was icy cold. It shocked her almost as if she had fallen into water. She shuddered, and became semi-conscious with fatigue. The blankets were heavy, heavy. She was dazed with excitement and wonder. She felt vaguely that Cicio was miserable, and wondered why.

She woke with a start an hour or so later. The moon was in the room. She did not know where she was. And she was frightened. And she was cold. A real terror took hold of her. Cicio in his bed was quite still. Everything seemed electric with horror. She felt she would die instantly, everything was so terrible around her. She could not move. She felt that everything around her was horrific, extinguishing her, putting her out. Her very being was threatened. In another instant she would be transfixed.

Making a violent effort she sat up. The silence of Cicio in his bed was as horrible as the rest of the night. She had a horror of him also. What would she do, where should she flee? She was lost—lost—lost utterly.

The knowledge sank into her like ice. Then deliberately she got out of bed, and went across to him. He was horrible and frightening, but he was warm. She felt his power and his warmth invade her and extinguish her. The mad and desperate passion that was in him sent her completely unconscious again, completely unconscious.

CHAPTER 15

The Place Called Califano

There is no mistake about it, Alvina was a lost girl. She was cut off from everything she belonged to. Ovid isolated in Thrace might well lament. The soul itself needs its own mysterious nourishment. This nourishment lacking, nothing is well.

At Pescocalascio it was the mysterious influence of the mountains and valleys themselves which seemed always to be annihilating the Englishwoman: nay, not only her, but the very natives themselves. Cicio and Pancrazio clung to her, essentially, as if she saved them also from extinction. It needed all her courage. Truly, she had to support the souls of the two men.

At first she did not realize. She was only stunned with the strangeness of it all: startled, half-enraptured with the terrific beauty of the place, half-horrified by its savage annihilation of her. But she was stunned. The days went by.

It seems there are places which resist us, which have the power to overthrow our psychic being. It seems as if every country has its potent negative centres, localities which savagely and triumphantly refuse our living culture. And Alvina had struck one of these, here on the edge of the Abruzzi.

She was not in the village of Pescocalascio itself. That was a long hour's walk away. Pancrazio's house was the chief of a tiny hamlet of three houses, called Califano because the Califanos had made it. There was the ancient, savage hole of a house, quite windowless, where Pancrazio and Cicio's mother had been born: the family home. Then there was Pancrazio's villa. And then, a little below, another newish, modern house in a sort of wild meadow, inhabited by the peasants who worked the land. Ten minutes' walk away was another cluster of seven or eight houses, where Giovanni lived. But there was no shop, no post nearer than Pescocalascio, an hour's heavy road up deep and rocky, wearying tracks.

And yet, what could be more lovely than the sunny days: pure, hot, blue days among the mountain foothills: irregular, steep little hills half wild with twiggy brown oak-trees and marshes and broom heaths, half cultivated, in a wild, scattered fashion. Lovely, in the lost hollows beyond a marsh, to see Cicio slowly ploughing with two great white oxen: lovely to go with Pancrazio down to the wild scrub that bordered the river-bed, then over the white-bouldered, massive desert and across stream to the other scrubby savage shore, and so up to the high-road. Pancrazio was very happy if Alvina would accompany him. He liked it that she was not afraid. And her sense of the beauty of the place was an infinite relief to him.

Nothing could have been more marvellous than the winter twilight. Sometimes Alvina and Pancrazio were late returning with the ass. And then gingerly the ass would step down the steep banks, already beginning to freeze when the sun went down. And again and again he would balk the stream, while a violet-blue dusk descended on the white, wide stream-bed, and the scrub and lower hills became dark, and in heaven, oh, almost unbearably lovely, the snow of the near mountains was burning rose, against the dark-blue heavens. How unspeakably lovely it was, no one could ever tell, the grand, pagan twilight of the valleys, savage, cold, with a sense of ancient gods who knew the right for human sacrifice. It stole away the soul of Alvina. She felt transfigured in it, clairvoyant in another mystery of life. A savage hardness came in her heart. The gods who had demanded human sacrifice were quite right, immutably right. The fierce, savage gods who dipped their lips in blood, these were the true gods.

The terror, the agony, the nostalgia of the heathen past was a constant torture to her mediumistic soul. She did not know what it was. But it was a kind of neuralgia in the very soul, never to be located in the human body, and yet physical. Coming over the brow of a heathy, rocky hillock, and seeing Cicio beyond leaning deep over the plough, in his white shirt-sleeves following the slow, waving, moth-pale oxen across a small track of land turned up in the heathen hollow, her soul would go all faint, she would almost swoon with realization of the world that had gone before. And Cicio was so silent, there seemed so much dumb magic and anguish in him, as if he were forever afraid of himself and the thing he was. He seemed, in his silence, to *concentrate* upon her so terribly. She believed she would not live.

Some times she would go gathering acorns, large, fine acorns, a precious crop in that land where the fat pig was almost an object of veneration. Silently she would crouch filling the pannier. And far off she would hear the sound of Giovanni chopping wood, of Cicio calling to the oxen or Pancrazio making noises to the ass, or the sound of a peasant's mattock. Over all the constant speech of the passing river, and the real breathing presence of the upper snows. And a wild, terrible happiness would take hold of her, beyond despair, but very like despair. No one would ever find her. She had gone beyond the world into the pre-world, she had reopened on the old eternity.

And then Maria, the little elvish old wife of Giovanni, would come up with the cows. One cow she held by a rope round its horns, and she hauled it from the patches of young corn into the rough grass, from the little plantation of trees in among the heath. Maria wore the full-pleated white-sleeved dress of the peasants, and a red kerchief on her head. But her dress was dirty, and her face was dirty, and the big gold rings of her ears hung from ears which perhaps had never been washed. She was rather smoke-dried too, from perpetual wood-smoke.

Maria in her red kerchief hauling the white cow, and

screaming at it, would come laughing towards Alvina, who was rather afraid of cows. And then, screaming high in dialect, Maria would talk to her. Alvina smiled and tried to understand. Impossible. It was not strictly a human speech. It was rather like the crying of half-articulate animals. It certainly was not Italian. And yet Alvina by dint of constant hearing began to pick up the coagulated phrases.

She liked Maria. She liked them all. They were all very kind to her, as far as they knew. But they did not know. And they were kind with each other. For they all seemed lost, like lost, forlorn aborigines, and they treated Alvina as if she were a higher being. They loved her that she would strip maize-cobs or pick acorns. But they were all anxious to serve her. And it seemed as if they needed someone to serve. It seemed as if Alvina, the Englishwoman, had a certain magic glamour for them, and so long as she was happy, it was a supreme joy and relief to them to have her there. But it seemed to her she would not live.

And when she was unhappy! Ah, the dreadful days of cold rain mingled with sleet, when the world outside was more than impossible, and the house inside was a horror. The natives kept themselves alive by going about constantly working, dumb and elemental. But what was Alvina to do?

For the house was unspeakable. The only two habitable rooms were the kitchen and Alvina's bedroom: and the kitchen, with its little grated windows high up in the wall, one of which had a broken pane and must keep one-half of its shutters closed, was like a dark cavern vaulted and bitter with wood-smoke. Seated on the settle before the fire, the hard, greasy settle, Alvina could indeed keep the fire going, with faggots of green oak. But the smoke hurt her chest, she was not clean for one moment, and she could do nothing else. The bedroom again was just impossibly cold. And there was no other place. And from far away came the wild braying of an ass, primeval and desperate in the snow.

The house was quite large: but uninhabitable. Downstairs, on the left of the wide passage where the ass occasionally stood out of the weather, and where the chickens wandered in search of treasure, was a big, long apartment where Pancrazio kept implements and tools and potatoes and pumpkins, and where four or five rabbits hopped unexpectedly out of the shadows. Opposite this, on the right, was the cantina, a dark place with wine-barrels and more agricultural stores. This was the whole of the downstairs.

Going upstairs, half-way up, at the turn of the stairs was the opening of a sort of barn, a great wire-netting behind which showed a glow of orange maize-cobs and some wheat. Upstairs were four rooms. But Alvina's room alone was furnished. Pancrazio slept in the unfurnished bedroom opposite, on a pile of old clothes. Beyond was a room with litter in it, a chest of drawers, and rubbish of old books and photographs Pancrazio had brought from England. There was a battered photograph of Lord Leighton, among others. The fourth room approached through the corn-chamber, was always locked.

Outside was just as hopeless. There had been a little garden within the stone enclosure. But fowls, geese, and the ass had made an end of this. Fowl-droppings were everywhere, indoors and out, the ass left his pile of droppings to steam in the winter air on the threshold, while his heart-rending bray rent the air. Roads there were none: only deep tracks, like profound ruts with rocks in them, in the hollows, and rocky, grooved tracks over the brows. The hollow grooves were full of mud and water, and one struggled slipperily from rock to rock, or along narrow grass-ledges.

What was to be done, then, on mornings that were dark with sleet? Pancrazio would bring a kettle of hot water at about half-past eight. For had he not travelled Europe with English gentlemen, as a sort of model-valet? Had he not *loved* his English gentlemen? Even now, he was infinitely happier performing these little attentions for Alvina than attending to his wretched domains.

Cicio rose early, and went about in the haphazard, useless way of Italians all day long, getting nothing done. Alvina came out of the icy bedroom to the back kitchen. Pancrazio would be gallantly heating milk for her, at the end of a long stick. So she would sit on the settle and drink her coffee and milk, into which she dipped her dry bread. Then the day was before her.

She washed her cup and her enamelled plate, and she tried

to clean the kitchen. But Pancrazio had on the fire a great black pot, dangling from the chain. He was boiling food for the eternal pig—the only creature for which any cooking was done. Cicio was tramping in with faggots. Pancrazio went in and out, back and forth from his pot.

Alvina stroked her brow and decided on a method. Once she was rid of Pancrazio, she would wash every cup and plate and utensil in boiling water. Well, at last Pancrazio went off with his great black pan, and she set to. But there were not six pieces of crockery in the house, and not more than six cooking utensils. These were soon scrubbed. Then she scrubbed the two little tables and the shelves. She lined the food-chest with clean paper. She washed the high window-ledges and the narrow mantelpiece, that had large mounds of dusty candle-wax, in deposits. Then she tackled the settle. She scrubbed it also. Then she looked at the floor. And even she, English housewife as she was, realized the futility of trying to wash it. As well try to wash the earth itself outside. It was just a piece of stone-laid earth. She swept it as well as she could, and made a little order in the faggot-heap in the corner. Then she washed the little, high-up windows, to try and let in light.

And what was the difference? A dank wet soapy smell, and not much more. Maria had kept scuffling admiringly in and out, crying her wonderment and approval. She had most ostentatiously chased out an obtrusive hen, from this temple of cleanliness. And that was all.

It was hopeless. The same black walls, the same floor, the same cold from behind, the same green-oak wood-smoke, the same bucket of water from the well—the same come-and-go of aimless busy men, the same cackle of wet hens, the same hopeless nothingness.

Alvina stood up against it for a time. And then she caught a bad cold, and was wretched. Probably it was the wood-smoke. But her chest was raw, she felt weak and miserable. She could not sit in her bedroom, for it was too cold. If she sat in the darkness of the kitchen she was hurt with smoke, and perpetually cold behind her neck. And Pancrazio rather resented the amount of faggots consumed for nothing. The only hope would have been in work. But there was nothing in that house to be done. How could she even sew?

She was to prepare the mid-day and evening meals. But with no pots, and over a smoking wood fire, what could she prepare? Black and greasy, she boiled potatoes and fried meat in lard, in a long-handled frying-pan. Then Pancrazio decreed that Maria should prepare macaroni with the tomato sauce, and thick vegetable soup, and sometimes polenta. This coarse, heavy food was wearying beyond words.

Alvina began to feel she would die, in the awful comfortless meaninglessness of it all. True, sunny days returned, and some magic. But she was weak and feverish with her cold, which would not get better. So that even in the sunshine the crude comfortlessness and inferior savagery of the place only repelled her.

The others were depressed when she was unhappy:

'Do you wish you were back in England?' Cicio asked her, with a little sardonic bitterness in his voice. She looked at him without answering. He ducked and went away.

'We will make a fire-place in the other bedroom,' said Pancrazio.

No sooner said than done. Cicio persuaded Alvina to stay in bed a few days. She was thankful to take refuge. Then she heard a rare come-and-go. Pancrazio, Cicio, Giovanni, Maria, and a mason all set about the fireplace. Up and down stairs they went, Maria carrying stone and lime on her head, and swerving in Alvina's doorway, with her burden perched aloft, to shout a few unintelligible words. In the intervals of lime-carrying she brought the invalid her soup or her coffee or her hot milk.

It turned out quite a good job—a pleasant room with two windows, that would have all the sun in the afternoon, and would see the mountains on one hand, the far-off village perched up on the other. When she was well enough they set off one early Monday morning to the market in Ossona. They left the house by starlight, but dawn was coming by the time they reached the river. At the highroad, Pancrazio harnessed the ass, and after endless delay they jogged off to Ossona. The dawning mountains were wonderful, dim-green and mauve and rose, the ground rang with frost.

Along the roads many peasants were trooping to market, women in their best dresses, some of thick heavy silk, with the white, full-sleeved bodices, dresses green, lavender, dark-red, with gay kerchiefs on the head: men muffled in cloaks, treading silently in their pointed skin sandals: asses with loads, carts full of peasants, a belated cow.

The market was lovely, there in the crown of the pass in the old town, on the frosty sunny morning. Bulls, cows, sheep, pigs, goats stood and lay about under the bare little trees on the platform high over the valley: someone had kindled a great fire of brush-wood, and men crowded round, out of the blue frost. From laden asses vegetables were unloaded, from little carts all kinds of things, boots, pots, tinware, hats, sweet-things, and heaps of corn and beans and seeds. By eight o'clock in the December morning the market was in full swing: a great crowd of handsome mountain people, all peasants, nearly all in costume, with different headdresses.

Cicio and Pancrazio and Alvina went quietly about. They bought pots and pans and vegetables and sweet-things and thick rush matting and two wooden armchairs and one old soft armchair, going quietly and bargaining modestly among the crowd, as Anglicized Italians do.

The sun came on to the market at about nine o'clock, and then, from the terrace of the town gate, Alvina looked down on the wonderful sight of all the coloured dresses of the peasant women, the black hats of the men, the heaps of goods, the squealing pigs, the pale lovely cattle, the many tethered asses—and she wondered if she would die before she became one with it altogether. It was impossible for her to become one with it altogether. Cicio would have to take her to England again, or to America. He was always hinting at America.

But then, Italy might enter the war. Even here it was the great theme of conversation. She looked down on the seethe of the market. The sun was warm on her. Cicio and Pancrazio were bargaining for two cowskin rugs: she saw Cicio standing with his head rather forward. Her husband! She felt her heart die away within her.

All those other peasant women, did they feel as she did?—

the same sort of acquiescent passion, the same lapse of life? She believed they did. The same helpless passion for the man, the same remoteness from the world's actuality? Probably, under all their tension of money and money-grubbing and vindictive mountain morality and rather horrible religion, probably they felt the same. She was one with them. But she could never endure it for a life-time. It was only a test on her. Cicio must take her to America, or England—to America preferably.

And even as he turned to look for her, she felt a strange thrilling in her bowels: a sort of thrill strangely within her, yet extraneous to her. She caught her hand to her flank. And Cicio was looking up for her from the market beneath, searching with that quick, hasty look. He caught sight of her. She seemed to glow with a delicate light for him there beyond all the women. He came straight towards her, smiling his slow, enigmatic smile. He could not bear it if he lost her. She knew how he loved her—almost inhumanly, elementally, without communication. And she stood with her hand to her side, her face frightened. She hardly noticed him. It seemed to her she was with child. And yet in the whole market-place she was aware of nothing but him.

'We have bought the skins,' he said. 'Twenty-seven lire each.'

She looked at him, his dark skin, his golden eyes—so near to her, so unified with her, yet so incommunicably remote. How far off was his being from hers!

'I believe I'm going to have a child,' she said.

'Eh?' he ejaculated quickly. But he had understood. His eyes shone weirdly on her. She felt the strange terror and loveliness of his passion. And she wished she could lie down there by that town gate, in the sun, and swoon for ever unconscious. Living was almost too great a demand on her. His yellow, luminous eyes watched her and enveloped her. There was nothing for her but to yield, yield, yield. And yet she could not sink to earth.

She saw Pancrazio carrying the skins to the little cart, which was tilted up under a small, pale-stemmed tree on the platform above the valley. Then she saw him making his way quickly back through the crowd, to rejoin them.

'Did you feel something?' said Cicio.

'Yes—here—!' she said, pressing her hand on her side as the sensation trilled once more upon her consciousness. She looked at him with remote, frightened eyes.

'That's good—' he said, his eyes full of a triumphant, incommunicable meaning.

'Well!—And now,' said Pancrazio, coming up, 'shall we go and eat something?'

They jogged home in the little flat cart in the wintry afternoon. It was almost night before they had got the ass untackled from the shafts, at the wild lonely house where Pancrazio left the cart. Giovanni was there with the lantern. Cicio went on ahead with Alvina, whilst the others stood to load up the ass by the highway.

Cicio watched Alvina carefully. When they were over the river and among the dark scrub, he took her in his arms and kissed her with long, terrible passion. She saw the snow ridges flare with evening, beyond his cheek. They had glowed dawn as she crossed the river outwards, they were white-fiery now in the dusk sky as she returned. What strange valley of shadow was she threading? What was the terrible man's passion that haunted her like a dark angel? Why was she so much beyond herself?

CHAPTER 16

Suspense

Christmas was at hand. There was a heap of maize cobs still unstripped. Alvina sat with Cicio stripping them, in the corn-place.

'Will you be able to stop here till the baby is born?' he asked her.

She watched the films of the leaves come from off the burning gold maize cob under his fingers, the long, ruddy cone of fruition. The heap of maize on one side burned like hot sunshine, she felt it really gave off warmth, it glowed, it burned. On the other side the filmy, crackly, sere sheaths were also faintly sunny. Again and again the long, red-gold, full phallus of corn came clear in his hands, and was put gently aside. He looked up at her, with his yellow eyes.

'Yes, I think so,' she said. 'Will you?'

'Yes, if they let me. I should like it to be born here.'

'Would you like to bring up a child here?' she asked.

'You wouldn't be happy here, so long,' he said, sadly. 'Would you?'

He slowly shook his head, indefinite.

She was settling down. She had her room upstairs, her cups and plates and spoons, her own things. Pancrazio had gone back to his old habit, he went across and ate with Giovanni and Maria. Cicio and Alvina had their meals in their pleasant room upstairs. They were happy alone. Only sometimes the terrible influence of the place preyed on her.

However, she had a clean room of her own, where she could sew and read. She had written to the matron and Mrs Tuke, and Mrs Tuke had sent books. Also she helped Cicio when she could, and Maria was teaching her to spin the white sheep's wool into coarse thread.

This morning Pancrazio and Giovanni had gone off somewhere, Alvina and Cicio were alone on the place, stripping the last maize. Suddenly, in the grey morning air, a wild music burst out: the drone of a bagpipe, and a man's high voice half singing, half yelling a brief verse, at the end of which a wild flourish on some other reedy wood instrument. Alvina sat still in surprise. It was a strange, high, rapid, yelling music, the very voice of the mountains. Beautiful, in our musical sense of the word, it was not. But oh, the magic, the nostalgia of the untamed, heathen past which it evoked.

'It is for Christmas,' said Cicio. 'They will come every day now.'

Alvina rose and went round to the little balcony. Two men stood below, amid the crumbling of finely falling snow. One, the elder, had a bagpipe whose bag was patched with shirting: the younger was dressed in greenish clothes, he had his face lifted, and was yelling the verses of the unintelligible Christmas ballad: short, rapid verses, followed by a brilliant flourish on a short wooden pipe he held ready in his hand. Alvina felt he was going to be out of breath. But no, rapid and high came the next verse, verse after verse, with the wild scream on the little new pipe in between, over the roar of the bagpipe. And the crumbs of snow were like a speckled veil, faintly drifting the atmosphere and powdering the littered threshold where they stood—a threshold littered with faggots, leaves, straw, fowls and geese and ass droppings, and rag thrown out from the house, and pieces of paper.

The carol suddenly ended, the young man snatched off his hat to Alvina who stood above, and in the same breath he was gone, followed by the bagpipe. Alvina saw them dropping hurriedly down the incline between the twiggy wild oaks.

'They will come every day now, till Christmas,' said Cicio. 'They go to every house.'

And sure enough, when Alvina went down, in the cold, silent house, and out to the well in the still crumbling snow, she heard the sound far off, strange, yelling, wonderful; and the same ache for she knew not what overcame her, so that she felt one might go mad, there in the veiled silence of those mountains, in the great hilly valley cut off from the world.

Cicio worked all day on the land or round about. He was building a little earth closet also: the obvious and unscreened place outside was impossible. It was curious how little he went to Pescocalascio, how little he mixed with the natives. He seemed always to withhold something from them. Only with his relatives, of whom he had many, he was more free, in a kind of family intimacy.

Yet even here he was guarded. His uncle at the mill, an unwashed, fat man with a wife who tinkled with gold and grime, and who shouted a few lost words of American, insisted on giving Alvina wine and a sort of cake made with cheese and rice. Cicio too feasted, in the dark hole of a room. And the two natives seemed to press their cheer on Alvina and Cicio whole-heartedly.

'How nice they are!' said Alvina when she had left. 'They give so freely.'

But Cicio smiled a wry smile, silent.

'Why do you make a face?' she said.

'It's because you are a foreigner, and they think you will go away again,' he said.

'But I should have thought that would make them less generous,' she said.

'No. They like to give to foreigners. They don't like to give to the people here. Giacomo puts water in the wine which he sells to the people who go by. And if I leave the donkey in her shed, I give Marta Maria something, or the next time she won't let me have it. Ha, they are—they are sly ones, the people here.'

'They are like that everywhere,' said Alvina.

'Yes. But nowhere they say so many bad things about people as here—nowhere where I have ever been.'

It was strange to Alvina to feel the deep, bed-rock distrust which all the hill-peasants seemed to have of one another. They were watchful, venomous, dangerous.

'Ah,' said Pancrazio, 'I am glad there is a woman in my house once more.'

'But did *nobody* come in and do for you before?' asked Alvina. 'Why didn't you pay somebody?'

'Nobody will come,' said Pancrazio, in his slow, aristocratic English. 'Nobody will come, because I am a man, and if somebody should see her at my house, they will all talk.'

'Talk!' Alvina looked at the deeply-lined man of sixty-six. 'But what will they say?'

'Many bad things. Many bad things indeed. They are not good people here. All saying bad things, and all jealous. They don't like me because I have a house—they think I am too much a *signore*. They say to me "Why do you think you are a *signore*?" Oh, they are bad people, envious, you cannot have anything to do with them.'

'They are nice to me.' said Alvina.

'They think you will go away. But if you stay, they will say bad things. You must wait. Oh, they are evil people, evil against one another, against everybody but strangers who don't know them—'

Alvina felt the curious passion in Pancrazio's voice, the passion of a man who has lived for many years in England and known the social confidence of England, and who, coming back, is deeply injured by the ancient malevolence of the remote, somewhat gloomy hill-peasantry. She understood also why he was so glad to have her in his house, so proud, why he loved serving her. He seemed to see a fairness, a luminousness in the northern soul, something free, touched with divinity such as 'these people here' lacked entirely.

When she went to Ossona with him, she knew, everybody questioned him about her and Cicio. She began to get the drift of the questions—which Pancrazio answered with reserve.

'And how long are they staying?'

This was an invariable, envious question. And invariably Pancrazio answered with a reserved—

'Some months. As long as *they* like.'

And Alvina could feel waves of black envy go out against

Pancrazio, because she was domiciled with him, and because she sat with him in the flat cart, driving to Ossona.

Yet Pancrazio himself was a study. He was thin, and very shabby, and rather out of shape. Only in his yellow eyes lurked a strange sardonic fire, and a leer which puzzled her. When Cicio happened to be out in the evening he would sit with her and tell her stories of Lord Leighton and Millais and Alma Tadema and other academicians dead and living. There would sometimes be a strange passivity on his worn face, an impassive, almost Red Indian look. And then again he would stir into a curious, arch, malevolent laugh, for all the world like a debauched old tom-cat. His narration was like this: either simple, bare, stoical, with a touch of nobility; or else satiric, malicious, with a strange, rather repellent jeering.

'Leighton—he wasn't Lord Leighton then—he wouldn't have me to sit for him, because my figure was too poor, he didn't like it. He liked fair young men, with plenty of flesh. But once, when he was doing a picture—I don't know if you know it? It is a crucifixion, with a man on a cross, and—' He described the picture. 'No! Well, the model had to be tied hanging on a wooden cross. And it made you suffer! Ah!' Here the odd, arch, diabolic yellow flare lit up through the stoicism of Pancrazio's eyes. 'Because Leighton, he was cruel to his model. He wouldn't let you rest. "Damn you, you've got to keep still till I've finished with you, you devil," so he said. Well, for this man on the cross, he couldn't get a model who would do it for him. They all tried it once, but they would not go again. So they said to him, he must try Califano, because Califano was the only man who would stand it. At last then he sent for me. "I don't like your damned figure, Califano," he said to me, "but no-body will do this if you won't. Now will you do it?" "Yes!" I said, "I will." So he tied me up on the cross. And he paid me well, so I stood it. Well, he kept me tied up, hanging you know forwards naked on this cross, for four hours. And then it was luncheon. And after luncheon he would tie me again. Well, I suffered. I suffered so much, that I must lean against the wall to support me to walk home. And in the night I could not sleep. I could cry with the pains in my arms and my ribs, I had no sleep. "You've said you'd do it, so now you must," he said to me. "And I will do it," I said. And so he tied me up. This cross, you know, was on a little raised place—I don't know what you call it—'

'A platform,' suggested Alvina.

'A platform. Now one day when he came to do something to me, when I was tied up, he slipped back over this platform, and he pulled me, who was tied on the cross, with him. So we all fell down, he with the naked man on top of him, and the heavy cross on top of us both. I could not move, because I was tied. And it was so, with me on top of him, and the heavy cross, that he could not get out. So he had to lie shouting underneath me until someone came to the studio to untie me. No, we were not hurt, because the top of the cross fell so that it did not crush us. "Now you have had a taste of the cross," I said to him. "Yes, you devil, but I shan't let you off," he said to me.

'To make the time go he would ask me questions. Once he said, "Now Califano, what time is it? I give you three guesses, and if you guess right once I give you sixpence." So I guessed three o'clock. "That's one. Now then, what time is it?" Again, three o'clock. "That's two guesses gone, you silly devil. Now then, what time is it?" So now I was obstinate, and I said *Three o'clock*. He took out his watch. "Why damn you, how do you know? I give you a shilling—" It was three o'clock, as I said, so he gave me a shilling instead of sixpence as he had said—'

It was strange, in the silent winter afternoon, downstairs in the black kitchen, to sit drinking a cup of tea with Pancrazio and hearing these stories of English painters. It was strange to look at the battered figure of Pancrazio, and think how much he had been crucified through the long years in London, for the sake of late Victorian art. It was strangest of all to see through his yellow, often dull, red-rimmed eyes these blithe and well-conditioned painters. Pancrazio looked on them admiringly and contemptuously, as an old, rakish tom-cat might look on such frivolous well-groomed young gentlemen.

As a matter of fact Pancrazio had never been rakish or debauched, but mountain-moral, timid. So that the queer, half-sinister drop of his eyelids was curious, and the strange, wicked yellow flare that came into his eyes was almost frightening. There was in the man a sort of sulphur-yellow flame of passion which would light up in his battered body and give him an almost diabolic look. Alvina felt that if she were left much alone with him she would need all her English ascendancy not to be afraid of him.

It was a Sunday morning just before Christmas when Alvina and Cicio and Pancrazio set off for Pescocalascio for the first time. Snow had fallen—not much round the house, but deep between the banks as they climbed. And the sun was very bright. So that the mountains were dazzling. The snow was wet on the roads. They wound between oak trees and under the broom-scrub, climbing over the jumbled hills that lay between the mountains, until the village came near. They got on to a broader track, where the path from a distant village joined theirs. They were all talking, in the bright clear air of the morning.

A little man came down an upper path. As he joined them near the village he hailed them in English:

'Good morning. Nice morning.'

'Does everybody speak English here?' asked Alvina.

'I have been eighteen years in Glasgow. I am only here for a trip.'

He was a little Italian shop-keeper from Glasgow. He was most friendly, insisted on paying for drinks, and coffee and almond biscuits for Alvina. Evidently he was also grateful to Britain.

The village was wonderful. It occupied the crown of an eminence in the midst of the wide valley. From the terrace of the high-road the valley spread below, with all its jumble of hills, and two rivers, set in the walls of the mountains, a wide space, but imprisoned. It glistened with snow under the blue sky. But the lowest hollows were brown. In the distance, Ossona hung at the edge of a platform. Many villages clung like pale swarms of birds to the far slopes, or perched on the hills beneath. It was a world within a world, a valley of many hills and townlets and streams shut in beyond access.

Pescocalascio itself was crowded. The roads were sloppy with snow. But none the less, peasants in full dress, their feet soaked in the skin sandals, were trooping in the sun, purchasing, selling, bargaining for cloth, talking all the time. In the shop, which was also a sort of inn, an ancient woman was making coffee over a charcoal brazier, while the crowd of peasants sat at the tables at the back, eating the food they had brought.

Post was due at midday. Cicio went to fetch it, whilst Pancrazio took Alvina to the summit, to the castle. There, in the level region, boys were snowballing and shouting. The ancient castle, badly cracked by the last earthquake, looked wonderfully down on the valley of many hills beneath, Califano a speck down the left, Ossona a blot to the right, suspended, its towers and its castle clear in the light. Behind the castle of Pescocalascio was a deep, steep valley, almost a gorge, at the bottom of which a river ran, and where Pancrazio pointed out the electricity works of the village, deep in the gloom. Above this gorge, at the end, rose the long slopes of the mountains, up to the vivid snow—and across again was the wall of the Abruzzi.

They went down past the ruined houses broken by the earthquake. Cicio still had not come with the post. A crowd surged at the post-office door, in a steep, black, wet sidestreet. Alvina's feet were sodden. Pancrazio took her to the place where she could drink coffee and a strega, to make her warm. On the platform of the highway above the valley, people were parading in the hot sun. Alvina noticed some ultra-smart young men. They came up to Pancrazio, speaking English. Alvina hated their Cockney accent and florid showy vulgar presence. They were more models. Pancrazio was cool with them.

Alvina sat apart from the crowd of peasants, on a chair the old crone had ostentatiously dusted for her. Pancrazio ordered beer for himself. Cicio came with letters—long-delayed letters, that had been censored. Alvina's heart went down.

The first she opened was from Miss Pinnegar—all war and fear and anxiety. The second was a letter, a real insulting letter from Dr Mitchell. 'I little thought, at the time when I was hoping to make you my wife, that you were carrying on with a dirty Italian organ-grinder. So your fair-seeming face covered the schemes and vice of your true nature. Well, I can only thank Providence which spared me the disgust and shame of marrying you, and I hope that, when I meet you on the streets of Leicester Square, I shall have forgiven you sufficiently to be able to throw you a coin—'

Here was a pretty little epistle! In spite of herself, she went pale and trembled. She glanced at Cicio. Fortunately he was turning round talking to another man. She rose and went to the ruddy brazier, as if to warm her hands. She threw on the screwed-up letter. The old crone said something unintelligible to her. She watched the letter catch fire—glanced at the peasants at the table—and out at the wide, wild valley. The world beyond could not help, but it still had the power to injure one here. She felt she had received a bitter blow. A black hatred for the Mitchells of this world filled her.

She could hardly bear to open the third letter. It was from Mrs Tuke, and again, all war. Would Italy join the Allies? She ought to, her every interest lay that way. Could Alvina bear to be so far off, when such terrible events were happening near home? Could she possibly be happy? Nurses were so valuable now. She, Mrs Tuke, had volunteered. She would do whatever she could. She had had to leave off nursing Jenifer, who had an *excellent* Scotch nurse, much better than a mother. Well, Alvina and Mrs Tuke might yet meet in some hospital in France. So the letter ended.

Alvina sat down, pale and trembling. Pancrazio was watching her curiously.

'Have you bad news?' he asked.

'Only the war.'

'Ha!' and the Italian gesture of half-bitter 'what can one do?'

They were talking war—all talking war. The dandy young models had left England because of the war, expecting Italy to come in. And everybody talked, talked, talked. Alvina looked round her. It all seemed alien to her, bruising upon the spirit.

'Do you think I shall ever be able to come here alone and do my shopping by myself?' she asked.

'You must never come alone,' said Pancrazio, in his curious benevolent courtesy. 'Either Cicio or I will come with you. You must never come so far alone.'

'Why not?' she said.

'You are a stranger here. You are not a *contadina*—' Alvina could feel the oriental idea of women, which still leaves its mark on the Mediterranean, threatening her with surveillance and subjection. She sat in her chair, with cold wet feet, looking at the sunshine outside, the wet snow, the moving figures in the strong light, the men drinking at the counter, the cluster of peasant women bargaining for dressmaterial. Cicio was still turning talking in the rapid way to his neighbour. She knew it was war. She noticed the movement of his finely-modelled cheek, a little sallow this morning.

And she rose hastily.

'I want to go into the sun,' she said.

When she stood above the valley in the strong, tiring light, she glanced round. Cicio inside the shop had risen, but he was still turning to his neighbour and was talking with all his hands and all his body. He did not talk with his mind and lips alone. His whole physique, his whole living body spoke and uttered and emphasized itself.

A certain weariness possessed her. She was beginning to realize something about him: how he had no sense of home and domestic life, as an Englishman has. Cicio's home would never be his castle. His castle was the piazza of Pescocalascio. His home was nothing to him but a possession, and a hole to sleep in. He didn't *live* in it. He lived in the open air, and in the community. When the true Italian came out in him, his veriest home was the piazza of Pescocalascio, the little sort of market-place where the roads met in the village, under the castle, and where the men stood in groups and talked, talked, talked. This was where Cicio belonged: his active, mindful self. His active, mindful self was none of hers. She only had his passive self, and his family passion.

His masculine mind and intelligence had its home in the little public square of his village. She knew this as she watched him now, with all his body talking politics. He could not break off till he had finished. And then, with a swift, intimate handshake to the group with whom he had been engaged, he came away, putting all his interest off from himself.

She tried to make him talk and discuss with her. But he wouldn't. An obstinate spirit made him darkly refuse masculine conversation with her.

'If Italy goes to war, you will have to join up?' she asked him.

'Yes,' he said, with a smile at the futility of the question.

'And I shall have to stay here?'

He nodded, rather gloomily.

'Do you want to go?' she persisted.

'No, I don't want to go.'

'But you think Italy ought to join in?'

'Yes, I do.'

'Then you *do* want to go—'

'I want to go if Italy goes in—and she ought to go in—'

Curious, he was somewhat afraid of her, he half venerated her, and half despised her. When she tried to make him discuss, in the masculine way, he shut obstinately against her, something like a child, and the slow, fine smile of dislike came on his face. Instinctively he shut off all masculine communication from her, particularly politics and religion. He would discuss both, violently, with other men. In politics he was something of a Socialist, in religion a free-thinker. But all this had nothing to do with Alvina. He would not enter on a discussion in English.

Somewhere in her soul, she knew the finality of his refusal to hold discussion with a woman. So, though at times her heart hardened with indignant anger, she let herself remain outside. The more so, as she felt that in matters intellectual he was rather stupid. Let him go to the piazza or to the wine-shop, and talk.

To do him justice, he went little. Pescocalascio was only half his own village. The nostalgia, the campanilismo from which Italians suffer, the craving to be in sight of the native

church-tower, to stand and talk in the native market-place
or piazza, this was only half-formed in Cicio, taken away
as he had been from Pescocalascio when so small a boy. He
spent most of his time working in the fields and woods, most
of his evenings at home, often weaving a special kind of fish-
net or net-basket from fine, frail strips of cane. It was a work
he had learned at Naples long ago. Alvina meanwhile would
sew for the child, or spin wool. She became quite clever at
drawing the strands of wool from her distaff, rolling them
fine and even between her fingers, and keeping her bobbin
rapidly spinning away below, dangling at the end of the
thread. To tell the truth, she was happy in the quietness with
Cicio, now they had their own pleasant room. She loved his
presence. She loved the quality of his silence, so rich and
physical. She felt he was never very far away: that he was a
good deal a stranger in Califano, as she was: that he clung
to her presence as she to his. Then Pancrazio also contrived
to serve her and shelter her, he too loved her for being there.
They both revered her because she was with child. So that
she lived more and more in a little isolate, illusory, wonderful world then, content, moreover, because the living cost
so little. She had sixty pounds of her own money, always
intact in the little case. And after all, the highway beyond
the river led to Ossona, and Ossona gave access to the railway, and the railway would take her anywhere.

So the month of January passed, with its short days and
its bits of snow and bursts of sunshine. On sunny days Alvina walked down to the desolate river-bed, which fascinated her. When Pancrazio was carrying up stone or lime
on the ass, she accompanied him. And Pancrazio was always
carrying up something, for he loved the extraneous jobs like
building a fire-place much more than the heavy work of the
land. Then she would find little tufts of wild narcissus
among the rocks, gold-centred pale little things, many on
one stem. And their scent was powerful and magical, like
the sound of the men who came all those days and sang
before Christmas. She loved them. There was green helle-
bore too, a fascinating plant—and one or two little treasures,
the last of the rose-coloured Alpine cyclamens, near the
earth, with snake-skin leaves, and so rose, so rose, like vi-

olets for shadowiness. She sat and cried over the first she
found: heaven knows why.

In February, as the days opened, the first almond trees
flowered among grey olives, in warm, level corners between
the hills. But it was March before the real flowering began.
And then she had continual bowl-fuls of white and blue
violets, she had sprays of almond blossom, silver-warm and
lustrous, then sprays of peach and apricot, pink and fluttering. It was a great joy to wander looking for flowers. She
came upon a bankside all wide with lavender crocuses. The
sun was on them for the moment, and they were opened
flat, great five-pointed lilac stars, with burning centres,
burning with a strange lavender flame, as she had seen some
metal burn lilac-flamed in the laboratory of the hospital at
Islington. All down the oak-dry bankside they burned their
great exposed stars. And she felt like going down on her
knees and bending her forehead to the earth in an oriental
submission, they were so royal, so lovely, so supreme. She
came again to them in the morning, when the sky was grey,
and they were closed, sharp clubs, wonderfully fragile on
their stems of sap, among leaves and old grass and wild peri-
winkle. They had wonderful dark stripes running up their
cheeks, the crocuses, like the clear proud stripes on a badg-
er's face, or on some proud cat. She took a handful of the
sappy, shut, striped flames. In her room they opened into a
grand bowl of lilac fire.

March was a lovely month. The men were busy in the
hills, she wandered, extending her range. Sometimes with a
strange fear. But it was fear of the elements rather than of
man. One day she went along the high-road with her letters,
towards the village of Casa Latina. The high-road was depressing, wherever there were houses. For the houses had
that sordid, ramshackle, slummy look almost invariable on
an Italian high-road. They were patched with a hideous
greenish mould-colour, blotched, as if with leprosy. It
frightened her, till Pancrazio told her it was only the copper
sulphate that had sprayed the vines hitched on to the walls.
But none the less the houses were sordid, unkempt, slummy.
One house by itself could make a complete slum.

Casa Latina was across the valley, in the shadow. Approaching it were rows of low cabins—fairly new. They were the one-storey dwellings commanded after the earthquake. And hideous they were. The village itself was old, dark, in perpetual shadow of the mountain. Streams of cold water ran round it. The piazza was gloomy, forsaken. But there was a great, twin-towered church, wonderful from outside.

She went inside, and was almost sick with repulsion. The place was large, whitewashed, and crowded with figures in glass cases and *ex voto* offerings. The lousy-looking, dressed-up dolls, life size and tinselly, that stood in the glass cases; the blood-streaked Jesus on the crucifix; the mouldering, mumbling, filthy peasant women on their knees; all the sense of trashy, repulsive, degraded fetish-worship was too much for her. She hurried out, shrinking from the contamination of the dirty leather door-curtain.

Enough of Casa Latina. She would never go *there* again. She was beginning to feel that, if she lived in this part of the world at all, she must avoid the *inside* of it. She must never, if she could help it, enter into any interior but her own— neither into house nor church nor even shop or post-office, if she could help it. The moment she went through a door the sense of dark repulsiveness came over her. If she was to save her sanity she must keep to the open air, and avoid any contact with human interiors. When she thought of the insides of the native people she shuddered with repulsion, as in the great, degraded church of Casa Latina. They were horrible.

Yet the outside world was so fair. Corn and maize were growing green and silken, vines were in the small bud. Everywhere little grape hyacinths hung their blue bells. It was a pity they reminded her of the many-breasted Artemis, a picture of whom, or of whose statue, she had seen somewhere. Artemis with her clusters of breasts was horrible to her, now she had come south: nauseating beyond words. And the milky grape hyacinths reminded her.

She turned with thankfulness to the magenta anemones that were so gay. Someone told her that wherever Venus had shed a tear for Adonis, one of these flowers had sprung. They were not tear-like. And yet their red-purple silkiness

had something pre-world about it, at last. The more she
wandered, the more the shadow of the bygone pagan world
seemed to come over her. Sometimes she felt she would
shriek and go mad, so strong was the influence on her, something pre-world and, it seemed to her now, vindictive. She
seemed to feel in the air strange Furies, Lemures, things that
had haunted her with their tomb-frenzied vindictiveness
since she was a child and had pored over the illustrated Clas-
sical Dictionary. Black and cruel presences were in the un-
der-air. They were furtive and slinking. They bewitched you
with loveliness, and lurked with fangs to hurt you afterwards. There it was: the fangs sheathed in beauty: the beauty
first, and then, horribly, inevitably, the fangs.

Being a great deal alone, in the strange place, fancies possessed her, people took on strange shapes. Even Cicio and
Pancrazio. And it came that she never wandered far from
the house, from her room, after the first months. She seemed
to hide herself in her room. There she sewed and spun wool
and read, and learnt Italian. Her men were not at all anxious
to teach her Italian. Indeed her chief teacher, at first, was a
young fellow called Bussolo. He was a model from London,
and he came down to Califano sometimes, hanging about,
anxious to speak English.

Alvina did not care for him. He was a dandy with pale
grey eyes and a heavy figure. Yet he had a certain penetrat-
ing intelligence.

'No, this country is a country for old men. It is only for
old men,' he said, talking of Pescocalascio. 'You won't stop
here. Nobody young can stop here.'

The odd plangent certitude in his voice penetrated her.
And all the young people said the same thing. They were all
waiting to go away. But for the moment the war held them
up.

Cicio and Pancrazio were busy with the vines. As she
watched them hoeing, crouching, tying, tending, grafting,
mindless and utterly absorbed, hour after hour, day after
day, thinking vines, living vines, she wondered they didn't
begin to sprout vine-buds and vine-stems from their own
elbows and neck-joints. There was something to her unnatural in the quality of the attention the men gave to the vine.

It was a sort of worship, almost a degradation again. And heaven knows, Pancrazio's wine was poor enough, his grapes almost invariably bruised with hail-stones, and half-rotten instead of ripe.

The loveliness of April came, with hot sunshine. Astonishing the ferocity of the sun, when he really took upon himself to blaze. Alvina was amazed. The burning day quite carried her away. She loved it: it made her quite careless about everything, she was just swept along in the powerful flood of the sunshine. In the end, she felt that intense sunlight had on her the effect of night: a sort of darkness, and a suspension of life. She had to hide in her room till the cold wind blew again.

Meanwhile the declaration of war drew nearer, and became inevitable. She knew Cicio would go. And with him went the chance of her escape. She steeled herself to bear the agony of the knowledge that he would go, and she would be left alone in this place, which sometimes she hated with a hatred unspeakable. After a spell of hot, intensely dry weather she felt she would die in this valley, wither and go to powder as some exposed April roses withered and dried into dust against a hot wall. Then the cool wind came in a storm, the next day there was grey sky and soft air. The rose-coloured wild gladioli among the young green corn were a dream of beauty, the morning of the world. The lovely, pristine morning of the world, before our epoch began. Rose-red gladioli among corn, in among the rocks, and small irises, black-purple and yellow blotched with brown, like a wasp, standing low in little desert places, that would seem forlorn but for this weird, dark-lustrous magnificence. Then there were the tiny irises, only one finger tall, growing in dry places, frail as crocuses, and much tinier, and blue, blue as the eye of the morning heaven, which was a morning earlier, more pristine than ours. The lovely translucent pale irises, tiny and morning-blue, they lasted only a few hours. But nothing could be more exquisite, like gods on earth. It was the flowers that brought back to Alvina the passionate nostalgia for the place. The human influence was a bit horrible to her. But the flowers that came out and uttered the earth in magical expression, they cast a spell on her, bewitched her and stole her own soul away from her.

She went down to Cicio where he was weeding armfuls of rose-red gladioli from the half-grown wheat, and cutting the lushness of the first weedy herbage. He threw down his sheaves of gladioli, and with his sickle began to cut the forest of bright yellow corn-marigolds. He looked intent, he seemed to work feverishly.

'Must they all be cut?' she said, as she went to him.

He threw aside the great armful of yellow flowers, took off his cap, and wiped the sweat from his brow. The sickle dangled loose in his hand.

'We have declared war,' he said.

In an instant she realized that she had seen the figure of the old post-carrier dodging between the rocks. Rose-red and gold-yellow of the flowers swam in her eyes. Cicio's dusk-yellow eyes were watching her. She sank on her knees on a sheaf of corn-marigolds. Her eyes, watching him, were vulnerable as if stricken to death. Indeed she felt she would die.

'You will have to go?' she said.

'Yes, we shall all have to go.' There seemed a certain sound of triumph in his voice. Cruel!

She sank lower on the flowers, and her head dropped. But she would not be beaten. She lifted her face.

'If you are very long,' she said, 'I shall go to England. I can't stay here very long without you.'

'You will have Pancrazio—and the child,' he said.

'Yes. But I shall still be by myself. I can't stay here very long without you. I shall go to England.'

He watched her narrowly.

'I don't think they'll let you,' he said.

'Yes, they will.'

At moments she hated him. He seemed to want to crush her altogether. She was always making little plans in her mind—how she could get out of that great cruel valley and escape to Rome, to English people. She would find the English Consul and he would help her. She would do anything rather than be really crushed. She knew how easy it would be, once her spirit broke, for her to die and be buried in the cemetery at Pescocalascio.

And they would all be so sentimental about her—just as Pancrazio was. She felt that in some way Pancrazio had killed his wife—not consciously, but unconsciously, as Cicio might kill *her*. Pancrazio would tell Alvina about his wife and her ailments. And he seemed always anxious to prove that he had been so good to her. No doubt he had been good to her, also. But there was something underneath—malevolent in his spirit, some caged-in sort of cruelty, malignant beyond his control. It crept out in his stories. And it revealed itself in his fear of his dead wife. Alvina knew that in the night the elderly man was afraid of his dead wife, and of her ghost or her avenging spirit. He would huddle over the fire in fear. In the same way the cemetery had a fascination of horror for him—as, she noticed, for most of the natives. It was an ugly, square place, all stone slabs and wall-cupboards enclosed in four-square stone walls, and lying away beneath Pescocalascio village obvious as if it were on a plate.

'That is our cemetery,' Pancrazio said, pointing it out to her, 'where we shall all be carried some day.'

And there was fear, horror in his voice. He told her how the men had carried his wife there—a long journey over the hill-tracks, almost two hours.

These were days of waiting—horrible days of waiting for Cicio to be called up. One batch of young men left the village—and there was a lugubrious sort of saturnalia, men and women alike got rather drunk, the young men left amid howls of lamentation and shrieks of distress. Crowds accompanied them to Ossona, whence they were marched towards the railway. It was a horrible event.

A shiver of horror and death went through the valley. In a lugubrious way, they seemed to enjoy it.

'You'll never be satisfied till you've gone,' she said to Cicio. 'Why don't they be quick and call you?'

'It will be next week,' he said, looking at her darkly. In the twilight he came to her, when she could hardly see him.

'Are you sorry you came here with me, Allaye?' he asked. There was malice in the very question.

She put down the spoon and looked up from the fire. He stood shadowy, his head ducked forward, the firelight faint on his enigmatic, timeless, half-smiling face.

'I'm not sorry,' she answered slowly, using all her courage. 'Because I love you—'

She crouched quite still on the hearth. He turned aside his face. After a moment or two he went out. She stirred her pot slowly and sadly. She had to go downstairs for something.

And there on the landing she saw him standing in the darkness with his arm over his face, as if fending a blow.

'What is it?' she said, laying her hand on him. He uncovered his face.

'I would take you away if I could,' he said.

'I can wait for you,' she answered.

He threw himself in a chair that stood at a table there on the broad landing, and buried his head in his arms.

'Don't wait for me! Don't wait for me!' he cried, his voice muffled.

'Why not?' she said, filled with terror. He made no sign. 'Why not?' she insisted. And she laid her fingers on his head.

He got up and turned to her.

'I love you, even if it kills me,' she said.

But he only turned aside again, leaned his arm against the wall, and hid his face, utterly noiseless.

'What is it?' she said. 'What is it? I don't understand.' He wiped his sleeve across his face, and turned to her.

'I haven't any hope,' he said, in a dull, dogged voice.

She felt her heart and the child die within her.

'Why?' she said.

Was she to bear a hopeless child?

'You *have* hope. Don't make a scene,' she snapped. And she went downstairs, as she had intended.

But when she got into the kitchen, she forgot what she had come for. She sat in the darkness on the seat, with all life gone dark and still, death and eternity settled down on her. Death and eternity were settled down on her as she sat alone. And she seemed to hear him moaning upstairs—'I can't come back. I can't come back.' She heard it. She heard it so distinctly, that she never knew whether it had been an actual utterance, or whether it was her inner ear which had heard the inner, unutterable sound. She wanted to answer, to call to him. But she could not. Heavy, mute, powerless, there she sat like a lump of darkness, in that doomed Italian kitchen. 'I can't come back.' She heard it so fatally.

She was interrupted by the entrance of Pancrazio.

'Oh!' he cried, startled when, having come near the fire, he caught sight of her. And he said something, frightened, in Italian.

'Is it you? Why are you in darkness?' he said.

'I am just going upstairs again.'

'You frightened me.'

She went up to finish the preparing of the meal. Cicio came down to Pancrazio. The latter had brought a newspaper. The two men sat on the settle, with the lamp between them, reading and talking the news.

Cicio's group was called up for the following week, as he had said. The departure hung over them like a doom. Those were perhaps the worst days of all: the days of the impending departure. Neither of them spoke about it.

But the night before he left she could bear the silence no more.

'You will come back, won't you?' she said, as he sat motionless in his chair in the bedroom. It was a hot, luminous night. There was still a late scent of orange blossom from the garden, the nightingale was shaking the air with his sound. At other times, honey scents wafted from the hills.

'You will come back?' she insisted.

'Who knows?' he replied.

'If you make up your mind to come back, you will come back. We have our fate in our hands,' she said.

He smiled slowly.

'You think so?' he said.

'I know it. If you don't come back it will be because you don't want to—no other reason. It won't be because you can't. It will be because you don't want to.'

'Who told you so?' he asked, with the same cruel smile.

'I know it,' she said.

'All right,' he answered.

But he still sat with his hands abandoned between his knees.

'So make up your mind,' she said.

He sat motionless for a long while: while she undressed and brushed her hair and went to bed. And still he sat there unmoving, like a corpse. It was like having some unnatural, doomed, unbearable presence in the room. She blew out the light, that she need not see him. But in the darkness it was worse.

At last he stirred—he rose. He came hesitating across to her.

'I'll come back, Allaye,' he said quietly. 'Be damned to them all.' She heard unspeakable pain in his voice.

'To whom?' she said, sitting up.

He did not answer, but put his arms round her.

'I'll come back, and we'll go to America,' he said.

'You'll come back to me,' she whispered, in an ecstasy of pain and relief. It was not her affair, where they should go, so long as he really returned to her.

'I'll come back,' he said.

'Sure?' she whispered, straining him to her.